Acclaim for Michael Isikoff's
UNCOVERING CLINTON

"Isikoff has written a lively, highly readable and attention-holding account, with much that is new, about how one of the strangest episodes in the history of the American presidency came about."

Elizabeth Drew, *Los Angeles Times*

"*Uncovering Clinton* reads like a detective novel in which almost everyone is partially guilty."

Chicago Tribune

"Here is a yarn to keep the juices flowing . . . Isikoff's tale is serpentine in two senses of the word: sinuous in its course and writhing with snakes in human guise . . . an impressive feat of investigative reporting."

Boston Globe

"Michael Isikoff has been the Woodward and Bernstein of the Clinton era. We loved [*Uncovering Clinton*] because it made us look at a story that we thought we knew far too well already in a completely different light. We found something startling on almost every page. We loved it for its narrative drive, its out-landish cast of characters, its Dickensian coincidences, and we suspect it will still be read as such long after Monica Lewinsky and Kenneth Starr are distant memories."

Book-of-the-Month Club

"*Uncovering Clinton* . . . is a stunning, suspenseful, marvelous and completely convincing rendering of William Jefferson Clinton's messy life and its corrosive effect on the American presidency. . . . a book of power and fairness that offers deep insights into Clinton, his victims, the grimy baseness of politics in Washington and provides what will surely be the first book historians of the next century turn to when they want to understand the Clinton impeachment."

Buffalo News

"Isikoff, like all great reporters, is just as good at telling a story as getting it. The book is well-written throughout, but the last fourth of it, dealing with Starr's fateful entry into the case, is absolutely gripping. . . . Isikoff deserves a wide audience. Sometimes the most important thing is not the story itself, but how and why it came out."

Cleveland Plain Dealer

"Isikoff writes smoothly and without malice. This is by no means a Clinton-hating book. For that reason, it is all the more devastating."

Lars-Erik Nelson, *New York Daily News*

"Isikoff's book is important because he, more than any other reporter, saw this story from the ground up."

USA Today

"Spectacular . . . The most compelling and important first-person 'big story' narrative any reporter has written since *All the President's Men*."

The Weekly Standard

"A no-holds-barred, definitive record of events . . . told by a reporter with no political ax to grind."

Virginian-Pilot

"A penetrating look at the most explosive presidential scandal since Watergate."

Associated Press

"Surely the best exposition so far of the Clinton crisis, filled with new revelations and insights. . . . a first-person whodunit depicting a demi-world of betrayal and mendacity."

Robert Novak, *National Review*

"An excellent, fast-moving, behind-the-scenes account . . ."

Pittsburgh Post-Gazette

"Uncovering Clinton is an extremely important book. It is an account of how things work inside the Beltway, and how events are—and are not—reported. It is a multileveled tale of deceit, duplicity, and corruption, and how they spread from the top down. . . . I know this sordid tale inside and out, chapter and verse, and I still couldn't put *Uncovering Clinton* down."

Bookreporter

"For sheer readability and thoroughness, it will probably be many years before anyone tops Isikoff's tale of l'Affair Monica. . . . His book becomes the absolutely essential narrative on the scandal, with revelations that no one would have thought possible in the aftermath of such a heavily reported story."

Journal News, Westchester County, NY

"This isn't just journalism. This is history . . . a fascinating, powerful and candid account of [Isikoff's] scandal-mongering at the *Washington Post* and *Newsweek.* . . . the definitive book on the most serious and surreal crisis since Watergate."

Madison (Wis.) *Capitol Times*

"Briskly written, revealing and insightful. . . . essential reading for anyone interested in the press, Clinton, and his presidency."

American Spectator

UNCOVERING
CLINTON

A Reporter's Story

MICHAEL ISIKOFF

 THREE RIVERS PRESS
NEW YORK

Published by Three Rivers Press, New York, New York.
Member of the Crown Publishing Group.

Originally published in hardcover by Crown Publishers in 1999.

Random House, Inc. New York, Toronto, London, Sydney, Auckland
www.randomhouse.com

Three Rivers Press is a registered trademark and the Three Rivers Press
colophon is a trademark of Random House, Inc.

Printed in the United States of America

Design by Barbara Sturman

Library of Congress Cataloging-in-Publication Data
Isikoff, Michael.
Uncovering Clinton : a reporter's story / Michael Isikoff.
1. Clinton, Bill, 1946– —Sexual behavior. 2. Clinton, Bill,
1946– —Relations with women. 3. Political corruption—United
States—History—20th century. 4. United States—Politics and
government—1993– I. Title.
E886.2.I85   1999
973.929'092—dc21   99-13056
                                                                     CIP

ISBN 0-609-80558-4

10 9 8 7 6 5 4 3 2 1

First Paperback Edition

For Lisa and Willa

AUTHOR'S NOTE

This is, in almost every respect, the same book as was originally published by Crown in hardcover in March 1999. A few small mistakes are corrected. A few new details are added toward the end of the narrative, mostly involving the handling of Linda Tripp's audiotapes in January 1998. This new material is derived from public testimony during pretrial hearings on Linda Tripp's indictment for violation of the Maryland wiretapping statute in December 1999.

A new Afterword also has been included, covering developments since the hardcover edition went to press.

CONTENTS

INTRODUCTION

"Hey, Isikoff, you might not want to go out that way."

It was Tom Sherwood, my old colleague from *The Washington Post,* now a local television ace, offering me a friendly heads-up. We were standing in a hallway of the NBC Washington bureau, just a few minutes after the taping of *Meet the Press.* I poked my head out the glass doorway to the lobby and saw the crowd—an unruly crush of TV cameramen, photographers and disgruntled correspondents stuck with Sunday stakeout duty.

So this was what they meant by the jackals of the press.

"What's that all about?" I asked Sherwood. "Who are they waiting for?"

"You," he said.

"Oh, for God's sake," I said. "This is ridiculous." Sherwood agreed, and we both sort of laughed. I was used to chasing newsmakers, not being one. There was a rough form of justice to this, of course: The hunter learns what it is like to be hunted. But it also seemed, like so much else that morning, surreal and extremely absurd.

It was Sunday, January 25, 1998. In the previous four days, Washington had gone mad. A scandal had erupted, seemingly out of nowhere, and turned American politics on its head. The president of the United States, it was alleged, had been having oral sex with a young woman, a former White House intern. He had lied about it— under oath. He had allegedly asked the young woman to lie about it, too, and gotten her a job to keep her quiet. There were tapes. The ever-vigilant independent counsel was investigating.

As it happened, I had more than a little to do with how this had come to pass. Four years earlier, I had looked into another charge of sexual misconduct against Bill Clinton, and had concluded that he was lying then too—that he probably had done something like what his accuser described. As time went on, a second accuser stepped forward and the trail twisted and turned until it led to the intern.

What it all added up to, I wasn't sure. The benign view—the one held by Clinton's more sophisticated defenders who weren't still in denial—was not much: The guy liked women. So what? The more troubling reading—the one I leaned toward—was that the president's private weakness had led inexorably to much larger public wrongs: lies to the public and to a court, the smearing of innocents, the deployment of an army of hardball litigators, private investigators and spin doctors whose primary purpose was to smash the accusers and destroy the president's enemies. James Carville, Clinton's most aggressive defender, had just summed it up for *Meet the Press* host Tim Russert: "There's going to be a war."

To be sure, many of Clinton's enemies were not pleasant people. Mean-spirited and mercenary, their zealotry gave comfort to the president's lieutenants that the fight was worth waging. But at what cost? It had begun to seem all-consuming. It had come to define the Clinton presidency.

In those days, there was much talk that he wouldn't survive. "Will the president be forced to resign or face impeachment?" Russert had just asked Senator Arlen Specter, the stern and censorious Pennsylvania Republican. Specter didn't want to speculate. "I do not believe the Congress is going to impeach the president unless there is an open-and-shut case," he said. (Then again, Specter said, if the charge of sex with the intern was true, "It may well be" enough to force him to resign.) I had been stunned a week earlier when one of my editors had first used the word "impeachment" in the context of this story. My *Newsweek* colleague Dan Klaidman and I had rolled our eyes, thinking it was being blown out of proportion. But by that Sunday morning, those inner doubts were submerged in the chaos of the moment. Clearly, I had underestimated how this would play. How can you tell?

A much more difficult concept for me—and one of more immediate concern that morning—was the idea that I was part of the story. I didn't like it. There is a principle in quantum physics—Heisenberg's Uncertainty Principle: The act of measuring the object changes the direction of the object being measured. My reporting had been the journalistic equivalent. The players in this saga—the accusers, the conspirators, even the president—had all at times calculated their actions in response to what they thought I might do. In 1994, the advisers for Paula Jones had shared her story with me as a way to get it publicized. When my editors balked, they filed a lawsuit. The conspirators, Linda Tripp and Lucianne Goldberg, saw me as their vehicle for exposing the president. Even the prosecutors working for independent counsel Kenneth Starr were forced to scramble when they learned that I had discovered their still-secret investigation. In the end, I had set Starr's deadline.

Along the way, I was forced to make choices—sometimes tricky ones. The professional terrain in reporting on such matters was treacherous; the rules were blurry and ever-changing. And yet my decisions, some of them made on the spur of the moment, had consequences. As a reporter, this made me distinctly uncomfortable. I don't want to influence the news. And I certainly don't want to make it.

Now, here I was, a player—one of the acts in the scandal circus. That morning on *Meet the Press* there was a gallery of them: William Ginsburg, the intern's lawyer. Specter, the potential juror. Carville, the attack dog. Then the reporters' roundtable: legal writer Stuart Taylor, *New York Times* columnist William Safire, Internet scribe Matt Drudge and me. Sitting opposite Drudge bothered me. Why are you going to have him on? I had complained to Russert a few days before. He's a reckless gossip merchant.

"He's part of the story too," Russert replied.

He was right.

For twenty minutes or so, Sherwood and I waited, hiding from the stakeout, hoping the lurking journalists would go away. A photographer came in to snap my picture, then went back to tell the crowd I was still there. Then Sherwood had an idea. Follow me, he said, and we padded through the recesses of NBC, down a long corridor, down some stairs by a loading dock in the back. NBC had provided cars for all the guests on the show. Sherwood fetched mine. I hopped in and drove away, feeling very weird as I glanced back at the outfoxed jackals, my brethren of the press.

Book One

PAULA JONES

February 1994–May 1994

1

"It's just a cheap political fundraising trick."

It didn't take Craig Shirley long to figure out that things weren't going well. The slight giggles, the hostile questions, the looks on the faces of the reporters listening to the odd woman at the podium, told him all he needed to know. The press conference Shirley had helped arrange—a press conference he hoped would embarrass and even humiliate the president of the United States—was starting to look like a train wreck.

Only a few hours earlier, Shirley—a charter member of what First Lady Hillary Rodham Clinton years later described as a "vast right-wing conspiracy"—thought things would be quite different. It was February 11, 1994, and a miserable winter storm had snarled traffic in the nation's capital. Shirley was helping to coordinate publicity for the Conservative Political Action Conference, an annual meeting of hard-line activists that had started the day before at Washington's Omni Shoreham Hotel. If there was any unifying theme to the event, it was the presumed defects—ideological, political, ethical—of William Jefferson Clinton. Few disdained Clinton more than Shirley, a veteran right-wing Republican strategist and political consultant. Like many of those present, he viewed the president as a moral leper, a man undeserving of the respect customarily afforded the occupant of the highest office of the land. But Clinton-bashing was to be expected at events like the CPAC conference. A cool pragmatist about the world of public relations, Shirley knew the usual anti-Clinton rants had little chance of making news. Then early

3

that morning, Shirley had huddled in a hotel suite with Cliff Jackson, a lanky lawyer from Hot Springs, Arkansas, and one of Bill Clinton's oldest and most bitter political enemies. Suddenly, Craig Shirley got very excited.

Jackson had been booked for a CPAC panel on media coverage of Clinton. He was invited to speak about his role in giving birth to Troopergate, the raucous mini-scandal that had erupted barely two months earlier when a group of Arkansas state troopers told stories about soliciting women and facilitating extramarital trysts for Clinton while he was governor. The stories were indeed extraordinary— at once shocking, nasty and, if true, disturbing. The troopers depicted Clinton as a terminal adolescent with a libido that was out of control, a man-child who plotted endlessly to conceal his escapades from the public and from his tempestuous wife. Jackson had a philosophy about how to handle stories such as these. When it came to exposing Clinton, he argued, conservatives had to overcome their distrust of the news media and reach out to mainstream news organizations. He had done precisely that with Troopergate, secretly arranging for the troopers to tell their stories to Bill Rempel, a ferocious investigative reporter with the *Los Angeles Times.* Reporters like Rempel had no qualms about going after Democrats like Clinton; they were "equal opportunity abusers" who had long since concluded that anything Clinton said had to be viewed with a healthy degree of distrust. Still, fearing that Rempel's editors might get cold feet, Jackson had arranged for an ideologically sympathetic "backup"—in this case the conservative *American Spectator*'s resident "hit man" David Brock—to be given the same stories on an embargoed basis. The strategy worked: when Rempel's nervous editors held his story, Brock rushed into print, thereby forcing the *Los Angeles Times* to publish its far more substantial account of Clinton's rampant womanizing. At least for a brief moment, the *Times* story gave Troopergate "legs." Rempel had done his homework: He had cell phone records documenting Clinton's repeated late night calls to one of his alleged paramours; he had one of the troopers recounting how Clinton, as president, had tried to entice him to keep silent by offering a federal job. It was, as Jackson saw it, a textbook example of how to work with, some might say manipulate, the mainstream media.

To spice up his presentation to the CPAC conference, Jackson had brought his troopers to Washington, where they would have a chance to repeat their accounts to what was sure to be a wildly appreciative audience. But that morning, Jackson briefed Shirley on somebody else he had brought along—a former Arkansas state worker. Her name was Paula Corbin Jones.

When Jackson relayed what Jones had to say, Shirley reported later, his jaw dropped. This, he thought, was going to be huge.

•   •   •

The press conference convened at one P.M. in the Omni Shoreham's shabbily elegant Diplomat Room. Within minutes, Shirley realized that nothing was going according to plan. Jackson's two troopers—beefy, vaguely menacing men—took their seats on the dais just a few feet from Jones and her entourage. Jackson, it turned out, wanted to use the press conference to make a fundraising pitch. A "Troopergate Whistleblower Fund" had been set up to handle the "legitimate job security" and "legal services" needs of his cops— and to encourage other whistleblowers to step forward and tell the truth about Bill Clinton in a "professional, dignified and non-tabloid manner." Jackson had set up an easel with a poster bearing an 800 number for benefactors to call. This was really stupid, Shirley thought. It was sure to turn off the press.

Then there was the lawyer Jackson had brought along, a bespectacled "good ol' boy" with an Arkansas drawl named Danny Traylor. Traylor was Paula Jones's attorney. Jackson described him as a "yellow dog Democrat." When he took the podium, he baffled everybody. He was, he said, just a "real estate lawyer" and he had not come to Washington to cause "any undue embarrassment to the First Family." He and his client just wanted to redress a grievance. The story Traylor told that afternoon was convoluted. "Mrs. Jones," as he called his client, had come to Washington to clear her "good reputation." She had been "defamed, libeled and slandered" by Arkansas state trooper Danny Ferguson in the Troopergate article written by David Brock and published in the *American Spectator.*

This seemed to make no sense. Cliff Jackson—the man who had just introduced him—was the impresario of the Troopergate article.

But Traylor insisted that on one point, the Brock article had got it all wrong. It quoted Ferguson, anonymously, describing how he had taken a woman identified only as "Paula" to a hotel room to meet Clinton. The article suggested that this woman had had a "consummated and satisfying sexual experience with Bill Clinton." It quoted her as volunteering to be Clinton's "regular girlfriend" after their meeting. The "Paula" in question was his client, Paula Jones, and she had indeed gone to meet Bill Clinton that day at the invitation of Trooper Ferguson. But the quote attributed to her was false; so, too, was any suggestion that the meeting had resulted in a "satisfying sexual experience." In fact, Jones's experience in the hotel room with Bill Clinton had been quite unpleasant.

"Ladies and gentlemen," Traylor said, "out of deference to the First Family [and] the presidency, I do not want to appeal to the prurient interests of us all." So he was instructing his client not to say precisely what happened when Bill Clinton met Paula Jones. "But let me assure you that what transpired in that room is the legal equivalent of on-the-job sexual harassment."

Jones herself seemed a puzzle. Slight, somewhat mousy, with long dark hair, she had a high-pitched, squeaky voice. She was twenty-seven years old, the mother of a young boy. She was accompanied by an angry-looking husband who remained resolutely silent. Jones looked nothing like Gennifer Flowers, the lounge singer with frosted hair who had rocked Clinton's campaign in 1992. When it was her turn to speak, she was maddeningly circumspect. "It's just humiliating what he did to me," she said.

What? reporters wanted to know. What had he done to you?

"He treated me in a most unprofessional manner."

Reporters hate nothing more than to be teased. The vagueness of Jones's account seemed to infuriate them. The questions, skeptical at first, grew hostile. Traylor and Jackson claimed that Jones had received no money to come to Washington to tell her story. Would she and her husband turn over their credit card receipts to verify that was the case? As for her allegations about the incident in the hotel room, the press corps demanded specifics.

"Was there any physical contact?"

"Was there any touching?"

"Was there any exposure of sexual parts?"

Jones huddled with Traylor. The lawyer decided to "open the door a bit" and let her give a few more details. Yes, Clinton had touched her. He had taken her by the hand and pulled her close to him. He had asked her for a "type of sex."

What did that mean? Nobody was satisfied, including Reed Irvine, the dyspeptic chief of Accuracy in Media—a conservative watchdog group. Irvine wanted Jones to tell all. That was the only way to make headlines, he knew. He thought he might smoke her out by asking a pointed enough question.

"You mentioned that he asked you to perform a sexual act," he shouted from the audience. "Was this something that involved taking his clothes off?"

The audience groaned.

Shirley watched the reporters glancing at each other and shaking their heads. He could tell: Nobody's buying it. He had begun the day hoping that CNN would carry Jones live; that the TV networks would report on her allegations that evening; that the major newspapers would carry her story on the front page the next day. CNN hadn't even bothered to show up. Now, Shirley wondered what, if anything, could possibly come of this.

Even Traylor, Jones's lawyer, seemed to have his doubts. By the end of the press conference, he was actually apologizing for even taking up the president's time with such a matter. He had no political agenda, he said. He and his client had no reason to embarrass the president or even to press the matter any further, even though, Traylor strongly hinted, they might well have a cause of legal action. But he had "lost a lot of sleep" over how to handle his client's needs and decided for now on a different course of action. He had written Ferguson a letter asking him to admit the truth. He had written the president a letter as well. All Clinton had to do was acknowledge his misbehavior, apologize to his client and set the record straight that there had been no sexual relations between the two of them.

Then he and Jones would go away.

Traylor closed with a quaint entreaty.

"We've got Bosnia," said Traylor. "We've got a health care crisis. We've got eighteen children living in a room without a father. Mr.

President, this is something that shouldn't occupy your energy and your attention. I would encourage you to come forward and . . . tell the American people what the truth of this matter is. If you made a mistake, the American people will forgive you."

Based on how the press conference had gone, there was little reason to think the White House would have to pay Traylor's request any heed. But years later, some said it was the soundest advice Bill Clinton would ever get.

●   ●   ●

To help drum up interest earlier in the day, Shirley had tipped off two reporters from *The Washington Post* to Jones's appearance. One was Lloyd Grove, a wry, acerbic writer for the paper's Style section who specialized in lampooning the idiosyncracies and idiocies of politicians of all stripes. Grove had watched much of the press conference with a bemused expression. What a joke this all was, he thought. Why would Jones choose to come forward at an event hosted by a Clinton enemy like Cliff Jackson and surrounded by people like Reed Irvine? And why was Traylor prattling on about a presidential apology? The whole thing illustrated the right wing's obsession with bimbos. He had been planning to write a Style article poking gentle fun at the CPAC conference and never imagined he would be handed such rich material.

I was the other *Post* reporter in the audience, and I had a somewhat different perspective. I was forty-one years old and on the national staff, assigned to cover the Justice Department—a prestige beat that was supposed to involve important national issues like affirmative action and the future of the criminal justice system. But for the past two years, I had carved out a far more entertaining subspecialty: investigating allegations of improprieties involving Bill and Hillary Clinton.

I had no particular ax to grind. As a college student, in the early 1970s, I had been inspired by Bob Woodward and Carl Bernstein as they uncovered the crimes of Richard Nixon. As a professional reporter, I had frequently had occasion to skewer Republicans, exposing the hypocrisies of the religious Right—many of whose leaders figured prominently at the CPAC conference. I had written extensively about the glaring weaknesses in gun control laws, earn-ing the enmity of one of Shirley's clients, the National Rifle Associa-tion. I was even, briefly, a small hero to the Clinton campaign's notorious "war room" when in the fall of 1992 I broke a series of front-page stories describing how Bush administration officials at the State Department had pawed through Bill Clinton's old passport files in search of political dirt.

But as a reporter, I don't think ideologically. The political intrigue of Arkansas fascinated me—the bizarre characters, the southern folklore, the strange mix of rumor, fact and tabloid fantasy. At the time, the Clinton White House seemed like a gothic ware-house filled with endless mysteries and intrigue. Lamps went flying in the middle of the night. Ushers and travel workers were fired for unexplained reasons. One sunny day the previous July, a White House lawyer—a childhood friend of the president's—had left work early, driven out to a park by the Potomac River and put a bullet through his mouth. Why? Why did these things happen?

Back in Little Rock that winter, odd characters kept popping up, talking about suspicious land deals and disappearing documents. Much of it was probably hokum cooked up by paranoids and far-right crazies. But all of it? Digging into Clinton's past was like walking into the pages of *All the King's Men.* You never knew what long-buried secrets you might stumble across.

I looked at Paula Jones and wondered: Could she be one of them?

•   •   •

As the press conference broke up, I decided to talk privately to Jackson. That morning, Shirley had told me what Jones would not say at the press conference: that Clinton had dropped his pants, exposed himself, and asked for oral sex. Now I wanted to hear this directly from Jackson. Was this really Jones's claim?

Yes, he assured me—and it's even better than that. He reminded me that the press kit he had passed out included sworn affidavits from two friends asserting that Jones had first told them all about this that very day—and that she was quite upset. That struck me as serious: real-time corroboration. I had helped cover the Clarence

Thomas–Anita Hill hearings for the *Post,* and I remembered how
feminist leaders had striven mightily to find witnesses who would
testify that Hill had told them about Thomas's behavior at some
point reasonably close to the time it had allegedly taken place. If
Jackson's affidavits were to be believed, they could be important evidence that bolstered Jones's story, establishing that her account
could not have been recently concocted to undermine Clinton's presidency.

I had gotten to know Jackson in 1992, when I first started chasing down Clinton scandal stories. There was no question he had an
agenda and a deep animus toward the president. They had known
each other for more than a quarter century and had actually once
been friendly at Oxford University, where Jackson was a Fulbright
Scholar while Clinton was a Rhodes. Clinton later had sought Jackson's help in contacting the leader of the Arkansas Republican Party
to get a crucial draft deferment. But at some point the two went
their separate ways. Over the years, a rivalry turned into a near
blood feud—at least on Jackson's side. I recalled having dinner with
Jackson along with a colleague, David Marannis, in early 1992 and
being struck by how personal it all seemed. Jackson was soft-spoken,
shy, socially inept—everything the fast-talking and personable Clinton was not. To Jackson, Clinton was a phony, a man who pretended
to be your best friend one minute and forgot you the next, a man
who would do anything to get ahead. Jackson, it was clear, burned
with resentment toward Clinton. He reminded me a bit of Messala,
the fictional Roman proconsul who, spurned by his childhood friend
Ben-Hur, plots eternal vengeance.

Still, unlike many other embittered Clinton enemies, and there
seemed to be quite a few of them in Arkansas, Jackson struck me as
worth listening to. He was, I thought, a more complicated and interesting character than the rabid hater depicted by the White House.
In my experience, Jackson didn't make things up; indeed, during the
1992 campaign he released letters stored in his attic that strength-
ened the case that Clinton had dissembled about his draft status. He
was also a veteran trial lawyer; a few years earlier, he had won a
multimillion-dollar sexual discrimination verdict on behalf of a
female employee of Texaco—not a case that would have attracted

many arch-conservatives. Jackson understood the rules of evidence—and the need of reporters to have solid sourcing. He assured me that he had personally spoken to Jones and her corroborators and could vouch for them.

I wanted to pursue this, I told him. Jackson was intrigued. To have *The Washington Post* take the story seriously would give the Jones allegations much more credibility. This, he thought, could be a repeat of his Troopergate strategy with the *Los Angeles Times.* Jackson took me aside, away from a group of reporters who seemed to be trying to listen in. In hushed, vaguely conspiratorial tones we talked some more.

Perhaps he could see to it that I could talk to Jones alone—and check out her story. Would I be interested?

Of course, I said. Let's do it.

Jackson gave me his room number at the Shoreham and said I should call him later.

•   •   •

But first I had a story to write—or at least so I thought. I arrived back at the *Post* newsroom about three P.M. and headed toward the national desk to brief my editors. Along the way, I ran into Robert Kaiser, the managing editor. With somewhat excessive enthusiasm, I gave him a quick fill: A new woman had just surfaced who was claiming Clinton whipped it out in a hotel room.

Kaiser, not surprisingly, glared at me disapprovingly. "What a worthwhile piece of news," he said, his voice dripping with sarcasm.

"Yeah, well, we'll see," I muttered, walking away. Kaiser, in my view, was a pompous snob; a Yalie, a former Moscow correspondent, the son of a member of the diplomatic corps who had served as an ambassador under John F. Kennedy and Jimmy Carter. Kaiser liked to propound grand thoughts about the serious mission we at the *Post* had to educate our readers. Not surprisingly, he didn't have much use for me; in truth, many editors didn't. I was known for my disheveled attire, messy desk and erratic work habits. Personnel evaluations dating back a decade invariably described me as "difficult"; I was an "uncommunicative" reporter who wandered off on his own without keeping his editors informed. At best, Kaiser tolerated me; every once in a while, my tenacity produced results. Most of the time, I was quite certain, he viewed me with utter disdain.

In any case, if Kaiser wasn't interested in the story, I was sure other *Post* editors would be. I was right. Within minutes, the news of a new sex charge against Clinton spread through the newsroom and I soon got the word "Len" wanted to be briefed right away. Executive Editor Leonard Downie, the boss, successor to the legendary Benjamin C. Bradlee, was in many ways the antithesis of Kaiser; in *Post* folklore, he was "Land Grant Len," an Ohio State grad who worked his way up, starting as a tireless, low-level metro reporter who was breaking stories of land fraud in Prince George's County before the world had ever heard of Woodward and Bernstein. Downie was an aggressive newsman and fiercely competitive. When it came to scandals involving a president of the United States, he was determined the *Post* would not be beaten.

Downie wanted to know what this latest charge was all about. One by one, the editors assembled in his office—Kaiser, Karen DeYoung, the *Post* national editor Fred Barbash, the deputy national editor, and a few others. I held court, laying out Jones's allegations and why I thought they were serious. Only a few months earlier, I explained, the paper had wrestled with what to do about the Troopergate allegations that Clinton had routinely used state police officers to procure women for sexual trysts. The White House had labeled the charges "ridiculous"; aides had demanded to know how come there wasn't a single woman who had stepped forth to confirm what the troopers were saying. The point had been taken up by Clinton's defenders in the news media. "Where are the women?" asked Joe Klein in a *Newsweek* column entitled "The Citizens of Bimboland" that derided the troopers' accounts as "trash."

Well, here was a woman, I told the *Post* editors. Jones said this happened to her.

I had brought along copies of the sworn affidavits from Jones's friends—I passed them around.

The editors looked uncomfortable. Barbash was the most openly dismissive. We can't trust these affidavits, he said, waving his arm with disdain. They look exactly alike, he pointed out. They were clearly written by somebody else—then handed to Jones's friends for their signatures.

Well, I started to say, they still signed.

Downie did not seem impressed with Barbash's point. That's the way these things are usually done, he pointed out. The lawyers prepare them—that doesn't mean much. Let's go ahead and report it out, he said. I should call the White House and draft a story.

Within minutes, I was on the phone with Clinton aide George Stephanopoulos. I had dealt with Stephanopoulos a bit during the campaign—and found him likable enough. He returned my calls relatively promptly and tried to be helpful. Now Stephanopoulos was irritated. He had watched Clinton almost sink under the weight of the Gennifer Flowers allegations in 1992 and then had spent considerable time during the campaign keeping the press from revisiting the issue. His primary weapon, captured brilliantly in the documentary *The War Room,* was shame. Serious journalists don't ask questions about stuff like this. "People will think you're scum," he could be heard telling a radio talk show host in *The War Room* who was threatening to air new sex allegations against Clinton.

He was only a bit more subtle with me. "You're not really going to write a story about this?" Stephanopoulos asked. It was obviously political, he argued. He pointed to Jackson's involvement and his advertisement to raise money for the "Troopergate Whistleblower Fund." He had already checked the story out. Clinton didn't even know this woman, he told me. She was being used.

Well, can I have a quote? I asked.

He hesitated. If he gave one, would that make it easier for the *Post* to run the story? I pressed. Downie has ordered me to write this, I told him. Grudgingly he gave one. The charge is "not true," he said. "It's just a cheap political fundraising trick."

There were a few other players who had to be called. One, of course, was the trooper, Danny Ferguson. It was Ferguson's comments in the *American Spectator* that had prompted Jones to come forward. Although he had not been named in the piece, Ferguson was the trooper who described bringing a woman named "Paula" to Clinton's hotel room. "Paula told him she was available to be Clinton's regular girlfriend if he so desired," the article reported. I tracked down Ferguson in his home in Arkansas that afternoon to ask him if he had been accurately quoted. "I'm not going to have anything to say," he told me.

Well, what about the author of the *Spectator* article? Young and cocky, Brock had already made a name for himself as a right-wing attack dog, even before his Troopergate scoop, his book *The Real Anita Hill,* had skewered the feminist icon. It seemed no small irony that Jones's main beef, or at least her reason for going public, was her distress at what she contended was the libelously inaccurate portrayal of her in Brock's piece. I got Brock on the phone and asked him: Did you get it wrong?

Brock got huffy. Not at all, he said. The Jones story "corroborates the essence" of what he wrote because it shows that the troopers actually did solicit women for Clinton.

Well, how about Jones's complaint that you portrayed her—wrongly, she contended—as a compliant sexual partner of Clinton?

"That seems a fairly minor point to me," Brock said.

What a sensitive guy, I thought as I hung up.

While I was writing, my *Post* colleague Lloyd Grove was sent back to the hotel by Downie to interview Jones. The *Post* wanted to know precisely what she was alleging. Grove found Jones in her room at the Shoreham. She was lounging on the bed. She was friendly, but Traylor refused to lift his instructions that she not talk about the events of the day in question. "She wouldn't tell me what happened," Grove said later. Grove got annoyed and frustrated. "I told her this is not credible, you're attacking the president of the United States. You've got to do a little better than this. This is really not a good way of getting your message out." Jones simply repeated the same limited account she had given at the news conference. After about an hour, Grove gave up and returned to the *Post.* His assessment: He had no idea whether or not she was telling the truth.

By now, it was getting close to deadline. By 6:30 P.M. I had written about eight hundred words—a relatively minor piece that I figured would run inside the paper somewhere. The story was low-key and, I thought, down the middle. Jones's charge was the lead, followed by a paragraph of context and Stephanopoulos's denial:

A former Arkansas state employee said yesterday that President Clinton made unwanted sexual advances during a 15-minute encounter in a Little Rock hotel room while he was governor in 1991.

The woman, Paula Jones, 27, provided her account of what she called "sexual harassment" at a Washington press conference sponsored by a conservative political group seeking to embarrass the president by reviving allegations of his sexual infidelity.

White House spokesman George Stephanopoulos flatly denied Jones's story, saying Clinton did not know the woman and that she was being used by the president's political enemies. "It's not true," he said of her account. "It's just a cheap political fundraising trick."

But Cliff Jackson, a bitter political enemy of the president who hosted the press conference, said that Jones's story provided important new corroboration for the recent accounts of two Arkansas state troopers that they were regularly instructed to solicit potential sexual partners for Clinton.

The story, I felt, played it straight. But was it fair? When the issue is something as highly charged and corrosive as sexual misconduct, do the usual rules apply? Is it responsible journalism to report sensational allegations simply because they had been aired at a public forum? I thought there was enough there—the sworn affidavits from Jones's friends, the rough tracking with the Ferguson version of the same story—to let the readers know what had gone on at the CPAC conference. But I realized it was going to be a dicey call.

No sooner had I finished than I picked up rumblings of what I was up against. Stephanopoulos had been on the phone with Ann Devroy, the paper's chief White House correspondent, lobbying hard against my story. Devroy apparently agreed—and talked to some of the editors on the national desk. Now, just as the paper was being laid out, Downie convened another meeting.

This time, the discussion was more pointed. Devroy, without mentioning her talks with Stephanopoulos, argued most forcefully. "How can we run this story?" she demanded. "We have no idea if any of this is true." The involvement of Cliff Jackson made the whole thing suspect. We hadn't even interviewed the woman ourselves, we still didn't know precisely what she was alleging; we knew nothing about her background and how she came to be at this gathering of Clinton enemies.

I was annoyed—more at the idea that another reporter was trying to suppress my story than at the points Devroy was raising.

Devroy was a dogged reporter, the best White House correspondent in the business. I didn't view her as a White House lackey. But I did think she wanted to control the paper's coverage of Clinton. If the *Post* was going to stick it to the president, she wanted to be the reporter doing it—on her terms. The press conference had been a public event; it was bound to be covered in most papers tomorrow and would probably get some TV coverage. "How could we not print anything?" I asked. Readers would hear something about Jones's charge and expect to learn something about it in their morning paper. "How can we just ignore this?"

For about half an hour, the debate went back and forth. Others joined in, mostly on Devroy's side. Downie listened—then ruled. We would not run the story—but not because we didn't take this seriously. In fact, he wanted it investigated thoroughly. Jones and her friends should be interviewed; we should look into who she was and how she'd come to make this charge. It was my job to get to the bottom of it.

Early that evening, I got back in touch with Jackson at the Shoreham. By now, he and his visitors from Little Rock—Jones, her husband and Traylor—were in the doldrums. CNN had ignored their press conference, and there was nothing on the network news. Now I was informing him that the *Post* wouldn't run anything. But I relayed Downie's charge to me: The story had to be investigated. I reminded him of our talk about the possibility of interviewing Jones in depth. Jackson seemed excited. If a "liberal" paper like the *Post* took an interest, that could change everything. Jackson, it turned out, had already talked to Traylor and Jones about my request. They, too, were interested. Of course, I explained, I wanted this to be exclusive. Nobody else should have access to Jones while I did what I had to do. Jackson understood. We worked out arrangements for me to come by the hotel and meet Jones the next morning.

Actually, I didn't wait that long to get to work. I had gotten the phone number of one of Jones's sisters that night—one she supposedly had spoken to at the time about her experiences with Clinton— and called her. Lydia Cathay, then twenty-nine and married, answered the phone and spoke to me at length. Yes, her sister had indeed told her all about the incident with Clinton the very night it happened. She came to the bedroom, shut the door, then plopped onto her bed and cried, Cathay said. "She was afraid she might lose her job."

I called Jones's mother, Delmer Corbin, who sounded somewhat confused. Still, her story tracked. "She didn't tell me near as much as she did her sister—I think because she knew how much it would hurt me," she said. Well, I asked, what did she tell you? "I just remember her telling me how Clinton was flirting around. I do remember her saying he put his hands on her and kissed her. . . . I was greatly surprised that the governor would act that way toward her." Paula didn't tell her more, Corbin said, because "I think Paula was afraid that it would hurt her mother. I've cried, and I've prayed about this—and it just hurts me. You know, she was brought up in church. I'm a Christian lady."

That night, I got a message that Downie wanted me to call him— at home. I'd never been asked to do that before. I rang, he answered. He wanted to know where we stood, what we'd learned—and what I planned to do next. I briefed him, told him about the plan to meet Jones on Saturday. I also told him about my interview with Jones's sister. "Well," said Downie, "that's a start."

2

"I mean the man is just a pervert!"

The paucity of news coverage of the Friday press conference was very much on the minds of Paula Jones and her entourage when I met them early Saturday morning at a suite in the Omni Shoreham. Two of the three television networks hadn't said a word about Jones's claims; a third, ABC, mentioned them briefly and then quoted the White House as calling her charges "pathetic." The *Post*, of course, carried nothing. Surprisingly, *The New York Times,* a paper traditionally far more reticent than the *Post* about such matters, carried a four-paragraph story, buried deep inside the paper, that reported allegations of "unwanted sexual advances" by Clinton. In the story, Mark Gearan, the White House communications director, was quoted as saying: "It is not true. He does not recall meeting her. He was never alone in a hotel with her."

"The nerve of that!" Jones said indignantly within moments of our introduction. "To say that he did not remember the meeting with Ms. Jones whatsoever. He knows exactly what I look like and who I am. He is not stupid. Can you believe the gall of that man?"

Jones, it was clear, was not exactly lacking in self-confidence. She was, in fact, quite chirpy and chatty, far more spontaneous than she had appeared at the press conference the day before. The daughter of a lay preacher in a fundamentalist church, Paula Corbin Jones had grown up in the tiny town of Lonoke, Arkansas, about an hour west of Little Rock. She was raised in a strict household where provocative dress and off-color language were forbidden. She had clearly strayed a bit, especially after her father died of a stroke in 1985. As the country would soon learn, thanks in large part to the arduous research of the president's legal team, Jones had begun a walk on the wild side. An estranged brother-in-law would regale reporters with tales of how Jones had pursued men and enjoyed a full range of sexual experiences.

By the time Jones met with me that morning in the winter of 1994, she had been married for nearly three years and was the mother of an eighteen-month-old boy, Madison, who was back in Arkansas being cared for by her sister Lydia. We talked a bit about Madison. She missed him. My daughter was nearly one, I told her. For a few moments, we had established some rapport.

Jones was not terribly well educated. She had a penchant for butchering verbs and mangling pronouns—"persuade" became "persuase," "himself" turned into "hisself." She also struck me as utterly guileless and unsophisticated—certainly about politics. "I've never been politically anything," she told me. Had her parents been Republicans or Democrats? I asked her. "I don't have any idea," she said, and then giggled. She supposed that maybe her daddy might have been interested in politics a bit. "I guess any man probably would be more than a woman," she said. But, she added, "That's just not my interest in life."

My interest, I explained to her, was to hear her story in detail. If it held up, *The Washington Post* might run a story about it. But only if what she told me checked out. She was, she said, more than happy to go along. She would tell all her friends to cooperate. "I'll give you their numbers and everything," she promised. Jones's husband, Steve, still looking glum, nodded his assent. He sat nearby, as did Traylor, the lawyer, who turned out to be quite entertaining. "Izzy! Please to meet you, Izzy," he said, adopting a nickname he came to use repeatedly. Cliff Jackson showed up briefly to say hello—then disappeared. He was smart enough to know that even the slightest attempt to coach Jones on what she should tell me would undercut the whole point of the interview.

Jones plopped down on the hotel bed, and for the next three hours, while my tape recorder ran, she chain-smoked cigarettes and recounted her story for the first time to an outsider.

She had been on the job only a few months, a secretary-typist at the Arkansas Industrial Development Commission, when she and her childhood friend Pamela Blackard got assigned to work the registration desk at the Quality Management Conference at the Excelsior Hotel. Clinton was supposed to speak in the morning, she said, but was late. Shortly after lunch, he walked out into the hallway and was hanging out, chatting with well-wishers. He was, said Jones, "just lollygagging around."

It was, she guessed, about 2:30 P.M. Soon, Trooper Ferguson came by to "chitchat" with Jones and Blackard. It turned out he also had a message to deliver from his boss: The governor said "I made his knees knock." Blackard said to her, "Paula, he [Clinton] is looking straight at us."

Jones said she and Blackard joked nervously about it—as did Ferguson—and then went back to work. Clinton continued to hang out in the hallway. Jones thought he was "trying to make sure nobody was around and stuff . . . to see when we were alone or something . . . trying to see I guess when he could get a chance to come over."

Then Ferguson came back and slipped her a note. "I said, what is this? I had it in my hand, I think it was just face up. It had a four-digit number. . . . He said, 'The governor would like to meet you up in his room and talk with you.' . . . And that's when me and Pam, oh we were weird. We didn't know what to believe."

Should she go up or not? According to Jones, she was reluctant. "Pam remembered this—Pam said that he [Ferguson] was trying to persuase [sic] me . . . lettin' me know, yeah, that we do this all the time for the governor. . . . We were kind of discussing it, me and Pam—Oh my God, he wants me to go up there, what do you think he wants? . . . And Pam said, 'Oh I don't know, Paula.'" Maybe, Blackard suggested, "You might get a job at the governor's office." Jones agreed. "What else would he want me up there for?"

For many, skepticism about Jones's story begins with her assertion that she agreed to go upstairs thinking it might lead to a better job. It struck me as a bit dubious: Surely there was ample reason to suspect that Clinton's interest in her was anything but innocent. What did she think Ferguson meant about Clinton's knocking knees?

"But I never thought he would actually do something," said Jones. "He's the governor! I thought maybe that he thought I was attractive. I didn't think he was going to go up there and do what he did."

"The guy's got a reputation," I said.

"I didn't know that. I had never heard anything."

"In retrospect, would you say you were probably a little naive?"

"Yes. I am very gullible and naive and I had a problem with that a lot. But that's just my raising. I was brought up to trust people and especially of that statue [sic], you know, a governor. I've never been in that type of situation before, but it's a shame you can't trust somebody like that."

Her account of what followed was, heard for the first time, a bit jarring. Ferguson took her upstairs in the elevator to the eleventh floor and pointed her to Clinton's room. She knocked, Clinton answered, and for the next few minutes they introduced themselves and made awkward small talk. Clinton asked how she liked her job. She asked about Hillary "working on something with the children in the school system or something. You'd think if I was up there to do something I'd mention his wife's name," she said. "You know, my goodness."

Jones said she also asked if Clinton was planning to run for president. "His face got red or something and he goes, 'I don't know yet or something or I hadn't decided or it hasn't came out yet.' In other words, he wasn't going to tell me anyway, put it that way."

It was, she said, about five minutes into the encounter when events took a decidedly darker turn. Clinton was standing by the windowsill, she said, when suddenly he "picked my hand up and just kind of like this, he wasn't grabbing it, you know, he just held it. He kind of pulled me over and he backed up just against the windowsill."

Jones said she "pulled away," walked to another part of the room and tried to divert his attention by "just talking about everything else." Clinton, she said, got "kind of flustered" and walked over closer to her, leaning up against a wing-backed chair. "I guess he was listening to me because he was going, oh, he just killed me with this look on his face. Yeah, yeah, yeah. I can just see him looking."

Jones turned to Traylor. "I will never forget the look on his face,

Danny! I will never! His face was just red, beet red, I swear it was. Oh, it was horrible!"

At this point, she said, Clinton reached over and slipped his hand up her culottes. "And I said, 'What are you doing? What is going on?' He was trying to nibble on my neck and I was trying to back off. I said, what is, I said, 'I don't want to do this.' . . . I backed away and then he started telling me, he said, 'I was just noticing downstairs. I was looking at your curves and the way you walked around the front of the table and I love the way your hair came down your back, the middle of your back and your curves.'"

Jones was now quite animated. She once again pulled herself away, she said, and sat on a couch on the other side of the room. "I was gettin' away from him. . . . And he could have caught the hint. I mean the man is just a pervert!

"I need to be going," she says she told Clinton. "Oh, he says, you don't need to go right now." Then Clinton—who had already taken off his sport coat and loosened his tie—sat on the couch beside her. When she looked over, she said, the governor of Arkansas had his pants down to his knees. "He had boxer shorts and everything and he exposed hisself with an erection to me on the couch. And I was literally just scared, shocked." Clinton was "holding it . . . fiddling it or whatever. And he asked me to—I don't know his exact word—give him a blow job or—I know you gotta know his exact words."

"Exact words," I said.

"He asked me to do something, I know that. I'll tell you, I was so shocked. I think he wanted me to kiss it. . . . And he was saying it in a very disgusting way, just a horny-ass way that just scared me to death."

"What do you mean in a very disgusting way?" I asked.

"Disgusting way, he just, it was *please, I want it bad*—just that type of way, like he was wanting it bad, you know." Jones said she "jumped up and said, 'Now, I don't do that, I'm not that type of person, I need to be going downstairs.' . . . And he said, 'Well, I don't want to make you do something you don't want to do.' But he said if you have any trouble—now that's when he pulled his boxer shorts up then—but if you have any trouble you have Dave Harrington contact me immediately. You won't be in trouble. But I left."

"But he did say, 'I don't want to make you do anything you don't want to do'?" I pointed out.

"Oh, wasn't that sweet of him? Asshole. That one little sayin' in there I guess will get him off the hook."

*   *   *

I encountered my first potential witness within a few minutes of leaving Jones's hotel room. At both the press conference and in my interview, Jones had recounted a curious coda to her encounter with Clinton. It was her job to deliver documents to the governor's office, a duty that regularly took her to Clinton's third-floor suite in the state Capitol. One day, some weeks after the incident, Jones said she had run into Clinton by the stairs of the Capitol rotunda. Clinton, accompanied by one of his troopers, gave her a big greeting: He put his arms around her, turned to his trooper and said, "Look at us, kind of like Beauty and the Beast, isn't it?" Jones thought the trooper in question was one of those at the press conference—one of Cliff Jackson's troopers, Larry Patterson. A large and gregarious man, Patterson was still an officer in the Arkansas State Police, although after Troopergate he had been transferred from gubernatorial security to the somewhat less lofty post of highway patrol administrator in the Used Car Licensing Division. That afternoon, I found him in the lobby of the Omni Shoreham, regaling the conservative activists with tales of Clinton's sexual adventures. I pulled him aside and asked about what Jones had to say.

"Oh yes," he said instantly. He remembered that episode well. It happened just as Jones said. "He gave her a big hug," Patterson said. Then he plopped his arm around her shoulder and made the "Beauty and the Beast" comment. That's just the way Clinton was, Patterson said. He would do that sort of stuff with women all the time. "It was common for him to walk up and hug or kiss or put his hands on some female," Patterson told me.

In the Troopergate articles, Patterson had been the source for the most sensational, on-the-record accounts of Clinton's womanizing (Ferguson ultimately refused to be quoted by name). Patterson had recounted, for example, how he once stood guard in the parking lot of Chelsea Clinton's elementary school while the governor received oral sex in the car of one of his many paramours. Patterson had also reported that Clinton told him how, after having "researched the subject in the Bible," he had concluded that oral sex did not constitute adultery—a Clintonian distinction that, years later, the world would hear much more about. Indeed, this seems to have been a topic of considerable discussion between the governor and his bodyguard. According to a later account by Patterson, Clinton had insisted that oral sex was the safest sex because stomach acids interacting with swallowed semen would neutralize the AIDS virus.[1]

On this day, however, for some reason that wasn't quite clear, Patterson quickly steered the conversation to a somewhat tamer subject: how Clinton used to give him remarkably successful tips on how to pick up women. Really? I said. Oh yes, said Patterson, Clinton had told him on more than one occasion about the best line to use whenever you see an attractive woman reading a book. You go up to her and, in an excited voice, say, "I can't believe you're reading this! This book changed my life." Patterson told me he had tried the line—and it actually worked. I thanked him for this helpful information and moved on.

I got back to the newsroom midafternoon and handed my tape to a *Post* transcriber. The newsroom is mostly empty on Saturdays. A small crew was putting the final touches on the Sunday paper. But a few editors knew what I was up to, and as portions of my transcript made their way into the computer system, some began calling it up. Was this for real? one colleague asked. Were we really going to publish this?

Beats me, I said. I had no idea.

•   •   •

The truth was I wasn't entirely sure at that point what I made of Jones's account. My instincts told me she was describing *something* that was real. Liars generally get fuzzy and dodgy when you press for details. Jones didn't; her account was studded with particulars that would have taken considerable rehearsal had it been concocted. Her story was also nuanced; Clinton's last-second soothing words—"I don't want to make you do something you don't want to do"—seemed out of place if the story had been invented to hurt him politically. There was no question that some parts seemed improbable, especially her insistence that she had no inkling of any sexual intentions on Clinton's part. Still, I reasoned, Jones had been on the job for just two months at the lowest possible rung of the state government. A state trooper had just informed her that the governor wanted to see her upstairs. What was she supposed to do? Tell him to get lost?

Jones's claim that Clinton had dropped his pants was bizarre. Clinton was an uncannily savvy politician who was legendary for his acute sensitivity to his environment. Nobody knew better than he how to take the temperature of an audience and play to the crowd. Could he have so badly misread the situation at the Excelsior that day? What was one to make of Jones's vivid descriptions of Clinton's actions and demeanor—slipping his hand up her legs, the "beet red" face, the "horny-ass" request for oral sex? Did Jones invent this stuff? Or was Bill Clinton more seriously disturbed than anybody had suspected? Even given the possibility of some embellishment on Jones's part, I thought it right that her charges be taken seriously. If she was telling the truth, then Clinton had treated her, a state employee, in a degrading and humiliating fashion, as a tool for his sexual pleasure.

* * *

Of course we were a long way away from establishing that. But if Jones's credibility deserved scrutiny, and perhaps some skepticism, Clinton wasn't exactly starting with a clean slate either. With much of the national press corps, certainly with reporters like me and my colleagues at the *Post*, he had a history—and that history unquestionably influenced how I approached the story.

Bright, articulate, personable and relentlessly ambitious, Clinton had been well-known for more than a decade to most of *The Washington Post*'s political reporters. He had received generally favorable coverage during the 1992 campaign; indeed, some of the dispatches written by David Maranniss (who would go on to write a critically acclaimed and authoritative biography, *First in His Class*) positively bubbled with enthusiasm: Here was a dynamic new Democrat who had the potential to reenergize American politics, a Baby Boomer who embodied the values of his generation, a southerner who on the really important questions—race, concern for the underprivileged— displayed genuine empathy. His could be a healing presidency. And yet, for all his brainpower and political talents, many of my colleagues harbored profound doubts—about his glibness, about his lack of political spine and, most important, about his tendency to fudge the truth and even flat-out lie, especially when it came to inconvenient questions about his past.

Inside the *Post* newsroom, the suspicions about Clinton were exacerbated by an incident during the presidential campaign. Dan Balz, the paper's lead reporter for campaign coverage and a journalist universally respected for his fairness, had interviewed Clinton about his draft history in December 1991. Rival campaigns were starting to whisper that Clinton might have a draft problem, and Balz wanted to nail the candidate down. Balz had a personal interest: He had graduated from college the same year as Clinton, 1968—the year graduate-school deferments had been eliminated. He knew how large the specter of Vietnam was for everyone in his class and, having pulled the candidate's Selective Service records, thought it odd that Clinton had managed to remain 1-A for a full year—from the summer he graduated to the fall of 1969. "It didn't quite add up," Balz would later recall thinking.

That December, Balz had a chance to question Clinton directly. In a televised debate, Clinton and Nebraska senator Bob Kerrey had gotten into an exchange about rival proposals for voluntary national service. One afternoon, as Clinton was about to leave Washington, Balz hitched a ride with him to National Airport and for twenty minutes questioned him about his draft history.

"You and I were in the same graduating class," Balz said. "How did you manage to not get called that year?"

Clinton casually brushed the question aside. It was kind of surprising, wasn't it? "As it happened, I told them I expected to be called while I was over there [at Oxford] the first year, but they never did," he said. It was, Clinton suggested, just a matter of luck. "I wound up just going through the lottery and it was just a pure fluke that I was never called."

George Stephanopoulos was sitting in the front seat, heard Clinton use the word "fluke" and wondered about it. Balz thought it strange, too, but decided to take Clinton at his word. Somebody tells you something, he thought, "you take it at face value."

In the same interview, Clinton also talked about his later decision to give up his ROTC deferment in the fall of 1969. He presented it as an act of conscience—and patriotism. Whatever personal doubts he had over the Vietnam War, Clinton suggested, he had been tormented over the idea of ducking combat when so many of his less fortunate high school classmates were being drafted. "Four of my classmates had died in Vietnam, including a boy that was one of my closest friends when I was a child," Clinton told Balz. "And so I asked to be put back in the draft." In fact, Clinton insisted, the head of his ROTC unit tried to talk him out of his decision. To which Clinton said he replied: "I just can't put it off. Call me. Let's go."

Balz wrote a story about all this—a front-page piece that ran January 18, 1992, comparing Kerrey's and Clinton's experiences during the Vietnam War. It quoted Clinton's account of his draft history as he had given it. At the paper, there was little interest in taking the story any further. Clinton had opposed the Vietnam War and avoided service the way millions of others did. He had given a plausible account of his actions. Was this really an issue?

But there was a problem. Almost nothing that Clinton had told Balz that day was actually true. Within a few weeks of Balz's piece, the real story began to emerge, dug up by *The Wall Street Journal*, the *Los Angeles Times* and other news organizations. Clinton, it turned out, had maneuvered mightily to avoid the Vietnam War. He had pulled influence with his local draft board—recruiting help from Arkansas senator William Fulbright and even Governor Winthrop Rockefeller's office—to avoid being called. He had enrolled in an ROTC program only after he had been classified 1-A and had done so for the express purpose of avoiding service in Vietnam. Clinton was correct when he had told Balz that he finally surrendered his deferment in October of that year and allowed his name to be put back in the draft. But he did so only after President Nixon had begun major troop withdrawals and his chances of being called had substantially diminished.

Clinton's claim that he finally said to his draft board, "Call me,

let's go," was especially fanciful. Having signed up for the ROTC program at the University of Arkansas, Clinton promptly dropped out of
the program and made plans to attend Yale Law School days after
pulling No. 311 in the draft lottery—a number that virtually guaran-
teed he would never get called. Two days after the lottery, he wrote
his famous letter to Colonel Eugene J. Holmes, director of the University of Arkansas ROTC program, in which he thanked him "for
saving me from the draft."

Even by the standard of political campaigns, where candidates
are expected to portray themselves in the most favorable light, Clinton's rewriting of his draft history was a maddening performance.
But that wasn't the end of it. Three months later, it appeared the
draft controversy had subsided. Clinton had weathered it as he had
all the other furors that had rocked his campaign. Balz was in Manhattan, covering the New York primary, when he got a call from the
Post late on a Saturday night: The Associated Press had dug up a
copy of Clinton's draft induction notice dated April 1969—the very
induction notice Clinton had insisted he had never gotten. Years
later, Balz remembered that evening quite clearly. "I was stunned, to
say the least," he recalled. Clinton hadn't just fudged his draft history—he had brazenly lied. Balz ran across the street and found all
the campaign aides huddled in Stephanopoulos's room, agonizing
over how to explain this latest example of their candidate's mendacity. For months, they had been defending Clinton against the charge
of draft-dodging and berating reporters who questioned Clinton's
account. Stephanopoulos himself later wrote that he felt sick over
the experience and stayed in bed the next morning, "unable to face
the world."

Soon enough, Mickey Kantor, the *éminence grise* of the Clinton
spin doctors, arrived on the scene and settled on the campaign's new
response—a shift that would be repeated over and over again by
Clinton aides whenever their man got caught shaving the truth. Kantor erupted in anger at Balz and other reporters who had gathered at
campaign headquarters. Why were you all still dwelling on these
matters? With all the problems of the world, why are you even bothering to ask questions about this sort of thing? What difference does
it make?

The next day, Balz accompanied Clinton to an African American church in Brooklyn and watched while Clinton fended off questions about the draft induction notice he had always denied getting. The notice was such a "routine matter" that he hadn't even thought about it before, Clinton told the reporters that day. His draft board had told him he wouldn't have to report until that fall—after he got back from England, so he just forgot about it. "It just never occurred to me to make anything of it one way or the other," he said, an explanation that almost nobody accepted.

Balz was a pro; he had long since learned to keep his personal feelings out of his coverage of any candidate. Still, the incident was embarrassing—as much for the paper as for him. The *Post* had relied on Clinton's word and ended up looking foolish. Clinton's explanation—that he had simply forgotten about it—was pathetic. When David Broder, the dean of *Post* political reporters, heard it, his immediate reaction was, "That's bullshit. Nobody forgets their own draft notice." For Broder, perhaps the city's most influential political reporter, it was a pivotal moment in his evaluation of Clinton. "That's when the lightbulb went off—that this is a guy who reconstructs his own history to suit his needs," Broder said years later.

•   •   •

There was another, more ambiguous, episode that subtly influenced how Clinton was viewed by the paper. It had taken place more than a year earlier, on March 23, 1991, during the Gridiron Dinner—a grand rite of spring where the pooh-bahs of the Washington press corps treat themselves to a lavish feast and satirical skits staged by well-known columnists and pundits. Broder had invited as his guests Clinton and two young reporters from the *Post*'s staff, Barbara Vobejda, the paper's education writer, and Laura Sessions Stepp, a soft-spoken religion reporter from the small town of Booneville, Arkansas. Broder had arranged for Clinton to sit between Katharine Graham, chairman of the board of the Washington Post Company, and Meg Greenfield, editor of the *Post*'s editorial page. But some thought Clinton seemed to take a special interest in the two younger female reporters Broder had invited.

When the dinner was over, the Arkansas governor came over to

shake Stepp's hand and—according to Stepp—wouldn't let go. Looking intensely into her eyes, Clinton told her that "you really have to
come see me" in Little Rock. Stepp lightheartedly tried to brush him
off. But Clinton persisted. He repeated his invitation, looking closely
at her, continuing to hold her hand even as she gently tried to
remove it. "I just thought he was coming on to me," concluded
Stepp. "I've shaken enough politicians' hands to know this was a little unusual." She felt unsettled enough that in the newsroom the
next Monday, she mentioned it to Broder. "I was sort of pissed,"
Broder said later. "It was clear that whatever had happened, it was
something that made her uncomfortable—and he was my guest."

As it happened, Broder had breakfasted with Clinton the morning after the Gridiron and remembered him saying that he had just
spoken to Hillary and told her all about the dinner. Was Clinton trying to cover for his misstep the night before? Inside the paper, the
Stepp incident made the rounds. Some thought Stepp must be exaggerating. But nobody could rule out the possibility that it was
exactly as she thought—and that Bill Clinton was stupid enough to
have made a pass at a *Washington Post* reporter.

•   •   •

I had my own experiences with Clinton, or more precisely his
operatives, that unquestionably influenced my own reaction to
the Jones allegations. In early July of 1992, I had been working on a
lengthy story about the use of private investigators in political campaigns. The story had been prompted by reports that Ross Perot had
retained detectives to investigate the business dealings of President
Bush's sons. After I completed it, though, I had gotten a tip about a
similar development in the Clinton campaign: Clinton operatives, I
was told, had hired a private investigator from San Francisco who
was flying around the country gathering "dirt" on women who might
allege romantic relationships with Clinton. The gumshoe was purportedly being paid out of campaign funds and reporting directly to
Betsey Wright, Clinton's longtime chief of staff in Little Rock.

I knew Wright: she was a canny political operator who knew
Clinton's vulnerabilities better than anyone. For reasons that nobody
had ever been able to fathom (an extremely fierce mothering

instinct seemed as good a bet as any) she had taken it upon herself to protect Clinton from the press—in short, to make sure that his manifest weaknesses as an individual never spilled over into public view. She, like me, also clearly relished the spy-versus-spy dimension of political campaigns. And she liked matching wits with reporters.

Back in March, we had lunch in Little Rock. She was pleasant and gracious but made it clear she was keeping a close eye on me. Weeks earlier, I had ventured down to the courthouse in Arkadelphia—about an hour and a half southwest of Little Rock—to check out a tip that a prominent Clinton supporter who had landed several no-bid state contracts supposedly had a drug record. My trip yielded nothing to support the allegation and I never wrote a story. I had not even called the Clinton campaign for comment. Still, Wright couldn't resist letting me know that her spies were everywhere.

"You should know," she whispered at one point, "I've finally figured out what you were doing in the Arkadelphia courthouse a few weeks ago."

Now, in July, armed with my tip about the private detective, I looked forward to the chance to retaliate. I got Wright on the phone and confronted her with my information about the private detective. Much to my surprise, she confirmed it—and proceeded to boast about it. The investigator, a renowned San Francisco detective named Jack Palladino, was needed to cope with an alarming development: claims by and about a plethora of women alleged to have had sexual affairs with Bill Clinton. There was, Wright explained, a sleazy tabloid culture that was degrading the political dialogue. Women—nineteen by her count—were being pursued by the tabloids, which offered juicy sums of up to $500,000 a pop to tell embarrassing stories about the Arkansas governor. "The gold-digger growth is enormous," Wright told me. "There is a whole industry being spawned."

The campaign needed to protect itself, Wright maintained. Palladino's assignment was to collect from the targeted women affidavits denying any romantic relationship with Clinton. If they were not so cooperative, he would take other steps, such as gathering information that would raise questions about their credibility or mental stability.

I asked Wright if she was using Palladino for research on any other topics. No, she said. "I don't think I've used him for anything except bimbo eruptions," she added. And with that utterance, a new phrase entered the political vernacular.

This, I thought, was surely a new wrinkle in American politics—a paid dirt-digger whose brief was, at least in part, to smear the reputations of women romantically linked to a presidential candidate. In one case I detailed in the article, Palladino had successfully suppressed a story about Sally Perdue—a former Miss Arkansas who claimed to have had a brief fling with Clinton in the fall of 1983—by furnishing the *National Enquirer* with signed statements from former associates and estranged relatives raising questions about her veracity. My story took no stand on whether Perdue or any of the others targeted by Palladino were actually telling the truth; indeed, I thought the story important even if they were not. The payments to Palladino came from campaign funds, which were federally subsidized. Equally important, they were being laundered: the initial payments, totaling $28,000, were made to a Denver law firm, which in turn passed the money to Palladino's agency in San Francisco. That way, only the name of the Denver law firm showed up on financial disclosure statements filed with the Federal Elections Commission. In the line where the campaign was supposed to list the purpose of the expenditure, officials had written simply "legal fees."

That little bit of subterfuge seemed the most significant part of the Palladino story: every trivial expenditure for postage and catering was routinely reported on Clinton's FEC report. But something truly worth knowing—the campaign's retention of a high-powered private detective—had been concealed. Working myself into high dudgeon, I proclaimed to anyone who would listen that this was an outrage: Didn't the name Donald Segretti mean anything to anybody around here? Didn't people have to obey the campaign disclosure laws anymore? But few of my colleagues seemed to share my passion.

Under the headline CLINTON TEAM WORKS TO DEFLECT ALLEGATIONS ON NOMINEE'S PRIVATE LIFE, the Palladino story ran on page 18 on July 26, 1992, two weeks after the Democratic convention in New York had nominated Clinton. I thought that if nothing else, it gave an unusually revealing glimpse of a secret political war between Clinton and his enemies over rumors about his sexual peccadillos. To put Palladino's retention in perspective, Wright had pointed me *toward* the activities of Larry Case, a dubious Little Rock private detective who had taped a thirty-eight-year-old Oklahoma City woman saying she had an extended affair with Clinton in the 1980s. The moment the Clinton campaign got wind of the story, Palladino hopped aboard a plane to Oklahoma City—and persuaded the woman to sign an affidavit claiming she had been "tricked" by Case because she suffered from "multiple personality disorder" triggered by recent brain surgery.

But this was not a subject the press corps at large wanted to touch. With these sorts of characters, who could possibly figure out what was true? Besides, Clinton's nomination was assured. Questions about his sex life seemed out of bounds. Even legitimate questions about the use of campaign funds for questionable purposes seemed irrelevant. Much to my frustration, the Palladino story got no bounce.

It did result, however, in one modest achievement. After it appeared, the campaign was prodded into publicly reporting its payments to Palladino. More than a year later, after Clinton was president, I waded through hundreds of pages of campaign reports at the Federal Elections Commission. The total Clinton campaign funds disbursed to Palladino had exceeded $100,000—with a large chunk of the payments delayed until after the election, one final layer of subterfuge.

I wondered: What exactly had he done for all that money?

•   •   •

Inside the *Post* newsroom, the questions about Bill Clinton's past lingered. In the fall of 1993, my colleague Sue Schmidt discovered that federal bank examiners in Kansas City had recommended that the Justice Department open a criminal investigation into Madison Guaranty Trust, a defunct Arkansas savings and loan that had been operated by James and Susan McDougal, the Clintons' colorful partners in a failed real-estate venture called the Whitewater Development Corporation. The Clintons' investment in Whitewater and their dealings with the McDougals had first been reported by *New York Times* reporter Jeff Gerth in a February 1992 article. The Clinton campaign had quickly mobilized to shoot down any suggestions of impropriety, and after a while the story died.

But inside the *Post,* there were always fears that the paper had blown it—that there was more there and, worse, that Gerth knew it and we didn't. The Clinton campaign's explanations about Whitewater never quite added up. Key documents requested by *Post* reporters, seeking to follow up on Gerth's scoop, never materialized. Now, with Schmidt's discovery, Downie ordered a full-court press. On November 3, 1993, the *Post* published a front-page story coauthored by me recounting new allegations by David Hale, a shady Little Rock businessman and recently indicted owner of a lending company, claiming that in 1986 Clinton had pressured him to extend a federally backed $200,000 loan to an apparently bogus marketing firm owned by Susan McDougal. (The White House flatly denied the story.) *The New York Times* published a similar account the same day. Suddenly, the national press corps was off on a wild chase through the far corners of Arkansas for new evidence on the Clintons' long-ago business affairs.

A few weeks later, with the *Post* pursuing Whitewater vigorously, David Gergen—an old Washington hand recently hired by Clinton— arranged a meeting with Len Downie and the editors and reporters working the story. Gergen hoped the meeting would clear the distrust that seemed to be building between the *Post* and the administration. He brought along Mark Gearan and another senior aide whose importance inside the White House was far greater than was generally understood: Bruce Lindsey. A slight, nervous and perpetually suspicious Little Rock lawyer, Lindsey had known Clinton for decades and was considered his most trusted and loyal confidant. He rarely talked to the press and was never seen on the Sunday talk shows. But Lindsey was always there in the background, whispering in Clinton's ear between campaign stops on official trips, gathering intelligence about stories the press might be working on and, not the least of his functions, always available to play a round of hearts with the president, no matter the hour. He was regarded as the keeper of all secrets, Clinton's all-purpose Mr. Fix-It.

The session was a disaster. Downie and other *Post* editors couldn't understand why the White House wouldn't answer specific questions about the Whitewater investment—or why it wouldn't turn over the documents requested more than a year and a half earlier. Gergen tried to pin down the editors on precisely what they felt they needed. But Lindsey would have none of it. "First, you tell us what story you want to write," he said. Then we'll tell you if we have anything that would help you.

Downie shook his head. No, he explained, it didn't work that way. The *Post* couldn't know for sure what it wanted to write until the reporters had a chance to review all the documents.

The meeting stretched on pointlessly for more than an hour, with Lindsey growing more agitated and resistant by the minute. His true attitude toward the *Post*—toward the press in general—bubbled to the surface. Lindsey was Clinton's political id, displaying the raw, instinctual hostilities that lurked beneath the surface of the president's and First Lady's public geniality. As he explained it that day, this focus on Whitewater was way out of line—symptomatic of the "gotcha" journalism that typified the national press. They had faced the same kind of nonsense during the campaign—reporters nitpicking over every little detail of Clinton's past, trying to find one scandal or another. "Why should we give you any of this?" Lindsey asked Downie at one point. "You'll just use [it] to write more stories."

Gergen looked embarrassed; his efforts at mediation obviously had failed. Gearan sat with a pained expression on his face. I sat quietly, too, pondering the strange spectacle of three senior White House aides dickering with *The Washington Post* over real-estate documents.

After the meeting, a few of the reporters who had sat in gathered around to talk. What is it with these people? we asked among ourselves. Why can't they ever give you straight answers? What are they hiding?

•   •   •

Over the next three months, the *Post* hit the Whitewater story hard, running sixty-two articles, sixteen of them on the front page. An entire Whitewater team had been created, and its regular meetings were chaired by Downie himself. Unraveling mysterious real estate transactions was a lot more respectable than chasing after Clinton's women. Stephanopoulos's "shame" card didn't work on this one. Still, some of us wondered quietly if we weren't over-doing it a bit. Greed did not strike me as Clinton's weakness. When I expressed my misgivings to DeYoung, she confided her own doubts but told me it didn't matter. Downie felt strongly about this. "Len thinks this is his Watergate," she said.

In the absence of full disclosure, who knew? There were always "unanswered questions," and every new development, however small, could be seen in a suspicious light. In mid-December, it was reported—first in the conservative *Washington Times*—that White-water documents had been "removed" from the offices of deputy White House counsel Vince Foster after his suicide the previous July. With a little perspective, the news might not have seemed so remarkable: the man had just died, and presumably somebody else was going to move in. Still, the story exploded like a neutron bomb. The White House response—refusing once again to release the docu-ments in question—only aggravated the situation. "These are their private records," Lindsey told the *Post*. "They see no reason to pub-licly release them." Justice Department officials, forced to respond to the uproar, subpoenaed them. Demands intensified for the appointment of an independent counsel. In January 1994, Attorney General Janet Reno appointed one, a respected former federal pros-ecutor named Robert Fiske. I wrote the *Post*'s front-page story on his appointment and noted prominently what struck me as an extraordi-nary development: In an attempt to give himself as much leeway as possible, Fiske requested—and received—a broad and essentially unfettered mandate to investigate virtually any potentially illegal matter he came across in the course of his inquiry. "There are," Fiske said that day, "no limits on what I can do."

•   •   •

On Monday, February 15, 1994, two days after I had interviewed Paula Jones in her hotel room, I picked up my copy of *The Wash-ington Post*—and was furious. There, in the Style section, was Lloyd Grove's story on the Conservative Political Action Conference. It was a typical Grove piece—funny and sarcastic, with a sneering line about the "seismic rumblings attending the promised eruption, yet again, of Mount Bimbo." Wright's memorable and dismissive label—"bimbo"—now had been hung around Paula Jones's neck. The story lampooned the press conference and seemed to make fun of Jones's allegations as well. There had been, Grove reported, "lots of tittering and chuckling from the 100 or so conference attendees gathered in back for this historic occasion." When I got to the office, I was livid. What the hell is this? I demanded of some of the editors on the national desk. They didn't know anything about the Style piece, they said. When Downie wandered by my desk, I registered my protest. I've been asked to go out and investigate this story because you decreed it should be taken seriously, I complained. And now here is the paper already dismissing it and branding Jones a "bimbo." Downie seemed unconcerned; he'd been off on Sunday and nobody had consulted him. But it didn't matter. Don't worry about it, he said. Just go out and do your job.

The next day I flew to Little Rock. As I did, I got word that Stephanopoulos—clearly watching events at the paper closely—had some information for me. I reached him by phone while waiting for a connecting flight. He couldn't believe I was still pursuing this Jones story, he said. But in any case, he had somebody for me to talk to: Phil Price, a former member of Clinton's staff who now worked for Clinton's successor as governor, Jim Guy Tucker. He was with Clinton at the Quality Management Conference that day and would tell me this was all bullshit. I promised to call him.

And another thing, Stephanopoulos said. Did I realize when this encounter with Jones was supposed to have happened? It was the day after Clinton had returned from giving the keynote speech at the Democratic Leadership Conference in Cleveland. Did I realize how significant that was?

I did. The DLC conference was the event that, for all practical purposes, had launched Clinton's campaign for the presidency. I had pulled the clips. CLINTON'S STAR RISES was the headline on the AP account the morning of May 8, 1991. Reporter John King quoted one party fundraiser describing Clinton's speech as "toe-tingling," an emotional appeal for Democrats to reach across the ideological spectrum and fashion new policies that would appeal to mainstream voters. Party strategist Bob Beckel called it "the best Democratic speech I've heard in ten years." Clinton's Cleveland trip had been a triumph, certifying him as bona fide presidential timber. When Clinton flew back to Little Rock the evening of May 7, he knew for the first time that he had a good shot at winning the Democratic nomination.[2]

Did I really think, Stephanopoulos asked, that Clinton would have been so crazy as to have done something like this right after Cleveland? To jeopardize everything that he had worked so hard for for so many years? It just didn't make any sense, he said.

3

"I know Paula's not lying."

amela Blackard sounded nervous. Blackard was one of Jones's two witnesses; her affidavit had been distributed by Cliff Jackson at the CPAC press conference. Nobody else had paid any attention to it. She had never before talked to a reporter and, I sensed, hoped she never would have to again.

Soft-spoken and earnest, Blackard spoke to me for about an hour over the phone. No, she didn't have time to get together while I was in Little Rock. She really didn't like being involved in all this. Why? I wondered. Had Paula pushed her into this against her better judgment? Perhaps, but another more obvious explanation quickly emerged. Blackard had been a secretary at the Arkansas Industrial Development Commission in 1991. Now, like Jones, she was married and a mother of small children. She had met her husband at AIDC, and he still worked there. Blackard's welfare, and that of her family, still depended on an Arkansas state agency controlled by Democrats loyal to Bill Clinton.

Blackard and Jones had been childhood friends. That winter, when her supervisor asked her to recommend someone to fill a slot as a secretary-typist, she had mentioned Paula. Jones had been on the job for only a few months when the two were asked to work the Quality Management Conference. Blackard remembered that day quite well, she said.

As Blackard told it, she and Paula were at the registration desk when she noticed Clinton had come out into the hallway, surrounded by a buzz of reporters and TV cameras. Clinton "kept looking over the cameras toward us," Blackard said. He seemed to be staring at Jones. "I said to her, 'Paula, he keeps looking at you.' She said, 'No, no.'" The reporters left, and then Blackard noticed Clinton talking to his trooper. "The next thing I know the bodyguard comes over and starts talking to Paula. He tells her, 'The governor wants to talk to you.'"

Blackard was worried that they might get in trouble if Jones left the desk. She got a bit testy with her friend. "I'm the one who asked for you to help out here," she said. "Find out what he wants and come right back." Blackard watched as Jones walked over to Ferguson so he could escort her upstairs.

"She was gone about ten minutes," Blackard continued. "When she came back, she was kind of walking very fast toward me. I asked her, 'What is wrong? You're shaking.'" Jones's demeanor had visibly changed. "I'll tell you in a moment, wait just a second," Jones said. "I've got to calm down." And then Jones said to her: "You're not going to believe what just happened."

As Blackard recalled their conversation, Jones then related most of the events she had outlined at the press conference and later provided to me in Technicolor detail. She told her about Clinton introducing himself, then trying to kiss her. Jones told Blackard "she pulled away" and asked, "What are you trying to do?" She then said Clinton had "pulled her close again." This time Jones said she had squirmed away and crossed the room to sit down in a chair.

What did she say happened next? I asked. "I can't say," Blackard replied. Oh, come on, this is important. She paused. "I can't say," she repeated. I let it go.[1]

Jones then made it clear that she wanted out of the room fast. "I'm getting out of here—I've got to get back downstairs," Blackard recalled Jones saying. Jones then confided that Clinton had said something else: "Don't worry, you won't lose your job. I'm the governor."

According to Blackard, the two sat for a while in stunned disbelief. "She said to me, 'Don't tell anybody what happened, just forget it.' I said to her, 'I can't believe he'd do that.' We were both kind of scared. We weren't thinking straight. I thought I could lose my job. She thought she could lose her job."

I asked Blackard if she had believed Jones's account. She hadn't been "in the room," she said, so of course she couldn't say for sure what happened. But, she then added: "I had no reason not to [believe her]. . . . We were pretty close." If Jones and Clinton had done something more, "she would have told me." After the incident, "we never really discussed it again," she said. Every once in a while, "she might walk by my office and say, 'Can you believe that happened,' and . . . I'd say no."

Then, a few weeks ago, Jones had called her up and asked if she had heard about her name being included in an article in the *American Spectator.* Blackard had no idea what she was talking about. But Jones, she said, was "real mad." Blackard was surprised: "I really thought she was willing to forget it."

Blackard emphasized again she was not at all happy about being pushed into the dispute with the president. "I'm really scared," she told me. "I just want to tell what I saw and get this over with."

Blackard's account—plainly rendered, without a trace of hyperbole—made a powerful impression on me. It was, I immediately thought, more important than Jones's. Whatever Jones's motivations in coming forward, telling her story at a press conference sponsored by Clinton's enemies, Blackard appeared to have little, if anything, to gain by backing her up. With her husband still working for the state of Arkansas, in fact, she had much to lose. She seemed a strong corroborating eyewitness to key portions of the encounter described by Jones.

• • •

The next day, I arranged to have lunch with Jones's other witness, Deborah Ballantine. Ballantine, then thirty-one, was an administrator with a prominent local engineering firm. Like Blackard, she was extremely nervous about talking to me; she asked me—and I agreed—not to use the name of her employer in any story we published. She had promised her boss that the company's name wouldn't appear. Still, she told me, she wasn't going to let Paula hang out there alone. "I know Paula's not lying," she said.

Ballantine's recollections were vivid, detailed and devastating. She had been at her office the afternoon of May 8, 1991, she told me, when Jones showed up unexpectedly and insisted they go someplace where they could talk. "She was very upset, something was really wrong," Ballantine said. The first thing Jones said was, "You're not going to believe what just happened to me."

The two went to a designated smoking area. Jones told her everything, Ballantine said—Trooper Ferguson's approach, the note he slipped her with Clinton's room number, Clinton's sexual advances in the room. As she related the story that day, said Ballantine, Jones was "breathing really hard, she was trembling." Unlike Blackard, Ballantine was explicit about the culminating event: "She said, 'Debbie, he pulled his pants down to his knees and he asked me to suck his dick.'"

Ballantine said she told her friend, "Paula, you need to tell somebody. She said, 'No, no, no, I could lose my job.'" She was also clearly worried about how her boyfriend, Steve Jones, would react. "She couldn't believe she was so stupid. . . . I said to her something like, 'Paula, don't you know he does stuff like this?' She said no, she didn't. She was really embarrassed."

And there the matter rested. Although the two would talk about the incident from time to time, especially when Clinton was running for president, Jones had no interest in going public—even when the tabloids were offering hundreds of thousands of dollars to women with Clinton stories. A cynic would say that Jones didn't have a story to tell about Clinton; what the tabloids wanted then were flesh-and-blood tales of sexual liaisons with the candidate, not a murky claim of a gross sexual pass gone awry. In any case, Jones was carrying on with her life—getting married, getting pregnant, moving to California.

One of the central mysteries of the case has always been what finally caused Paula Jones to step into the limelight. Jones's assertion that it was the reference to "Paula" in Brock's article seemed a bit strange. Was Paula Jones a regular reader of the *American Spectator*? Given her acknowledged ignorance of politics, it seemed unlikely that she would have been scouring a conservative monthly that is most intensely read by political activists and journalists inside the Washington Beltway. But Ballantine told me that day that she could explain it.

It was she who had come across the *Spectator* reference to "Paula." She immediately knew that the trooper was talking about her friend. She knew Paula was in town visiting her family for Christmas. She called Jones at her mother's house and read her the relevant portion. Jones, she said, seemed horrified. "Oh my God, it's complete bullshit! That's a complete lie!" Jones said. Jones had no idea what the *American Spectator* was. But that meant she might well have imagined the story was being read by the entire world—and everybody she ever worked and partied with in Arkansas.

Events took an even more improbable turn when, according to Ballantine, the two old friends arranged to get together a few nights later with their babies at the Golden Corral steakhouse in north Little Rock. There they were—two young mothers, toddlers squirming in their high chairs, gossiping and swapping baby stories—when Jones looked up and froze. There, sitting five tables away, was Danny Ferguson, the very trooper who had escorted Jones up to the hotel room to see Clinton. Jones stopped talking and stared. "Oh my God," she whispered. "You're not going to believe who that is."

Should Jones confront him? The idea crossed both their minds when suddenly Ferguson noticed Jones. Jones motioned him over. Ferguson was immediately apologetic. "Now, Paula, I got dragged into that deal and I never gave out your last name—so nobody knows who you are," he said. Then Ferguson volunteered something: "Clinton told me you didn't do anything anyway." Jones grew indignant. "Well, I didn't—but it wasn't because he didn't want me to." Ferguson told how the media had been hounding him and his family ever since the article. It was then, according to Ballantine, that the discussion turned to money.

"If you decide to go public with this, the *Enquirer* would pay you a million dollars," said Ferguson.

Jones was incredulous. "A million dollars!"

"Oh yeah, but you have to remember, they'll destroy you. If you do, they'll dig up your past."

Jones insisted, "I don't have a past. I was only twenty-four." In any case, she asked, why should that make a difference? "It's all true."

And Ferguson replied: "I know it's all true and you know it's all true, but everybody else doesn't. And he always gets away with it."

It was the first reference to money—which for the next three years, Clinton's lawyers and spin doctors insisted was Jones's main motivation in coming forward. But according to Ballantine, it was Ferguson—not Jones—who had raised the issue. Still, the thought of personal enrichment might well have been planted in Paula Jones's mind.

•   •   •

The money issue came up again the next day. I drove to Lonoke for breakfast with another of Jones's sisters, Charlotte Brown, and her husband, Mark. Charlotte was dour and plump, as retiring as Paula was bubbly. She offered a different take on the events surrounding her younger sister.

After the encounter at the Golden Corral, Paula had called Charlotte. "There could be big money in this story," Paula said, according to Charlotte. "Whichever way it goes, it smells big money." Charlotte was sure the allure of cashing in was what had motivated her sister to speak out.

In undercutting her sister, Charlotte seemed to be egged on by Mark, a bearded, somewhat ornery man in his mid-thirties who looked as though he were on break from a bike tour with the Hell's Angels. Mark was unemployed—he and Charlotte and their children lived off the Social Security disability checks Mark had started receiving after brain surgery a few years back. Mark, it was clear, wasn't real fond of Paula.

Paula was a "flirt" who liked to dress provocatively and come on to men, he said. One of Paula's boyfriends had once taken nude pictures of her—he'd seen them. Paula was always chasing guys with money. One of his friends had gone out with Paula, and she had treated him shabbily, dumping him for someone with a better job. Paula was a conniver, Mark said, and what she was saying about Clinton was disgraceful.

For me, the most important question was what, if anything, they could tell me about the actual incident itself. On this point, Charlotte's recollections were important—and at odds with the story she and her husband later told the national media. Paula had insisted to me that Charlotte was one of the people in whom she had confided immediately after her encounter with Clinton. Was this true? I asked. Yes, Charlotte said. Paula had come by her house that night. As she was leaving, she told her the story.

What story? I asked.

"She told me the bodyguard came up to her and told her that Bill Clinton wanted to see her." When she went up to his hotel room, Paula had said, Clinton "asked her to have oral sex and she refused."

Paula hadn't told her any more details; indeed, Charlotte said, she was upset that she had told her younger sister, Lydia, a lot more. There was another difference. Lydia had recalled Paula sobbing on her bed. Charlotte thought Paula hadn't seemed particularly upset that evening. "She didn't really act nervous," Charlotte said. She had told her in a "matter-of-fact" way.

I asked Mark directly what I thought was the most important question about his sister-in-law. Had he ever known her to out-and-out lie—just make something up? He paused. No, he said, he hadn't.

On balance, I thought, Charlotte had added weight to Paula's story. Her account was one more piece of evidence that Jones had not, as the White House wanted me to believe, invented this story in 1994. What I failed to see, of course, was how this wouldn't matter: how under the massage of shrewd White House spin, the resentments of Charlotte and Mark would be used to undermine Paula.

There was other work to do. Traylor had signed a waiver that allowed me to review Jones's personnel records at AIDC. I was looking for any evidence of disciplinary actions, alcohol or drug abuse or any other employment problems that might suggest Jones was a disgruntled former employee with a grudge.

On the contrary, Jones's record seemed utterly unremarkable. She had won polite praise from her supervisors for being "anxious to please," having good "calligraphy skills" and a "cheerful personality on the phone."[2] She had received three pay raises, including a merit increase, and been promoted from a $10,270-a-year documents examiner to a $12,800-a-year secretary before resigning in February 1992, when she and her husband moved to California. In the future, those raises would come back to haunt Jones—they severely undercut her legal claim that she suffered in the workplace because of her refusal to provide oral sex to Clinton. But this wasn't yet a legal dispute, and Jones had not really made that claim. This was a journalistic inquiry into her credibility—and the merit raise seemed to take away one possible basis for questioning her motivations.

There were two more people I wanted to see before leaving Little Rock. One was Trooper Danny Ferguson. The day after the Jones press conference, the *Los Angeles Times* had quoted previously unpublished material from reporter Bill Rempel's interview with Ferguson the previous summer. Ferguson had said then that Clinton had dispatched him to bring Jones up to his room after saying she had "that come-hither look." That was important. It meant that I was no longer relying solely on the account of the highly suspect David Brock. But Ferguson refused—repeatedly—to see me. One night, when he was working the night shift, he suggested I swing by the governor's mansion at midnight. "There's a lot more to this story," he hinted over the phone. But when I got to the mansion, he refused to come out. I went by his house—nearly an hour outside Little Rock—a few days later. His wife refused to let me in. "I have to think about my family," Ferguson later said over the phone, explaining why he wouldn't talk to me.

The other person I needed to question was Phil Price, the man Stephanopoulos claimed could prove the entire event never happened. Price had been the economic aide who had accompanied Clinton to the Quality Management Conference the day of the Jones encounter. I had already gotten Clinton's schedule for that day. (Clinton ordered Stephanopoulos to dig it out as well.) It showed him giving a speech at the conference in the morning. His attendance in the afternoon was listed as "optional." Did he go or not? Price was now working for Clinton's successor, Jim Guy Tucker. He remembered the Quality Management Conference: he had helped organize it. After his speech, Price said, Clinton had left to host a luncheon at the governor's mansion. He had been "within five yards" of Clinton the entire time and could say with certainty that nothing like what Jones described ever took place.

Moreover, Price insisted, it was impossible to believe that Clinton had returned to the conference in the afternoon; otherwise, he—

Price—would have returned with Clinton, and he hadn't. Jones's story was obviously a lie, Price said. He knew. He was there.

•   •   •

I didn't realize it, but Price's account was straight from the playbook of Betsey Wright's "bimbo suppression" operation. The very first sex allegation to hit Clinton's presidential campaign was not Gennifer Flowers's claim, in January 1992, that she had carried on a twelve-year affair with the governor of Arkansas. It came in the fall of 1991. An article in *Penthouse* recounted the memoirs of a rock groupie named Connie Hamzy—an account that, in some respects, paralleled the story later told by Paula Jones.

Hamzy had kept a diary about her days following around such bands as the Eagles and Grateful Dead. It was filled with wild accounts of sexual escapades and drug taking. But the writer hired by *Penthouse* to put it into readable prose noticed an odd entry for a spring day in 1984. While hanging around a Little Rock pool, she had been approached by an Arkansas state trooper, who asked if she would like to meet the governor of Arkansas. According to Hamzy, she and Bill Clinton then scampered around the pool, looking for a bit of privacy—but none of the cabanas were empty. The account had a certain authenticity: Hamzy had written it at a time when she had no idea who Clinton was—fully seven years before he launched his campaign for the presidency. Still, the Clinton campaign moved quickly to squelch it. Clinton had told Stephanopoulos that Hamzy had come on to him—flipping down her bikini top and exposing her breasts. "We have to destroy her story," Hillary Clinton coldly ordered, according to an account Stephanopoulos wrote years later. He did. An Arkansas legislator and a Clinton aide named Michael Gaines signed affidavits saying that they had been with Clinton the entire time and that Hamzy's account was fiction. It stopped the story cold.[3] Was that what Phil Price was trying to do?

Whatever my suspicions about Price's account, however, I was stumped. Clinton had what looked like an airtight alibi. My interviews with Blackard, Ballantine and all the other Jones corroborating witnesses didn't matter. If Phil Price was to be believed, the

Paula Jones story would die right there. There was no way the *Post* could run it.

•   •   •

hen I got back to Washington, I started scouring the list of atten-dees at the Quality Management Conference—businessmen from around the country—to determine whether anybody remembered seeing Clinton there in the afternoon, as Jones claimed he was, or only in the morning, as Price insisted. It seemed futile. I reached about a dozen of those present. While most remembered seeing and hearing Clinton at the event, none could say with any certainty three years later what time of day it was.

Then, late one night, I finally got through to the person I wanted to speak to the most—Jim Harrington, a management consultant to the international accounting firm of Ernst & Young. Harrington had been listed as the conference's afternoon speaker that day. His address was scheduled to start at 1:15 P.M. If anyone could remember whether Clinton had been present in the afternoon, surely it was he.

Jim Harrington couldn't have been more helpful. Did he remember seeing Clinton around the time of his speech? I asked. Without any idea why I wanted to know, he answered: Why, of course. He had even chatted with Clinton shortly before he started his address; they had talked about whether Clinton was going to run for president. Harrington recalled seeing Clinton in the audience during his talk. "He was there for my speech and then he sort of drifted out. . . . He was just milling about," he told me. I thought immediately of Jones's description of Clinton in the lobby, around 2:30 P.M., just "lollygagging around."

I was now incensed. Price, Stephanopoulos, the Clinton White House—they had all misled me and *The Washington Post*. No, they had lied! These were government officials on the public payroll![4]

In my opinion, it was also reason enough to publish the Jones story. I approached Marilyn Thompson, my assignment editor on the national desk. Thompson hadn't been there the day of the original Jones press conference, but she was now directly overseeing my reporting. She had a passion for investigative reporting and a visceral disdain for White House spin efforts. Like me, she was instinctively skeptical of the self-serving stories of government officials. When I explained how the Price story Stephanopoulos had fed me had collapsed, she—like me—was exercised. "That's outrageous," she said.

I was ready to draft a story—a story that I thought would be fairly strong. The story I began writing emphasized the strength of Jones's supporting witnesses: she had told no fewer than five friends and family members about the alleged incident soon after it happened. It quoted Blackard and Ballantine prominently, pointing out their common descriptions of Jones's distress immediately after her meeting with Clinton. It played up Harrington's account—and how it contradicted the official White House line that Clinton hadn't even been in the hotel when Jones said the encounter took place.

As I was pulling the story together, I was checking back with Jones's lawyer, Danny Traylor. I sort of liked Traylor. He made little effort to disguise the fact that he was in way over his head. "Tell me, Izzy, what are the big boys back there in Washington saying about all this?" he would ask me. As far as I could tell, he had no real political affiliations—certainly none to the right-wing activists to whom he had delivered his client back in February.[5]

As I was going over a few final details, I noticed something. Traylor early on had turned over a copy of the contingency-fee contract he had signed with Jones on February 7, 1991, just four days before the CPAC press conference. Reviewing it one last time, I homed in on something deep in the fine print that I had missed the first go-round: the fourth page, subsection 3(b). It called for Traylor to "negotiate and arrange"—with a one-third cut of the proceeds—"any and all television, radio, or movie contracts."

Movie contracts? From day one, Stephanopoulos had insisted that Jones, just like Gennifer Flowers, was making her claims in order to cash in with the tabloids. This was, for the White House, an article of faith: all bimbos come forward in exchange for money. Therefore they can't be believed. When I had told Stephanopoulos that there wasn't a shred of evidence of that in this case—indeed, that Jones and Traylor had specifically denied receiving so much as a single penny in return for making their charges—he had retreated only slightly. Yeah, he said, but what about down the road? It's about future book and tabloid deals.

This seemed to lend support to Stephanopoulos's theory. I called Traylor. What was all this about magazine and movie contracts? He got a bit defensive. Oh that, he said. That was Cliff Jackson's idea. Jackson had given him a copy of the contract he had signed with his troopers, and it contained that "boilerplate" language about movie deals. He used it—and didn't think Paula had even bothered to read it. Besides, Traylor asked, what's so wrong with that? "Izzy," Traylor said, "we wasn't in this deal for the tabloids. But I do hope to earn a fee for all of this misery I'm putting my family through. It seems to me if downstream there are some public appearances—if there's an honorarium or a fee for appearing—that I'm entitled to a piece of that action."

Well, it's going in the story, I told him. Sure, no problem, he said. I then called Paula and asked her to explain again. Charlotte told me she had said something about smelling money. Now this contract with its talk of movie deals. Did she or did she not expect to profit from all this? "I really don't," she replied. "I don't think I could get any unless you went to these stupid magazines like the *Enquirer* and stuff, and I would never do it. It ruins your credibility and makes it look like you're in it for the money." No, Jones repeated, this had nothing to do with money. It had to do with Bill Clinton—and telling people the truth. "I can't stand the man personally because of what he did to me," she said. "And I think people have a right to know who is sitting up there and running our country today."

Later, the presumptive allure of money loomed ever larger in Clinton's defense against Jones's charges. The president's lawyers hired The Investigative Group, a blue-chip international investigative firm headed by ex-Watergate lawyer Terry Lenzer. Lenzer's sleuths put Jones's finances under a microscope. They found evidence that she and her husband were in debt at the time she came forward at the CPAC conference. They discovered a few months earlier that Jones had even missed a rent payment for their apartment out at Long Beach. The president's defenders, his lawyers and spin doctors, suggested—time and again—that Jones was just trying to hustle cash by making outrageous charges against the president.

Actually, Jones had acknowledged some of her money problems

to me from the start. She had told me about her credit card debts, a few thousand dollars' worth. I didn't make that much of it. Lots of people, including me, had credit card debts. But the contingency contract with Traylor did bother me. It suggested, at a minimum, that Jones might have been less than candid about her motivations. I also knew that Stephanopoulos and the White House would make much of it. It would give them just enough to go after Jones's story.

But at the end of the day, I thought it far from dispositive and no reason to ignore the rest of my reporting. You judge people by what they do, not what you think they might be thinking. And the fact remained: Jones had come forward that day in February without receiving payment from anyone. She was telling her story at length to *The Washington Post,* a newspaper that didn't pay for interviews, rather than to a tabloid that did. Her actions over time would prove inexplicable if her sole goal was to maximize compensation. Indeed, three years later, Jones's reluctance to cash in—to accept a lucrative cash settlement when it was offered in lieu of vindication on the facts—would lead directly to the greatest calamity of Bill Clinton's presidency.

Slowed only slightly by the discovery of the contingency-fee contract, I finished my story over the last weekend in February. On Monday, national editor Karen DeYoung came to my desk. She would like to see memos on my interviews with all the sources I had seen in Little Rock. She had asked for them earlier—and I hadn't been giving them to her. She was annoyed. Memos? I said. We don't need memos. I've already written the story—and it's ready to go in the paper. One look at her face made it clear that without reading a word I had written, she wasn't going to agree.

•   •   •

Karen DeYoung was a cautious woman—and still skeptical about Jones. For another opinion, she called in *Post* staff writer David Marannis, who was then at home working on his landmark biography. Marannis understood Clinton as well as anybody; he had done prodigious research stretching back into his childhood. Is Clinton really capable of doing what Jones alleges? DeYoung asked him. Marannis was unsure. Clinton was sexually reckless, there was no question about that. But the behavior Jones had described seemed out of character to him. There must be more to the story. Jones and Clinton were probably both lying. "It didn't seem to me in keeping with Clinton's normal pattern to drop his pants like that without any indication that the other person was willing," Marannis later recalled telling DeYoung. DeYoung agreed—and repeated that assessment to the senior editors.

Within a few days, Len Downie called a meeting to assess my progress.[6] The talk wandered all over the map. The contingency-fee contract was duly noted, but nobody dwelled on it. Had we tried hard enough to reach the state trooper, Danny Ferguson? Downie wanted to know. Ferguson's comments were obviously crucial; he's the one who purportedly told Brock and Rempel that he had taken Paula up to the room. He's also the one who suggested Paula was excited when she left—very different from the descriptions by her friends. Did he stand by that account or not?

Forget it, I said. He's not going to talk. I've called the guy repeatedly. I had been to his house. His wife had slammed the door in my face.

Downie was undeterred. Maybe we ought to have somebody else try to contact him.

What good would that do? I said.

We have to try everything, he said brusquely.

I was starting to get impatient. I now made with more force and evidence the same argument I had made the very first Friday of Jones's press conference. We now had strong reason to believe that the very essence of the Troopergate charge—that Clinton had used his bodyguards as, well, pimps—was true: Jones said she was taken by a state trooper to a hotel room for a sexual encounter with Clinton. Ferguson said he took her there. Pamela Blackard said she watched it happen. Ballantine said Jones told her that day about Clinton's behavior and described her as "trembling" and worried that she might lose her job if she told anyone.

Nobody bit. The meeting started to break up—inconclusively, I thought.

What about my draft? I asked Downie, who had it on his lap.

"Well," said Downie, glancing down at it, "this is closer."

Closer, I wondered, to what? I walked out convinced this was going nowhere.

4

"Hey, Mike . . . is there anything we can do to help?"

The *Washington Post* now faced a quandary similar to those confronting press and government investigators throughout Bill Clinton's presidency. There had been an allegation of misconduct against Clinton. The *Post* had found compelling reason to believe there was something to the charge. But there was some evidence that cut the other way—and the undeniable taint of politics surrounding the original accusation. We couldn't prove it. In fact, the charge was, by its very nature, unprovable.

At that point, there were two choices. The *Post*'s editors could have said: Case closed. Move on to other things. If they had done that, I'm fairly certain that I would have objected to the editors, whined to my colleagues and generally made a nuisance of myself for a week or so. Then life would have gone on. I would have gone back to covering the Justice Department, trolling for scoops that had nothing to do with Bill Clinton's sexual antics.

The other alternative was to forge ahead. Bring in more manpower. Do more reporting—reporting that probably had no real hope of turning up anything that was going to make the ultimate choices any easier.

Downie chose option two. He ordered up more work. He expanded the scope of the inquiry. He brought in additional reporters. And the stakes, inevitably, got higher.

•   •   •

53

B ob Kaiser, the managing editor, whose distaste for the story was palpable at every meeting we had, was by now suspicious that I had too much invested in it. He wanted somebody to give the editors another perspective. The reporter chosen for this task was Charlie Shepard. An unusually thoughtful and sharp-eyed observer, Shepard worked for the paper's investigative unit, headed by Bob Woodward. He had come from the *Charlotte Observer,* where he had won a Pulitzer Prize for his reporting on Jim and Tammy Bakker's troubled ministry. He even had some expertise in the subject matter at hand: in November 1992, he had helped break the story of Senator Bob Packwood's serial harassment of staff members, a story that eventually led to the Oregon Republican's resignation.

At first, I wondered what I needed him for. In early March, he asked me for Jones's number. I put him off. I would have to check with Paula first, I said. Then, after a few days, I figured, What the hell. The editors wanted me to cooperate with him. "See what you think," I told Shepard. Over the next week or so, Shepard questioned Jones on his own. He flew to Little Rock, where he retraced her steps at the Excelsior Hotel. He interviewed her family members. He obtained Clinton's cell-phone records for the day in question. And he soon concluded that Jones seemed pretty believable. Everything Jones said seemed to check out—even her description of the eleventh-floor hotel room where the encounter with Clinton allegedly had taken place. "She's as credible as any of the women we interviewed for the Packwood story," he said.

Shepard, like many others, was conflicted. He had voted for Clinton. He wanted Clinton to succeed. He even liked the guy. At a White House correspondents dinner the previous year, Clinton had personally given Shepard an award for his investigative reporting on financial abuses at the United Way. But if Paula's account was true, he thought, we had no choice but to report it. I soon got over my annoyance about his being brought in to work on my story. Indeed, by mid-March, Shepard had become one of a small group of newsroom allies who advocated publishing the story.

Another was my assignment editor, Marilyn Thompson. Intense, nervous and deeply suspicious of power, Thompson was convinced that Clinton's conduct toward women was scandalous. Even before the Paula Jones press conference, in the wake of the Troopergate flap, Thompson had marched into Downie's office and argued that the paper had to follow up. "This is about the misuse of office. It's about accountability," Thompson told him. "We can't ignore this." Downie seemed to agree. But nothing ever happened. Thompson was sorry she was off the day of the press conference; she would have pushed for the paper to run the story.

With my more expanded version of the Jones story stalled, Thompson became obsessive. She dug out files from the 1992 campaign and was astonished to find that the paper had killed a story, written by national staff writer Bill McAllister, detailing how Clinton had helped arrange a state job for Gennifer Flowers. Flowers, a part-time cabaret singer, had finished ninth out of eleven candidates on a state merit test. A middle-aged African American, a state worker named Charlotte Perry, had applied for the same position and been passed over. She had filed a grievance. The grievance officer ruled in Perry's favor, finding that state officials had restructured the qualifications to suit Flowers's limited credentials (a background in "public relations" was added as a new requirement) and improperly given Clinton's alleged paramour the $17,524-a-year position with the Arkansas Appeal Tribunal. But the grievance officer was overruled by one of Clinton's political cronies, the head of the state agency that hired Flowers. McAllister, of course, hadn't proved Clinton's underlying sexual relationship with Flowers. And he had assembled the story weeks after the Flowers episode had faded as a political issue. Still, Thompson was incensed. How could the paper not have run this?[1] It wasn't about Clinton's sex life. It was about what Clinton had done *in office.*

Convinced the paper had blown it, Thompson contacted Gennifer Flowers, talked to her for hours and arranged to get all of the surreptitious tapes she had made while talking to Clinton. The full set had never been released during the 1992 campaign—perhaps because, in their entirety, they were as revealing of Flowers's duplicity as they were of Clinton's infidelity. In any case, once she started listening, Thompson couldn't hear enough. Every night, she would pop one into the tape deck of her Honda Accord as she drove home. Much of the talk was raunchy; some she found simply hilarious. The

Clinton on these tapes was, she thought, unvarnished: arrogant, crude and profane, he was an entirely different person from the Rhodes Scholar/policy wonk the public was accustomed to seeing. He was, Thompson thought, a "total hick."

On the tapes, Clinton could be heard talking about the physical attributes of rumored girlfriends of U.S. senators. He could be heard grossly mocking his political enemies and members of the media. "A real scumbag," he says about a local TV newscaster in one December 1990 conversation. "I stuck it up their ass," he gloats a few moments later, describing how he had outfoxed local Republicans trying to nail him on his womanizing. Clinton tells Flowers how he caught his GOP nemesis Sheffield Nelson dispatching a lawyer to a state prison to "try to get inmates . . . to trash me." Nelson was forced to call Clinton to deny his complicity in the sordid scheme—a conversation Clinton evidently enjoyed. "I mean, I know he lied," Clinton says. "I just wanted to make his asshole pucker. But I covered you. . . ."

A recurring theme throughout the tapes is Clinton's never-ending scheming to conceal their affair and portray any allegations about it as part of a scurrilous Republican plot. A subtheme is his obsession with figuring out who had leaked Flowers's name to his enemies. "The night watchman—that's who did it to us," he says during an October 1991 conversation, referring to the security guard at the Little Rock apartment complex where Flowers had lived. Flowers is, at this point, feeling under siege from the ever-ravenous press. Clinton says, "You call me anytime. . . . If somebody contacts you, I need to know." His message is unequivocal. "All you got to do is deny it." "Hang tough," deny everything, the press can't prove anything. "As long as everybody hangs in there, we're in the clear." When Flowers worries about the state job Clinton arranged for her, he is at first concerned. "Yeah, I never thought about that," he says. But then he adds: "If they ever asked if you'd talked to me about it, you can say no."[2] In the meantime, he says, it might be helpful if Flowers signed an affidavit, to be kept on file, "explaining that, you know, you were approached by a Republican."

Thompson found the gap between the public and private Clinton so striking that she was convinced the paper had an obligation to dig deeper. The crude Clinton of the Flowers tapes reminded her of a story she had been working on for more than a decade. As a young political reporter in her native South Carolina, Thompson had heard rumors that the state's senior senator, Strom Thurmond, had once fathered an illegitimate child. The girl had supposedly been born in the 1920s, when Thurmond was a superintendent of schools in a rural area and an African American housekeeper—the purported child's mother—was working in his home. After looking into it, Thompson became convinced the story was true and chased it with dogged tenacity—even though colleagues told her no paper in the state would ever print it. Thurmond, she discovered, had kept in touch with the girl, lending her money, helping pay for her education and even visiting her from time to time.[3] But at each step of the way, Thurmond and his minions had clouded the truth, describing the woman as an old family friend and nothing more. The South Carolina press corps became complicit in concealing this secret in the aging segregationist's distant past. For Thompson, Clinton's messy private life was a lot like Thurmond's purported love child: a continuing political embarrassment protected by a bodyguard of lies.

At the end of February, Thompson pressed Downie to reopen the subject of Clinton's private behavior. Paula Jones, she argued, should be seen in the context of a broader pattern—a pattern of abusive conduct, the use of troopers to procure women, the dangling of jobs to buy silence, the expenditure of government dollars to facilitate reckless trysts. Uncomfortable with the idea of basing a story on the account of a single woman, Paula Jones, Downie authorized Thompson to oversee a wide-ranging inquiry. A third reporter, Sharon LaFraniere, was brought in. LaFraniere was instructed to go back to Gennifer Flowers, Sally Perdue and every other woman alleged to have had sexual affairs with Clinton. The troopers, too, should be interviewed again. The *Post* would reevaluate all their claims.

• • •

One of the country's preeminent newspapers was in effect launching an open-ended investigation into the president's sex life. Years later, there was considerable second-guessing about the media's role in pursuing allegations about Clinton. In the view of the critics, there was no predicate for any of these inquiries. Should private conduct be explored at all, they asked, if it has no demonstrable effect on the performance of public duties? Is it the role of reporters to function as a roving sex police, exposing every private indiscretion by any public figure?

When the issues are framed like that, the answers seem simple: Of course not. It is our job to report public, not private, business. But the truth is there are no fixed rules on where to draw the lines, and what rules there were had been steadily changing. The press had ignored John F. Kennedy's private indiscretions while president only to learn, more than a decade later, that his conduct had been truly scandalous: he had struck up a sexual relationship with the girlfriend of a Chicago mobster who had been secretly under contract with the CIA to assassinate Fidel Castro. The potential for blackmail was so great that even loyal friends acknowledged Kennedy's affair with Judith Campbell Exner might well have been grounds for impeachment, had it been reported at the time.

Over time, the views of the press toward such matters began to change. A series of sex scandals hit Capitol Hill over the next few years, leading to the demise of two powerful House members, Wilbur Mills and Wayne Hays. (The immortal line of Elizabeth Ray, the girlfriend Hays had placed on the public payroll—"I can't type, I can't file, I can't even answer the phone"—helped define the potential for abuse in such arrangements.) Then, in 1979, a young feminist writer, Suzannah Lessard, touched off a media brushfire with an article she originally wrote for the *New Republic* arguing that Senator Edward Kennedy's rampant philandering was a legitimate issue that ought to be explored in his upcoming presidential campaign. Lessard conceded that the protection of privacy was an important public principle that should be breached for only the most compelling reasons. But in Kennedy's case, Lessard argued, his sexual liaisons were so chronic and manipulative that they raised serious questions that ought to be deeply troubling to women. ("It gives me the creeps," Lessard wrote; "the constant pursuit . . . of semi-covert, just barely personal and ultimately discardable encounters is a creepy way to act.") After it had been approved by the magazine's editors, the *New Republic*'s owner, Martin Peretz, a Kennedy supporter, killed the piece, prompting a rancorous debate in the capital's journalistic community. The rival *Washington Monthly* then published Lessard's article in its entirety, accompanied by an editorial introduction concluding that it had "important and wise things to say about women and their relationship to" the Massachusetts senator.[4]

The shift was readily apparent by the spring of 1987, when the *Miami Herald* got a tip that Democratic presidential front-runner Gary Hart was involved with an aspiring actress named Donna Rice. In every profile of him written that political season, the Colorado senator had adamantly denied he was having extramarital affairs and even challenged the press to prove him wrong. The *Herald*'s reporters did. When Hart withdrew from the race weeks later, the consensus of the political community was that his dalliance exposed grievous defects of judgment that were far worse than whatever it said about his personal morality.

Among those who privately endorsed that view was Bill Clinton. According to David Marannis's biography, Clinton and Betsey Wright had debated whether he should carry through with his own plans to run for president that year in the wake of Hart's downfall. Clinton, Wright told Marannis, wanted to believe that Hart's private conduct was irrelevant. But Wright argued it had a significant bearing because "it raised questions about his stability." Any previous affairs might have been irrelevant, she said, but "to have one while he was running was foolhardy." Clinton agreed: Hart was foolish to flaunt it.

Another complicating factor was the rising public awareness of sexual harassment, culminating in the Senate hearings on Clarence Thomas's nomination to the U.S. Supreme Court. The furor over Anita Hill's allegations, and the seriousness with which they were taken by the press at the time, made it crystal clear that sexual harassment was an important political issue. Jones's charges were different from Hill's, of course, but they were no less serious—and arguably more so. Even by Hill's account, Thomas never touched her. According to Jones, a state worker at the time, Clinton had summoned her to his room, pawed her and then exposed himself. Because the public was always disinclined to believe Jones, it was reluctant to face the consequences inevitably posed by the possibility that she was telling the precise truth: Clinton's conduct, as alleged, was bizarre, perverse, near pathological. Does it make a difference if the man the voters have elected president is given to behavior like that? Even then, in the winter of 1994, the issue wasn't whether Clinton had ever committed adultery. The charges against Clinton—running from Flowers and the troopers to Paula Jones—pointed to something more fundamental: a continuing pattern of reckless and even compulsive behavior that, if true, would almost surely affect the course of his presidency.

•   •   •

But the fact is none of this was debated vigorously within the *Post* newsroom at the time. If there was queasiness about delving so deeply into Clinton's sexual past, it was expressed only obliquely. After all, the paper wasn't committed to publishing anything. It was only asking questions, trying to determine the truth about Bill Clinton. Did the president have a serious problem in this sphere of his life or not? The White House position was that all the sex charges against him were "ridiculous" lies. Clinton's minions were not saying: We don't have to answer any of these questions because they are irrelevant. They were saying: The charges are false. In the world of the Clinton spinmeisters, Flowers was a tabloid hustler, the troopers were embittered, sex-obsessed liars, Jones was a tool of the president's enemies. The White House counterattack left open two stark possibilities: Either the charges were malicious smears, concocted by Clinton's antagonists, or the spin doctors themselves were engaged in an orchestrated cover-up.

For my part, I was fixated on one small part of the Troopergate allegations that had received relatively little attention. One of the troopers, later identified as Ferguson, had recounted sneaking one of Clinton's supposed girlfriends past the Secret Service for a farewell rendezvous at the governor's mansion on the day Clinton left Little Rock for his inauguration in Washington. Could this possibly be true? This was a year after Gennifer Flowers had nearly derailed his presidential campaign, a year after the pivotal *60 Minutes* interview in which he confessed to causing "pain" in his marriage, two months after he had been elected president. After all that, could Clinton possibly have continued his reckless ways? Even some of the president's defenders—political allies and pundits who had denounced the Troopergate stories as politically inspired tall tales—found that prospect troubling. "It would bother me greatly if Clinton was still messing around after the *60 Minutes* interview—let alone after the election," wrote Michael Kinsley in a December 1993 *Washington Post* column. "That would reveal a brutal willingness to deceive the public—way beyond the normal politician's cynicism—as well as a frightening lack of self-control." But Kinsley added he didn't believe there was any reason to think that was the case.

Mostly on utilitarian grounds, I was ambivalent about the direction of the paper's inquiry. We were, I thought, mixing apples (Clinton's prior consensual affairs) with oranges (a specific, and I thought, credible claim of sexual harassment). Either way, knowing how high the bar was for publishing any stories that involved Clinton's sex life, I thought we were unlikely to find out anything that would make its way into print. Editors always wanted to know these things. They hardly ever wanted to publish them.

In any case, I was given a narrower charge in the paper's expanded project: See if there was any evidence that Clinton, like Packwood, had engaged in other acts of harassment. Right, I recall saying at the time. How exactly am I supposed to do that? Take out an ad in our paper saying if you've been harassed by Bill Clinton, call Michael Isikoff? I protested: The odds against our finding another woman like Paula Jones, who would freely talk about such experiences—and risk the full wrath of the White House attack machine—seemed pretty formidable.

Still, if that's what the editors wanted, I would give it a try. One of the people I called was Cliff Jackson. Surely, I said, with all your dealings with the troopers, you might have some names for me. I'm looking for a pattern similar to what Jones has described. Jackson pondered for a moment. Well, he said finally, I might have some leads for you.

•   •   •

Cyd Dunlop had been the wife of a Clinton campaign contributor in the Arkansas town of West Helena near the Tennessee border. She had since divorced him and married a wealthy Mississippi businessman who was active in Republican politics. Jackson had heard about Dunlop after Troopergate broke. He gave me her number and suggested I give her a try. Friendly and engaging, Dunlop, thirty-two, took my phone call without any reticence. Sure, she knew Bill Clinton. Yes, she said, she did have a story to tell about him. It was more amusing than anything else, but she would be happy to share it.

As Dunlop explained it, her ex-husband, besides being active in Clinton's gubernatorial campaign organization, had also served as director of the West Helena airport. Whenever Clinton came to town in the early 1980s, he would make a point of seeing her husband. He even stopped by the house once to talk about airport issues and politics—and flirted with her a bit.

Then, in November 1986, Dunlop and her husband, Daryl, drove to Little Rock to attend Clinton's reelection victory party at the Excelsior Hotel. It was a festive event; Clinton was rolling up a landslide victory over a token Republican opponent, and already his allies were talking him up as presidential timber in 1988. Dunlop, wearing a new red dress and red shoes, was having a grand old time. An exuberant Clinton found her on the dance floor that night—as he did many other women—and twirled her around a few times. Sometime after midnight, Dunlop recalled, she and her husband retired to their room.

This is how she remembered what happened next:

They were fast asleep when the phone rang. Dunlop, half-conscious, reached for it. "Hello," she said, wondering what this could be all about.

"Cyd," said the hushed voice on the other end, "it's Bill."

"Bill who?" Dunlop asked.

"Bill, the governor," replied Bill Clinton.

Dunlop glanced at the clock radio next to the bed. It was after two A.M. She asked Clinton what he could possibly want at this hour.

"I just wanted to hear the sound of your voice again," said Clinton. "Can you get out of your room?"

At this point, Dunlop recalled, her husband awoke briefly, rolled over and groggily asked what was going on. It's a wrong number, honey, go back to sleep, she said. He did. Dunlop couldn't believe the situation. She considered herself a polite southern girl. She tried to be gentle about responding to Clinton's question.

"No, I don't think so," she said. "Daryl knows I wouldn't do that."

Clinton apparently was not willing to take no for an answer. "Just tell him you need to be by yourself and think for a while," Clinton told her.

At this point, Dunlop got a bit firmer. "I can't do that," she said.

Still, Clinton persisted. "Can you go for a jog with me in the morning?" he said.

Dunlop reminded him that the only shoes she had with her were her red pumps. Clinton laughed—and again returned to the issue at hand. "What time are you leaving in the morning?" he asked her. "Can you meet me at the old statehouse in the morning at around six?"

Finally, Dunlop said yes—just to get him off the phone. Then she went back to sleep.

The next morning she and her husband had breakfast with another couple, the mayor of West Helena and his wife. Dunlop joked about Clinton's phone call. Everybody had a laugh. Then they all headed home. Whether Clinton actually waited for her at the old statehouse that morning, she had no idea.

Dunlop was entertaining, and she sounded believable. I called the mayor of West Helena and got his wife. Yes, she did remember Dunlop telling them something about Clinton over breakfast that day. Dunlop's story was, in its limited way, revealing. On the night in question, Clinton was forty years old. He had just been elected governor of Arkansas for the third time. He was chairman of the National Governors' Association and a potential candidate for president in two years. Yet according to Dunlop's account, there he was acting like some oversexed adolescent, carousing in the early hours of the morning, badgering the wife of one of his campaign supporters for a date. It certainly seemed, well, peculiar. But when I asked Dunlop whether she felt harassed by Clinton, she laughed heartily. No, she didn't. "I just thought he was an idiot," she said. Maybe he was even drunk, she speculated. Whatever it demonstrated, Dunlop's story was not precisely what I was looking for. I wrote a memo to the editors—and moved on.

• • •

One evening, my colleague Sari Horwitz was having drinks with one of her sources, Karen Hinton. Horwitz was a reporter on the *Post* metro staff, assigned to cover the Washington, D.C., school system. Hinton was the school system's director of public affairs. Hinton liked to give Horwitz a hard time for never writing anything positive about the city's troubled schools—and this evening was no different. But somehow the conversation eventually got around to the president. Hinton had heard about the Jones allegations and mentioned she had no doubt that Jones was telling the truth. Really? Horwitz asked. How would you know that? Well, Hinton told her, I've had my own little experience with Bill Clinton.

A few days later, Horwitz arranged for me to meet Hinton for coffee. She was a striking woman, tall and blond. She had long been active in Democratic Party politics. After a stint as a newspaper reporter in the 1980s, she had gone to work for Robert Clark, a state legislator from the Mississippi Delta who was running for Congress. Hinton, a committed liberal, felt strongly that her native state should have a black congressman. Clark, she hoped, would become the first. That was reason enough, Hinton thought, to drop her career in journalism and become his press secretary.

In the summer of 1984, after appearing as the guest speaker at a Mississippi Democratic fundraiser, Clinton showed up at a popular local eatery in the town of Greenville for a little glad-handing. Hinton and a group that included Willie Morris, the former editor of *Harper's* magazine, were already there when the Arkansas governor and his entourage walked in and headed over to their table. When he was introduced to Hinton, Clinton stared at her, eyed her from head to legs, and instantly made her uncomfortable. "This is the first time I've ever seen him," Hinton told me. "It's hard to describe, but the way he looked at me—nobody could have missed it—it was a direct flirtation. He made direct eye contact, he looked me up and down—it was very clear." Clinton then invited Hinton, Morris and the rest of their group to join him for dinner. As Hinton told it, Clinton maneuvered to sit next to her. For the next thirty minutes, she said, the Arkansas governor engaged her in lively conversation, soliciting her views about teenage pregnancy, education and assorted other social issues. Hinton forgot about Clinton's leer—and was dazzled. "This man is giving me his undivided attention. Here I am, this twenty-four-year-old, and I'm captivated by the fact that he's sitting there listening to me."

Clinton finally out took his pen, wrote something on a napkin, folded it and pushed it over to her. Hinton opened it and saw Clinton's room number at the Holiday Inn that evening—and a question mark. "I folded the napkin up and I didn't look up and it all started to sink in. Here I'd been talking to him for all this time, thinking he was interested in what I had to say and all he's thinking of is how could he get his hand up my dress." After a while, Clinton went to the other end of the long table and was "gazing at me like he wants some kind of response." She avoided eye contact and never went to his room.

Clinton had never said anything directly suggestive—nor had he touched her. Still, the entire incident bothered Hinton. The folded note with the room number—hadn't Paula Jones said that was what the trooper handed her? How could Clinton just do that—with somebody he didn't even know? How do you call yourself a supporter of women's rights—and then treat people that way? "I was offended," Hinton told me. "I felt a bit humiliated." From then on, Hinton kept her distance from Clinton—and never hesitated to tell her friends in the Democratic Party. One of them was the daughter of a prominent southern politician. Hinton's friend wasn't surprised at all by her experience. One night, when Clinton was visiting her friend's father at home, he had made a direct pass—and invited Hinton's friend to sleep with him. In her father's house! Hinton's friend, in her early twenties, chastised him. "Do you know what you are doing?" she had asked.

Hinton couldn't get over it. What is it with this guy? It was a question she talked about repeatedly among her colleagues at the Democratic National Committee's press office between 1989 and 1991, and later when she was a volunteer in Bob Kerrey's presidential campaign. Everybody at the DNC knew about Clinton's womanizing, she told me. It was indiscreet, blatant. "People were always sort of joking about it," she said. "Nobody could ever imagine that he could be nominated because of it." One of those who joined in—who would snicker at how Clinton's behavior would sink him sooner or later—was the DNC press secretary at the time, Mike McCurry.

But Hinton didn't think it was a joke. In fact, over the years, she became somewhat passionate on the subject. "It used to drive me crazy," she told me. "I used to say to people, Why doesn't anybody take this seriously? Why doesn't it matter that we have a president who walks into a room and sees an attractive woman and proceeds to hit on her without any concern how that woman might feel about it?"[5]

•   •   •

For a while, Kristy Zercher looked as though she might actually add up to something a lot bigger. A former flight attendant on the Clinton 1992 campaign plane, Zercher had been dating a Dallas businessman. She would tell him about Clinton's behavior on his campaign plane—how he flirted with all the stewardesses, made lewd and suggestive comments and propositioned them. The Dallas businessman, a roguish entrepreneur named Ken McKay, got excited. McKay was quite a character in his own right: a defrocked Assembly of God minister who had gotten caught in a sexual dalliance with a member of his congregation, McKay loved mischief. Late in the campaign, he contacted someone high up in the Texas Republican Party and told them he had a brilliant idea that would save the election for George Bush: They should sting Clinton. He would use his girlfriend, Zercher, to entrap the candidate, get pictures of the two in a compromising position, then leak the whole thing to the press. According to McKay, his Republican contact got back to him within a few days and told him to forget it: his idea was too risky.

Still, the story made its way to me. I tracked down McKay, an amiable raconteur and part-time oilman who seemed to work exclusively from his cell phone. Zercher and he had stopped dating more than a year earlier, he said; he thought she might be in New Jersey. But he did happen to have a number for her mother.

I called Zercher's mother and asked how to get in touch with her daughter, explaining it was very important that I speak to her. She was suspicious but promised to take my number and pass it along to Kristy. Tell her I'm a friend of Ken McKay, I said.

It worked. A few days later, Zercher called me at home. Why did I want to talk to her? I explained that we were doing some research on Clinton and wanted to hear about some of her experiences on the campaign plane.

What sorts of experiences?

Well, I mumbled, we've heard that some of what Clinton did might have been offensive to some of the flight attendants and we weren't jumping to any conclusions but it was important that . . . Even as I spoke, the line went dead.

A few days later, McKay called. He had heard from Kristy. She was very nervous about talking. But if *The Washington Post* would pay to fly her down to Dallas, she would see me there—so long as McKay was present. Otherwise she wouldn't feel comfortable. There were a couple of other things I should know, McKay added. Kristy had a new boyfriend in New Jersey. He was a former pit boss in an Atlantic City casino who was now a hairdresser, and he was "mobbed up."

What do you mean, "mobbed up"? I asked.

Well, according to Kristy, after her boyfriend's dad had died a few weeks earlier, FBI agents were crawling all over the funeral, watching everybody who showed up. Mobbed up like that.

And another thing. Right after my phone call, Kristy got a phone call from some guy at the White House.

Who? I asked.

Lindsey, he said. Bruce Lindsey. He told her he understood she had been contacted by a reporter and it might be a good idea if she kept her mouth shut.

Oh, and one more thing, the businessman told me. Kristy had pictures.

Pictures of what? I asked.

Pictures of her and Clinton, McKay said, and I think you'll find them interesting.

When McKay hung up, I was quite excited. According to what the guy had just told me, a top White House aide had been calling the home of a New Jersey mobster to try to get the mobster's girlfriend to keep her mouth shut about the president of the United States. I thought of John Kennedy—and Judith Campbell Exner and Sam Giancana. I thought of a really big scandal that went far beyond a three-year-old case of sexual harassment. Okay, maybe I had gotten a little ahead of myself. But why did my phone go dead that day? Was Zercher's phone being tapped? Was mine? And how could Bruce Lindsey possibly have known that I had tracked down Kristy Zercher?

After I relayed this to the *Post* editors, Downie approved my proposal that the *Post* fly Zercher to Dallas.

• • •

It didn't take long after I got to Dallas to realize that this was not the scoop of the century. Zercher, an attractive thirty-year-old blonde, McKay and another young woman all showed up at my hotel in Dallas that night, apparently quite excited about the idea of having a great time on the *Post*'s dime. They had some fancy restaurant they all wanted to go to. I suggested we have drinks first—and I get a chance to learn a bit more about Zercher. A farm girl from Celine, Texas, she had worked as a topless dancer for a high-class Dallas strip joint before landing a job with Express One, the airline charter company retained by the Clinton campaign. The very first time she met Clinton, she told me, he came on to her. It was on the campaign plane in February, just weeks after Gennifer Flowers had nearly torpedoed his candidacy. Clinton wandered back to the galley of the plane, looked closely at her and said something like, "Oh, those blue eyes. Let's just blow the campaign and go to Bermuda." Throughout the rest of the campaign, she said, Clinton kept up a steady verbal banter with her and her two fellow flight attendants, one of whom, Deborah Schiff, now worked as an Oval Office secretary. He would comment on their clothing, saying things like, "You don't know what that outfit is doing to me." During one such talk, she said, Clinton asked for intimate details about her two prior marriages. On another occasion, he dozed off to sleep with his head on her shoulder. Late in the campaign she was posing for a picture with Clinton in the galley of the campaign plane when he "completely grabbed me, like a bear hug. . . . I was just shocked. It caught everybody off guard."

Clinton's flirtations with Zercher and the other stewardesses clearly worried his confidant and perennial sidekick, Lindsey. It was quite customary for Clinton to invite Zercher, Schiff and a third flight attendant named Angie Fields to work out with him at the

YMCA when they landed in Little Rock. Invariably, a nervous Lindsey would advise the women "it would not be a good idea" if they actually accepted Clinton's invitation. According to Zercher, Lindsey would also insist that they never exit the plane at the same time Clinton did or even appear on the tarmac when he was there—lest there be a picture in the paper the next day of the candidate standing near the comely stewardesses.

But in the end, said Zercher, nothing actually happened: she had never had any sexual relationship with Clinton. And when I questioned her closely, she acknowledged that she and the other flight attendants never objected to Clinton's flirtations. "I just laughed it off," Zercher said.

That ruled out any idea that Zercher was going to confirm a pattern of harassment similar to that of Paula Jones. But what about her boyfriend, the alleged mobster—and the phone call from Lindsey? Zercher said it was true about her boyfriend; she was quite certain both he and his father had been players in the Colombo crime family. That sounded intriguing, even more so when she told me that her boyfriend was part owner of a newly formed private investigative firm that had just submitted a proposal to the United States Justice Department to work under a new federal law tracking down "deadbeat dads" who don't pay child support. I scribbled down all the information Zercher could give me about the company and made a mental note to check it out as soon as I got back to Washington. I was unable to discover any evidence documenting that Zercher's boyfriend at the time had any connection to organized crime.[6]

Then I pressed Zercher on what I thought was the most intriguing part of her story, the supposedly uninitiated phone call from Bruce Lindsey. I couldn't understand, I told her, how Bruce Lindsey at the White House would have known that I was trying to track her down.

Zercher tried to explain. It seemed that before she called me, Zercher had called Debbie Schiff, her old buddy from the campaign plane. She might have mentioned that a reporter from the *Post* was trying to get in touch with her. Right after that, Lindsey had called. "I've heard some reporters are trying to get in touch with you," he said. "Did you talk to them?" When Zercher said she did talk to one—me—"very briefly," Lindsey pumped her for information. "What did he want to know? Did he want to know if Clinton flirted with you?" Zercher told him she didn't tell the reporter anything. He seemed relieved—then added: "It might be a good idea if you talk to any of these people to say all positive things."

More intriguing, perhaps, was the phone call Zercher got a few days later. It was Schiff again—and she couldn't have been friendlier. Schiff invited Zercher to get together in New York City the following week, when Clinton was going to be in town for an event at the Sheraton Hotel. Zercher accepted. She and Schiff went shopping; Schiff cleared Zercher past the Secret Service to see the president's speech and graciously invited her down to Washington, offering to get her seats in presidential boxes at the Kennedy Center.

Was Schiff just being friendly to an old colleague from the campaign plane? Or had she been deputized by Lindsey to make sure Zercher stayed on warm and fuzzy terms with the White House—and kept her mouth shut when questioned by snoopy reporters? Zercher didn't seem to have any idea.

By now, we had finished dinner. Zercher and McKay decided they wanted to have some fun—and took me to the Men's Club, the topless establishment where Kristy had once worked. We got a choice table, and after a while, I found myself looking up while an extraordinarily large-busted woman in an extremely skimpy blue outfit performed something resembling a lap dance within a foot or so of my face. I had never experienced this before and was uncertain of the proper etiquette. I noticed she had $20 bills stuffed in her panties. I took a twenty out from my wallet and delicately added it to the others, fretting a bit about how I would record this on my expense account. She smiled—and danced even closer. She was now within inches of my glasses, the country rock music blaring, the atmosphere giddy. I extended my left arm and started to gently touch her shoulder, thinking that was what you were supposed to do. I was wrong. She slapped my arm. "No touching!" she barked.

"Oh," I said sheepishly. "I didn't know that." Zercher and McKay burst out laughing, clearly enjoying my humiliation.

I had come to Dallas imagining myself Seymour Hersh. Instead, I was starting to feel like Geraldo Rivera. I went back to my hotel late that night and went straight to sleep, deeply depressed.

*   *   *

hen I got back to Washington, I briefed Thompson. She thought Zercher's account of her phone call from Bruce Lindsey was incredible—further confirmation of her theory that the White House was engaged in an ongoing cover-up. "We have got to get that in the paper," she told me. I wasn't so sure. By Zercher's account, she might well have prompted the phone call by contacting Schiff in the first place. I had also secured the campaign pictures that McKay had told me about. They were indeed fascinating glimpses of the sexually charged, lighthearted frolic aboard the campaign plane. One in particular stood out: a red-faced Clinton with an enormous grin, his shirt hanging down outside his pants, his arm draped around Zercher, his right hand almost, but not quite, touching her breast. When Thompson and I examined it, we both thought of the same thing: the unforgettable picture that first ran in the *National Enquirer* of Donna Rice on Gary Hart's lap aboard the good ship *Monkey Business*. It was the picture that, for all intents and purposes, finally sank Hart. This may not have been quite as damning, but it seemed illustrative nonetheless. Clinton looked like a rowdy frat rat at a college beer blast. And this guy was president? Here, we thought, was photographic evidence suggesting that the contrite Clinton of the *60 Minutes* interview was a fraud, that months after his nationally televised confession that he had caused "pain" in his marriage, he still was not taking the concerns raised about his private behavior the least bit seriously. It also occurred to both Thompson and me that if Zercher's interests were pecuniary, she had probably made a mistake by giving the picture to *The Washington Post*. Some tabloid would almost surely have paid big money for it.

But in order for the *Post* to run the picture, it would need a story to go with it—and I wasn't sure I had one. My "other women" reporting was, I thought, a window into a side of the president the public had never seen. But if the goal was to establish a pattern of harassment, it was nowhere near conclusive. Dunlop's story was, I thought, amusing, but her claim of an annoying late-night phone call couldn't plausibly be presented as analogous to Jones's allegations. The same went for Zercher's account of the antics on the campaign plane. Hinton, because of her background in Democratic politics, was probably the most credible, and certainly the most indignant, of the three. But her story of Clinton's unwanted advance was modest, and in any case, she made it clear that, for now, she didn't want her name used. I suggested we might throw together Dunlop and Zercher in a sidebar that could run with the story on Jones—presuming, of course, that there ever was a story on Paula Jones.

• • •

Meanwhile, I faced another, more pressing problem. Under the original arrangement negotiated through Cliff Jackson, Traylor and Paula Jones had agreed to talk exclusively to me and *The Washington Post.* But how long they would stick to the bargain was far from clear. By mid-March, they were getting antsy. Traylor began pestering me. "Izzy—what's going on, Izzy?" Traylor asked one day in his ingratiating southern twang. "Are you all going to publish anything or not?"

"Sure we are, Danny," I told him. "You just have to understand that this is one of those sensitive stories."

"Are your editors giving you a hard time?" he asked. "Do they not believe Paula's story?"

"Well, it's fair to say that there is considerable debate about how to proceed on this. But don't worry. I think we can work it out."

• • •

In truth, I was far from confident. Among the reporters and editors now working on the Clinton "project," tensions were increasing. For me, the issue was not so much that the story was being suppressed as that the *Post*'s editors couldn't make up their minds what precisely they wanted. We were, I thought, flailing away, with no clear strategy for bringing this Jones matter to an end. Out of frustration, Shepard and I discussed taking a different approach—perhaps a feature story that reported Jones's full allegations and the evidence supporting them but discussed them in the context of the difficulties in writing about such issues. We envisioned the story as a thoughtful essay on a journalistic dilemma. We thought it might run in the paper's Style section or maybe as a magazine piece. It was, in retrospect, a foolish idea—the *Post* would never publish shocking allegations of sexual impropriety by the president as a Style feature story. Still, Shepard had discussed the idea with his editor, Steve Luxemberg, Woodward's deputy on the investigative staff and a man highly respected for his judgment. On Tuesday morning, March 15, the day after filing a front-page piece about the resignation of Associate Attorney General Webster Hubbell, I talked to Luxemberg about it as well and later brought the subject up briefly with Downie. He suggested Shepard and I write a short synopsis of how we might handle it.

What happened next was in retrospect ridiculous—and a painful lesson in my own ineptitude at personal relations and newsroom politics. The next morning, I approached Marilyn Thompson—perhaps the newsroom's greatest champion of the Jones story—and a bit too brusquely informed her that Shepard and I had talked with Luxemberg about an alternative approach that might run in Style or the magazine. Thompson fumed; she immediately concluded that she was being cut out of the process. The *Post* is a bureaucratic fiefdom where the editors of the various sections jockey for position every day and vie ceaselessly over turf. Thompson was an editor on the national desk; as she saw it, I was suggesting that we place a national desk story in a rival section. She complained to her superiors, the national editor DeYoung and her deputy Barbash, who immediately perceived an act of treachery on my part. Barbash and I had clashed repeatedly over the past year, and he was sick of me. Within minutes, I was summoned into his office, where, in Thompson's presence, he let me have it.

"What do you think you're doing, Isikoff, operating *sua sponte?*" he shouted. Barbash was a former Supreme Court reporter. He liked to use Latinisms. I turned to Thompson and asked her if she happened to know what that meant, because I surely didn't.

"It means acting on your own, acting like a freelancer," Barbash continued. That was the problem with me, he continued. I was always acting as though I didn't need any editors, going behind people's backs, trying to get stories into the paper on my own. I had been doing this since day one on this story, he declared, shopping it around the newsroom.

Before long, I was shouting back at him. I called him a "fucking asshole." He ordered me out of his office. I stayed where I was. For a moment, we were eyeball to eyeball—as close, perhaps, as the lap dancer and I had been in Dallas. I blinked first and left, sensing I was now in big trouble.

I was right. That morning, Barbash took the Isikoff problem to his ally Kaiser and demanded that I be fired—or at least be asked to find another job. It was, he argued, the final straw. I was a problem employee who was causing more trouble than I was worth. Downie ordered an internal inquiry into my behavior. The next week, he announced that he had no choice but to suspend me for two weeks for my "insubordination."

The disciplinary action was mostly a side show to the main debate over the Paula Jones story. It had grown largely out of the long-standing clash between myself and Barbash. In a dynamic not exactly unknown in newsrooms, or in any workplace, for that matter, I felt underappreciated; Barbash felt disrespected. But events were about to take a bizarre twist that neither I nor the *Post* editors ever anticipated.

•   •   •

Reporters may well be the biggest gossips of any profession short of Hollywood agents. By the day after Downie suspended me, word of the flare-up had leaked out. Worse, it had leaked to exactly the wrong people. Right-wing activists in Washington heard of my dust-up with Barbash and put their own political twist on this dreary personnel matter: The *Post*, they concluded, was covering up for Bill Clinton.

I realized this on the afternoon of March 24, when I checked my voice mail and heard a message from Floyd Brown. A big right-wing entrepreneur with an almost childlike enthusiasm for political dirt, Brown was a figure of considerable notoriety in Washington political circles: it was he who, during the 1988 presidential campaign, devised the infamous Willie Horton attack ads that struck many critics as a naked appeal to racist fears. Brown's forte was the "independent expenditure"—supposedly third-party political attack ads that invariably took the low road and operated outside the purview of the campaign finance laws. He had used the same tactics in 1992, sponsoring "independent" political ads that featured the Gennifer Flowers tapes. He had even tried to market the tapes, setting up a 900 number so callers could hear them.

I returned Brown's call with some trepidation. He came right to the phone and in a solicitous tone asked: "Hey, Mike, are you okay? Is there anything we can do to help?"

"I'm fine, Floyd," I told him without confirming anything. I promptly put down the phone and shuddered at what I realized was about to happen.

The next day, my clash with Barbash was splattered across the front page of the conservative *Washington Times*. POST SEX STORY ABOUT CLINTON GETS THE SPIKE, blared the headline on the March 25, 1994, story. The paper reported that I had been suspended "after a heated confrontation with editors" and went on to say: "Two sources at the paper said Mr. Isikoff was upset because he thinks the *Post* is burying his findings about sexual harassment charges leveled at Mr. Clinton by Paula Corbin Jones.... Mr. Isikoff, reached at his home yesterday afternoon, said he did not want to talk about the situation." That was bad enough. Within days, I was being hailed—much to my chagrin—on conservative radio talk shows across the country. I was, it was said, a journalistic hero who courageously battled with his editors over their attempts to conceal the truth about Clinton. Jerry Falwell took up my cause. Reed Irvine of Accuracy in Media resurfaced and launched a public relations offensive—complete with advertisements on *The New York Times* op-ed page and in the *Post* itself—demanding that the paper publish my suppressed story. POST COVERS FOR CLINTON ON SEX HARASSMENT CHARGE, read the headline in the cover story of the April 15, 1994, issue of the conservative weekly *Human Events*. Inevitably, the account grew in the telling. Within a few days, the *New York Post* was reporting that I had "pinned Barbash to the wall" out of anger for his attempts to "spike" my story.

I was, to say the least, mortified by my newfound celebrity. This was not exactly how I envisioned making a name for myself in the world of journalism. Still, the whole thing had a "theater of the absurd" quality: my fight with Barbash certainly had grown out of weeks of internal debate over the Jones story. But it was actually triggered by a dispute about bureaucratic etiquette, exacerbated by the fact that Barbash and I could barely stand the sight of each other. It didn't matter. The idea that this was a case of a crusading reporter censored by craven editors made a far more interesting story line and gained wide currency.

More important, it had consequences. The publicity over my battle with my editors created new anxieties among Traylor and his client. "Oh man—sounds like you had quite a dust-up there, Izzy," Traylor said to me a few days after the suspension hit the news. I tried to mollify him, assuring him that the reporting was continuing on track. But it was really Paula and her husband I had to worry about. Paula was despondent. Nobody was believing her. Steve Jones, who had said nothing in the February press conference and very little when I interviewed his wife the next day, became furious.

About that time, a right-wing California filmmaker named Patrick Matrisciana contacted the Joneses at their apartment in Long Beach. He invited them out to dinner and told them they were getting a raw deal: the *Post* was never going to run their story. What's more, he said, their lawyer, Danny Traylor, didn't know what he was doing. They deserved better. Matrisciana assured Paula and Steve that he could help them. He offered them some money—$1,000—to help with their debts. He also asked them to appear in a little film about Bill Clinton he was putting together.

On a windy day that spring, Paula and Steve Jones were videotaped by Matrisciana as they stood on the balcony of their apartment building overlooking the Pacific Ocean. Steve Jones worked as a ticket agent for Northwest Airlines, but he was also a frustrated actor. He had most recently played an Elvis impersonator in a dream sequence in the movie *Midnight Blues* by the director Jim Jarmusch. Now, for Matrisciana's film crew, he poured it on—an angry husband breathing indignation, defending the honor of his aggrieved wife. With his arm around Paula, Steve talked about how Michael Isikoff of *The Washington Post* had checked out Paula's story, but his editors wouldn't run it. He railed against the hypocrisy of the liberal news media. "The media jumped on that Anita Hill–Clarence Thomas deal right from the start," Steve Jones said. They had jumped on the Packwood story, too. "I'll tell you what the position of the editors of *The*

Washington Post is—their position is under the left foot of Bill Clinton. Every time I look at Clinton I see him with his pants down in front of my wife. . . . God, it really infuriates me!"

Matrisciana's film—including a clip of Steve Jones talking about me—started out as an anti-Clinton infomercial that was marketed by the right-wing televangelist Jerry Falwell. It was soon expanded into a notorious documentary called *The Clinton Chronicles.* With eerie music playing in the background, Matrisciana's lurid film accused the president of being at the center of a giant conspiracy that included drug running and murder—a conspiracy so immense that it could suppress stories in *The Washington Post.* The film became a cause célèbre, the video bible for Clinton haters. More than 150,000 copies were sold.

The battle lines for Jones vs. Clinton were drawn.

5

"Ms. Jones can identify certain distinguishing characteristics."

etsey Wright was indignant. "I've just been stunned at how you decide you've got facts worthy of pursuit," she berated her visitors. The recipients of this lecture were the *Post*'s Charlie Shepard and Sharon LaFraniere. While I was out on suspension, they were pursuing the story of Paula Jones and the broader questions about Clinton's private behavior. Who better to answer them than Wright—now a Washington lobbyist, but still Bill Clinton's de facto bimbo-suppressor-in-chief?

Wasn't it obvious that the Jones story was a lie? Wright asked. Just like all the other lies that have been spread about Clinton's private life? She knew, Wright said. She had looked into Paula Jones. She had talked to some people back at the Arkansas Industrial Development Commission, Jones's old agency, and she was apparently a "pretty interesting co-worker for a lot of folks."

What does that mean? the reporters wanted to know.

Well, Wright said, they had to institute a new dress code there because of Paula Jones. And the woman was a "real gossip" who was "always bragging about this, that or the other thing." Jones had a "reputation" for telling stories, for "gossiping and exaggerating in her own office." Therefore, Wright suggested, if there had actually been an encounter with Clinton, it surely would have come to her attention before.

The reporters were put off. Shepard, in particular, had heard this sort of thing before—when he was working the Packwood story. The

Oregon senator and his aides had come to *The Washington Post* shortly before election day in 1992, asking the paper to hold off on its story accusing Packwood of harassing women. They raised the same sorts of questions about the senator's accusers—questioning their character, their reputations, their past sexual histories.

Shepard and LaFraniere pressed Wright for evidence, for the names of people at AIDC who could corroborate what she was saying. But Wright wouldn't play. Look, she explained, she had tracked down—and discredited—every possible sex charge against Clinton during the 1992 campaign. The Jones story had never turned up. "There was no way that we could have gone through that '92 campaign with as much of a premium as people were putting on hearing bimbo stories and bimbos trying to get their claim to fame and never heard of this woman," Wright said. Therefore, Jones's charge must be a lie—or, as Wright put it, a "brand new story," a "pure fabrication" invented this year to harm Bill Clinton. "The entire whole cloth was woven and spun in '94," she said.

The longer the interview continued, the more emotional Wright grew. LaFraniere asked about Sally Perdue, the former Miss Arkansas who had recently claimed she had been intimidated to keep silent about an affair with Clinton. Perdue is a "very sad and very sick character," said Wright. LaFraniere asked about a Little Rock lawyer—identified by the troopers as one of Clinton's girl-friends—who had been appointed a state judge. Tears welled up in Wright's eyes. "I mean, it is very difficult to maintain my composure with these questions. I don't understand what they have to do with anything."

The reporters tried to explain. What she had done in 1992—the whole operation with the detective Palladino—was extraordinary. The compiling of lists, the investigating of women, the attacks on the character—didn't that go too far? Was it really possible that all of these stories about Clinton's womanizing were false? That there wasn't a kernel of truth in them somewhere?

"I feel assaulted by your questions," said Wright, by now sobbing openly. "I did a defense job about complete fabrications. That word is spelled f-a-b-r-i-c-a-t-i-o-n-s. And you keep coming back and asking me about truth. I worked against lies and fabrications. That's what I did. I worked to insert truth into stories about the state I loved, and the record of Bill Clinton as governor."

Wright wanted to know why any of this should matter. She didn't understand what the *Post* was even doing here. Shepard returned the discussion to Paula Jones. This is not enjoyable for any of us, he said. But the Jones charges raised issues of "character," and that can "eventually suggest something about suitability to serve in public office. And the Jones case, I think, for example, raises an issue of someone's appetite for risk—an incredibly risky behavior which, if the story she was telling is true, I think one could argue that Bill Clinton is willing to take extraordinary risks."

Don't talk to me about character, Wright said. Character is about many different things, and it's a lot bigger than this. "I don't believe you have any interest in knowing anything about the man." She knew Bill Clinton, she knew him very well. They didn't. The reporters left, themselves a bit shaken by Wright's outbursts, feeling no more enlightened than when they went in.

•   •   •

Inside the *Post*, the Jones story was about as dead as it could get. I returned to work in early April. Shepard and I, with some help from LaFraniere, tried one more time to draft a version of the story that might pass muster. It outlined Jones's charges, explored questions about her credibility, evaluated the evidence that both supported and detracted from her account. In the end, I wasn't happy with it. It left the reader with no idea whether to believe her or not. I thought it hedged so much that it no longer made sense. If there wasn't a presumption that at least some elements of Jones's story had more substance than the White House conceded, what was the point of running anything at all?

In any case, the question was moot. After reviewing the last draft Shepard and I had labored over, Bob Kaiser wrote a lengthy memo arguing that no version of this story ought to see the light of day. "The Team" had made a valiant effort, he proclaimed. But we hadn't proved the case. The story simply did not meet the standards of *The Washington Post.*

To hell with it, I thought. I was weary of the whole business—and ready to move on to other matters. I began looking around for a dif-

ferent subject and soon found one that intrigued me—an unprece-
dented increase in court-authorized FBI wiretaps by the Clinton Justice Department. I thought the story raised some interesting privacy
issues. It would certainly be a welcome relief from the line of inquiry
I had been pursuing lately.

•   •   •

That April, Danny Traylor was in a bind. Paula and Steve Jones
hadn't even told him about the interview with Matrisciana; he
found out by seeing a promo for *The Clinton Chronicles* on television.
This was just what he'd tried to avoid: turning the case into a political cause. He immediately called Paula. They had an agreement,
Traylor told his client. She wasn't supposed to say anything about
the case—at least not without clearing it with him. It was an emotional phone call. The baby wailed and Steve yelled in the background; Paula cried and apologized. Traylor concluded that Paula
didn't fully appreciate what she had done—that she had been
manipulated by a hustler with a political agenda. He forgave her but
realized that he didn't want much more to do with this case. He
vowed to get rid of it as soon as he could.

Traylor, thirty-eight, knew he was miscast as someone butting
heads with the president of the United States. He was a small-time
solo practitioner, whose bread and butter was real estate closings and
insurance claims. In fact, he hated lawsuits. "I try to stay out of court-
rooms," he liked to say. Since graduating from the University of
Arkansas Law School in 1982, he had barely argued a case before a
jury. He believed in settling differences, not litigating them. "My first
partner"—a wizened fellow named H. Clay Robinson—"taught me
good lawyers always try to settle," Traylor once told me. "You don't
put life, liberty or property in jeopardy by going into a courtroom if
you can help it."

Even before the disastrous CPAC press conference, Traylor had
called George Cook, a local businessman who he thought had an
"in" with the White House, explaining that he had a client with a
problem that could be embarrassing to the president. By Traylor's
account, he never demanded anything: "I told him that I was going
to leave it to their imagination what they wanted to do." But his
client had been "damaged" by the president's conduct toward her,

Traylor told Cook. Her husband was an aspiring actor in California, he added; maybe there was something the president's friends could work out that would make his clients happy and avoid a fuss. Traylor's entreaty arguably had the smell of blackmail, but Traylor seemed oblivious of the implications. As he saw it, this was the sort of thing lawyers are supposed to do. You quietly try to work out your differences before everybody goes off and starts filing lawsuits.

I called Cook. He told me he never took Traylor's proposal seriously. He hadn't even bothered to pass it along to the White House. "I would have been embarrassed to do that," Cook said. He considered Jones's allegations too ridiculous. Traylor, however, remembered their conversations quite differently. He and Cook had talked four times. Cook had told him he needed to check with somebody at the White House. A few days later, on Monday, January 24, Cook called him back. "I'm going to tell you the fucking story," Cook said. He had checked with his friend at the White House, who, before deciding anything, had wanted to look at some polling data on whether the Troopergate allegations from the previous month had hurt the president's standing. The polling numbers had come back, and it was clear that "we haven't been hurt by it." In fact, after consulting with his White House friend, Cook told Traylor that the White House didn't care about any of this stuff. "My guy has looked at this, and shit, man, they can't even get their stories straight," Cook told him, according to Traylor. "Your girl is saying one thing and the trooper is saying another." Traylor said he was "really pissed" by Cook's response. "Well, my gal is going to take this public, then," Traylor told Cook. After a long pause, Cook dismissed him. "Well, okay, we're going on down the road, then."

Cook would not identify his friend at the White House to Traylor. But four years later, in a sworn deposition, he did identify him. It was Bruce Lindsey.

•   •   •

Traylor had hoped a big story in *The Washington Post* would force the White House into some kind of settlement before any lawsuit had to be filed. But it was by now clear that wasn't going to happen. Jones had missed her chance to file a formal sexual harassment complaint under federal law. That would have required action within 180 days of the alleged incident. But she could still file a civil suit under Arkansas law, which gave her until May 8, 1994—the third-year anniversary of the encounter at the Excelsior Hotel. Realizing he was well out of his depth, Traylor began reaching out for help to big-name litigators and women's groups around the country.

But nobody wanted to touch it. Traylor called Gerry Spence in Wyoming. He called Anita Hill in Oklahoma—and sent her a package of material—but she wouldn't even return his phone calls. He called the National Organization for Women, and someone sent him back a kit on how to file a lawsuit. A handful of other conservative activists, working through Cliff Jackson, began looking in other directions. "There was a frantic effort to get Traylor out of it," Jackson recalled much later. "He knew he was in over his head."

One of Jackson's first calls was to Peter W. Smith, a prominent Chicago investment banker and conservative financier. In 1993, Smith—a major financial backer of GOPAC, the political action committee identified with Newt Gingrich—had given David Brock a $5,000 stipend for research into stories about Clinton's sex life. Later, after the Troopergate stories broke, Smith contributed $25,000 to Jackson's "whistleblower fund" to provide support for troopers Patterson and Perry. Smith put Jackson in touch with Richard Porter, a young former aide to Vice President Dan Quayle. Porter had recently joined the blue-chip Chicago law firm of Kirkland & Ellis as an associate. He specialized in commercial transactions and was, at the time, trying to schmooze Smith for some business. Porter couldn't take the case—for one thing, he wasn't a litigator—but as he later explained it, he wanted to prove to Smith that he could make things happen. He quickly thought of a friend of his, a fellow classmate and *Law Review* colleague from the University of Chicago Law School named Jerome Marcus. Intense and prematurely balding, Marcus had worked as a lawyer in Ronald Reagan's State Department (where he specialized in the law governing international arms control treaties) and later as a federal prosecutor in the U.S. Attorney's Office in Philadelphia. He was a man of strong convictions, political and personal. Raised in a relatively liberal, affluent

Jewish Democratic family (his father was a well-known Philadelphia businessman who founded Crazy Richard's Peanut Butter), Marcus became an observant Jew who kept a kosher home. At Chicago, he had majored in political philosophy and turned toward conservatism (although he stayed a registered Democrat). Most important to Porter's request, he also was now a litigator with a Philadelphia firm that specialized in class-action lawsuits.

The founding partner of the firm, David Berger, was a prominent Democratic fundraiser and Clinton supporter. Even so, Marcus was intrigued. "I can't put my name on this stuff, but I'll help," he told Porter. Porter and Marcus placed a conference call to Jackson, who briefed them on the case. He then put Marcus in touch with Traylor, who faxed him the affidavits of Jones and her friends, along with other material. After looking it over, Marcus was satisfied that Jones had a credible complaint. He was especially struck by one line in Jones's account—her recollection of what Ferguson had said when he asked her to meet Clinton upstairs: "Don't worry, we do this for the governor all the time." "That phrase really stuck in my craw," Marcus said years later. "I thought it told you a lot about who Bill Clinton really is." For Marcus, the opportunity to expose what he viewed as the fraudulence of Clinton's public persona was, he said, what animated him about the Jones case. He wrote an unpublished essay that described his thinking about the subject: It was called "The Mask." "I thought this [case] really was an exercise that had value for the country," he said. In late April, from the study of his home in Philadelphia, Marcus wrote the first draft of the first civil suit ever filed against a sitting president of the United States.

In later years, defenders of the president would search for the conservative cabal they were certain was behind the Jones case. They weren't entirely off base; indeed, many of these same players would appear much later in critical behind-the-scenes roles. But at the start, this was a cabal with a subtext: the revenge of the University of Chicago Law School, with its conservative academic tradition, against what its acolytes no doubt perceived as the liberal relativism of Yale Law and its most prominent graduate. And it would soon draw in a third player. Porter and Marcus still needed to find Jones some lawyers who could put their names to the case. They placed a conference call to a third University of Chicago alumnus, Nelson Lund, who had served as a lawyer in the Bush White House and clerked for Sandra Day O'Connor at the Supreme Court and was now teaching at the George Mason University Law School. Within a few days, Lund got back to Porter with a name: Gil Davis, a portly, easygoing attorney with a largely civil practice in northern Virginia. Davis was a former federal prosecutor, a moderate Republican. Traylor liked that—and soon he and Davis were talking. Davis had a colleague who shared space in his Fairfax office and who wanted to help out: an ambitious former Justice Department tax lawyer named Joe Cammarata. Neither Davis nor Cammarata was a big name. Neither was an expert in sexual harassment law. But for the conservatives, and certainly for Traylor, they were smart enough. And they seemed eager. They certainly knew how to file a lawsuit.[1]

Inside the White House, where the Jones matter had been largely dismissed as inconsequential, anxiety was rising. In morning meetings for the senior staff, the issue began to crop up. How big was this going to be? Deputy Chief of Staff John Podesta in particular was now eyeing it closely, peppering aides for the latest intelligence on Jones's intentions. "Does anybody know if she's going to file?" he would ask. Would she call another press conference? To be sure, nobody in the meetings took Jones's claims seriously as a legal matter. "There was an assumption that she was a wacko . . . that she was trash," said Jane Sherburne, an assistant White House counsel who had just joined the staff and was a bit puzzled when the matter first came up in the staff meetings. Still, the White House had to be concerned. There was no way to tell how an actual lawsuit against the president would play.

While Stephanopoulos had assumed the role of watching the *Post*'s reporting, David Kendall, the president's private lawyer at the Washington firm of Williams & Connally, had formal responsibility for monitoring legal developments. For Kendall, a brainy and somewhat stuffy litigator who was allergic to talking to the press, the Jones charges were largely a distraction. He had been hired to represent the First Family in the investigation into the Whitewater land deal. Kendall was of the old school: he believed lawyers should talk in the courtroom and nowhere else. But the president's political advisers—Podesta, Harold Ickes and Stephanopoulos—and his new White House counsel, Lloyd Cutler, were getting worried. The Jones case seemed to them largely political, and they thought it needed to be fought on those terms. Sensing that the story was about to burst into public view, Cutler in particular began urging the president to hire a lawyer who could fight fire with fire. In early May, just a few days before the statute of limitations expired, Clinton hired Robert Bennett.

SUPERLAWYER TO BOLSTER CLINTON DEFENSE; PRESIDENT TURNS TO BENNETT AS PAULA JONES PREPARES HARASSMENT SUIT. The headline was stripped across the front page of the *Washington Times* on the morning of May 3, 1994. Inside the *Post,* the news changed everything. Bennett was, at the time, perhaps Washington's hottest criminal defense lawyer. Short, garrulous and pugnacious, Bennett was full of moxie, a former amateur boxer from the streets of Brooklyn. He was also a formidable presence in Washington political circles. Bennett loved to schmooze with pols and the press. Everybody knew him. He got his clients off—before they ever had to go to trial. He had represented Caspar Weinberger in the Iran-contra affair and helped win him a pardon. He was, at the time, representing Dan Rostenkowski, the chairman of the House Ways and Means Committee— the man widely viewed as key to the fate of Clinton's health care reform package—in a criminal investigation into abuse of the House franking privileges.

The fact that the president would hire Bob Bennett to represent him against the claims of Paula Jones bestowed official legitimacy on a story that, until then, the *Post* had been afraid to touch. It showed the White House was worried about Jones—and meant the public had a right to know what her claims were all about. The morning the story broke, all the *Post*'s senior editors were out of town on a management retreat. But having learned the news, Downie ordered Shepard and me to get our story into shape for the next day.

One of the first things I did was call Bennett. This lawsuit is bullshit, he told me. You're way off base on this. He gave me a quote: "It's really just an attempt to rewrite the results of the election." The right wing had jumped all over it and now were trying to use it to stick up the president. What's more, he said, it was extortion, and he, Bennett, could prove it.

How's that? I asked him.

Bennett had a sworn affidavit from a guy named George Cook.

Cook? I said. I know Cook.

Well, you should take a look at what he has to say.

Bennett faxed me an affidavit that had been signed in Little Rock that morning. It made Jones—and, more especially, Traylor—look like little more than crass extortionists. According to Cook's affidavit, Traylor had threatened the president, telling him if Paula Jones "did not get money . . . she would embarrass" Clinton publicly. Cook also claimed that Traylor conceded he knew his case was weak, but he "needed the client and he needed the money out of it." Finally, Cook claimed Traylor had told him "it would help if President Clinton would get Paula a job out in California"—an idea Cook asserted he rejected because "that would be illegal."

That's not quite how Cook—much less Traylor—had described their discussions to me a few weeks earlier. Cook had never said anything to me about considering Traylor's proposal "illegal"—much less that the lawyer had claimed he "needed the money out of it." Either Cook then had played down their discussions in order to avoid embarrassing Traylor, or now he had ratcheted up his account to suit the needs of the president's lawyers. It didn't matter. It was close enough to the truth to give the press-savvy Bennett his first shot in the coming PR war over the Jones lawsuit.

Bennett said something else to almost every reporter he talked to that day. He said it off the record, of course, because lawyers like him like to get messages across without leaving any fingerprints. "Do you know," he asked, "that there are nude photographs of Jones?" Bennett actually had never seen any such pictures. But inside the *Post* we had a pretty good idea where he had heard about them. Mark Brown, Jones's burly brother-in-law, had mentioned them to me back in February. Now, he was trying to discredit Jones and had already begun meeting with Bennett's associates, dishing out tales of sexual escapades involving the president's accuser.

Brown was, at best, a questionable source. Unemployed and resentful, a former country music disc jockey and Marine Corps dropout, Brown had recently been evicted from a local city council meeting for shouting vulgarities. Reporters never would have relied on him had he been making similar charges against Clinton. But

Bennett had no hesitation about spreading Brown's claims to every reporter who called him without making the least effort to check them out.

The sliming of Paula Jones had begun.

•   •   •

T he next day, May 4, the *Post* published the Paula Jones story—a lengthy piece that ran on the front page under an unusual triple byline: Isikoff, Shepard and LaFraniere. Most of it came from the reporting I had done back in February. The story reported in detail, for the first time, Jones's claims: that Clinton, despite her expressed lack of interest, had allegedly taken her by the hand, kissed her on the neck, put his hand up her culottes, dropped his trousers and underwear, then asked her to perform oral sex. Pam Blackard was quoted as saying she saw Clinton stare at Jones that day, watched Trooper Ferguson escort her upstairs and witnessed her return "walking fast" and "shaking." Deborah Ballantine was quoted recounting how Jones came to her office and "told her the story." The story also quoted Bennett's flat denial—"this event, plain and simple, didn't happen"—and noted how the allegations of extreme behavior by Clinton were a "departure from past allegations about Clinton's personal conduct."

Because the events described by Jones took place while she was allegedly alone with Clinton, the story said, it was "impossible to independently resolve what, if anything, happened between them."

•   •   •

O n Thursday, May 5, I went to Little Rock—along with hundreds of other reporters. The statute of limitations for Jones to file her lawsuit ran out on Friday. Would Clinton become the first president in U.S. history to be sued in office? Would a Democratic president—a president whose wife had hailed Anita Hill as a modern American heroine—be formally identified as a defendant in a sexual harassment lawsuit? The ironies and potential embarrassments for the White House were rich. The front-page *Post* story had bestowed new legitimacy on Jones's claims and put them "into play." The aggressive effort by Clinton aides to shame the press out of writing about allegations of sexual misconduct looked as if it were coming to an end.

Also flying into Little Rock that week were Jones's new lawyers, Davis and Cammarata. They met for hours with their client in Traylor's seventeenth-floor office; they reviewed, step by step, her allegations and began rewriting the draft complaint. Cammarata questioned Jones closely about precisely what she saw when Clinton had exposed himself. Jones recalled something that she had once mentioned to Ballantine—but not to me. Clinton's penis, she said, seemed to hang downward. She and Ballantine joked that it looked "like the leaning Tower of Pisa." Lydia Cathay, Jones's sister, would later say that Jones had talked about it with her as well, describing Clinton's penis as "crooked" and "gross."

Traylor had heard this—he remembered well the "leaning Tower of Pisa" joke—but never made much of it. Jones, by her own account, had only a split-second glance, and if her eyes weren't deceiving her, it could have been no more than a partial erection. Nonetheless, Cammarata was excited. He remembered a case that had been prominently in the news that year: how lawyers for a fourteen-year-old California boy allegedly molested by pop star Michael Jackson had claimed his client had knowledge of unique features of Jackson's anatomy. Only four months earlier, Jackson had agreed to pay a reported $15 million or more to settle the case.[2] Here was something that could smoke Clinton out, Cammarata thought. He quickly relayed the observation to Davis, who was sitting at Traylor's desk in the office next door. "I was thrilled," Davis later recalled. "This helps put him in the box." Other than "a couple of follow-ups" to make sure she understood him, Cammarata never extensively questioned Jones on the subject or explored other possibilities. Instead, the two lawyers quickly wrote a new paragraph into the complaint—a paragraph that would forever distinguish the Jones lawsuit. It was paragraph 22. "There were distinguishing characteristics in Clinton's genital area that were obvious to Jones," it read.[3]

Traylor had publicly suggested that Jones might file her claim that afternoon. By two P.M., a huge throng of reporters gathered at the courthouse steps. Reporters for *The New York Times, The Wall Street Journal* and the *Los Angeles Times* mingled with hacks from the British tabloids and representatives of sleazy television shows like *Hard Copy* and *A Current Affair.* When I arrived, there was a buzz. Many of those present, I noticed, had copies of the *Post* story and had underlined key passages. "That's Michael Isikoff," I heard one young TV producer say. Once again, I felt faintly ridiculous.

The media crush was no doubt a warning to the White House: This case is about to explode. In Washington, Bennett decided he should try to settle the case. He taxied over to the White House, moved into Stephanopoulos's quarters just outside the Oval Office and started a series of conference calls with Davis and Cammarata in Little Rock. Bennett knew Davis. They had been federal prosecutors together years earlier during the Nixon administration. When the two spoke for the first time that morning, Bennett started off with his usual bravado and bluster. "You don't have a case," he told Davis. "I've talked to my client for hours, and he doesn't even know this woman. He absolutely denies this happened."

All Davis could think was: You've talked to your client *for hours.* About this?

Bennett then added the line he had been sharing with every journalist he talked to. "I understand there are some nude photos of her."

If Bennett was trying to play hardball, Davis and Cammarata were prepared to retaliate in kind. "Well, Bob," said Davis, "might it affect your thinking if I told you that Ms. Jones can identify certain distinguishing characteristics in the president's genital area?"

There was a long pause. "Goddammit, Gil," Bennett finally said. "We're lawyers—and here we are talking about the president's privates. . . . Well, I guess this is not your usual personal injury lawsuit."

With their opening shots fired, the sides began intense negotiations. Bennett made it clear that the president was not going to pay Jones any money. That's fine, Davis replied. His client wasn't seeking any. She wanted only to "redeem her reputation." Bennett suggested he might have a statement that could do that, a statement Clinton might be willing to issue. Inside the West Wing of the White House that day, Bennett worked on it as a bevy of aides—Lloyd Cutler, Stephanopoulos and Harold Ickes—looked over his shoulder and weighed in. Even Clinton himself kept stopping by, asking how it was going. Cutler, in particular, was a proponent of settlement. You never knew what dangers lurked in the course of civil litigation. Clinton seemed tentatively to have bought the idea of getting rid of this thing. By late afternoon, Bennett had drafted something that he thought might pass muster and faxed it to Traylor's office in Little Rock. It was, in the context of the time, a remarkable concession. In it, the president would declare that he had "no recollection" of meeting Jones "in a room," but then add: "I do not challenge her claim that we met there."

When Jones and her lawyers first saw it, they were upbeat. It was, they thought, practically an admission of at least the core elements of Jones's story. The statement went on to say that Jones "did not engage in any improper or sexual conduct. I regret any untrue assertions that may have been made about her." Bennett had built in some lawyerly wiggle room, of course. The statement refers to "a" room, not "the" hotel room where Jones claimed the encounter had taken place. Still, after months of White House claims that nothing like the incident had ever taken place, it gave Davis and Cammarata almost enough to declare victory.

Given the attacks on Jones's character that had emanated from the White House, Davis wanted to make sure the statement got maximum attention. Bennett offered to have White House press secretary Dee Dee Meyers read it.

Davis said no—it had to be the president.

Bennett said, Wait, he's right here in the room, let me check.

Davis cupped his hand over the receiver and whispered, "He's in the room." Everybody looked at each other. "My God," Cammarata later remembered thinking, "we're negotiating directly with the president of the United States." He looked at Jones. She looked awed.

Bennett got back on the line. "No problem," he told Davis.

There were a few more details to iron out. Davis and Cammarata wanted to tweak the language a bit, see if they could come up with something that would at least acknowledge the president actually knew Jones. Clinton's insistence that he didn't was what seemed to bother Jones the most. They also wanted to work out strict "no comment" language that would make sure White House aides would keep their mouths shut about the case and not try to "spin" the deal to the detriment of Jones once it was struck. To ensure that, they wanted a "tolling agreement" that would permit Jones to revive her claim just in case the White House started trashing her again after settlement. But Bennett, after consulting with Cutler, was particularly resistant on this point. A "tolling agreement," he told Davis, was a "deal breaker." It would mean Jones and her advisers could revive the lawsuit at any time.

At Bennett's request, Davis and Cammarata agreed to put off filing the lawsuit. They hoped everything would be nailed down in the morning. Traylor, watching the throng of reporters outside the courthouse from his office window, thought chances were good that they would.

But then everything began to unravel. On its news show that night, one of the local Little Rock TV stations featured an interview with Jones's own sister Charlotte Brown and her ubiquitous husband, Mark. Charlotte claimed that she had spoken to Paula when she was in town over the Christmas holidays and that Jones had told her about her plans to press her claims against Clinton, adding that "whichever way it went, she smelled money." That much, of course, Brown had said before to me. But on the TV news that night, Charlotte and her husband now strongly suggested that they believed Jones was lying about the whole thing. Charlotte described Paula as being "thrilled" when she told her of the encounter with Clinton that day. Thrilled? Only two months earlier, when we had breakfast at the roadside coffee shop, Charlotte Brown had said her sister told her of the encounter in a "matter-of-fact" way. Watching the TV in Traylor's office, Davis thought the interview with Charlotte and Mark had been staged. Jones, for her part, burst into tears. "Why is she saying that?" Jones wailed. "Why?"

Watching the same interview back in my room at the Capital Hotel, I immediately saw the fine hand of Clinton's lawyers. I was right. Mark Brown, I later learned, had gone that week to the Little Rock office of Stephen Engstrom, a longtime lawyer for the Clinton family. There to debrief him was Mitch Ettinger, one of Bob Bennett's law partners. The Browns' story hadn't entirely changed after this meeting with Clinton's legal squad. But it had hardened.

From there, things only got worse. Someone at the White House leaked word to CNN that Jones had delayed filing her lawsuit because she had no case and because her family didn't believe her—a reference to the Browns' press conference. Jones and her lawyers were "shocked" and "furious" when they watched the report; there had been an explicit agreement with Bennett that the negotiations would be conducted in secret. Bennett was upset, too. He thought he was close to a deal. Now the White House spinners—he suspected Stephanopoulos, although the White House aide later denied it—couldn't control themselves. It had been ingrained in them since the campaign that you have to "win" every news cycle. Their victory was Pyrrhic; the negotiations were now effectively ended.

On Friday, Davis and Cammarata reassembled with their client and her now quite agitated husband. They discussed how the events of the preceding evening proved that the White House couldn't be trusted. Even if they reached an agreement, the other side would continue to trash Paula. And at that point, with the statute of limitations run out, they would have forever surrendered their right to sue. Steve Jones, it was clear, was ready to go. He hated Clinton—with a passion—and wanted to stick it to him.

But Davis needed to hear it directly from Paula. She hadn't been talking much. He sensed she felt uncomfortable.

"Now, Paula," the avuncular Davis told her. "I want to review this with you one more time. When we go, your life is going to be an open book. This has got to be your decision—not mine, not Steve's. I believe you're a courageous person, but I will think nothing less of you if you decided not to pursue this. If you want, we can just drop it and forget it."

Jones looked pained and nervous. To Davis, it was now clearer than ever that she was not at all relishing this, that maybe things had gotten out of hand.

"I really don't want to have to do this," she finally said.

She paused—and then continued. "But I don't see that I have any choice."

"Are you authorizing me to go forward?"

Yes, she said, she was.

That morning, Davis and Cammarata walked down to the U.S. courthouse a half mile away and handed a copy of their complaint to the clerk of the court. It accused Bill Clinton of "odious, perverse and outrageous" conduct that caused Paula Corbin Jones "severe emotional distress." It accused Clinton and trooper Danny Ferguson

of defaming Jones and damaging "her good name, character and reputation." It charged that Clinton conspired with Ferguson to violate
Jones's rights under the "due process and equal protection provi-
sions of the United States Constitution." The complaint asked for
$700,000 in compensatory and punitive damages.

As Davis and Cammarata left the clerk's office that day, they
were followed by reporters and photographers. As they emerged
from the courthouse, the throng grew larger and more unruly. The
TV cameras followed every move they made. The photographers
clicked one shot after another. The reporters shouted questions.
Davis laughed at first: he had never seen anything quite like this.
Then he had what he would later describe as an epiphany. "In most
other countries, you go after the head of state, you'd be met with a
barrage of bullets rather than cameras," Davis thought. "Here any
citizen can redress his or her grievance by filing a lawsuit—even if
it's against the president of the United States."

Davis reflected on this as he stood in the middle of the media
circus outside the Little Rock courthouse. "What a great country," he
thought.

•   •   •

Back in Washington, no sooner was the lawsuit filed than Bennett
rushed out of his office to hold an impromptu press conference.
Seething with indignation, he denounced the lawsuit as "tabloid
trash with a legal caption on it." The president would never capitu-
late, he said. The case was purely and simply "about money. It's
about TV contracts, it's about movie contracts, it's about book contracts." At the White House, senior staffers gathered around a TV set
in communications director Mark Gearan's office to watch Bennett
and practically cheered. The lawsuit had struck them as repugnant,
its contents vile and repulsive. Some of the White House staffers
were saddened. How low had American politics sunk? they wondered. Were there no depths to which Clinton's enemies would not
sink? Bennett's righteous indignation gave voice to their inner feelings. He was expressing their own anger, standing up for decency in
the face of naked political sleaze. Bennett reinvigorated them. "We
thought Bennett had hit a home run," said Jane Sherburne, the new
White House lawyer.

• • •

T hat morning, I picked up a copy of the nineteen-page complaint at the Little Rock courthouse and then rushed back to the hotel to write my story. As I flipped through the document, I focused on two allegations. The first was Jones's claim of being able to identify "distinguishing characteristics" on Clinton's private parts. Jesus, I thought, I never heard that before. How the hell am I going to get that into the paper?

Further along, the complaint charged that after the alleged incident Jones was "treated in a hostile and rude manner" by her superiors at the AIDC, that she was denied merit increases and, after her maternity leave, placed in a new job with no opportunities for advancement. This too was new.[4] In the nearly three months I had been talking to Jones, she had never complained about suffering in the workplace after her encounter with Clinton. On a couple of occasions, she had indicated that she thought others in the office might have known about the incident, and she wondered if that hadn't held her back in her otherwise unremarkable, low-level career at the AIDC. Davis and Cammarata had seized on this speculation and shoved it into the lawsuit. Jones's post-incident treatment, the suit portentously charged, had subjected Jones to a "hostile work environment"—a quid pro quo punishment for refusing Clinton's sexual demands that violated her constitutional rights.

From a strictly legal perspective, the claim that Jones had suffered in the workplace might have made sense—at least in the short term. By giving greater weight to her suit, it made it harder for the president's lawyers to get a quick dismissal. It made the case look more like a classic sexual harassment claim. And the lawyers were not unmindful of their interests: the count alleging civil rights violations, if ultimately upheld, would require the defendant to pay not just damages to Jones, but attorneys' fees as well.

I pointed out this new dimension to Jones's allegations in the story I was writing that afternoon, explaining Jones's previous failure to mention suffering on the job. But tipped off by Traylor and Jackson, I was more focused on what I was learning about the secret negotiations between Bennett and the Jones lawyers. Even while the president's lawyer was denouncing the lawsuit as "trash," he was

quietly trying to settle it by making an arguably key concession—
that the president and the plaintiff might well have met at the
Excelsior Hotel that day. The fact that Bennett had been willing to
acknowledge as much seemed astounding to me—especially after
the endless claims by Stephanopoulos, Betsey Wright and Phil Price
that the entire event had been manufactured out of whole cloth. I
included it prominently in my story.

The story also noted the potential political pitfalls for Clinton if
the case were to move forward. Federal court rules, I wrote, "may
give Jones's lawyers the opportunity to take sworn depositions from
witnesses, including former members of Clinton's gubernatorial
security detail who have said they solicited women for the governor.
This process could keep alive for some time politically damaging
questions about the president's private conduct."

After filing, I rushed to the airport to make a late Friday afternoon flight back to Washington. When I landed, I checked in with the
Post, and my nemesis Barbash came on the line. He, too, was incredulous that Clinton had actually been willing to concede having met
with Jones.

Go back to Bennett and check this again, he ordered.

I called Bennett from the airport. He confirmed the secret Thursday talks and also a detail I hadn't known: that Clinton had specifically authorized him to conduct the negotiations, even though
Bennett insisted, "I didn't run [the draft statements] by the president. These were two lawyers who were talking." Given where we
started—the White House insistence that Jones's entire claim was a
scurrilous fabrication—I felt modestly vindicated.

•   •   •

But I was also still stewing over my experiences with the *Post.* I
thought the editors had come down too hard on me over the
clash with Barbash. The bad blood from the incident hadn't dissipated. At the time of my suspension in March, I had called up a number of editors at other publications. One of them was Evan Thomas,
then the Washington bureau chief of *Newsweek.* I knew Thomas
through mutual friends and had played in his intensely competitive
Sunday morning football games until I decided there were more

relaxing ways to spend my weekends. Thomas seemed encouraging when I talked to him about coming to *Newsweek*, which, although owned by the Washington Post Company, was an entirely independent news operation. I had told him in March that I didn't want to leave until the Jones story was resolved one way or another. Now, in May, it was. I told him I was ready to jump ship. Because of the common corporate ownership, Thomas and Ann McDaniel, the *Newsweek* chief of correspondents, had to get approval from *Post* editors. No one objected. In mid-May, after a thirteen-year career at *The Washington Post*, I quit the paper and moved to *Newsweek*.

Book Two

KATHLEEN WILLEY

September 1996-August 1997

6

"I had a similar thing happen to me when I worked at the White House."

When Bill Clinton contemplates the scandals that could ruin his second term, what worries him most is not the vast machinery of the special prosecutor investigating Whitewater or the potential for endless congressional hearings over shady contributions to his presidential campaign. His real concern, say his friends, is the sexual-harassment suit filed against him by Paula Jones. Legally, most experts agree, the case has some holes. But it still has the potential to make Clinton's life hellish in the months and years ahead.

So proclaimed *Newsweek* in the January 13, 1997, cover story entitled: "Should She Be Heard? Clinton v. Paula Jones Goes to the Supreme Court." The decision to put Jones on the cover just two weeks before Clinton's second-term inauguration was controversial. Indeed, it enraged the White House. Yet the piece, written by Evan Thomas, was remarkably prescient—and if anything, it understated the dangers to the Clinton presidency. Within a year, the Jones case would merge with "the vast machinery of the special prosecutor" and make Clinton's life far more hellish than we at *Newsweek* or anybody in the White House could possibly have envisioned.

•   •   •

I n the fall of 1996, I got a call from a Washington writer named Stuart Taylor Jr. I had, by that time, more than adjusted to my switch two years earlier from *The Washington Post* to *Newsweek*. After nearly two decades in daily journalism, I had quickly learned to appreciate the more leisurely pace of a newsweekly, not to mention the higher pay and added perks. More important, as one of the magazine's two "investigative correspondents," I'd had a chance to work on a broad range of stories: I had reported extensively on the Oklahoma City bombing, the Ruby Ridge FBI debacle and the 1996 presidential campaign. With my sidekick Mark Hosenball, I had also worked on a number of investigations, including one about a Pat Robertson business scam that sent the conservative televangelist into paroxyms of rage.[1]

I had not forsaken the Clinton "scandal" beat: I had been the magazine's lead reporter on the long-running Whitewater investigation, which had led the previous spring to the criminal convictions of the Clintons' former business partners, Jim and Susan McDougal. The idea that turning over some new rock would bring the entire Clinton presidency tumbling down was by now deeply ingrained in the psychology of the Washington press corps. But the Paula Jones case and its unappetizing side issues were well off my radar screen— at least until Taylor asked me to revisit the subject over lunch.

Taylor was the ace legal affairs reporter for the minimedia empire of Steve Brill. A Princeton grad who finished first in his class at Harvard Law School, he was an intense iconoclast who relished puncturing Washington's conventional wisdom. After eight years at *The New York Times,* where he covered the Supreme Court and other legal matters, he had left in 1988 to exploit his formidable polemical skills in spirited and exhaustively researched pieces for Brill's publications. A massive 1994 article for the *American Lawyer* had especially impressed me. Iraqgate—the grab-bag name for a rash of allegations about duplicitous dealing between the Bush administration and Saddam Hussein in the years before the Persian Gulf War— had obsessed many in the press during the 1992 presidential campaign. It had been championed by a bipartisan collection of scandal-mongers, ranging from *New York Times* columnist William Safire to vice-presidential candidate Senator Albert Gore Jr. of Tennessee, who proclaimed it "a bigger cover-up than Watergate ever was." Taylor's piece, "Anatomy of a Feeding Frenzy," dissected the Iraqgate charges in the light of new evidence released by the Clinton Justice Department—and concluded that the affair was largely bogus. There was no proof that senior Bush administration officials had been complicit in a scheme to arm Iraq, and not a shred of evidence that the Bush Justice Department had obstructed justice. It was, Taylor argued, typical of the "phony scandals" that had become a permanent feature of the political landscape.

Over an expensive lunch courtesy of Brill, Taylor explained that he owed the *American Lawyer* another long piece—and was thinking about examining the Paula Jones lawsuit. Clinton's claim of immunity while in office was due to be argued early in the next Supreme Court term, and Taylor thought it was time to take a fresh look at the entire matter. He remembered vaguely the publicity about my experiences at the *Post* and was curious. What did I think? How legitimate were her claims?

As a legal matter, I said, the Jones suit was probably borderline at best. But when it came to the actual incident at the Excelsior Hotel, there was a lot more evidence to support Jones's account than most of the media had ever accepted. In particular, there were these witnesses, Pamela Blackard and Deborah Ballantine. They were much stronger than anybody realized—and as far as I knew, no one but me had bothered to talk to them. Taylor seemed intrigued. I told him I would try to dig out some of my old notes.

A few days later, Taylor came by my office. I showed him a few internal memos I had written back in 1994 about the witnesses in the Jones case, and he quickly got a lot more excited. He couldn't believe the *Post* hadn't made more of this stuff. He wanted to talk to these witnesses himself.

Taylor had to call repeatedly, but eventually he got through. The result was a powerful 15,000-word piece in the *American Lawyer*'s November 1996 issue entitled "Her Case against Clinton." The article argued that Jones's claim of "predatory, if not depraved, behavior by Bill Clinton is far stronger than the evidence supporting Anita Hill's allegations of far less serious conduct by Clarence Thomas."[2] Taylor chided Clinton's lawyers for using an endless arsenal of delaying tactics to avoid confronting the evidence. He attacked *The Washington Post* for not showcasing more of my reporting in 1994. And he railed against the "hypocrisy (or ignorance) and class bias of feminists and liberals" who had embraced and even lionized Anita Hill, only to dismiss Jones's charges of "far more serious (indeed criminal) conduct as unworthy of belief and legally frivolous." He also made a more subtle point: Even if Jones's motives were as impure as the White House had suggested, and even if her backers were politically motivated, her core charges about Clinton's behavior might be true.

Touting the piece in a brief cover letter, Brill mailed it to scores of opinion makers and journalists one week before election day. The article was long and intimidating, and at first, hardly anybody noticed. But in the days after Clinton's triumph over Bob Dole, it got read. The popular radio talk show host Don Imus started to mention it. William Safire plugged it in a December column. An idea was entering the conversation of the chattering class: On the Jones case, the press might have given Clinton a pass.

One of those struck by Taylor's piece was *Newsweek*'s Evan Thomas. With his Andover-Harvard background and WASP pedigree, Thomas was sensitive to Taylor's charge of class bias—a sensitivity that may well have been passed down from his grandfather, Socialist Norman Thomas. Moreover, he felt especially vulnerable on this one: As a regular on the talk show *Inside Washington,* he had once derided Jones as "some sleazy woman with big hair coming out of the trailer parks," a sneering description for which he had caught some grief. What was more, Taylor was a regular in Thomas's Sunday football games, and he had been lobbying Thomas to give the article a close look.

Thomas did—and was instantly impressed. Jones, he thought, might really have a case. Thomas, a newsmagazine veteran who had worked at *Time* before moving to *Newsweek,* was a talented storyteller always on the lookout for a good yarn. He quickly sensed one here, and in late December, he proposed it at a *Newsweek* cover conference. Maynard Parker, the magazine's editor, had already talked with National Affairs editor Jon Meacham about doing a story in light of the Taylor piece. Parker and Ann McDaniel, the new Washington bureau chief, tentatively endorsed Thomas's idea.

When McDaniel called me at home a few days after Christmas and told me of the magazine's plans, I groaned. I was immersed in what looked to me like a far juicier scandal: the millions of dollars in foreign contributions that had poured into Democratic Party coffers during the 1996 campaign. I had no interest in delving back into the Jones case and mildly resisted, especially after I learned that Thomas planned to include me and my reporting at the *Post* in the article.

I was overruled. You are part of the story, Thomas said later. In any case, there was a compelling news peg: After nearly two and a half years of wrangling, the Supreme Court was to hear Clinton's lawyers argue that presidents should be immune from civil litigation while in office. It was a novel claim, and a growing number of legal scholars were saying the president's chances were dicey at best. And if Clinton lost, the Jones case—after a long absence from the front pages—would finally proceed.

•   •   •

Nobody was grumpier about *Newsweek*'s decision to put Jones on the cover than White House press secretary Mike McCurry. Clinton chewed him out about it the day it came out. The *Newsweek* editors hadn't even given him the courtesy of a heads-up. How could they give credibility to this sleazy case? he grumbled to regulars in the White House press room. *Newsweek* had taken the Jones story, a story that belonged in the tabloids, and injected it into the mainstream. Jones was now staring out from every newsstand at every airport in the country, featured in a magazine that was mailed to three million homes every week.

McCurry was skilled at his job. He conveyed a sense of competence and even *gravitas,* making him the perfect public face for an administration that, in its early days, had been perceived as chaotic and filled with amateurs. But while the McCurry of the TV news briefings was good-natured and personable, he was not above browbeating reporters or undercutting them with their colleagues when it served the president's interests. Now, incensed about *Newsweek*'s move, McCurry began a low-level whispering campaign. This was all the work of that renegade Isikoff. He's a zealot on this issue. He got into trouble over at the *Post*. McCurry voiced some of those senti-

ments to *Newsweek*'s new White House correspondent, Karen Bres-
lau, when she stopped by a Thursday afternoon briefing for the
weeklies. "Your editors have clearly made an investment in this
story," McCurry said. You've even got a correspondent who's dedicated to investigating the president's sex life and who attracts all the
scumbags who deal in this stuff. McCurry let it be known that Bres-
lau shouldn't be expecting any exclusives from the White House
staff for some time to come.

• • •

If McCurry was feeling vengeful, Joe Cammarata was just
delighted with the *Newsweek* cover. A fast-talking and likable
scrapper, the Brooklyn-born Cammarata reminded some reporters of
the Joe Pesci character in *My Cousin Vinnie*. The image was somewhat
deceptive: Cammarata had a shrewd legal mind honed in the mid-
1980s, when he pursued tax cheats for the Reagan Justice Department. Still, he unquestionably loved the limelight. Cammarata went
to Georgetown, twelve years after Clinton, and ran for school office
there, on a slate that billed him as "the Disco King."

An experienced civil litigator, Cammarata had the instinct for the
jugular developed in a courtroom. The "distinguishing characteristics" affidavit proved that. As shaky as it was, the gambit probably
had achieved its purpose of spooking the president's high-priced
lawyers. While he publicly dismissed the claim as fraudulent, Robert
Bennett, the president's chief lawyer, had privately agonized over the
allegation and consulted with Clinton's doctors at Walter Reed Naval
Hospital to figure out what Jones had in mind. Still, what worked brilliantly in high-profile celebrity cases such as the Michael Jackson sex
suit seemed inappropriate for solemn litigation involving the nation's
chief executive. In the court of public opinion, Bennett had clobbered
the Jones team over the "distinguishing characteristics" affidavit,
making it Exhibit A in his charge that the entire case was little more
than "tabloid trash."

But if Cammarata had misfired on the issue of Clinton's private
parts, it didn't matter that week. He was in heavy demand—and loving it. Taylor's article had played to the media elite; the *Newsweek*
cover story conveyed the same thoughts to a much broader audience.

It featured quotes from Cammarata. It carried a picture of him with Davis. Reporters from major news organizations were bombarding him with calls. The TV bookers were besieging him. By late morning on Friday, January 10, 1997, Cammarata was slated to be on all three major network Sunday talk shows—an inside-the-Beltway royal flush.

• • •

In the midst of the most tumultuous week of his life, Cammarata was prepping for the Supreme Court, poring over briefs in his chaotic cubbyhole of an office, when his secretary told him there was a woman on the line who wanted to talk to him. Cammarata groaned. He was too busy. Getting your picture in a national newsweekly can be a mixed blessing. "Tell her I'll call her back," he said.

"No—she's called several times before, and she doesn't want to leave a number."

All right, he said with some exasperation—put it through.

Was this the Joe Cammarata who represented Paula Jones? the woman asked.

"Yeah," he said, vaguely impatient. "What can I do for you?"

Well, there's something you should know. "I had a similar thing happen to me when I worked at the White House in 1993."

For the next fifteen minutes, the woman talked and Cammarata listened. She and her husband had been fundraisers for Bill Clinton in 1992 and had even flown to Little Rock on election night. She later went to work at the White House, first as a volunteer in the social office and later as a secretarial assistant in the office of the White House counsel. In November 1993, she said, "my marriage was deteriorating." Her husband had gotten into some legal trouble. She went to see the president about a permanent job. During the meeting, the president took her into a small hideaway office, where, the woman told Cammarata, "it got physical." "He pulled me to him, he kissed me." Clinton touched her breasts and put her hand on his penis. The session was interrupted when an aide began knocking on the door.

Cammarata was too experienced a trial lawyer to get overly excited. Still, the woman sounded convincing. How could he get in touch with her? She wouldn't say. But she dropped a few hints. The day after the president's advances, she learned that her husband had killed himself with a shotgun. Her husband's suicide had since been mentioned in right-wing conspiracy literature, she said, as one of the many "strange" deaths associated with Bill Clinton's presidency. There was a bulletin that kept track of these things—the *Guarino Report*—and it mentioned her husband. There was also a reference to him on *The Clinton Chronicles.* After her husband's suicide, the woman said, she briefly landed a position at the White House counsel's office. And in 1995, she had traveled to Copenhagen and Jakarta as a member of State Department delegations.

The woman dropped one more clue. After she left the Oval Office that day, she went to see a friend—a member of the White House staff—and told her about the incident. Another witness was out there, Cammarata thought, somebody who might corroborate this story.

Please, said Cammarata—let me know how I can get in touch with you. No, she said, she would call back. Cammarata was taking notes. He just might be able to use this.

Since taking over the Jones case in May 1994, Cammarata and Davis had been flooded with tips about other alleged adventures by the president. They had even briefly toyed with the idea of hiring a private detective to track them down. But the Jones Legal Fund, set up by a friend of Davis's in 1994, hadn't raised nearly enough money. And in any case, the tips they had to go on were invariably second- or third-hand hearsay—someone said she had a girlfriend who once had a roommate who had slept with Clinton fifteen years before. Most reporters, including me, had heard the same stuff, and we generally tended to dismiss it. It was ancient history—tales from long ago in Arkansas. But here was something quite different: an apparently first-person account of an improper sexual advance by Clinton while he was in the White House. Cammarata sensed it might one day prove important. But right now, he had other things to worry about.

•   •   •

First and foremost, of course, were the upcoming arguments in *Jones* v. *Clinton* before the United States Supreme Court. The fight for Paula Jones's day in court was a matter of legal principle laced with political mischief. Members of the conservative legal community had long been skeptical of the emerging case law in sexual harassment; they were virtually to the man and woman defenders of Clarence Thomas against the allegations of Anita Hill. But if Clinton was wrong on his constitutional claim of immunity, why not hoist the liberals by their own petard with the Paula Jones case? Even before the president had formally staked out his position, a conservative legal titan—Kenneth Starr, a former solicitor general and federal appeals court judge—had volunteered to write a friend-of-the-court brief supporting Jones's position that her case should go forward. Although Starr was nominally going to file on behalf of a conservative women's group, the Independent Women's Forum, he and Davis spoke a half dozen times that June. (Davis's billing records show the talks consumed four and a half hours and Davis charged his client $775 for the time.) They discussed legal theories and arguments the Jones attorneys could use to beat back Bennett's immunity claims. Then in August 1994, Starr was selected to replace Robert Fiske as the independent counsel investigating the president's Whitewater land deals, and his legal help for the Jones team ended.

After Starr's exit, Cammarata and Davis continued to receive secret legal help from Marcus and, to a lesser extent, Porter, the two conservative lawyers who, through their law-school classmate Nelson Lund, had recruited them to be Jones's public lawyers in the first place. By now, however, their ranks had been augmented by yet another conservative lawyer—a brilliant young New York litigator named George Conway.

A graduate of Harvard College and Yale Law School, Conway was, in his mid-thirties, a million-dollar-a-year partner at one of the city's most prestigious law firms, Wachtell, Lipton, Rosen & Katz. Ironically, one of the partners he worked most closely with was Bernard Nussbaum, Clinton's first White House counsel and a colleague of Hillary Clinton's during the Nixon impeachment case. Conway was active in the Federalist Society, an organization of right-leaning legal scholars who attended annual conferences in swank hotels and plotted political strategy amid airy debates over constitutional theory. Short and pudgy, with an impish laugh, Conway was a consummate gossip who loved to swap stories about Clinton's foibles. In the summer of 1994, he had submitted to the *Los Angeles Times*—on spec—an op-ed piece attacking Clinton's immunity claim. The piece ran, and soon Cammarata and Davis were reaching out to him. Ever since, Conway had played consigliere to Jones's lawyers, conducting behind-the-scenes research and, together with Marcus, drafting Jones's legal briefs on the immunity issue.

Conway's role had never been made public—and for good reason: He was quite certain his pro bono freelancing would not go down well with Nussbaum and others at his predominantly Democratic firm. Still, in the early days of January, Conway—like the rest of the Jones camp—was quite busy. He had arranged a "moot court" to help prepare the Jones lawyers for what was sure to be the biggest oral argument of their lives. He had called in the heaviest conservative legal guns he could find: former solicitor general Robert Bork, whose 1987 confirmation battle for the Supreme Court had been a bitter milestone in the political wars of that decade, and Theodore Olson, a Justice Department official under Ronald Reagan and now a top partner in the Washington office of Gibson, Dunn & Crutcher. The session was designed to mimic the often intimidating atmosphere of Supreme Court arguments. Bork and Olson were to hurl hostile questions at Davis and test his ability to fire back persuasively. The genial Davis showed up late, toting a bulging briefcase, and quickly suggested that he'd prefer not to do things the way Conway had envisioned. "Instead of presenting an argument, I thought it would be better if we just sit down and talk about the case," Davis said, according to Conway. Conway felt ill. He wondered how much Davis had even prepared his case. "Here we had dragged out two of the leading lights of the D.C. bar for this, and he just seemed to want to shoot the breeze," he said. (Davis, for his part, later said he had already spent days in "full dress rehearsal" for the oral arguments and, in any case, it was Bork who suggested the more informal approach.)

The session proceeded. Olson kept pressing Davis on one point: If the Supreme Court allowed the case to proceed, how would the judge manage a civil suit in which the defendant was the president of the United States? The Jones camp was arguing that—as a matter of principle—Bill Clinton could not put off a suit simply because he was president. That was fine; there was nothing in the Constitution that protected the president from the obligations of every other citizen. But as president, Clinton had certain special obligations as well—to run foreign policy, for example, and to oversee defense in times of national emergency. What if the two conflicted in the course of the lawsuit? Say the president's deposition were scheduled for a certain day. What if he couldn't make it? "You have to be clear about what actually happens when the case goes back to the district court," Olson warned him. "What if the president just refuses to show up?" Olson suggested some answers—the courts could easily schedule the proceedings to accommodate the president's schedule and his duties. Depositions and trial dates are rescheduled all the time, Olson coached; just stress that you will be accommodating. Davis nodded. Conway wondered if he really got it.

The following week was momentous for Cammarata and Davis—and embarrassing for the White House. The Supreme Court arguments over the Jones case received saturation coverage; a swarm of reporters descended on the courthouse to listen to Washington superlawyer Bennett, Solicitor General Walter Dellinger and Davis duke it out over whether an obscure woman had a right to press her claim that the president of the United States had once implored her to provide him with oral sex. No cameras are permitted inside the majestic courtroom, but CNN and its upstart competitor, MSNBC, provided hourly bulletins from the courthouse steps. That night, the Jones case was the lead story on all the broadcast networks. In the view of most observers, Davis had stumbled badly in the oral argument: he seemed confused by the justices' questions and, when pressed by Justice Sandra Day O'Connor, got tripped up over precisely the issue Olson had warned him about. Still, Bennett and Dellinger had also gotten a tough grilling. The justices seemed skeptical of Bennett's arguments that a civil lawsuit would impose too heavy a burden on the president's time. "We have seen presidents riding on horses, chopping wood, playing golf," Justice Antonin Scalia said. "The notion that he doesn't have a minute to spare is not credible." The betting odds were that the Court would have a hard time overturning the proposition that no citizen, not even the chief executive, was above the law.

•   •   •

A few days later, I called Cammarata. When Ann McDaniel had told me to do fresh reporting for the *Newsweek* cover on Jones, one of the first things I did was get reacquainted with him. Now

I wanted to touch base, to get his sense of how the oral arguments had gone.

Cammarata was excited. He seemed emboldened by the arguments of commentators that feminist groups were hypocritical for not speaking up on behalf of Jones's right to her day in court. He had just had a private meeting with Patricia Ireland, president of the National Organization for Women, and sensed she might be under some pressure to be more sympathetic to his client.

Cammarata's machinations involving the feminists didn't interest me much. Look, I told him, at the end of the day, this case still comes down to Paula Jones's word against the president's. The only way perceptions would change was if there were evidence that Clinton did this to other women.

Something went off in Cammarata's mind. "What if there was?"

"Do you know of something?" I asked. "Are we talking another consensual affair in Arkansas—or an actual case of harassment?"

"An unwanted sexual advance."

"When did this supposedly take place?"

"While he was president."

Cammarata then described the mysterious phone call. I dropped by his office the next day, and Cammarata started reading from the notes he had taken. This was weird, I thought. The caller had imparted a hell of a lot of detail. Cammarata, for his part, was more than happy to let me figure it out. If I could track this woman down, he reasoned, I'd probably pass it along to him. Then he could subpoena her. As he saw it, I would save him some legwork.

That, of course, is not quite how I saw it. Events would turn out to be a lot more complicated.

•   •   •

At first, the idea of a credible claim of harassment inside the White House seemed a bit farfetched. Surely Clinton couldn't have been stupid enough to do anything like what the woman had claimed? Still, this story had far more clues than those peddled by most blind callers, and I was intrigued by the challenge of trying to figure out who this person was.

I first focused on the reference to the *Guarino Report,* one of the more obscure purveyors of Clinton conspiracy theories. Guarino is a former Arkansas businessman and self-described TV host who devotes his time to exposing the sinister side of American politics—events purportedly ignored by the mainstream media. I had heard of him but had no idea where to find his publication. I called Philip Weiss, a gadfly reporter for the *New York Observer.* We had spoken just a few weeks earlier. Weiss was doing a story on "Clinton haters" for the *New York Times Magazine,* and he wanted to know why reporters like me didn't pay them much attention. Well, I told him, because I thought at bottom their theories were nutty. He didn't seem to like that and pressed me about some minutiae in the Vincent Foster case. I wondered whether the *Times Magazine* was really going to publish an article sympathetic to the "Foster was murdered" school of thinking. Still, we parted amicably, and when I called to inquire about the *Guarino Report,* he just happened to have a recent issue on his desk—and agreed to send it to my office in Washington.

"Murder in the First Degree"—a report by "The Wall Street Underground"—arrived in the mail a few days later. It was utterly ridiculous. Part one was entitled "An Interim Report on the Death of Commerce Secretary Ron Brown," advancing the theory that the plane crash that killed Brown was in fact a political assassination ordered by the Clinton White House to prevent Brown from fingering the president in various campaign finance investigations. Gee, I thought—and the thirty-four other people on the plane were just collateral damage. The second part of "Murder in the First Degree" was what I wanted: "A Summary of the 56 Clinton Dead: The Unknown and Deadly Side of the Whitewater Scandal." I went down the list, looking for clues to Cammarata's mystery caller.

It was a familiarly loony litany. There was Vince Foster, of course ("Victim No. 3"), and Jerry Parks ("Victim No. 1"), a former security guard at the Clinton campaign office whose murder on the streets of Little Rock, the theory went, was ordered by Clinton henchmen when they discovered he had secret files on the president's love life. There was Barry Seal, the international drug smuggler (and "Victim No. 9"), gunned down by Colombian hit men in Louisiana in 1994. The alleged Clinton connection? He had flown drugs out of Mena,

Arkansas, a rural airstrip—operated by the CIA, of course—that Clinton had supposedly protected as governor. Ronald Rogers, an obscure dentist from Royal, Arkansas, had met his maker when his twin-engine Cessna went down in Oklahoma—a crash the intrepid Guarino linked to the allegation that he was about to "reveal some dirt on Clinton" to a British journalist.

I was starting to wonder if I'd gotten a bum steer when I came across a name I hadn't heard before: Ed Willey, "Victim No. 20." He was described as "the manager of Clinton's presidential campaign finance committee, who, according to a reliable source in Texas, was involved with shuttling briefcases full of cash, [who] supposedly shot himself on Nov. 30, 1993."

The entry was, on its face, silly. Nobody named Willey was ever "the manager of Clinton's presidential campaign finance committee" or even played a prominent role. But even the wackiest conspiracy theories often contain a grain of truth, and a quick Nexus check of the *Richmond Times-Dispatch* found the nugget in Guarino's account. A Richmond lawyer named Ed Willey Jr., the scion of a prominent Virginia political family, had indeed been found dead in a wooded area outside Richmond on the day in question. The state police pronounced it suicide. The *Times-Dispatch* accounts gave a perfectly plausible explanation that had nothing to do with shuttling "briefcases full of cash" for Clinton: Willey had been caught in an embezzlement scheme and was being pursued by the victims—the owners of a Richmond produce store—for return of some $279,000 he had stolen while representing them in a case.

I then checked back copies of the Federal Staff Directory, a fat red book that lists everyone who works for the U.S. government. There was no Willey listed for 1993. But in the 1994 book, under White House Counsel's Office, I found the name Kathleen Willey. By the 1995 edition, the name had disappeared. I took the name to William Rafferty, the *Newsweek* librarian and a master at tapping into public databases. Within a few minutes, he handed me two printouts showing me a Kathleen E. Willey at an address in Midlothian, Virginia, just outside Richmond, and a phone number.

How do you approach somebody like this? If Willey was indeed Cammarata's mystery caller, she clearly was not panting to go public;

she had refused to give him her name. On the other hand, the mere act of calling the lawyer suggested she was at least ambivalent—and just might be willing to talk if she felt comfortable enough. My own experience told me people don't generally open up about sensitive personal matters with strange reporters over the telephone. In this case, even an unsolicited knock on the door might be too jarring. So I decided to drop her a brief note.

"Dear Ms. Willey," I wrote on January 31. "I plan to be in the Richmond area in the next week or so and would like to get together with you for a brief chat to discuss a matter of mutual interest. Would you mind giving me a call in the next few days . . . so we can, hopefully, arrange a time and place to meet." I included my office phone number. Actually, I had no plans to be in Richmond at all unless she would agree to see me. The "mutual interest" line was designed to hook her interest, figuring it might at least get her to give me a call to find out what I was talking about.

A few days later, she did.

•   •   •

Hi, my name is Kathleen Willey, and I just got this letter from you," said a barely audible voice. "What do you want to talk to me about?"

Startled, I stammered something about how there had been a change in my Richmond plans. I was stalling. She insisted again she wanted to know what this was about. I told her I really needed to talk to her in person. A journalistic dance between aggressive reporter and reluctant source began—a dance that was to continue for months.

Our first meeting was in late February in a coffee shop off I-95, halfway between Richmond and Washington. Willey arrived a half hour late. An attractive, soft-spoken woman dressed in a professional suit, she seemed nervous. "The moment I got your letter, I said, 'Oh shit,'" she told me. "Where did you get my name?" I described the phone call to Cammarata and explained my reason for thinking it was her. I watched closely for her reaction. If all this was a wild and unfounded rumor, the natural response would be, "You're out of your mind." At first, she said nothing. That was not she who had called

Cammarata, she insisted. Okay, I said, but it sounds to me like the woman described by the caller sure fit her situation.

Hadn't her husband committed suicide? Hadn't she worked in the White House counsel's office in 1994?

She seemed to nod. She wouldn't confirm anything about the encounter with Clinton. But her body language told me it was true— true, that was, that she had at least told somebody about such an incident. I pushed. I needed to hear this story from her.

"What would you do with all this?" she asked. "How big a story would it be?"

I didn't know, I told her. I couldn't possibly answer the question unless you told me the whole thing. Why don't you talk off the record? She balked. "What about Chelsea?" she asked. "What impact would a story like this have on her?" She didn't want to hurt the president.

Our meeting was at an impasse. Willey said she had a lawyer and wouldn't do anything more without checking with him. We walked to my car. All I want to do is hear your story, I said again. She understood. She said good-bye. As she did, she was standing just a tad closer than I was accustomed to standing to a source.

•   •   •

The dance continued on March 19, when I drove to Richmond and met Willey at the office of her lawyer, Dan Gecker. Gecker, polished and professional, was a partner at a medium-size firm in the heart of Richmond's financial district. We had worked out the ground rules beforehand. Everything would be off the record. I couldn't publish a word Willey said until she gave the green light.

At this point, I had done a little homework. Ed and Kathleen Willey had been a political couple. Ed was the son of one of the most powerful and respected members of Virginia's General Assembly, Ed Willey Sr. For years, Ed Sr.—a white-haired autocrat whose principal goal was protecting the business community from burdensome taxation—had chaired the Senate Finance Committee. Ed Jr. appeared to be something of a disappointment. His obituary in the *Times-Dispatch* described a gregarious real-estate lawyer who enjoyed the trappings of politics—the fundraisers and the parties— and who also liked the high life. The Willeys took fishing vacations in Bermuda and skied every winter at their condo in Vail. For Christmas, they would fly off to Australia. According to the paper's accounts, Willey Jr. had fallen on hard times. There were a few more details of the embezzlement scheme that led to his demise. He had robbed a client's escrow account to pay off $542,000 in federal tax liens. His defrauded clients sued—and were threatening to file a complaint with the Virginia Bar. Facing imminent disgrace, he had taken his life.

Now, nearly four years later, his widow was filling in the blanks. Calmly and convincingly, Kathleen Willey recounted how, as active fundraisers, she and her husband had met Bill Clinton at a 1991 party hosted by Virginia tycoon John Kluge. The young Arkansas governor was just starting his campaign for the presidency, and the Willeys were enthusiastic: the following spring, Virginia's first Clinton for President headquarters opened in Ed Willey's law office. Meanwhile, although Kathleen didn't say so, she must have caught Clinton's wandering eye. At a fundraiser that June, Clinton made a point of saying he hoped to see her the next month at the Democratic Convention in New York.

That October, Willey said, when Clinton flew into Richmond for a nationally televised debate with George Bush and Ross Perot, she had joined a group of local Democrats, led by Lieutenant Governor Don Beyer, to greet him at the airport. Clinton spoke to the small throng. As she was getting ready to leave, a Clinton aide approached. It was Nancy Hernreich, Clinton's office manager in Little Rock, later director of Oval Office operations. The governor wanted the Willeys' phone number.

Willey gave it. That afternoon, Clinton called. Willey relayed it this way: He could barely speak, he was suffering from laryngitis—a problem played up in all the news accounts of the day. "It was really good to see you," Clinton told her.

"It sounds like you need some chicken soup," Willey replied.

"Would you bring me some?" Clinton asked.

Willey was taken aback. "I don't really know about that," she stammered. Then, Willey said, she heard noise in the background. Some aides had apparently entered the room. "I'll have to call you back," Clinton said hurriedly. "I'll call you at six."

At five to six, the phone rang again. It was Clinton. Willey by now had made up her mind what to do. She had a friend listening in on her end of the conversation, a woman named Julie Hiatt Steele. "I'm staying right here," she told Clinton. There was going to be a fund-raiser that night after the debate. "I'll see you there." Willey then explained to me her decision. "I was starting to get the drift."

By itself, the vignette didn't prove much. Still, if true, it was plausible evidence that Clinton's penchant for chasing women had continued right through his presidential campaign—a campaign that almost was aborted in its early days because of allegations about his private life. Moreover, the story seemed eminently check-able. Video footage from that day shows Willey embracing Clinton at the airport and Clinton, moments later, turning to Beyer and ask-ing who she was. "Willey, Kathy Willey," Beyer can be seen telling Clinton. And Clinton's phone records for that day, obtained later by the FBI, showed the Democratic candidate making two phone calls to Willey's home that afternoon, just about when Willey said he had.

Despite "the drift" of Clinton's intentions, the Willeys were unflaggingly enthusiastic about his candidacy. On election night, they flew to Little Rock to celebrate the victory of the first Demo-cratic president in twelve years. Then in April of 1993, Willey told me, she landed a volunteer job in the White House social office. Three days a week, she would take the train up from Richmond. She helped plan the first White House Jazz Festival and that year's Christmas party in between such pedestrian duties as screening high school bands and organizing tour group visits to the White House.

•   •   •

Willey wasn't telling me everything. According to the testimony of two of her former co-workers, during this period she was openly flirtatious with the president and went to unusual lengths to gain his attention. Such assertions are always a matter of impressions, of course, and Willey later insisted that she simply considered herself a political friend of the president. Still, White House correspondence and phone records do seem to document that Willey rarely lost a chance to remind Clinton of her presence: she sent him a tie as a pres-ent, along with a note congratulating him on his performance at the

White House correspondents' dinner (May 3, 1993); she sent him a note of condolence on the death of Vince Foster (July 21, 1993); she called to wish him happy birthday (August 19, 1993); she sent him a copy of a new Jeffrey Archer novel she had just read called *Honor Among Thieves* (October 12, 1993). But the same records also suggest Willey's efforts were not exactly rebuffed. Most illustrative is a handwritten note from Willey to the president, dated August 4, 1993, inviting him to spend his winter vacation in Vail. In the letter, in a tone of cozy familiarity, she touted Vail's scenic virtues and amenities—the golf courses, "beautiful hiking trails" and "wonderful outdoor restaurants." She mentioned, with no reference to her husband, that she planned to be there in mid-December and offered to help if White House advance needed any assistance making arrangements for a presidential visit. On Willey's letter, Clinton scribbled a note to Nancy Hernreich: "Get me her Vail #."

●　　●　　●

Within two months of that letter, Kathleen Willey's life began to fall apart. Her husband's embezzlement had come to light; the creditors were closing in. As she told it that day in Dan Gecker's office, on the Sunday after Thanksgiving, at a family pow-wow, she announced: "I'm going to go to Washington. I'm going to speak to the president, and I'm going to get a paying, full-time job. I'm going to get us out of this."

Willey related what followed in gripping and microscopic detail. Hernreich had promised her an appointment in the Oval Office for Monday, November 29, 1993. That afternoon, Hernreich asked her to come on over. She sat across from Clinton's desk. "I've got something I need to talk to you about," she said. He asked her if she wanted a cup of coffee and then led her into a small hallway into his private hideaway office. There was a little galley kitchen across the hall, and Clinton poured her a cup of coffee in a Starbucks mug. Then he escorted her around the hideaway office, pointing out his collection of political buttons. Willey said she brought up a problem in the White House Social Office involving the mistreatment of one of the employees, a former nanny of Chelsea's in Arkansas. Then she got to her own situation: "I've got a really serious problem. I need to talk to you. There's something going on in my life. Ed has gotten himself into some financial trouble, and I'm really kind of desperate. The bottom line is, I need a job," she told him.

"I was pretty much in tears," Willey continued. Embarrassed, she said, "I've got to go"—and then walked into the hallway and put her hand on the closed door to the Oval Office. At that point, she said, Clinton hugged her. "I'm really sorry this has happened to you," he said. Then, while her back was up against the Oval Office door and she was still holding the Starbucks mug, Clinton kissed her.

"I was shocked," Willey said. "It was like an out-of-body experience. He had his hands in my hair. My back was up against the wall. All I remember is I didn't want to spill the cup of coffee." Then, said Willey, she tried gently to push him away. Clinton looked at her intently. "You have no idea how much I wanted you to come to Williamsburg and bring me that chicken soup."

"I said to him, 'Wait a minute, aren't you afraid there are people around here?'" Willey recalled. Clinton, with his arm over her head, glanced at his watch. "Yeah, I've got a meeting, but I can be late."

Now, Willey told me, Clinton took the coffee mug out of her hand and put it on a shelf. He pulled her to him again and said, "I've wanted to do this ever since the first time I laid eyes on you." She went on: "He had his hands on my hair and he kissed me again. His hands were everywhere. He put his hands up my skirt." His hands were on her breast. She grew reticent.

What else? I asked, recalling the phone call to Cammarata. Did he put your hands on his penis?

Yes, she said, he did.

Was it erect? Yes, she said, it was.

"I'll tell you how I know Paula Jones is telling the truth," she added. "His face was beet red."

The next thing she remembered, Willey said, was a knocking on the door to the Oval Office. She recognized the voice. It belonged to Andrew Friendly.

"Mr. President! Mr. President! Mr. President!"

She pushed him away. "Look, I've got to go. You've got a meeting." Willey recalled grabbing the coffee mug off the shelf and walking through the Oval Office and out the door. As she did, she saw Treasury Secretary Lloyd Bentsen, Office of Management and Budget director Leon Panetta and Council of Economic Advisers chairman Laura Tyson waiting in the lobby.

Willey had told the story so convincingly, with such rich detail, that it was hard to imagine her making this up. I looked to Gecker. He looked uncomfortable, almost sheepish. "Not exactly an impeachable offense," he said, breaking the silence.

Maybe not, I told him. "But this is pretty bad—a lot worse than I thought. She goes to see him about a job and he hits on her? If the CEO of any corporation did that, he'd lose his job."

Gecker didn't respond. I got the distinct impression he was not eager for his client's story to come out.

Could any of this story be corroborated? I pressed Willey on this. Did she tell anybody right away? Yes, she said: After leaving the Oval Office, she went to see a friend who worked in the White House counsel's office. Her name was Linda Tripp. I vaguely recalled the name. Tripp had surfaced briefly during the Senate's Whitewater hearings. As a secretary in the counsel's office, she had been the last person to see Vince Foster alive.

According to Willey, when she left the Oval Office that day, she had been "shaking. I just wanted to get out of that hall without seeing anybody." As soon as she saw Tripp, "the first thing she said was, 'Where's your lipstick?' " Willey told her she needed to talk, and the two went outside and sat at a picnic table on the White House lawn. She then told Tripp the whole story. As she did, Willey recalled, Tripp kept shaking her head and saying, "I could always tell the president wanted you." Willey said she became indignant and reminded her, "That's not why I went into his office this afternoon."

Where is Tripp now? I asked her. She thought maybe the Pentagon, although she wasn't sure.

Anybody else?

Yes, she said. Her friend Julie Steele, the woman who was there when Clinton had called the day of the Richmond debate. She had gone to Steele's home the night she got back from Washington and told her what had happened.

Willey was now in a hurry. We had been there for more than two hours, and she had a dentist's appointment. She excused herself. I chatted for a moment with Gecker.

"Have you heard this story before?"

"Oh yeah," he told me. "But she's never going to tell it publicly unless she's dragged kicking and screaming."

•   •   •

Late that afternoon, I headed out to the home of Julie Steele, Willey's friend. Willey had set up the appointment, calling from Gecker's office while I was there. I got on the phone, and Steele gave me the directions to her house.

Steele seemed friendly, if somewhat daffy. She offered me something to drink and began talking nonstop—about her young son, Adam, about her decade-long friendship with Willey, and about her personal views of Bill Clinton (not especially favorable). She invited me into her living room. I got out my notebook and began taking copious notes. She had indeed been at Willey's home when Clinton, suffering from laryngitis, called the day of the debate. "I personally didn't like that," she told me. It was "inappropriate" for someone running for president of the United States to do something like that.

We got to the events of November 29, 1993, and Steele had quite a bit to say. About 8:30 P.M., Willey just "showed up" at her home. She was upset. She had been trying to reach her husband all day by phone and had gone straight to his office when she got back to Richmond. He was nowhere to be found. Willey had reason to be worried, Steele suggested. The day before, Willey and her husband had gotten into a huge fight because Ed had pressured her to co-sign the note by which the Willeys promised to return the embezzled funds. Willey had even thrown her husband out of the house. Then she vowed to go see the president.

That night, Steele told me, Willey "told me everything" about what happened next. Nancy Hernreich had gotten her the appointment. Now Steele repeated to me what she said Willey had told her that night: "He took her to his private office and she told him she needed a paying job. He was supportive. Then he walked her to the door. He gave her a hug, then he started kissing her." Soon, Steele added, "she told me he had his hands up her skirt, in her hair, on her breasts, all over her." As Willey related this, Steele said, "she was humiliated, scared, embarrassed and in major disbelief. I said to her,

'You're kidding.' I couldn't believe it. It seemed like not the time he would take advantage of somebody like that." I repeatedly pressed Steele for details: What precisely had Willey told her Clinton did? Where exactly did she say Clinton put his hands? Willey seemed genuinely "shocked" by Clinton's behavior, said Steele. But, she added, whatever distress Willey felt about Clinton's alleged advances were secondary to her primary concern that night: "Where in the world was Ed?"

The next morning, Willey learned her husband was dead. She was traumatized. Steele, a few days later, had to put her in the hospital for treatment. When she recovered, her situation was more desperate than ever. She repeatedly pressed the White House for employment, Steele told me, and she briefly landed the position in the counsel's office. But that dried up in less than a year, and nothing else came through. Finally, the White House sent her on those State Department missions to Copenhagen and Jakarta. That was really something, Steele suggested. Willey had no business being on those trips. She had no qualifications. "I told her, 'This is just trying to keep you quiet,'" she said. Willey didn't get it. They gave her blank expense checks. On one of the trips, Willey even had an affair with a member of the U.S. delegation, Steele said. Steele couldn't remember who.

The whole thing was "just appalling," Steele told me. Willey had "just adored" Clinton. She used to have pictures of him all over her walls. "We're talking about a fallen hero here. She thought this man was God's gift to the country."

After about an hour, I got in my car for the drive back to Washington. What sort of story did I have, if any? Willey was off the record, of course, and even if I could persuade her to change that, I would still need plenty more corroboration. I wasn't quite sure what to make of Steele; although she basically confirmed Willey's version of events, her vagueness about some details bothered me. I also realized there were aspects of her account that could undercut Willey. The fact that hours after the incident with Clinton she was emotionally traumatized by her husband's suicide put a different cast on events. Steele had taken her to the hospital—understandable under the circumstances, but just the sort of thing the president's lawyers could seize on to suggest her memory was clouded and confused. Here, they would argue, was a troubled woman. And if Clinton was, as Steele suggested, a "fallen hero," what exactly was it that had stung Willey about the president? The way that he had treated her that day in the Oval Office? Or the fact that they had never come through with a job at the White House?

Willey's story was intriguing. But she was at that point a mystery. I wasn't sure what I had.

7

"The story is not what you think it is."

As surprising as it may sound, the schedule of the president of the United States is not a public document. Each day when the president is in Washington, the White House press office releases a list of public events he plans to attend. In some cases, press aides will tell reporters about significant or newsworthy private meetings. But not much more than that—especially if they think the reporters are up to something that might prove embarrassing.

This was a lesson I relearned with some irritation when I decided to check out Willey's account of a sexual encounter with the president. Willey had given me the date of her alleged meeting with Clinton—November 29, 1993—and even an approximate time, mid to late afternoon. What was Clinton doing that day? With whom was he meeting? I called the White House press office, and a helpful secretary pulled the public releases.

Clinton was indeed in town and had a leisurely day-after-the-holiday routine. President Clinton Attends Breakfast with Religious Leaders, read the headline of one White House press release. The president had a "social lunch" with Attorney General Janet Reno. He signed some less than notable documents: a proclamation declaring November National Hospice Month and an executive order relating to federal pay. As for the president's activities that afternoon, the public file was silent.

I called back to see if I could get a bit more and got through to

Barry Toiv, a deputy to White House press secretary Mike McCurry. When I explained what I was looking for, Toiv was suspicious.

Why do you want to know? he asked.

I was checking out a story involving some people who contended they met with the president that day, I said.

Who are these people? he asked.

I'd rather not say, I replied.

Well, Toiv said, I suggest you take your questions to Lanny Davis in the counsel's office. I knew Davis. He was the aide designated to deal with the press on the campaign finance investigation, the subject of upcoming Senate hearings, and he assumed my call had something to do with that. I told him it didn't. He told me he was sorry, he couldn't help me. "We don't release the president's private schedule," he said.

It appeared that I was stumped. Then I remembered what Willey had said about who was waiting outside the Oval Office when she left that day: Lloyd Bentsen, Leon Panetta and Laura Tyson. Bentsen was long gone from Treasury, but I had always gotten along well with Jack Devor, his longtime press secretary, who was now in Austin, Texas, working as a political consultant. I tracked him down and asked if there was any way I could get my hands on Bentsen's schedule for 1993. If Devor was curious about why I was asking, he didn't show it. Sure, he said, all Bentsen's papers had recently been turned over to the Center for American History at the Lyndon Baines Johnson Library at the University of Texas in Austin.

I thought briefly about hopping on a plane to Austin. A few phone calls told me it would be a waste of time. The Bentsen papers, it turned out, were not yet public—and wouldn't be for several years. A team of archivists had just begun the tedious task of indexing them. I finally reached one of the archivists, Elisabeth Switek. I understood the papers weren't public. But would it be possible for her to check this one small matter that I needed for some research? What did Bentsen's schedule show for the afternoon of November 29, 1993? Did he have a meeting with President Clinton?

Switek said she would take a look, and after a few days, she called back. She had Bentsen's daily briefing schedule for November 29, 1993. That afternoon, she said, Bentsen and the rest of the National Economic Council—a group that included OMB director

Panetta and Council of Economic Advisers chair Tyson—had a meeting with President Clinton in the Cabinet Room just outside the Oval Office. It was scheduled to start at 3:00 P.M., within the approximate time frame that Willey said she had walked past the three economic advisers after allegedly squirming out of the president's clutches in his private hideaway office.

•   •   •

On the morning of March 24, 1997, I asked my colleague John Barry, *Newsweek*'s senior defense reporter, for some help. Barry, an amiable Brit, knew his way around the Pentagon better than anybody. I wanted to track down a woman who I understood worked there, I told him—a former White House aide named Linda Tripp. The Pentagon telephone operator didn't seem to have a current number for her. I also didn't have a Pentagon press pass. Could he perhaps help me? No problem, he said. He would be going over that afternoon, so why didn't I just tag along and he would sign me in?

That afternoon, Barry and I traipsed through the cavernous hallways of the U.S. government's biggest building, looking for Linda Tripp. The directories showed that she was assigned to the Pentagon public affairs staff, but the room she was last listed as working in seemed literally to have disappeared—apparently the result of some recent remodeling. We tried offices nearby. Nobody had any idea where or who she was. After wandering aimlessly for a half hour or so, Barry ran into somebody he knew—Lynn Reddy, a public affairs officer. Reddy knew Tripp and pointed us toward a basement corridor that housed something called the Joint Civilian Orientation Conference (JCOC), an obscure division of DOD public affairs that arranged tours of military facilities for business and civic leaders.

Barry peeled off. I was directed to a small cubicle.

"Are you Linda Tripp?"

A somewhat annoyed-looking, heavyset woman with disheveled hair looked up.

"Yeah," she said testily, "what do you want?"

I identified myself and asked if I could talk to her for a few minutes. It was kind of important, I explained, and we needed some privacy.

Tripp glared at me. She later testified that she assumed I was trying to sandbag her—*60 Minutes* style—for an exposé on the JCOC. "I'm thinking that he was trying to do a slam dunk on the program," Tripp told a federal grand jury. "So I was thinking, Oh, I can take you on."

Well, all right, she said, wait outside. I'll see you in a few minutes when I take a cigarette break.

When she emerged, Tripp took me to an outdoor courtyard. "I know who you are," she said. She had been at the Bush White House, she told me. It was during the last days of the 1992 campaign, and you were writing all those stories about how Bush people had been rifling through Clinton's passport files. "People used to be afraid of your phone calls," she said.

I was flattered.

"So what do you want to talk to me about?" she asked.

I told her I had some questions about a woman named Kathleen Willey and a meeting she was supposed to have had with the president on November 29, 1993. Tripp looked alarmed. "Have you actually talked to her?" she asked.

"Yes, I have."

"Well, what—what did she tell you?"

I didn't want to color her comments if I could help it. What I really wanted to know, I said, is what she told *you.*

"I'm not going to talk about it—not until I talk to Kathleen first."

She demanded again to know what it was Willey had told me and how her name had gotten into the mix. Concluding that it was the only way to move the ball forward, I gave Tripp some details: Willey had contended that the president had made unwelcome sexual advances and that she, Linda Tripp, was the first person she told about it.

"Well, is it true?" I asked.

Look, Tripp said, she really had to talk to Willey.

I had thought that afternoon's mission would probably come to nothing—that once I found Tripp she would tell me I was crazy, that she didn't have any idea what I was talking about and I should just get lost. That was what usually happened with these long shots. Instead, Tripp's uncomfortable reaction to my questions gave me every indication I was on to something.

As we started to walk back toward her office, Tripp continued to speak.

"There's something here, but the story is not what you think it is," she said cryptically. "You're barking up the wrong tree."

My first thought was: What the hell does that mean?

*   *   *

After I left, Tripp later testified, she immediately tried to page Bruce Lindsey at the White House. When he didn't respond, she left a message on his beeper: "Urgent. Matter of potential national media significance." Lindsey knew Tripp from her days in the White House counsel's office. They had once been fairly friendly, but Lindsey later testified that he was wary of Tripp. He remembered some vaguely embarrassing testimony she had given before the Senate Whitewater committee and that she was suspected of leaking to the press during the early days of the controversy. It is also possible Lindsey was just too busy. For whatever reason, he did not respond to Tripp's messages.

It was a slight that bothered Tripp. As she saw it, she was trying to do him and the White House a favor, giving them a heads-up on some potential trouble. And he didn't even bother to call back.

That night, Tripp looked up Willey's number in Richmond. They talked for twenty minutes or so, and Tripp told Willey about the visit from me. They talked about the incident they first discussed that afternoon in 1993. Now, in the spring of 1997, they had very different memories of their conversation.

Surely, Kathleen, you can't be contending that what Clinton did to you that day was unwanted, Tripp said.

Absolutely, Willey replied.

That's not the way you described it at the time, Tripp said.

You must be misremembering, Willey told her.

In the middle of this awkward conversation, Willey heard a click. Wait a second, Tripp said. Somebody's on the other line. A second or so later, she was back.

"Monica?" Tripp said.

"No, it's me, Kathleen," Willey replied.

"Oh, sorry. Look, can I call you right back?"

Sure, Willey said as Tripp got off the line to take her other call. Monica? Willey wondered. Who's Monica?

•   •   •

T he relationship between Tripp and Willey turned out to be a lot more complicated than I suspected, as did Linda Tripp herself. Then forty-seven, Tripp was the divorced wife of a retired army officer, the mother of two college-age children, a skilled and wily bureaucratic survivor. She was, by most accounts, an efficient worker with a stern sense of rectitude. She was also, many colleagues said, a nosy and judgmental gossip with a somewhat exaggerated sense of her own importance. She was intimately familiar with what she liked to call "the covert side" of the Defense Department. In the course of a twenty-year career as a secretary, following her husband around the United States and Europe, she carried a top-secret security clearance and had worked for U.S. Army Intelligence and later for the Delta Force, a counterterrorist unit so sensitive the Pentagon will not publicly acknowledge its existence. In 1990, she separated from Lieutenant Colonel Bruce Tripp and landed a job as a "floater" in the secretarial pool of the White House under President George Bush.

There, Tripp was introduced to a glamorous new world. She forged friendships with a number of notable players, including speechwriter Tony Snow and Dorrance Smith, assistant to the president for media affairs. Smith found Tripp to be a hardworking, extremely competent, if sometimes high-strung secretary who showed some savvy in dealing with media celebrities such as Barbara Walters and Sam Donaldson. Others were less impressed. Billy Dale, then director of the White House travel office, recalled that Tripp was once assigned to the travel office while he was overseas with the president. When he got back, he said, his staffers complained that Tripp spent most of her time chatting with friends. Dale made a point of asking that she not be assigned to his office again. Still, Tripp continued to come back and try to chat with him and others. She seemed to prowl for tidbits on White House staffers. In Dale's view, Tripp suffered from a disease he had seen among many who passed through the building: "White House–itis," he called it. Its main symptom was an inflated sense of one's role in the vast scheme of things. Another was a tendency to drop names. "If she came in contact with some members of the senior staff," Dale recalled, "she wasn't shy about letting you know she had."

Tripp, a registered independent, grew to cherish her days working for the Bush crowd and to revere the Republican president. Smith, a former TV news producer, recalls once asking her to bring an Emmy from his office to show the president. She seemed "awestruck" at being in Bush's presence, said Smith: "She was hyperventilating. I thought she was almost going to pass out."

Tripp stayed on after the change in administrations and landed a job as executive assistant to Bill Clinton's first White House counsel, Bernard Nussbaum. Feared as a cutthroat New York litigator, Nussbaum was also a funny and somewhat bumbling fellow who initially endeared himself to Tripp. But, like many career White House workers, Tripp soon grew disenchanted. She was offended by what she perceived as the arrogance of the Clintonites and their lack of reverence—their casual dress, their nonchalant attitude toward security procedures. There was a small fraternity among career White House employees—men and women who had worked for Bush, and Reagan before him. Like many in this group, Tripp would "roll her eyes" at the behavior of the Clintons, according to Gary Aldrich, an FBI agent who was friendly with Tripp and who ultimately wrote a scandalous—and highly questionable—book attacking the mores of the Clinton White House.

Aldrich later denied that Tripp was a source for his book, portions of which were quickly discredited.[1] But there is no question Tripp grew to have a decidedly dim view of her new co-workers. In 1995, she was deposed by Senate investigators looking into the handling of documents after the death of deputy White House counsel Vince Foster. Within the first few minutes, Tripp unloaded on Betsey Pond, one of the secretaries in the counsel's office. Pond, Tripp volunteered, was "incompetent" and had a "severe drinking problem." Another secretary, Deborah Gorham, had spent an "inordinate" amount of time working for Foster on the Clintons' personal legal affairs—something, Tripp said, that never would have happened in the Bush White House. Discussing another "very low-level staffer"

whom she knew from the Bush days, Tripp gratuitously remarked: "This administration saw fit to give her more responsibility of which I'm not certain she is capable."

The death of Foster was a watershed event for Tripp. Her desk was right outside his office, and she may well have been the last person he spoke to before he killed himself. About one P.M. on July 20, 1993, Foster stopped by Tripp's desk, lifted some M&M's from a bowl and said: "I'll be back." He never returned. Tripp got a call late at night at home about Foster's suicide and later testified she was "traumatized." But her grief was mixed with stern disapproval at the actions of White House aides during the chaotic days that followed. The morning after Foster's death, Tripp arrived at the office to find that Foster's office had not been sealed off by investigators—and that fellow secretary Pond had already entered it to "straighten up papers" on Foster's desk. Tripp, whose years in the military taught her the importance of following procedures, berated Pond. The next week, she carried on a running e-mail conversation with Gorham about the belated discovery of a torn-up note in Foster's briefcase. In one of her messages, Tripp referred to Nussbaum and two other White House lawyers as "the Three Stooges." In another, she wrote: "So it took until Monday to figure out it [the briefcase] should be looked at? Christ. And we're the support staff?"

One of those to whom Tripp voiced her frustrations about the Clinton White House was Kathleen Willey. As Willey later told it, Tripp befriended her in the early days of 1993 when Willey was starting out as a volunteer. Tripp was funny and engaging and full of flattery. She was not unmindful of the fact that Willey, through her political connections, knew President Clinton well enough to speak with him in the hallways. "She latched on to me right away," Willey later said. "She would say things like, 'I think you're too smart for this job, you need to get a better job.'" Tripp was full of praise for Willey, commenting on her clothes and her "wonderful voice." In time, Tripp opened up about the things in the White House that bothered her—the messy dress, the arrogance of some staffers, the incompetence of some of the support staff. Willey remembered Tripp indignantly telling her about how she had been dispatched one day to McDonald's to fetch cheeseburgers for the president—a mission she clearly felt was beneath her.

Willey, in turn, began to confide in Tripp, talking even about her marital difficulties. "She's really good at roping you in and making you think she's your friend and that she's your biggest ally," Willey said later. "She was a master at manipulation."

Tripp later told the grand jury much more—including how Willey was smitten with the president. Sorting out the women's conflicting accounts is next to impossible. In Tripp's version, Willey was on a single-minded mission to ensnare Clinton. In Willey's, Tripp was consumed with the notion of a romantic attachment between the two and was constantly egging her on. At the going-away party for Nussbaum, Willey said, Tripp watched the president intensely, then whispered to her: "Look at him, he's looking right at you and nobody else in the room." Willey insisted she had no idea what Tripp was talking about.

Still, by late February 1994, after the death of Willey's husband and the dismissal of Nussbaum, the two were still friendly. It was then that Tripp had a brainstorm. The two of them had to make a personal pitch to retain their jobs at the White House counsel's office—otherwise they would be forced out by the new team. A friend of Willey's, Harolyn Cardozo, helped set up a meeting for Tripp and Willey with Washington superlawyer Lloyd Cutler, the new White House counsel. One day that winter, Willey and Tripp paid a visit to the venerable Washington law firm of Wilmer, Cutler & Pickering and were ushered into Cutler's elegant corner office. Cutler wasn't quite sure why he was supposed to be meeting with these White House functionaries; always cautious, he asked his longtime personal secretary, Cheryl Poole, to sit in. Tripp did almost all the talking, explaining somewhat officiously why it was important that Cutler retain them. She seemed to be selling herself and Willey as a package. She also seemed to suggest that she understood the personalities of the Clinton crowd and could help Cutler navigate them. Cutler was put off, finding Tripp a bit overbearing. In any case, he had an out. He planned to take Poole to the White House as his main secretary. While he politely explained that he would consider their request, he made clear that he couldn't give them any guarantees.

As it turned out, Willey—who had been a volunteer—was permitted to stay on and was even put on the White House payroll. Some in the counsel's office assumed it was out of compassion in light of the recent death of her husband. Poole—facing formidable new duties during Cutler's first few weeks—had recommended that both Willey and another unpaid White House volunteer be given temporary positions to lighten the workload. But there was neither office space nor budget for the more highly paid Tripp—who was furious when she was told she had to leave. She berated Poole, accusing her and Cutler of lying and stringing her along. She gave Poole the cold shoulder and treated her rudely. Poole, a reserved southerner, at one point ran into White House lawyer Jane Sherburne's office in tears. "I had never been exposed to anything like it," Poole would later say about Tripp's behavior. "I was afraid of her."

Tripp also resented Willey—and not entirely without cause. While Willey was personally well liked within the office, it soon became clear that the Richmond socialite had virtually no secretarial skills, could barely use the computers and frequently garbled office messages. Tripp saw only one possible explanation for why such a woman would be put on the payroll. Late in April, during Tripp's last days in the counsel's office, she asked Willey to step outside. As Willey recalled it, Tripp was extremely agitated. "Don't you think for one minute I don't know what's going on around here," Tripp told her. "Don't you think I don't know why I'm getting fired and you're getting my job."

Willey tried to calm Tripp down. "What are you talking about?" she asked.

"I know they want you because the president wants you around," said Tripp.

Tripp's last day in late April was especially ugly. As she walked out for the last time, she turned to her now ex-friend Willey and loudly proclaimed: "I will get you if it's the last thing I do." Poole heard the remark and was stunned. Only a few weeks earlier, Willey and Tripp had seemed the best of pals. She wondered if Linda Tripp wasn't possibly becoming unhinged.

•   •   •

In late March and early April 1997, intrigued by her parting comments to me that day in the Pentagon, I pursued Linda Tripp. I called her office several times. She chewed me out for leaving a message and quickly gave me a code name to use when calling her at work: "Harvey." She finally agreed to see me—first over drinks at a Washington restaurant, then at her home in Columbia, Maryland, where we talked late into the night. Manipulative and perpetually suspicious, Tripp dribbled out an amazing story: Many lies had been told about the Clinton White House, she said. There were many cover-ups. She herself had been asked by her White House–provided lawyer not to volunteer information about a memo she had seen about the White House travel office that implicated First Lady Hillary Rodham Clinton.

As for the president's sexual behavior, Tripp said, it was worse—far worse—than anybody realized. There were, she said, a whole bevy of White House staffers known as the "graduates": women who had had affairs with Clinton and got cushy jobs in the West Wing. Everybody knew who they were.

And there was something else. Something that was going on as we spoke. The president was having an affair with a twenty-three-year-old former White House intern.

As Tripp told it, the young woman was a friend of hers. She had landed a position at the White House through a close family friend, a wealthy campaign contributor. He was a big insurance executive, Tripp explained, and he was especially close to Mrs. Clinton. Meanwhile, the young intern had been thrown out of the White House. Too many people were on to her, and they were trying to keep her away from the president. They had gotten her a job at another federal agency. Tripp wouldn't tell me which one. But, she said, the woman had told Tripp many details of the affair—how she would meet with the president in a small hideaway off the Oval Office and service him with oral sex, how they would have phone sex in the early hours of the morning, with the intern talking provocatively while the president masturbated. Tripp recounted conversations in which Clinton had confessed his deep-seated sexual problems, how he had had "hundreds" of affairs and was so congenitally unfaithful to his wife that, as a therapeutic device, he circled on a calendar the days he had been "good." After his presidency, he had said, he expected to be "alone"—a comment that led the young woman to believe that she might have a future with the most powerful man on the planet.

Many of these details came late one night in April when I visited Tripp at home. The house was cluttered, the atmosphere a bit chaotic. Tripp's golden retriever, Clio, followed me everywhere. A few minutes after we sat down in Tripp's living room, the phone rang and Tripp went into a study to take it. Then she imperiously snapped her fingers, gesturing me to come in. She held up the phone so I could listen.

It was the voice of an excited and somewhat whiny young woman complaining about another woman named "Marsha." I listened for a few seconds and then walked away.

That was she, Tripp told me after she got off. That was the young woman she had been telling me about. "Marsha" was Marsha Scott, the president's longtime personnel aide. When Tripp's friend was forced out of the White House last year, Clinton had promised that Scott would get her back after the election. But nothing was happening. Marsha Scott was giving the woman the runaround.

Tripp had other things to show me that night. She took out some pictures—photos of Nussbaum, Lindsey and other White House aides, some of them from a Halloween party. I was impressed; the pictures seemed evidence that Tripp had once enjoyed some kind of intimacy with the Clinton crowd. She also showed me a copy of a letter she had written to Leon Panetta upon her departure from the White House that seemed, obliquely, to describe something inappropriate between the president and an unidentified woman. But the talk kept coming back to the intern and the president.

Tripp talked about the relationship with such minutiae that it was hard to doubt her. Her story confirmed my sense that Clinton was troubled, a man whose sexual compulsions were far greater than anybody suspected. It explained, I thought, how it was that this president—such a gifted and accomplished politician—kept getting himself into political trouble over sex. It also explained the need for aides like George Stephanopoulos, Betsey Wright and Bruce Lindsey to be constantly covering up for him, devising cover stories and false alibis, digging up dirt on his accusers. It may well have been the key to understanding much of his presidency—explaining the mutual suspicion that pervaded his relations with the news media as well as his fear and loathing of his political enemies.

Still, I'm a reporter, not a voyeur. After a while, I put down my notebook. I realized there was nothing I could do with this information. Tripp wouldn't give me the ex-intern's name or the agency she worked for. And anyway, she made it clear that the young woman would never talk about her relationship with the president. And suppose the young woman could be persuaded to talk: how would I be able to prove such a story was not the fantasy of some disturbed stalker? Tripp was certain the relationship was entirely consensual. If anything, the young woman was the pursuer. That, it seemed to me, placed it outside the scope of the Paula Jones lawsuit—my main justification for proceeding down this path.

What I was interested in was Willey. Her allegations of unsolicited advances, if true, constituted a case of misconduct by Clinton that was squarely relevant to the Jones case. And Tripp had a lot to say about Willey that night. Willey had indeed told her immediately about a sexual encounter with the president in the hideaway office. But Tripp's version was not what Willey had described. Willey was excited, Tripp said. This woman had been pursuing the president ever since she got to the White House. She consulted Tripp about ways to get his attention, about what outfits she should wear in his presence. She was, Tripp told me, a woman "on a mission." After the encounter, Willey wanted to know what Tripp thought it had meant and how she should pursue the relationship. There was, Tripp insisted, no harassment whatsoever.

This was not the first time Tripp had told this story. In the spring of 1996, after she left her job at the White House counsel's office, Tripp had the idea of writing a book about the Clinton presidency—an inside, tell-all account patterned after the one by Aldrich. Tripp called an old friend from the Bush White House, the columnist Tony Snow, who recommended that he get in touch with a New York literary agent named Lucianne Goldberg. When Goldberg heard Tripp's idea, she was wildly enthusiastic. She filled Tripp's head with ideas of big money—advances as high as $500,000. She got Tripp a ghostwriter, a conservative young Yale graduate named Maggie Gallagher, to work up a proposal. Goldberg sensed that Tripp was worried about the consequences for her government job and came up with what she thought was a brilliant marketing ploy: Tripp would write under a nom de plume. It would be "Joan Dean," a play on John Dean, the White House lawyer who brought down Richard Nixon. The working title for the book was *Behind Closed Doors: What I Saw at the Clinton White House.*

That summer, Gallagher and Tripp worked on the proposal. Then Goldberg set up a meeting with Richard Vigilante, the editor of Regnery, the firm that had published Aldrich's book. But after a five-hour session, Vigilante sensed that Tripp wasn't really prepared to go through with the idea. She seemed too concerned about the threat to her career and the inevitable upheaval in her life if she went public. He was right. In late August 1996, after she got a raise at the Pentagon, Tripp called Goldberg and told her to forget it. She wasn't quite happy with what Gallagher had put together, she said. It was too sensational. And the money just wasn't enough. Tripp later testified that she felt manipulated by Goldberg—that Goldberg had promised Gallagher a larger cut of the advance than Tripp had thought she'd have to pay. In any case, the whole thing was "way too dangerous." "It's not worth the risk," Tripp later testified she told Goldberg. "It's not worth the gamble."

Goldberg was quite miffed, Tripp later recalled. "Who do you think you are, the queen of England?" the literary agent said. Then she slammed down the phone.

Tripp also had to break the news to Gallagher, who didn't take it much better. Gallagher had spent some twenty hours on the proposal—and she hadn't been paid a dime. "I got stiffed," Gallagher said later. "I was pissed. I thought we had a pretty hard deal, and she just walked away from it." Gallagher understood Tripp's job concerns and was not unsympathetic. Still, she remembered telling Tripp: "If you don't do this, you're going to regret it for the rest of your life."

The night I visited Tripp, she got out the proposal Gallagher had drafted. She let me see one chapter, a copy of which I later secured from other sources. It was entitled "The President's Women," and it offered Tripp's original account of the Willey story, complete with pseudonyms as told by "Joan Dean."

"The President's Women" described a woman, "call her Brenda," close to fifty, who worked as a volunteer in the White House social office, who "always dressed to kill and had a body teenagers would die for." Brenda was on a "mission" to get the president's attention. One day a disheveled-looking Brenda ran up to "Joan" in the White House and told her about a sexual encounter with the president in the hallway outside the Oval Office. As the Tripp/Gallagher manuscript described it, it had gone this way:

"What if Hillary comes in?" she [Brenda] had asked Bill, terrified.

"I've got that covered," the president told her huskily.

The aftermath of Brenda's encounter, Tripp and Gallagher wrote, was "very sad and sort of funny and in some ways typical." According to this account, Brenda had gone home that night and told her husband of twenty-five years that she wanted a divorce. The husband "promptly left the house" and committed suicide. "The publicity apparently scared the president off, which frustrated Brenda to no end. She was effectively barred from the president's presence."

There was no doubt that "Brenda" was Willey and "Joan" was Tripp. There was also no doubt that Joan and her ghostwriter had a key detail wrong: Willey's husband had already killed himself by the time Willey got back to Richmond that night. Still, what was most revealing about the book proposal was the spin it put on this episode. In the Tripp-Gallagher rendition, the real victim of Clinton's sexual dalliance was not "Brenda" or even Brenda's cuckolded husband. It was Joan Dean. According to the proposal, feeling sorry for Brenda, Joan had arranged for her friend to get a volunteer position in the counsel's office. A few months later, Brenda was "promoted to a paid position." Joan, on the other hand, had to leave the White House—a presumptive casualty of the sexual discrimination at the Clinton White House.

Tripp's book proposal—written some eight months earlier—seemed to rule out the possibility that Tripp and Willey had recently connived to cook their accounts for my benefit. That, I thought, was fairly important. It meant that Clinton, despite all the political trouble his womanizing had caused him, had not abandoned his wayward ways—a conclusion that appeared to be further confirmed by what Tripp had told me about the intern. But the premise of the piece I thought I was working on—that the experiences of Kathleen Willey might be part of a pattern of harassment that would plague the president in the Paula Jones case—now seemed hopelessly clouded.

•   •   •

That spring, in my spare time, I did some further work on the Willey story. I nailed down that she had indeed gone on two State Department missions—to Jakarta, Indonesia, and Copenhagen, Denmark—at government expense. State Department records showed that the White House personnel office had arranged for her to go on both trips even though she didn't have the slightest qualifications for either one. (The Jakarta trip was for a conference on biodiversity, and the Denmark trip was on social development. The total cost to the taxpayers for Willey's airfare and expenses was about $7,000.) That struck me as worth an explanation. I asked Frank Provyn, director of the State Department Office of International Programs, why he thought Willey was on the trips in view of her lack of background in the subjects being discussed. He had no idea, he told me. Willey's name had been forwarded by the White House. "A good way to get yourself into a jam is to ask too many questions when someone comes from the White House," he said.

Still, it was far from enough to hang a story on, and Willey, in any case, was still resolutely off the record. Between Willey and Tripp, I had no idea whom to believe. Willey's perceptions of the incident could have changed over time; Tripp could have misinterpreted Willey's mood and reaction at the time.

In either case, it didn't matter. I was immersed in other stories—primarily, coverage of the impending Senate campaign finance hearings. I hadn't even bothered to mention the Willey story to my editors. I had, however, talked about it with my two closest colleagues, Mark Hosenball and Danny Klaidman. How's that story going? Klaidman asked one day that spring. "That story," I replied, "is a muddle."

8

"Linda Tripp is not to be believed."

O n May 28, 1997, Bill Clinton's world—and the course of his presidency—changed irrevocably. In a surprising 9–0 ruling, the U.S. Supreme Court summarily rejected the president's claim to be immune from civil litigation while in office. The Paula Jones case could proceed forthwith. Not only would the Jones lawyers get to start deposing witnesses under oath, the Court ruled, but the case could even go to trial while Clinton was president.

That morning, I was asked to do an analysis of the Supreme Court ruling on MSNBC, the fledgling all-news cable network that is a joint venture of Microsoft and NBC News. While at the NBC studios in Washington, I checked in with my bureau chief, Ann McDaniel. *Newsweek* would likely want to do another cover story, she said. I should drop my reporting on campaign finances and start crashing on the Jones case. I mentioned that there was something else she should be aware of—and it was probably best that we talk about it in person. That afternoon, for the first time, I told McDaniel about the three women whose existence I had become aware of in the course of my reporting.

This was strictly confidential, I told her. I didn't want other reporters in the bureau or editors in New York gossiping about this. Then, without providing any names, I described what I'd found out during the past five months. McDaniel quickly got confused trying to keep the three women straight, so we started to refer to them by number: "woman number one"—a Richmond socialite who claimed to have been groped by the president during a meeting in the Oval Office in 1993; "woman number two"—a government employee and former White House secretary who corroborated a sexual encounter between Clinton and "woman number one" but insisted it wasn't harassment; and "woman number three"—a twenty-three-year-old former intern who was having an ongoing affair with Clinton. McDaniel, as is her way, took notes, shaking her head in astonishment. Unlike me, still primarily focused on woman number one (Kathleen Willey), McDaniel was most struck by the idea that Clinton was carrying on with a young woman barely half his age. She thought it had the potential to be explosive. We both realized that *Newsweek* was not going to print any of this without overwhelmingly solid evidence, which clearly didn't exist at this point. What would be our justification for printing any of this? McDaniel asked. The lawsuit, I told her. Clinton's sexual behavior was inevitably going to be front and center if the case proceeded. McDaniel agreed I should keep reporting. We both realized that the Jones case could be the catalyst that brought all these allegations to light, and she wanted *Newsweek* to be there first, with the most complete story.

The next day, McDaniel flew to New York for her weekly visit to *Newsweek*'s headquarters and met with Maynard Parker, the magazine's editor. She briefed him on our conversation, stressing that she had promised me absolute confidentiality. McDaniel explained that the magazine did not have to make any big decisions about this right away—only a small one: to give me the green light to continue to look into the matter. Parker was a risk taker. He loved big stories, and he had brilliant instincts for what would turn into one. But in recent years, he and the magazine had been burned badly by controversy. The previous summer, *Newsweek* had investigated a story about allegations that the chief of naval operations, Admiral Mike Boorda, had been wearing war decorations to which he was not entitled. Boorda killed himself just as two of *Newsweek*'s correspondents were arriving at his office to interview him about it. Although the reporters had been pursuing legitimate questions, some commentators blamed the magazine for hounding a good man to his grave.

Parker agreed with McDaniel that I should pursue the story. But if word were to leak out that *Newsweek* was reporting on this, he warned, it was almost the same thing as publishing it. They talked about a story *The Washington Post* had wrestled with during the final weeks of the 1996 presidential campaign—the account of a woman who allegedly had been Bob Dole's mistress during the 1970s. Len Downie chose not to run the story, concluding it had taken place too long ago and was of questionable relevance. Like my original Paula Jones piece, the story had divided the newsroom—and news of the debate had inevitably leaked out, embarrassing the paper. McDaniel assured Parker that Isikoff would be careful.

That week, I got back in touch with Paula Jones for a brief interview to go with *Newsweek*'s second cover story on her case. We had not spoken in three years, but she sounded positively bubbly on the phone. "Hi, Mike!" she said. "Can you believe it?" After all the trashing of her that had taken place, her right to a trial had been affirmed by the highest court in the land. Jones felt vindicated. I asked her the questions she had been asked a hundred times before: What did she want from all this? What did she hope to achieve? Might she agree to settle the case? "I'm not giving up," said Jones. "I just want him to admit what he did." Of course, she never expected him to confess to everything that went on that day at the Excelsior Hotel. But he should at least admit that he met with her, Jones said. Her first statement—"I just want him to admit what he did"— accompanied Jones's photograph on the cover of *Newsweek* the following week.

I made another call that week—to Kathleen Willey. "Do you realize what this means?" I said to her. "Do you realize you're almost certainly going to get a subpoena?"

"I know," she said.

Is there any chance you might now be willing to go on the record? I asked.

Nope.

Come on, I said. Your story is going to have to come out. It's inevitable.

No, she said firmly.

A few days later, I got a phone call from Cammarata. Did you ever find that woman I told you about? he asked.

Maybe, I replied.

You going to do a story?

Not right now. She doesn't want to go on the record.

Cammarata told me he wanted to talk to her, maybe off the record—get a sense of what she might testify to. That way he wouldn't have to subpoena her. Could I maybe arrange a telephone conversation? I said I didn't think I could help him.

He sounded surprised, somewhat agitated. "What are you talking about? Why not? I gave you this tip."

"I understand that," I told him, "but I can't be in a position where I become your private investigator." Cammarata was annoyed. All right, he said, he would find her on his own.

Over the next several weeks, Cammarata reached out to his network of helpers across the country. He called a private investigator in Arkansas. He had somebody run through *The Clinton Chronicles*. He hired an ex-FBI agent in Virginia. By late June, word of Cammarata's search for another woman—a woman who had talked to Isikoff of *Newsweek*— was starting to circulate among the supporters of Paula Jones.

*   *   *

On Friday afternoon, June 27, Steve Tuttle, the magazine's computer maven, popped into my office. "Drudge is in the office," he announced. "Drudge" was Matt Drudge, Washington's hottest journalistic and political phenomenon, the author of a racy Internet gossip column called the Drudge Report. I wandered out to meet him.

Patterning himself after Walter Winchell, Drudge, then thirty, churned out a steady stream of salacious tidbits about Washington politics, Hollywood and the media. In the Drudge Report, you could read "exclusives" you'd never find anywhere else—like the one announcing the imminent indictment of Hillary Rodham Clinton. Drudge was often little more than a scavenger—picking up stories, or whiffs of stories, that other news organizations were working on. And while his exclusives were often demonstrably false, they were usually entertaining and he was right just often enough so that most politicos—especially wishful conservatives—would wonder if there wasn't some kernel of truth to what he was reporting. Drudge was unquestionably an oddball; he lived and worked out of a $600-a-month apartment on a grungy stretch of Hollywood Boulevard in Los Angeles. But on the night before he came to *Newsweek*, the right-wing writer David Brock and conservative pundit Laura Ingraham had co-hosted a grand dinner party for him at Brock's George-town home. A star-studded cast of political and journalistic notables was on hand—including *Newsweek*'s Howard Fineman. At one point, amid the cigar smoke and gossipy chatter, Drudge said he planned to be making the rounds of Washington news organizations while he was in town. Fineman casually suggested that he stop by *Newsweek*.

So he did. Several of us chatted amiably with him in the hallway. He was, with his signature fedora, every bit the eccentric the media had portrayed. He also had the trademark instincts of a good gossip columnist: he gave the impression he knew much more than he was telling. He seemed to take a special interest in me. So, what did I hear about what was going on in Starr's office? He was hearing big things—and the action was going to be right here in Washington, not in Little Rock. Indictments may be coming, he suggested.

I, of course, couldn't let it look as if Drudge knew something I didn't. So I blurted out a bit of nonpublic—if innocuous—informa-tion. At long last, Starr was about to come out with his report on the death of Vince Foster, I told Drudge. It would confirm that Foster's death was a suicide, but it would have some new pieces of evidence that might surprise some people. I was hyping the new evidence stuff in part to tease Drudge. The basic tidbit—that the report was finally slated to be released—was true enough, but hardly headline news.

Still, Drudge got excited. Do you realize this will be the first report Starr has issued since his investigation began three years ago? he asked. Was I going to report this? I wasn't sure, I told him. I realized I had probably made a mistake by telling Drudge anything. When he left the bureau, I called after him: "Now you can't use that thing about the Starr report on Foster." He mumbled something non-committal.

Just how big a mistake I had made quickly became clear. That evening, I was finishing work on a story about new developments in Starr's investigation. It had nothing to do with Vince Foster. Bob Woodward, *The Washington Post* investigative reporter of Watergate fame, had broken a big story that week: FBI agents working for Starr had been questioning former Arkansas state troopers about Clin-ton's sexual liaisons. The story had caused an uproar: Why was the special prosecutor investigating the president's sex life? Starr's staff tried to squelch the controversy, explaining that the prosecutors were simply trying to compile a complete list of potential witnesses to events relating to Whitewater and had to include everyone Clinton had been in contact with during that time. The explanation was lame: Did Starr's agents really believe Clinton had mumbled something meaningful about Whitewater during bouts of furtive sex? Starr had been hurt by the story—and we at *Newsweek* thought we had to cover this apparent case of investigative excess.

About seven P.M., Tuttle came by. You might want to take a look at Drudge, he said. I called up his Web site. Drudge had a red police-siren logo flashing atop the Drudge Report—a siren reserved for supposedly hot breaking news. Foster Report Imminent! it read. Drudge went on to say that *"Newsweek*'s Isikoff" would report on the Foster report in the magazine's issue due out Monday and that there would be new information about the events that led to the White House lawyer's death. This put me in something of a bind. The story I was writing included no reference at all to the report on Vince Foster. As my unwritten "scoop" rocketed through cyberspace, I reviewed my options. Should I hastily type it into the story before my editors in New York read about it in Drudge? Or should I leave it out and make Drudge look stupid? But what if my competitors at *Time* read the Drudge Report and slipped a reference to the Foster report into their story? My colleagues were much amused by all this. Political reporter Matt Cooper, the office comedian, speculated about other Washington Post Company subsidiaries I might go to work for. "Perhaps Stanley Kaplan has got a slot for you," he said, referring to the Post-owned firm that teaches high school students how to boost SAT scores.

Finally, I stuck a line about the Foster report into the Starr sex story. On Monday, I found that *Time* had done the same.

The following Thursday, July 3, Drudge left a message saying he needed to talk to me about another story. I called back, mainly to tell him what a sleazebag he was for stealing other reporters' stories.

"I'm surprised you called me back," he said.

"I probably shouldn't have," I replied.

Drudge then said he had heard I was working on a story involving another woman who had been harassed by Clinton. My heart momentarily stopped. Where are you hearing this? I asked. What, exactly, were you told? In retrospect, I realize I displayed a bit too much alarm.

Well, I guess there must be something to this, he said.

I made it clear to him that I wasn't confirming a thing and slammed down the phone, fearing the worst.

• • •

In fact, there was much going on that I was unaware of. Events were coming together in ways nobody could have anticipated. Earlier that week, Kathleen Willey—nervous about having talked to me at all—concluded she might perhaps use her dalliance with me to her advantage. Perhaps she could get back in good graces with the White House. So she called her old pal Nancy Hernreich, director of Oval Office operations—the same Nancy Hernreich who had asked Willey for her phone number that day at the Richmond airport in 1992 to give to Bill Clinton. Nancy and Kathleen had gotten to know each other at the White House and always gotten along.

"Michael Isikoff of *Newsweek* has been calling me up and he's on to something," Willey said. "I think the president should know this."

Hernreich said she would make sure he knew. Willey explained nothing. She didn't have to.

"I am just so sorry you have to go through this," Hernreich said.

Willey's fears were justified. Cammarata was closing in fast, intent on serving the elusive Willey with a subpoena. His ex-FBI agent investigator had traced her to her house outside Richmond. To make sure he was right, the ex-agent had somebody call Willey's home, pretending to be from the power company and asking about hours that she might be home. Suspicious, Willey jotted down the number from her caller ID. She called it. She got a recording that said there was no such number. Willey was spooked—and reported it to the sheriff's office. Then, early on July 4, Cammarata called Willey at home. Willey again looked at her caller ID, recognized Cammarata's name, and this time didn't pick up. Instead, she immediately called her lawyer.

• • •

That same morning, at 8:51, Linda Tripp's friend twenty-three-year-old Monica Lewinsky—a former White House intern assigned to the Office of Legislative Affairs—was ushered past the White House gates on her way to a meeting with President Clinton. Fourteen months earlier, Lewinsky had been exiled from the White House and dispatched to the Pentagon public affairs office after a senior White House staffer, Deputy Chief of Staff Evelyn Lieberman, decided she was spending too much time hanging out near President Clinton. Devastated, Lewinsky had complained to the president, who promised to bring her back right after the 1996 election. But he hadn't delivered.

The day before, Lewinsky had fired off an angry letter to Clinton that had a vaguely threatening tone. If she was not going to be permitted to return to the White House, she wrote, then she would "need to explain to my parents why that wasn't happening." The president was not pleased. Lewinsky wasn't supposed to say anything—to anybody. "It's illegal to threaten the president of the United States," Clinton scolded when Lewinsky entered his private study on July 4.

Lewinsky burst into tears. Clinton embraced her and tried to console her. As they hugged, Clinton spotted a gardener through the window. As Lewinsky later described the scene, she and the president then moved into the hallway to avoid being seen. Clinton became affectionate, toying with her hair, stroking her arm, kissing her neck. They discussed whether they might ever have a future together. Clinton repeated a line he had used before—that in three years he might well be "alone." Lewinsky told him they would make a "good team." Clinton joked, "Well, what are we going to do when I'm seventy-five and I have to pee twenty-five times a day?" Lewinsky assured him that "we'd deal with that." As they talked, Lewinsky became convinced of something she had always before doubted: "I just knew he was in love with me."

Just as she was about to leave, Lewinsky told Clinton that there was "something serious" she needed to talk to him about, something she had learned from a friend. A reporter for *Newsweek,* Michael Isikoff, was working on a story alleging that the president had sexually harassed a woman named Kathleen Willey outside the Oval Office in 1993. Lewinsky was concerned that Willey might become another Paula Jones and thought the president might offer her a job to keep her happy. Clinton told her not to worry. The harassment claim was ludicrous, he told her: he would never be interested in a small-breasted woman like Kathleen Willey.

Besides, Clinton assured Lewinsky, he already knew all about this. Willey had warned Nancy Hernreich that a reporter was badgering her.

Still, Clinton may have been a bit concerned. Within a few minutes after Lewinsky left that morning, he called Bruce Lindsey. It is likely it was then that he learned about an item that had just moved on the Drudge Report.

•   •   •

At just about the same time Clinton and Lewinsky were embracing in the White House, my colleague Mark Hosenball called me at home. Have you seen this thing on the Drudge Report? he asked. He then read it to me. Isikoff of *Newsweek* was "hot on the trail" of another woman who had been harassed by Clinton "on federal property." Drudge didn't have anybody's name, thank God, and he didn't know any details. But he knew enough to cause trouble. This was bad, I said to Hosenball. This was very bad.

I wasn't the only person who was alarmed. That afternoon, White House lawyer Cheryl Mills, alter ego of presidential confidant Bruce Lindsey, called White House special counsel Lanny Davis. Davis had once described me to Mills as "an old friend"; years before, as a lawyer-lobbyist, he had been a source of mine on stories about alleged contract fraud at the Pentagon. Now Mills wanted Davis to check with me. Was *Newsweek* really about to publish something? Davis was in his car, on the way to the White House to watch the July Fourth fireworks. He reached me just as I was leaving with my family to watch the fireworks from *Newsweek*'s balcony.

"What's this all about?" he asked. Was I working on any story about a new woman that was about to come out?

I brushed him off. "Come on, Lanny, you're asking me about something in an Internet gossip report?"

•   •   •

When I returned to work the following Monday, I was on edge. Would Drudge have any more? I checked. Nothing beyond his sketchy July 4 item. I breathed easier. But before long, I got another unexpected phone call—this one from Linda Tripp.

I should know, she said, that my good source Kathleen Willey was two-timing me. Just last week, she had called Nancy Hernreich and complained about me. She told her all about what you're doing, said Tripp, and how you're trying to get her to talk. This woman Willey is just playing two sides off against each other.

How can you possibly know that? I asked.

Easy, Tripp explained. She had heard about it from her friend, the former intern.

And how in the world would she know? That, too, was easy, said Tripp. The president told her.

I called Willey.

Well, yes, it was true, she said. She had called Hernreich.

Why? I wanted to know. I thought you were angry at the guy because he harassed you. Why are you trying to protect him?

I just did, Willey said. I don't know.

I was annoyed. What kind of game was being played here? I expressed my disappointment. She assured me again that her story about what happened that day outside the Oval Office was completely true. Then Willey wanted to know something.

How in the world did you find out I called Nancy? she asked.

I mumbled something about having good sources and hung up. I felt distinctly uneasy. What in God's name was I in the middle of?

The bizarre game of telephone was not over. Sometime after I hung up, Willey was back on the line—to Nancy Hernreich, reporting that the reporter Isikoff knew all about her earlier phone call. Hernreich consulted with the president. It is reasonable to assume that the pieces of a puzzle began to come together in Bill Clinton's mind.

•   •   •

A few days later, Dan Gecker, Willey's lawyer, placed a call to Bob Bennett, the president's lawyer. He explained that he was representing Kathleen Willey, whom the Jones lawyers wanted to subpoena. What does she have to say? Bennett wanted to know. Gecker was cagey. He didn't know whether Clinton would deny meeting with Willey or even knowing her. Before he exposed her to the famed White House spin machine, he wanted to know exactly what Bennett and the president would say.

Bennett couldn't ask his client immediately. Bill Clinton was in

Europe. So was Monica Lewinsky, part of an entourage accompanying Secretary of Defense William Cohen on a tour of NATO nations.

Clinton returned to Washington on Saturday, July 12. Two days later, an exhausted Lewinsky got back—and promptly went to sleep. About 7:30 P.M., she was awakened by a phone call from the president's secretary, Betty Currie. The president would like to see her—that night.

At 9:30 P.M., Lewinsky arrived at the White House—and was immediately ushered in to see the president in Nancy Hernreich's office. Clinton was cold and distant. He had a question. Was the friend Lewinsky had mentioned the last time they met, the friend who had told her about Kathleen Willey's being pursued by that *Newsweek* reporter, was that friend by any chance Linda Tripp?

Yes, Lewinsky replied. It was.

Had Lewinsky told Tripp about Willey's phone call to Nancy Hernreich?

Lewinsky didn't know what to say. Clinton would be furious if he thought she was blabbing to her friends what he told her. He would surely wonder what else she had revealed. Clinton interjected that Willey had called Nancy Hernreich again to say Isikoff knew about her first call. How could that have happened? Only four people knew about that call: Willey, Hernreich, Lewinsky and himself.

Somehow, Clinton and Hernreich had pieced it together. Willey had been friends with Linda Tripp at the White House. Now Linda Tripp was in the same office as Lewinsky at the Pentagon.

Lewinsky acknowledged that she must have told Tripp.

Do you trust Linda Tripp? Clinton asked her.

Yes, Lewinsky said.

Have you told her about our relationship? Clinton asked.

No, Lewinsky lied.

In the midst of this tense conversation, Clinton had to leave the room—for a conference call with Bob Bennett. When he returned, he asked Lewinsky to tell her friend Tripp to call Bruce Lindsey. Lewinsky should call Betty Currie back the next day and tell her whether Tripp would agree to do that.

On Tuesday, Lewinsky did as Clinton requested. But Tripp had no interest in talking to Lindsey. In her own mind, she had crossed a

Rubicon. That night, the president called Lewinsky at home to find out what had happened—and was told of Tripp's recalcitrance. Lewinsky later described Clinton's mood during this brief conversation. It was, she said, "shitty."

• • •

On Friday, July 25, Joe Cammarata struck. Having finally identified Kathleen Willey as his mystery witness and tracked her to her secluded home in Virginia, he sent lawyer Dan Gecker a subpoena for Willey to testify as a witness in the Paula Jones case.

At the time, Cammarata wasn't really thinking about eliciting Willey's testimony. He was thinking of a settlement. Ever since the Supreme Court ruling, Cammarata and Davis had been negotiating secretly with the president's lawyers. Much of the impetus for these talks had come from two insurance carriers, Chubb and State Farm, which until now had been paying the president's hefty legal bills under a standard liability clause the First Family had in two policies. The companies were in no mood to foot the bill—certain to run into the millions—for the long process of civil discovery followed by a trial. Davis and Cammarata, lawyers for the insurance companies, and Bennett and his partner Mitch Ettinger were beginning to hash out a deal.

From the start, Bob Bennett's goal had been, first and foremost, to minimize political damage to the president. When he was defeated on his immunity claim to the Supreme Court, he told reporters privately that it didn't matter; he had actually "won" by tying up the case for so long and pushing it back until after the 1996 election. Publicly, after the Supreme Court defeat, he was all bluster—threatening to rake over Jones's sex life if the case proceeded. But privately, he was showing increasing flexibility. He had been instructed by the president's political advisers to explore a deal, and he was trying to deliver. And he wanted it done quickly—before discovery began and the Jones lawyers had a chance to start mucking around in the president's past.

Still, by the third week in July, the deal was not clinched. Hillary Clinton, in particular, was balking, recoiling at any capitulation to the president's political enemies. Bennett was ducking and dodging about precisely what the president was prepared to say. So Cammarata thought he would give the Clinton camp a nudge by suggesting the prospect of a damaging new claim—an incident inside the White House.

When Bennett learned about the Willey subpoena that Friday, he exploded. The president of the United States could not appear to cave in to blackmail. He warned Cammarata and Davis: Don't push this—or all deals are off. But by now, Cammarata was used to Bennett's bluster. After that tirade, he talked to Bennett's back-channel negotiating partner. Don't worry, he assured Ettinger. Nothing about this has to be public.

Another lawyer willing to go along with this strategy, apparently, was Dan Gecker. He wanted, most of all, to protect Willey's privacy, and a settlement would achieve that purpose. But first he wanted to make sure that Bennett and the president's vaunted spin machine were not about to trash his client. After receiving Cammarata's subpoena, Gecker told Bennett that if he promised that there would be no attacks on his client from the White House, Willey would stay silent. He would even file a motion to quash Cammarata's subpoena on the ground that Willey had no information "relevant" to the Paula Jones case.

What no one counted on was Matt Drudge.

•   •   •

On the morning of Tuesday, July 29, I was covering the campaign finance hearings chaired by Senator Fred Thompson. For three weeks, Drudge had not printed a word that suggested he or anybody else knew about Kathleen Willey. I still harbored hopes of a scoop—although it was far from clear what the story would be. I believed something had happened between Willey and Clinton, but beyond that I was fuzzy. In the meantime, I was still focused on other matters. During a break in the hearings, I ducked out to get my messages, expecting no more than a handful.

The first sign that something was afoot was the recording "Your mailbox is full." I started going through them. My buddy Glenn Simpson of *The Wall Street Journal* was the first. "Hey, have you seen Drudge? Give me a call." Tripp followed soon after. "I need to talk to you right away," she barked. "Where are you?" I ducked out of the hearings and headed back to the office.

Drudge had struck again—and this time he had done real damage.

WILLEY'S DECISION: White House
Employee Tells Reporter That
President Made Sex Pass
★★WORLD EXCLUSIVE★★

So read the headline in that morning's Drudge Report. Drudge had Willey's name, of course, and the barest outline of her claim— that she had gone to see the president "a few years ago" about work at the White House and Clinton "fondled" her. "Isikoff has held back on the explosive story because the woman has refused to go on the record with her account," he wrote. "Nevertheless, the events surrounding Willey have become the talk of the Washington underground and threaten to undermine President Clinton's defense in the ongoing Paula Jones sexual harassment case."

I was furious. Six months of work—and it came out like this? I figured this had to be coming from the Jones camp—after all, Cammarata knew Willey's identity and had probably told his coterie of loose-lipped supporters. The only other suspect was Tripp. When I finally tracked her down, she sounded irate—and accused *me* of leaking to the Internet scavenger.

I erupted. "Are you goddamn crazy? Are you insane? Why would I fucking give my reporting to him?" She backed down. But by then, she had already planted the idea that I was the culprit. At the Pentagon public affairs office, Lewinsky had run into her office that morning—"agitated beyond belief," as Tripp later put it. Now, she really had to call Bruce Lindsey, Lewinsky said. Otherwise, the White House would think it was she, Tripp, who had leaked to Drudge. Tripp had to set the record straight and show she was a "team player." Tripp reluctantly had agreed—and finally called Lindsey. Lindsey took notes of their conversation, jotting down the most salient snippets. One of Tripp's goals was to throw suspicion away from herself. "I think Isikoff leaked it," Lindsey wrote as he listened to what Tripp had to say.

Over the next few days, the Willey story gathered momentum. On Wednesday, July 30, CBS White House correspondent Bill Plante reported the subpoena by the Jones lawyers on the network's evening newscast. The next morning, Willey's name was everywhere; she was the subject of a story in *The Washington Post,* the wires were carrying her name, the cable networks were speculating wildly about what she might say and how much damage she could do the president. It was an unusual position for most news organizations, of course, since no reporters had actually talked to her, so nobody had any reliable source upon which to speculate. Nobody except me.

Meanwhile, Drudge was following up with more. He had been "fully briefed on the nature and details of Ms. Willey's off the record conversations with *Newsweek*'s once ace reporter Michael Isikoff," he wrote on July 31. "And when under oath, if Willey tells lawyers the same story she has told Isikoff—Washington will be rocked." I was now bombarded with calls. David Bloom of NBC News pleaded with me to give him some guidance. Clinton-friendly journalists wanted me to dump on Drudge and discredit what was surely another right-wing fabrication. I told everybody I had nothing to say—and consulted with McDaniel.

We at *Newsweek* were the only ones who could shed any light on this matter. We couldn't quote Willey. But we could cobble together a story—using Tripp, Julie Steele, and my other reporting about Willey's White House employment and subsequent overseas trips—to elucidate a potentially important development in the Paula Jones case. Was this justified? Only a few days earlier, we had no intention of writing a story about Kathleen Willey. Were we—as some critics later charged—using a scurrilous Internet gossip column as a pretext for publishing something that didn't meet the magazine's usual standards for what is fit to print?

It was a tough call. But two things had happened that completely changed the equation. The first was that Drudge's account, rightly or wrongly, had unleashed widespread public speculation about who Willey was and what she might have to say about the president. Second, and more critical, was Cammarata's subpoena. Willey was now a witness in a lawsuit involving the president of the United States. And while we couldn't resolve the murkiness surrounding her account, I knew enough to suspect that Drudge might be right about one thing. If Willey did testify—a distinct possibility—Washington would be "rocked."

McDaniel, who had covered the Justice Department and the Bush White House, was a cautious professional. But she sensed that this might be significant. She thought of the other woman Tripp had told me about. She made a tentative decision: We would try to publish a story for the next week's issue.

•   •   •

Over the next few days, I called Willey repeatedly. She didn't answer. I called Gecker and asked whether his client would now be willing to put our interview on the record. No, he said. He planned to fight the subpoena all the way.

Given Willey's recalcitrance, there were two key sources with whom I needed to get in touch. One was Tripp.

The other was Julie Hiatt Steele, Kathleen Willey's friend in Richmond. But when I called Steele to go over how I planned to quote her, she balked. Are you going to put my name in there? she asked. Yes, I said; that was important. I also recalled that she had said she had a picture of Willey with the president. I asked if we could have it for the story. Steele started to sound nervous. She needed to talk to me—in person. Could I come to Richmond? I didn't know if I had time, I told her. I would see.

Later that day, Steele called back. Did I remember all that stuff she'd told me back in March—how Willey had come to her house and was so upset about Clinton? Yes, I said, I had quite detailed notes. Well, she said, it's not true. Kathleen had called while I was on the way to her home and had asked her to tell me that. Kathleen hadn't come to her house at all that night in November 1993. She hadn't told her any of that. "She asked me to lie," Steele said. "God, I'm so embarrassed—I just didn't want you to have egg all over your face."

I was utterly perplexed. Was this woman telling me the truth now or had she been telling the truth last March? There was only one way to handle this, I told Steele: It would have to go into the story. You're not still going to put me in there, are you? Steele asked. Yes, absolutely, I answered. What you just said clearly casts new doubt on

Willey's credibility. The readers had a right to know. I also pressed Steele again for the picture of Willey and the president. She said she would get back to me.[1]

Early Friday morning, I again touched base with Tripp. We needed to work out exactly how she would be quoted. This was a matter of some importance. With Steele a riddle, Tripp might well wind up as the most crucial source for the story. But Tripp had a scheduling conflict. The only time and place she could meet me was that morning at a Georgetown salon.

"I can't interview you there—while you're having your hair done," I sputtered. "It's far too public." Tripp was unmovable. So late that morning, I wandered into the salon, feeling faintly ridiculous. Tripp was there, a diminutive foreign beautician working on her hair. I started talking to her about the Willey story—and grew distinctly uncomfortable, nodding toward the hairdresser.

"Don't worry about him," Tripp said. "He doesn't speak a word of English."

Then, as if on cue, I heard: "Michael Isikoff, what are you doing here?" It was Anne Farris, a *Washington Post* researcher who, being from Arkansas, had been assisting on Clinton scandal coverage.

"I am really impressed," said Farris. "You'll go anyplace for a story."

"I was just stopping by to see somebody," I mumbled. I whispered to Tripp that I had to get out of there; I'd meet her outside when she was finished. After I left, I peered back through the window. Farris had moved in on Tripp.

Twenty minutes later, Tripp emerged and we reconnoitered at a nearby coffee shop. Farris, Tripp said, had asked if she were Kathleen Willey. What did you say? That I was a friend of an uncle of yours. Did she believe you? Yeah, she went away. She even talked about what a tenacious reporter you were.

I took out my notebook. Exactly what can I quote you saying about your meeting with Willey that day? Tripp spoke carefully and deliberately; she seemed to be repeating a script she had already gone over in her mind. When she saw Willey in the West Wing that day, Willey was "disheveled—her face was red and her lipstick was off. She was flustered, happy and joyful." Then they had gone outside to a picnic table, and Willey had told her that the president had made sexual advances. Tripp said she was coming forward for one reason and one reason only—"to make it clear that this is not a case of sexual harassment."

It was stronger than I had expected. Tripp, a government official, was confirming that a former White House employee, a subpoenaed witness in a lawsuit against the president, had had a sexual encounter with Clinton outside the Oval Office.

Tripp told me something else: Bob Bennett, the president's lawyer, was extremely anxious to meet with her. She and her lawyer agreed that she should refuse.

That afternoon, I met with McDaniel and Evan Thomas. We went over what we had—and why we were doing the story. Thomas was uncomfortable. He didn't like stories like this. *Newsweek* stories, at least almost all sensitive ones, are usually the product of consensus. We thrash them out in editorial meetings in McDaniel's office; debate the main points and work out an outline. But now, as we went over the points the story would cover, Thomas began to get nervous. "Wait a second, all we've really got here is one source—Linda Tripp," he said.

No, it's actually more than that, I argued. We have a subpoena. We have a woman who we know has accused the president of very serious misconduct—and who will probably testify to that if she is forced to. We have her flying around the world at taxpayer expense. And we have a Pentagon official confirming that something took place between that woman and the president—even if the something is different from what the woman says. McDaniel agreed. I was told to start calling the White House and the president's lawyer for comment.

That afternoon, I called Mike McCurry. The White House press secretary had told reporters at his daily briefing that he would not address questions about Willey. The subtext was clear: This stuff was beneath contempt. "Responsible" news organizations have to "make editorial judgments" about these sorts of things. In cutting off all questions, McCurry was aided greatly by a statement Gecker had released on Thursday. Ms. Willey was "outraged" that her privacy was being invaded, Gecker said, and she had "absolutely no knowledge or information of any relevance regarding Paula Jones or her allegations." The statement was a dodge, of course. Relevant according to whom? But if Willey wouldn't say what allegedly happened, then what could reporters write?

McCurry was cordial enough but gave me the same line. He would not even consider answering any questions about Willey until he heard from a senior editor of *Newsweek* that we were seriously considering a story on this matter. I told him that wouldn't be a problem, but I had specific questions for him. I asked about Willey's overseas trips—to Copenhagen and Jakarta—and why the White House had arranged for her to go on them. These were publicly funded foreign missions. The public had a right to know how somebody without any apparent qualifications had been sent. McCurry paused. I had taken him by surprise. He agreed that perhaps those questions were legitimate. But he still needed to hear from one of my editors. I told him McDaniel would be calling shortly.

I had already contacted Bennett, who had been, as usual, all bluster and bravado. "I smell a rat," the president's lawyer said at first. Look, he argued, this is all a lamebrained ploy by the Jones lawyers to try to force a settlement. "I've looked into this matter and I can tell you that absolutely nothing happened between them," Bennett told me. Clinton had "no specific recollection" of even meeting with Willey, but he did have a "very dim" memory of consoling her after her husband's suicide. He then spoke carefully and slowly, to make sure I got his precise words: "It is preposterous to imagine that the president of the United States would make an improper advance toward this woman at the time he was consoling her about her husband's death."

There was a problem, I told Bennett. The meeting in question took place the day *before* Willey learned about her husband's death. We knew. We'd checked. Ed Willey's body wasn't discovered by the Virginia state police until November 30, 1993. The meeting between Clinton and Willey was November 29. Bennett didn't seem to hear me—or if he did, he chose to ignore what I'd just said.

I moved on to Linda Tripp—and informed him of what she was saying about all this. Bennett told me he knew all about Tripp. He had, after all, done his own investigation, he told me. I can tell you she has told different versions of this story, he said. I noted that she had told me one consistent version, and it seemed to suggest that there had been a sexual encounter between the president and Willey that day.

"Linda Tripp," Bennett scoffed, "is not to be believed."

But Bennett knew, or suspected, more than he was letting on. Later that day I called back—to go over his quotes and iron out some details. We chatted awhile—and he suddenly grew quiet. He sensed we were going to go ahead with the story, that there was no way to stop it—and for the first time, he sounded worried. As we were about to hang up, he tried to reason with me.

"Don't write this story," he said softly. "Don't write it. The punishment is too great. The president doesn't deserve this."

I was taken aback. Bennett may have been trying to use a different tack to try to stop me from writing the story. But, that's not how I took it. Bennett knows it is true, I thought. He knows that this happened.

•   •   •

That Sunday, the *Newsweek* publicity department released advance copies of my story, which ran under the headline "A Twist in the Paula Jones Case." The article started with the strange call to Cammarata the previous summer—a woman claiming she was the victim of unwanted sexual advances in a small private hideaway just outside the Oval Office. It explained how that call led the Jones lawyer to Kathleen Willey. It quoted Gecker as saying his client had nothing to say and was "outraged" at being drawn into the case.

It then included Linda Tripp's on-the-record comments about a "disheveled" Willey emerging from the Oval Office and telling about a sexual encounter she had just had with Clinton. This was clearly the strongest part of the piece. Then it quoted Julie Steele, Willey's friend, as saying Willey asked her to lie to support a claim of harassment. What, readers were likely to ask, was that all about? And it included my reporting on Willey's work history at the White House and her overseas trips to Denmark and Indonesia. Interesting, perhaps, but most readers were likely to wonder what on earth it all meant.

The story was closely read by the political community in Washington and by other journalists. It even got some slight praise. Conservative media critic Terry Eastland called it a "well-executed piece of investigative journalism." *Washington Post* media reporter Howard Kurtz, in a story about Drudge, called it "well-researched and solid." But hardly anybody wanted to touch the substance of the article. The *Washington Times* ran a brief story in its Monday editions about Tripp's allegation of seeing Willey emerge from the Oval Office with her lipstick smeared—and telling her about a sexual encounter. But *The Washington Post, The New York Times* and all three networks ignored it. That Monday afternoon, CNN's *Inside Politics* devoted the top of its show to the marital infidelity of a leading politician, raising the question whether it really mattered. The politician in question was New York City mayor Rudy Giuliani. *Vanity Fair* had come out with an article that same day claiming Giuliani had been engaged in a longtime affair with his communications director. Giuliani had denied it. The program said not one word about my piece about Clinton.

Among the president's advisers, there was relief. They had been anxious about the Willey piece. Bennett had wanted it faxed to him at home on Sunday. On Monday, he took a phone call from James Carville, Clinton's pit bull campaign consultant, to assess the damage. They both agreed. By all appearances, Clinton yet again had dodged a bullet.

•   •   •

Tripp read the article carefully—and fixated on Bennett's quote about how "she was not to be believed." She discussed it with her friend Monica Lewinsky. Lewinsky was upset. Linda couldn't let this story go like that. She had to protect herself.

Tripp agreed. She had some ideas about how to protect herself—ideas she didn't share with Lewinsky.

Somebody else also read the piece carefully. Later that week, I was sitting at my desk when the phone rang. A woman was on the line. You know that story you had in the magazine this week about the woman Clinton made sexual overtures to in the hideaway office? she asked.

"Yes," I said. "What about it?"

"That's exactly the same thing that happened to me," she said. She paused. "It was pretty awful."

We spoke for the next half hour. The caller was articulate and well educated, a professional woman probably in her mid- to late thirties, married and involved in politics. She wouldn't give me her name. She couldn't, she said. Her husband was a player in the Democratic Party. But she wanted me to know something. "There are a lot of us out there who are not bimbos," she said.

The story she told was chilling. She had met Clinton over the years at political events and would get invited to come see him at the White House when she was in Washington on business. Clinton's attention was "pretty flattering. . . . He's very charming." One day, about a year and a half before, she had gone by to see him and he had taken her into the hideaway office—the same one described in my article. They chatted. Clinton started getting physical, trying to kiss her, touching her breasts. The woman said she was stunned. She had no idea how to respond. "I've never had a man take advantage of me like that," she said. "I haven't felt that way since high school."

As Clinton pressed himself on her, she said, she resisted—and finally pushed him away. What happened after that? I asked. Clinton turned away, she said. She hesitated, and she said softly and with apparent discomfort, "I think he finished the job himself." The image lingered. The woman left the White House humiliated and repulsed. Clinton acted as if nothing had happened. The woman told no one except her sister. Then Clinton started calling her at work. There would be a flurry of calls at strategic times—usually when there were developments in the Jones case. He called many times in January, around the time of his inauguration—just as the Jones case was being argued in the Supreme Court. The calls were embarrassing; she worried that her colleagues would start to wonder about them. There didn't seem to be any point to Clinton's calls. He just wanted to chat, to see how she was doing.

I pointed out that the timing was the key; he must have been worried about what she might say. Look, I told her, it's really important that we get together and talk about this. There are so many people who have been attacked by the White House, so many people who are worried about being slimed for daring to tell the truth about this guy. You owe it to yourself, you owe it to all the others.

No, she couldn't do that, she said. "If my husband knew I was talking to you, he'd kill me," she said. She mentioned an administration official she knew who had told her about Clinton slipping his hands up her leg. She too would never say anything. It was just so awful. I pleaded for her name. I begged her to meet me. She would think about it, she said. She would be in Washington soon to meet with a "client," and maybe she would consider giving me a call.

After she hung up, I was shaken. That woman sounded to me as credible as any of them, more so, really, and her story was in some ways the most horrifying of all. Who was this guy Clinton? What demons possessed him? And how many more of them were out there—women too terrified and too smart to open their mouths? A few minutes later, I wandered back to McDaniel's office.

"In case you had any doubts about the Willey story," I told her, "let me tell you about the phone call I just got."

McDaniel listened. She shook her head sadly. "I didn't have any doubts," she said.

The woman never called back.

Book Three

MONICA LEWINSKY

August 1997-December 1997

9

"She was so crazy about him."

One of the unexpected by-products of the Kathleen Willey story was that it gave me a welcome opportunity to take the journalistic high road. While ignoring the question of whether something actually happened in the White House that day, commentators were fascinated by the role of Drudge in briefly creating a media firestorm. Not surprisingly, a few called me for comment—and I jumped at the chance to publicly slam him. "He's a menace to honest, responsible journalism," I told *The New York Times*'s Todd Purdum. He was digging through unverified reporting—"like raw FBI files"— and shoveling it onto the Internet, I told *The Washington Post*'s Howard Kurtz. Within weeks, Drudge proved me right. He posted— then hastily retracted—a ridiculous item accusing White House aide Sidney Blumenthal of beating his wife. Blumenthal sued. I looked prescient. Not long after that, I ran into Blumenthal at a party and went out of my way to say hello. "We have a common enemy," he said. Yes, we do, I replied.

In fact, my own thinking was moving in a direction that would have appalled the president's ardent defender. When Linda Tripp first told me about her young friend the previous April, I had felt ambivalent about whether such a consensual sexual relationship was worth going after. By August, however, I was starting to think that it was. In the end, I thought, Clinton's serial indiscretions really did matter. They mattered not simply because they had continued well into his tenure in the White House—behavior that, as Michael Kins-

167

ley had written four years earlier, would reveal a "brutal willingness to deceive the public." And they mattered not only because, I was now convinced, Clinton was far more psychologically disturbed than the public ever imagined. They mattered because private misbehavior on Clinton's scale required routine, repetitive, and reflexive lies to conceal itself. Clinton had been able to survive the wave of womanizing allegations—Gennifer Flowers, the troopers, Paula Jones and now Kathleen Willey—only by brazenly lying about them. The lies were told at first by Clinton and then spread and magnified by everybody around him—his top aides, his lawyers, his spin doctors. The lies were easily rationalized on the grounds that it was Clinton's private life that was at issue—a matter of no public consequence. But lying, engaged in often enough, can have a corrosive effect. The essential moral calculus had long since been established. If lies were needed to avoid political embarrassment, then lies—or at least extremely mangled versions of the truth—would be told. A culture of concealment had sprung up around Bill Clinton and, I came to believe that summer, it had infected his entire presidency.

The best evidence for this was the endless drip of scandals that bedeviled the White House—Whitewater, the travel office affair, Hillary Clinton's billing records, the campaign fundraising imbroglio. Inside the White House, these were all portrayed as minor infractions that had been blown far out of proportion by the president's political enemies and a scandal-obsessed Washington press corps. In short, the argument went, it was Washington, not Clinton, that was sick. There may have been some truth to this. Certainly, none of the abuses were of Watergate dimensions, and some of the charges appeared to melt away under close scrutiny. But not all of them. And the failure to play straight—the tendency to give false or misleading answers that invariably had to be revised upon the discovery of new evidence—had created an atmosphere of mistrust that caused many of us in the press to suspect that the truth was always much worse than we were seeing.

I came across a small example of this while covering the campaign finance mess. The scandal, in its totality, struck me as serious: In their hunger for reelection, Clinton and his top aides had audaciously stretched the campaign laws to their outer limits, accepting millions of dollars in suspicious foreign contributions and exploiting the White House for crass fundraising purposes—sleep-overs in the Lincoln Bedroom, kaffeeklatsches for fat cats in the map room—in ways that no previous administration had ever dared. That fall, I got a tip from a congressional investigator, who suggested I contact a retired investment banker in South Carolina named Richard Jenrette. Jenrette, I was told, could clear up a minor mystery: Did Clinton, like Vice President Al Gore, personally make fundraising calls from the White House?

The official White House line through the spring and summer of 1997 was that there was no evidence that he had. This was in part a legal issue: there was an antiquated and rarely enforced federal statute that barred solicitation of campaign contributions on federal property. Whether the statute—enacted before the widespread use of telephones—applied to phone solicitations was a matter of debate. But there was still a question of propriety here. The idea of a president picking up a White House telephone and dialing for dollars seemed unbecoming. Even if the pitch was low-key, how do you tell the president no, you'd rather not give him any money? And what if the prospective donor happens, as is often the case, to be a corporate executive with business before the federal government? Can it plausibly be argued that such pitches, no matter what the precise language of the request, do not amount to a form of strong-arming?

When asked directly if he ever made calls, Clinton responded—at a press conference in March 1997—that he couldn't remember. He then, characteristically, clouded the issue with a rush of seemingly helpful but utterly meaningless verbiage. In the course of a 289-word answer, he explained that 1) "I don't like to raise funds in that way"; 2) "It wasn't a practice of mine"; 3) "I prefer to meet with people face-to-face, talk to them, deal with them in that way"; and 4) "I also, frankly, was very busy most of the times that it's been raised with me." In fact, he did remember one time— "*in particular,*" he said. They asked him to make fundraising calls, "and I just never got around to doing it."

There the matter rested—for months. A Senate committee subpoenaed documents. The Justice Department interviewed prospective donors. But while Gore was getting raked over the coals for hitting up contributors from his White House office, nobody could establish whether Bill Clinton had done the same thing. White

House special counsel Lanny Davis sparred with reporters over the issue. If the president really had made any such calls, how come no donors had come forward to say they received them? (Shades of Joe Klein's "Where are the women?" line after Troopergate.)

That fall, I tracked down Jenrette. Did he remember getting any phone calls from the president asking for money? I asked. Why, of course he did. He knew exactly when, too: October 14, 1994. He had even sent the president a letter about it. He faxed it to me. "In response to your request, I wanted you to know that I am sending checks totaling $50,000 to the Democratic National Committee," Jenrette had written. "You said you wanted to raise $2 million from 40 good friends—by my Wall Street math, this comes out to $50,000."

In the days that followed, the White House conceded that Clinton probably did call Jenrette and perhaps a half dozen other Democratic donors that same day. The president's lawyer, David Kendall, insisted that Clinton didn't remember any of the calls. (Clinton's memory was indeed a wondrous thing: he remembered, *in particular,* the calls he never made. He couldn't, for the life of him, remember the calls he had made.) No other evidence of Clinton's fundraising calls ever surfaced, and the issue soon blew over. Neither Jenrette nor anybody else was willing to say he felt unduly pressured by Clinton.

Still, I found the matter fascinating. If Clinton was calling forty "good friends," as Jenrette's letter suggests, what happened to the thirty-nine others? Even more curious: The White House and the DNC had been subpoenaed for every scrap of paper involving campaign fundraising, and hundreds of thousands of pages of documents had been turned over. Yet the one letter that conclusively showed the president's personal involvement in a fundraising call had somehow vanished and had to be produced by Jenrette himself. How *exactly* does this happen?

It may seem a leap to connect Clinton's fundraising calls and his womanizing. But to me, the connection looked very real. The closer you got to Clinton, the more impenetrable were the barriers that had been erected to protect him. Whether the question was Clinton's ties to the Indonesian billionaire James Riady or the First Family's strange dealings with the McDougals of Arkansas, the principle for his White House always seemed to be the same: That which is embarrassing (or worse) was to be concealed. The question in my mind was how far he and his coterie of loyal aides would go to make sure that happened.

It seemed to me that the Jones lawsuit was a pretty good chance to find out. Here, more than anywhere else, I *knew* Clinton was vulnerable. Witnesses were about to testify. Questions were going to be asked—under oath. How would Clinton and his lawyers handle that? What would they do?

This, I thought, was going to be interesting to watch.

•   •   •

In the late summer of 1997, there were few people watching more closely than Monica Samille Lewinsky. For eighteen months, between November 15, 1995, and May 24, 1997, Lewinsky had enjoyed an improbable sexual relationship with the president of the United States. Barely twenty-two years old when it started—a White House intern fresh out of Lewis and Clark College in Portland, Oregon—Lewinsky would arrange through the president's private secretary, Betty Currie, for visits to the study outside the Oval Office, where she would perform oral sex on Clinton.[1] They had many phone conversations too; Clinton would call from the road, often early in the morning, and the two would have sexually charged conversations until they both stimulated themselves to climax.

Then on May 24, 1997, Clinton had seemed to cut things off. He couldn't do this anymore, he told her during a rendezvous just three days before the Supreme Court announced its ruling in the Jones case.[2] It wasn't right, he said. Lewinsky, at first devastated, clung to the hope that it wasn't really over—a hope sustained by the fact that Clinton maintained contact with her. (Even after their two White House conversations on July 4 and July 14, they met again in the Cabinet Room on July 24 so that the president could give Lewinsky a birthday present, and then again on August 16 so that Lewinsky could return the favor.) Whatever the president's true intentions, Lewinsky made clear to many of her friends during this period that she was still madly in love with Bill Clinton and very much wanted to protect him.

That was one reason why Lewinsky was so upset by the quotes Linda Tripp had given me for the Kathleen Willey article. They threatened the president with political damage. They also, Lewinsky thought, were harmful to Tripp. From the day the story came out, Lewinsky kept urging Tripp to retract the quotes attributed to her. "You have to fix this," she said. Lewinsky also tried to fix it herself. The Monday the article appeared, she placed an anonymous phone call to Kirby Behre, Tripp's lawyer, and told him the article had misquoted Tripp. He ought to issue a statement correcting it, Lewinsky said, then hung up.

In making that call, Lewinsky was acting true to form. She had something of a history of hurling herself emotionally into the affairs of others, then getting herself tangled in efforts to clean them up. Lewinsky was the product of a troubled upbringing, the daughter of wealthy Beverly Hills parents who quarreled relentlessly and divorced when she was fourteen. In 1992, fresh out of high school, she had begun a sexual relationship with Andrew Bleiler, a married, pony-tailed theater technician at Beverly Hills High School. The next year, Bleiler told Lewinsky he was looking for work in Portland, Oregon. Without telling Bleiler, Lewinsky hastily applied to Lewis and Clark College in the same city and arranged with Bleiler's uncle to work as a baby-sitter. The position permitted her to continue to see Bleiler when he moved there. According to Bleiler's later account to the FBI, Lewinsky would sexually proposition him in his uncle's home. Bleiler also said she ingratiated herself with his wife and showered their children with expensive gifts.

In the spring of 1995, Bleiler and his wife were involved in a bitter court fight for custody of his wife's daughter, Bleiler's stepdaughter. Bleiler, out of work at the time, needed to establish that he had some prospect of employment. Lewinsky took it upon herself to help. Using pilfered stationery from the Lewis and Clark College Theater Department, Lewinsky typed a letter purportedly from the department manager, David Bliss, alluding to work assignments he was offering Bleiler. She then forged Bliss's signature—and dropped it in the mail.

But Lewinsky's plotting blew up in her face. The letter was returned to the purported sender. Bliss was furious. He wrote a stern letter to Lewinsky, threatening to inform the college authorities about what she had done if she didn't promptly apologize. "Forgery is nothing to play around with," Bliss wrote. "If I don't hear back from you within two weeks I will pursue more formal actions regarding this dilemma." Lewinsky, by her own account, was "mortified." Two days later, she wrote Bliss an abject letter of apology, trying to explain her actions and begging his forgiveness. She felt "horrible and humiliated," Lewinsky wrote. All she was trying to do was help: "In all honesty, I never imagined that doing what I thought would be a kind, helpful thing for one of my closest friends would turn out to be one of the biggest nightmares of my life thus far."

After she sent the letter, Lewinsky also pleaded with Bliss to meet with her. As Bliss later recalled it, Lewinsky "seemed scared" when they met. She told him she was about to graduate and move to Washington, where she would be a White House intern. She was afraid that if Bliss took things any further, it might upset her plans. He agreed to let the matter drop.

Three years later, Bliss wondered whether he had done the right thing.

•   •   •

Linda Tripp agreed with Monica Lewinsky about one thing: The *Newsweek* story did not help her. She authorized Behre to release a statement making it clear that she didn't actually witness any encounter between Willey and the president. (The story didn't say she had.) But the statement got little play; only the *Washington Times* ran a piece about it. Lewinsky and Tripp agreed that Tripp had to do more. She had to be seen as a "team player," Lewinsky told her. The next week, Tripp wrote a letter to the editor of *Newsweek*. Lewinsky made editorial suggestions while looking over Tripp's shoulder at Tripp's Pentagon cubicle. When it was completed, Tripp called and said she wanted me to take a look at something. She faxed me a copy.

When I looked it over, I was not especially happy:

I take exception to the manner in which Newsweek *reporter Mike Isikoff presented my involvement in his recent "exclusive" concern-*

ing Kathleen Willey. The reader is led to believe that I came for-
ward and volunteered information damaging to the president. The
truth is that Isikoff appeared, uninvited and unannounced, in my
office at the Pentagon in late March 1997. I was compelled to
respond when he asserted that Ms. Willey had given him my name,
as a contemporaneous witness who could corroborate her new claim
of "harassment" or "inappropriate behavior" on the part of the
president. My response then, as it remains today, was that this was
completely inaccurate and that her version in 1993 and her version
in 1997 were wholly inconsistent.

Whatever happened that day in the Oval Office, if anything, is
known to only two people. One must wonder, however, how such dis-
parate allegations spanning a period of four years could have much,
if any, credibility.

Regarding the comment made by the president's attorney about
me, which appeared in the same article, I am acutely disappointed
that my integrity has been questioned.

Linda R. Tripp
Washington, D.C.

So, what you do you think? Tripp asked.

What I really thought was, What are you criticizing me for? What I said was: You start out by taking exception to the way I presented your "involvement" in the Willey matter. But you aren't really chal-lenging any facts in the piece. You're just clarifying things.

Well, what should I say, then?

This was a bit unusual. I don't usually get invited to edit letters attacking me.

Of course, you can say whatever you want, I told her. But then I thought, As long as she's asking, what the hell?

Why don't you leave my name out of it, I suggested. Why don't you say you just want to "clarify" some points about the article? Why don't you change that stuff about the reader being "led to believe" something? It implies we misstated the facts, and we didn't.

I could hear Tripp typing away on her computer keyboard. She proceeded to rewrite the first two sentences to read: "I would like to clarify the questions that have arisen about my involvement in the matter reported by *Newsweek* in the August 11th edition. Contrary to the perception held by many that I granted *Newsweek* an 'interview' for this story, the truth is the reporter appeared, uninvited and unannounced, in my office at the Pentagon in late March 1997."

I gave Tripp the fax number for *Newsweek*'s Letters to the Editor department in New York. I told her I didn't have the power to get it printed but promised to alert the letters department to it—and did. However, the letter never ran.[3]

About this time, Tripp said something that gave Lewinsky a jolt. As they discussed whether Tripp's quotes would jeopardize her employment at the Pentagon, Tripp said that if she ever did lose her job, she might just write a "tell all" book. Lewinsky was alarmed. Would Tripp ever consider . . . ? No, Linda wouldn't do that. She had promised. Lewinsky wrote it off as an offhand remark and forgot about it.

Tripp didn't. She was mulling over the whole situation—the nightly calls from Monica, the Willey subpoena, her new fears, fueled by her young friend, that she might have antagonized the president of the United States. And she got an idea. She called her friend Tony Snow, the former Bush speechwriter who two years earlier had put her in touch with Lucianne Goldberg. Tripp had a favor to ask. Would he find out whether Goldberg would still be willing to talk to her?

Snow called Goldberg on August 20, 1997. Goldberg was about to leave for Scotland for two weeks. She would deal with this when she got back, she told Snow.

• • •

By this time, Monica Lewinsky was in a state of pretty much perpetual emotional crisis. Her experiences in Washington had turned bittersweet—and painful. She wanted more than anything to return to work at the White House. Clinton had promised. She had met in July with presidential aide Marsha Scott, who suggested she might be able to arrange to detail Lewinsky to her staff on a temporary basis. Lewinsky got her hopes up. And then—nothing.

Over Labor Day weekend, Lewinsky poured out her frustrations to yet another older friend—an engaging forty-nine-year-old businesswoman from Scarsdale, New York, named Dale Young. Young and

Lewinsky had met in the summer of 1995 at the Hunter Mountain Valley Spa, a rustic Catskills resort that specialized in weight reduction. Young was taken by the young Lewinsky, finding her warmhearted and pretty and fun. They struck up a friendship that also included Lewinsky's mother, Marcia Lewis, whom Young had met separately. During one of her visits to the resort, over Memorial Day 1996, in the midst of a long walk through the woods, Lewinsky stunned Young by telling her she was performing oral sex on the president. (She stunned her almost as much by telling her the president put limits on how far he would go. "She told me he didn't even come," Young later recalled.)

On the Sunday of Labor Day weekend 1997, Lewinsky stopped off at Young's Scarsdale home after a few days at another weight reduction resort. They again took a long walk, and Lewinsky told her she was still in love with Clinton, but that he had tearfully broken off their affair. Clinton gave as one reason that he wanted Chelsea to be proud of him, Lewinsky said. Young, no fan of Clinton's, was disgusted. "I said my heart goes out to him," Young said. "He should have thought of this before." Lewinsky also said she still believed Clinton would come through on his promise to get her back to the White House.

Young said she tried to instill "a sense of reality" in Lewinsky. The idea that Clinton was trying to get her a job in the White House was "bullshit," she told her young friend. "'He's the most powerful man in the world, and you're going to tell me he can't get you in if he wants to?' I said to her, 'Monica, if he wants you there, there are ways that he can say things to people to get you in. He does not want you in the White House.' What I was trying to do was help her with closure, to get out of this thing. Because it was preoccupying her. She was so crazy about him."

As one measure of her preoccupation, Young said Lewinsky didn't say one word about the shocking news reported that weekend: the death of Princess Diana in a high-speed chase through the streets of Paris. It was the biggest news event of 1997, and Monica Lewinsky didn't notice it, so consumed was she by her relationship with Bill Clinton.

Lewinsky stayed at Young's house that night and left early the next morning for Washington. When she returned to work on Tuesday, she had a forty-seven-minute conversation with Marsha Scott, who told her the slot they had talked about in July wasn't going to work out. Lewinsky was devastated. The next day, September 4, she wrote Young a note, giving her an update and thanking her for her hospitality and her "good advice." It looked as if she wouldn't be getting back to the White House "any time soon," she explained.

"I think the end of this whole trauma is over," Lewinsky wrote that day. "I just wish my heart didn't have to be broken in all of this."

The real trauma, of course, was just beginning.

10

"There are lots of us busy elves working away in Santa's workshop."

During these weeks, unbeknownst to the rest of the world, the lawsuit known as *Jones* v. *Clinton* had once again come tantalizingly close to being resolved. Despite Bob Bennett's warnings, the Willey story had done little to slow the momentum for a settlement that had been quietly building. On the evening of August 5, lawyers for both sides met for six hours late into the night at a conference room in the Washington offices of Skadden, Arps. It went well. Mitch Ettinger and Cammarata peeled away to type some language. Davis and Bennett repaired to Bennett's office. "I'm tired of this case, Gil," Bennett told Davis. "I just want to get it over with." At four P.M. on August 15, Bennett and Ettinger messengered over to the Jones lawyers a two-page proposal entitled "Stipulation of Settlement."

Had reporters gotten wind of it at the time, they would have found the "stipulation" astonishing. It called for the two insurance companies that were footing the president's legal bills in the case—Chubb and State Farm—to pay Paula Jones $700,000 "in full satisfaction of all claims for damages." It further stated that the "parties agree that Paula Corbin Jones did not engage in any improper or sexual conduct on May 8, 1991, and that the allegations and the inferences about her published in January 1994 in the *American Spectator* are false and their adverse effects upon her character and reputation regrettable."

Bennett later adamantly denied that any such offer was formally on the table. But that was only partly true. It was always understood

178

among the lawyers that the White House never could be seen to publicly offer a deal only to have it rejected. (Privately, Ettinger told Cammarata that Bennett wanted to get a deal wrapped up before he left for a vacation in Australia the last week in August.) Still, Davis and Cammarata saw the proposal as a breakthrough. For the settlement of a sexual harassment lawsuit, $700,000 was an exceedingly generous payout. The statement addressed Jones's originally stated motivation for coming forward in 1994: to correct the misimpression that she was a loose woman who willingly complied with Bill Clinton's sexual demands. Davis and Cammarata strongly urged her to accept the proposal.

But there was a problem: Paula and Steve Jones didn't like it. Where was the apology? Where was the admission from Clinton? For Steve Jones, the case had long since turned into a personal vendetta. As he saw it, he and his family had been put through a living hell. His wife had been slimed on national television, made the butt of jokes by Jay Leno, ridiculed and lampooned—and all because of what "the pervert" had done to her. And now the guy was going to get off scot-free—no admission of wrongdoing, no punishment? Clinton wasn't even going to have to cough up a dime, Steve Jones complained; the insurance companies were going to cover everything. And there was another problem: Under Davis and Cammarata's proposal, Paula wasn't going to see that much anyway: the lawyers were going to take two-thirds of the payout in fees, plus a piece of any book or TV deals, until their full bill—nearly $800,000—was paid off.

Davis and Cammarata were exasperated. They had put three years into the case. They faced the real prospect of not only getting clobbered in court, but, like Paula, walking away with nothing. In a letter dated August 19, they poured it on strong: "There is a substantial possibility you may lose this case," they warned Paula. In the meantime, other possibilities for financial enrichment for Jones, and for them, would slip away. "You will lose all prospect of financial reward from the selling of your sealed affidavit," they wrote, referring to the document identifying Clinton's alleged "distinguishing characteristics."[1]

Such was the state of play when the lawyers congregated in Little Rock on August 22 for a conference before Judge Susan Webber

Wright, the first hearing on the case since the Supreme Court had ruled. Reporters and TV crews mobbed the courthouse; the session got blanket coverage on CNN and MSNBC. Judge Wright rejected Bennett's latest legal maneuver—an attempt to get the case tossed out on the ground that Jones's allegations didn't rise to the level of an actionable tort—and set a brisk schedule for discovery to be followed by a relatively early trial date of May 27, 1998. That seemed a huge victory for Jones and a nightmarish scenario for the White House.

But for the lawyers, the real action was in the details of Wright's ruling—and it was a disaster for everybody. While permitting the heart of the lawsuit to proceed, the judge had tossed out some of the lesser counts in Jones's claim. One alleged that the president had defamed Jones when White House aides depicted her as untruthful. It was hardly central to Jones's case, but it meant a lot to the lawyers. Because the Clintons hadn't taken out their State Farm policy until February 1992, well after the incident at the Excelsior, the defamation count was the only one keeping State Farm in the case. As soon as Wright ruled, Cammarata knew what it meant: State Farm was off the hook for any settlement money. Then, after the clerk passed out a copy of Wright's decision and the lawyers started poring over it, Cammarata and Ettinger exchanged worried glances. Wright had also tossed out Jones's claim alleging that Clinton had falsely imprisoned her in the hotel room that day. It was the technical count under which the other insurance company, Chubb, was primarily obligated to pay the president's legal costs—or the cost of any settlement. After the hearing, as the network correspondents rushed out of the courtroom to tell the world of the triumph for Jones, Cammarata slipped over to Ettinger's table.

"I think Chubb may be gone," Ettinger whispered.

"Oh my God," replied Cammarata. "Now what do we do?"

●　　●　　●

Wright's ruling made Davis and Cammarata even more frantic to get Jones's agreement quickly—before the insurance companies formally notified Bennett they were withdrawing their coverage of the president. But by now the Joneses had their backs up—and they were being egged on by a formidable new player, Susan Carpenter-McMillan.

A brash right-wing activist and TV commentator, Carpenter-McMillan, fifty-one, had recently become Paula Jones's new best friend. The two women had met over dinner three years earlier after Carpenter-McMillan volunteered to help out with publicity for the case. By the summer of 1997, they were virtually inseparable. Carpenter-McMillan took Paula on shopping trips, advising her on new outfits and hair-dos. They chatted three or four times a day, gossiping about the case and the various personalities showing up as talking heads on the tube. For Paula, isolated in her small Long Beach apartment, stuck at home with two small children, the blinds drawn to keep away the press, her new friend was a lifeline—and an entrée to a far more glamorous world. Susan was slender, perfectly manicured and fabulously wealthy (her husband was a successful malpractice lawyer). She drove a Mercedes and lived in a palatial French Provincial estate in San Marino. She showed champion bichon frise dogs. "She was all of the things that Paula dreamed of being," said Cindy Hays, a friend of Gil Davis's who ran the first Paula Jones Legal Fund.

She also drove Joe Cammarata crazy. From the moment Carpenter-McMillan started showing up on TV, describing herself as Jones's "spokeswoman" and then "adviser," Cammarata saw her as an irritant who was making a mess of his efforts to work out a settlement. (Her tendency to call the president "a little slimeball" during her many television appearances was especially unhelpful.) On the morning before the conference with Judge Wright in Little Rock, Cammarata had decided to draw his own line in the sand. As the Jones team assembled in a hotel room that morning, Cammarata took Steve Jones aside and gave him a firm order: Susan couldn't be in the car with Paula when she drove to the courthouse with her lawyers. She couldn't be anywhere in sight when they came out of the courthouse. Steve Jones then relayed this to Carpenter-McMillan, who seethed. That little control freak, she fumed. "Well," she told Steve Jones, "we'll work this out later." After that, she recalled, "I blew a gasket."

A week later, back in California, Carpenter-McMillan was exacting her revenge. She urged Paula and Steve to hold fast to their principles. Don't get pushed around by these lawyers, she told them. They're just looking for a cheap and easy way out.

During this time, Davis and Cammarata were constantly on the phone to Long Beach, practically begging Paula to reconsider the offer. They offered to cut their own fees—to one-third of the $700,000. When she still resisted, they played hardball. On August 29, they wrote her a second letter. If Paula didn't accept the offer by September 2, they would no longer be able to represent her—and she would be stuck with their full outstanding bill of $800,000.[2] Paula was devastated and sobbed uncontrollably. Steve was furious. Don't worry, kids, Carpenter-McMillan told them, I'll find you new lawyers. What she didn't tell them—at least at first—was that she had already started looking. Two weeks later, Davis and Cammarata, citing "fundamental differences" with their client, filed a motion with Wright to withdraw from the case.

●   ●   ●

In late August, I was asked to appear on CNBC to provide analysis on Judge Wright's ruling permitting the case to proceed. Like the rest of the press, I had no inkling of the melodrama being played out in Little Rock and California. But in the green room that afternoon, I ran into somebody who seemed to know a lot more than I did. Ann Coulter was an ardently right-wing lawyer and columnist for *Human Events* who had already carved out a niche among the all-news cable networks as a reliable purveyor of outrageously provocative views. She had a respectable legal résumé: she had clerked for a U.S. Court of Appeals judge, a Reagan-appointed conservative named Pasco Bowman (who authored the first appellate court opinion rejecting Clinton's claim of immunity in the Jones case) and later served on the staff of the Senate Judiciary Committee. But in Coulter's worldview, there were no nuances, no shades of gray. All was certainty. Clinton was a liar and a lecher, and that was that. We started to chat about the Jones case that evening, and Coulter kept dropping hints suggesting inside knowledge about Jones's legal strategy. I remarked on this. Oh yes, she said with a laugh. "There are lots of us busy elves working away in Santa's workshop."

Busy elves? I remembered hearing something about George Conway in New York. Now Coulter. Who else? And what were they doing?

The next day I looked up Conway's number at Wachtell, Lipton in New York and caught him off guard at his desk. How did you get my name? he answered, sounding startled.

Well, I just did. We started to talk.

• • •

onway and Coulter were fast friends who were close to obsessed with the Jones case. They were an odd duo. Coulter, the daughter of a wealthy corporate executive from Greenwich, Connecticut, was tall, blond, rail thin and very loud. Conway, the son of an electrical engineer, had grown up in a middle-class Boston suburb; he was short, pudgy, soft-spoken and somewhat shy. But they bonded over their common disdain for Clinton, and they loved nothing more than to gossip late into the night about the latest developments in the Jones lawsuit. They sent nonstop e-mails back and forth on the subject. They plotted strategy the Jones lawyers could use to expose the president. But by mid-September, they were worried. After the withdrawal of Davis and Cammarata, there were reports that Carpenter-McMillan's husband, Bill, a more reasonable figure than his volatile wife, was talking to Bennett about a possible settlement after all. "A deal!" Coulter shouted to Conway. "What a fucking disaster!" There would be no chance to disgrace Clinton. No chance to prove to the world what a lying, horny hick he was. "We were terrified that Jones would settle," Coulter later explained, offering an unusually candid and only half-joking description of her motives. "It was contrary to our purpose of bringing down the president."

So Coulter decided she would undertake a little black op to make sure that didn't happen. Through his contacts with Cammarata and Marcus, Conway had learned the details of Jones's secret "distinguishing characteristics" affidavit. Conway and Marcus had even scouted for possible medical experts who could testify at trial about the president's alleged condition, consulting at one point with a friend, Andrew Schlafly, son of conservative leader Phyllis Schlafly, general counsel to the Association of American Physicians and Surgeons. Now, faced with the dismal prospect of a settlement, Coulter had a brainstorm. She would leak a description of the "distinguishing characteristics" claim to the press. Once that became public, she reasoned, "it would humiliate the president." Then he couldn't possibly settle.

Ever since the claim was first filed in 1994, on the Internet, in the tabloid press, in conservative salons, there had been much speculation about what Jones was referring to. It was a mole. No, it was a scar.

No, the presidential penis was unusually small. Drudge reported it was an eagle tattoo. In mid-September, Coulter called Richard Johnson, editor of the *New York Post*'s gossipy Page Six. It was something else entirely, she told him—then proceeded to explain.

Johnson, ever hungry for an exclusive, bit. He made a few calls. He consulted a textbook. Within a few days, he had assembled an item reporting that the Jones team believed the president was suffering from a condition described in 1743 by a French scientist named François Gigot de la Peyronie. Now known as Peyronie's disease, it afflicted one out of every one hundred men between the ages of forty-five and sixty and was marked by curvature of the penis. In some cases, the discomfort was so great that intercourse was impossible.

As a piece of medical detective work, the Peyronie's disease diagnosis was little more than farfetched theorizing. It was based entirely on Jones's fleeting glance of an organ the sight of which, her lawsuit claimed, had repulsed and humiliated her. How reliable could that be? Still, based on Jones's observation that Clinton's member was "crooked," Davis and Cammarata had concluded that the Peyronie's diagnosis was worth a shot. Clinton's refusal to release his medical records during the 1996 presidential campaign gave them some encouragement. It was in hope of bolstering this hypothesis that— with Conway and Coulter's help—Cammarata had tried to recruit Dr. Tom Lue, a prominent urologist at the University of California in San Francisco, as an expert witness for Jones. The doctor had turned Cammarata down.

Johnson found it all hilarious and wrote it up, thinking he had a juicy item. "I was very proud of the story," he said. But his editors balked—and ultimately killed the item. Too tasteless, they said. Johnson argued: "Look, if we don't do the story, somebody else will." That was fine, they replied. Let somebody else break this one. Johnson, sheepishly, called Coulter. "I'm sorry, I did my best," he told her. Coulter was outraged. A few days later, the item was leaked to Don Imus, the morning radio talk host. And shortly after that, it showed up in the *Washington Times,* stripped across the front page.

About a week before the *Times* story, I was offered the same information. I listened, alternately fascinated to learn such an obscure piece of medical arcana and repelled by the use to which it was being put. It took me about two seconds to conclude this was one part of the Paula Jones case I wanted no part of.

• • •

The resort to lowball tactics was hardly the monopoly of Clinton's adversaries. After the Supreme Court ruling, Bob Bennett—under pressure from feminist groups—had publicly foresworn any attempt to delve into Paula Jones's sexual history. "We have absolutely no intention of dragging out Paula Jones's prior sex life or invading her privacy," the president's lawyer said on ABC's *Nightline*. Not only would his wife and three daughters "kick me out of the house," he added, but he had a client "who has done more for women than any president in the history of this country," and "he wouldn't permit me."

But in mid-September, when Jones was without lawyers and a judicial gag order cloaked all discovery efforts from the prying eyes of the press, Bennett aggressively moved to do in private precisely what he had promised in public he would never do. Culling the files compiled over four years, he arranged for Bill Bristow, Danny Ferguson's lawyer, to subpoena a half dozen young men in Arkansas who he believed could testify about the promiscuous past of Paula Jones. (Bristow provided Bennett with a thin cover. As would later be demonstrated in court papers, Bennett and his legal team played the primary role in locating and developing the witnesses for this part of the case.) The centerpiece of Bennett's efforts revolved around one witness in particular: Dennis Kirkland, who was friends with Mark Brown, Jones's disaffected brother-in-law. Kirkland had a somewhat questionable background. A convicted forger, he also had a history of drug abuse. Still, he served Bennett's interests well. Kirkland had told the president's lawyers about attending a high school graduation party in 1987 and meeting Paula Corbin, then a teenager. According to Kirkland, he and Paula went outside to a car, where she performed oral sex on him. Kirkland later claimed that four of his friends got the same treatment from Paula that night.

For months, the president's allies spread Kirkland's claims of serial fellatio throughout Washington. Virtually every reporter who cov-

ered the case had at some point heard hints about the alleged incident. We've got an affidavit proving that Jones gave "five blow jobs"
in the backseat of a pickup truck, Bennett told three Washington
journalists in January 1997. Bennett would usually add that he
would probably never use such information—somehow overlooking
the fact that he just had. And in August, he threatened Davis and
Cammarata during settlement talks: If the case didn't settle, he told
the Jones lawyers, their client had much to lose. According to Cammarata, Bennett then described how there would be testimony about
"five simultaneous blow jobs—one after the other."

But when Bennett dropped these hints and threats, there was
much he failed to disclose. Kirkland's name, for instance, and his
somewhat checkered background. That made it impossible for the
press to verify the story. Bennett also failed to mention the fact that
none of the four other alleged participants in the group fellatio said
they had been part of the incident Dennis Kirkland described.[3]

● ● ●

On September 10, John Whitehead was at his home outside Charlottesville, Virginia, when he spotted a *Washington Post* article
reporting that Davis and Cammarata had quit the case. He tore out
the article and took it to the office. Whitehead was, by his own
description, a former cocaine-snorting hippie who found Jesus Christ.
He now ran an unorthodox legal foundation called the Rutherford
Institute. Named after Samuel Rutherford, an obscure eighteenth-
century Scottish philosopher who proclaimed the primacy of God's
law over man's, Whitehead's institute financed a variety of conservative, religious-oriented litigation. A typical Rutherford case was a
lawsuit it filed defending the right of college football players to kneel
in prayer in the end zone. Whitehead had been hoping for some time
to expand a bit, and he thought Paula Jones's lawsuit might provide a
good opportunity. Exactly why would become a matter of dispute.
Whitehead later told reporters that as he saw it, Jones and her sexual
harassment claims amounted to a "human rights issue." Cynics
argued that until there was an opportunity to bash Bill Clinton, neither Whitehead nor his institute had ever shown an interest in this
particular subcategory of the rights of humanity.

Whitehead had in mind just the lawyer to handle the matter. Donovan Campbell Jr. was a member of Rutherford's board of directors as well as one of the institute's premier litigators. Whitehead liked to compare him to his Jack Russell terriers, which would tear through his drainpipes and much of his backyard in search of their quarry. Campbell had made a name for himself in a number of high-profile cases, including a tenacious and ultimately successful defense of Texas's anti-sodomy law. An intense workaholic whose scowling exterior masked a caustic sense of humor, Campbell was also a man of deep religious convictions. He believed homosexuality a sin. He believed the gay rights movement threatened to corrupt the American family. He felt just as strongly about adultery. "The last I checked," he liked to say, "the Seventh Commandment is still in the Bible." Among the Rutherford cases of which Campbell was most proud was his defense of a church sued for defamation after its pastor denounced a member of the congregation as an adulteress. Campbell depicted the plaintiff as a promiscuous woman whose conduct was so flagrant, her character could not possibly have been besmirched.

In the spring of 1992, Campbell had bolted from the prominent Dallas law firm of Locke, Purnell in part because of his disgust with the conduct of some of his senior partners. A sexual harassment lawsuit had been filed against the firm by a woman associate, and the discovery process had produced allegations of other sexual liaisons at the firm. Campbell's newly formed firm, which included two other breakaways from Locke, Purnell, was called Rader, Campbell, Fisher & Pyke. A relatively small commercial litigation boutique, Rader, Campbell reflected the "Christian principles" of its members, Campbell's partner David Pyke later explained.

To outsiders, it might seem odd how easily Christian principles and professional ambition can be reconciled. As soon as Campbell got the call from Whitehead that day in mid-September asking if he was interested in representing Paula Jones, he wandered into the office of another partner, a hungry young lawyer from Little Rock named Wes Holmes, and told him about it. Neither Campbell nor Holmes was under any illusions about the Jones case. It would involve the firm in an ugly lawsuit that would be fought out in large part over the seamy details of the sexual histories of the principals. It would also mean, almost certainly, taking a financial bath and putting much of the rest of the firm's practice on hold. Nonetheless, Holmes recalled, he could barely control his excitement. "We have got to take that case," he told Campbell. "There's just no question about it." This was a chance to get the firm on the map. A chance for the partners to make a name for themselves. A chance to take the first-ever civil deposition of a sitting president of the United States. It was historic, Holmes thought.

A few days later, Campbell, Holmes and another partner, a mild-mannered, born-again Christian named Jim Fisher, flew out to California to meet Paula. They spent hours questioning her about her story and immersing themselves in the details of everything that had transpired. Back at the hotel room, the three of them prayed together for spiritual guidance. When they were through, they knew what they were going to do. Paula had new lawyers.

Within days, the Christian litigators of Rader, Campbell, Fisher & Pyke were preparing for all-out, brass knuckles litigation against the formidable legal team of the president of the United States. It looked daunting. But then again, they had no idea how much help they were about to get.

11

"My tabloid heart beats loud."

When the phone rang at 10:23 P.M., Linda Tripp was waiting for it. It was the call she had asked her friend Tony Snow to arrange. "Hi, dear. How are you?" asked a beguiling Lucianne Goldberg. Thanks for calling, said Tripp. She felt a bit awkward, Tripp explained. Their last conversation had ended so unpleasantly. Forget it, said Goldberg. She was not one to hold a grudge—not when there was hot new material about Bill Clinton on hand, which Snow had assured her there was.

Tripp got quickly to the point. "I wanted to chat with you about something that's—completely ridiculous," she said, sounding quite nervous. There was a young woman, a former intern, twenty-three years old. Tripp had become her confidante, and it appeared that she was a "very close girlfriend of the big creep."

Goldberg fixated on one question right away. Where does this happen? In the office, Tripp answered, meaning the White House. "Yikes!" exclaimed Goldberg.

"This is so explosive," said Tripp. "It makes the other little thing, which was nothing, you know, pale."

For eighteen minutes, the two women talked—and quickly started gaming Tripp's options. They talked about how best to expose the president and worked out a tentative strategy: to feed a limited amount of the story to me at *Newsweek* in order to "titillate the public." Then Goldberg would hustle Tripp to a book publisher so she could cash in with a more complete version. They even talked about

189

using the Paula Jones sexual harassment lawsuit to force the story out. It was September 18, 1997, and for all intents and purposes, the plot that would threaten Bill Clinton's presidency was hatched that night.

As Linda Tripp later told it, her decision to reach out to Lucianne Goldberg was the result of enormous pressures and very real fears. Having been thrust into the middle of *Newsweek*'s Kathleen Willey story, then denounced by the president's lawyers, Tripp felt her career in government was threatened. It was inevitable, she insisted, that she would be subpoenaed to testify in the Paula Jones case. Once that happened, she would be forced to choose between lying under oath or telling the truth about Clinton's conduct with Kathleen Willey—facing brutal new attacks from the president's lawyers and spin doctors. "I'm an average American who found herself in a situation not of her own making," Tripp said after her final grand jury appearance on July 29, 1998. She turned to Lucianne Goldberg, she told the FBI, for "advice and protection."

What Tripp didn't know when she offered these explanations was that her initial conversations with Lucianne Goldberg had been secretly taped—by Goldberg. It is one of the supreme ironies of the entire Clinton-Lewinsky drama. Those tapes were not included during independent counsel Kenneth Starr's initial release of evidence in September 1997, and they received scant public attention when congressional investigators released them three months later. For Tripp, that was a good thing. The tapes show precisely how these two women created and then sought to manipulate the very situation Tripp claimed was "not of her own making." They also reveal a far more complicated and somewhat less flattering portrait of Tripp's motives. Tripp was moved, it appears, not so much by fear and a desire to protect herself as by anger, even disgust, at Bill Clinton. As a parent of college-age children, she thought the president's behavior with her young friend was "appalling," and she wanted it exposed to the world. "It's so sickening," she told Goldberg during the first few minutes of their conversation. "He has got to get his comeuppance," she added later.

But coexisting with Tripp-the-avenger was Tripp-the-aspiring-author. Spurred by dreams of personal enrichment, Tripp and Goldberg immediately plotted ways to use the new material about the intern to revive the book deal that, little more than a year earlier, had imploded. Indeed, some of the women's actions over the next few months could be construed as part of a strategy designed, at least in part, to maximize Tripp's marketability.

That is not to dispute that Tripp was at times fearful. Tending to view the world through a melodramatic lens, she was given to flights of paranoia. At one point, in another conversation secretly taped by Goldberg, Tripp even speculated that she might be the target of a murder plot by the president's friends—a fear Goldberg quickly tried to quell. But when it all began, Tripp's worry about possibly losing her political job at the Pentagon appears to have been a secondary concern. In fact, the September 18 tape suggests she was already planning to leave that job; by spring, she hoped to be "out of here." In any case, she told Goldberg that night, "If I lose my job, I lose my job."

Of course, if they went forward with their plan, there was something else she should be ready to lose, Goldberg warned: "You have to be ready to lose her [the young woman] as a friend."

"Oh," Tripp replied, "I have already made that decision."

•   •   •

The fact that Tripp turned to Lucianne Goldberg was always a tip-off that her motives were not entirely public-spirited. A tall, husky-voiced, fun-loving blonde, Goldberg had spent a lifetime trafficking in political gossip—spreading it, promoting it, profiting from it and on more than a few occasions landing smack in the middle of it. A onetime researcher and press agent for the Democratic National Committee and—briefly—the Kennedy White House, Goldberg had drifted over to the Republican camp by the early 1970s—in part through an association with a friend of her second husband's. The friend was Victor Lasky, a strident right-wing columnist and author of several books harshly attacking the Kennedys. It was Lasky who introduced Goldberg to Murray Chotiner, a longtime political operative for Richard Nixon. This led to Goldberg's first foray into political espionage. Armed with a fake press pass, Goldberg was deployed in 1972 as a $1,000-a-week Nixon spy on George

McGovern's campaign plane. Every night, after fraternizing with the rest of the press corps, Goldberg covertly dictated memos to Chotiner's secretary in Washington. The intelligence in Goldberg's memos was fairly tepid: advance copies of McGovern press releases and last-minute changes in the campaign schedule. But Goldberg spruced them up with dirty jokes she had picked up on the plane and with salacious tidbits about drug use and sexual dalliances among esteemed members of the Fourth Estate. Goldberg says she was told that every night her memos were driven over to the White House, where they were delivered straight to the "insomniac" in the Oval Office. "What Nixon really wanted to hear," said Goldberg, "was the dirty jokes."

Goldberg's ability to entertain—to enliven the humdrum of politics, government and book publishing—served her well over the years in a colorful and multifaceted career. She was an author who penned steamy novels about sexual high jinks involving politicians, journalists and the literary set (among her titles: *Madame Cleo's Girls* and an antifeminist tract, *Purr, Baby, Purr*). She was a literary agent who carved out a niche as a specialist in conservative books, preferably with a sensationalistic bent. About the same time that Goldberg first talked to Linda Tripp about an exposé of the Clinton White House, for example, she was also shopping around a proposal by Dallas lawyer Dolly Kyle Browning, who had written a fictional account of a longtime romance with a southern governor who bore a striking resemblance to Bill Clinton. During repeated talks, Browning told Goldberg that her novel was essentially true—that she and Clinton had indeed had a love affair that stretched back to the 1960s, when they were in high school together in Hot Springs, Arkansas. (Although the president's lawyers later attacked her credibility, suggesting that she was unstable, Browning had kept extensive correspondence from Clinton that, while not conclusive, gave her claims more than passing plausibility.)

Goldberg tried to persuade Browning to make her book nonfiction, saying that was the only way it would sell. Browning refused, but Goldberg nonetheless leaked to *Esquire* magazine an item about her alleged affair with Clinton. Placing such items was part of Goldberg's modus operandi; it helped to pique interest in her properties. It was also one of her greatest pleasures. "I love dish! I live for dish!"

she liked to tell reporters. Sometimes, she even got paid for it. For some time, Goldberg had been receiving a monthly stipend from Rupert Murdoch's News Corporation, owner of the *New York Post*. Ostensibly, the retainer was for scouting out potential book excerpts for the *Post*'s weekend supplement, a job that took her, she would say, all of about five minutes. In reality, it was for Goldberg's role as tipster—steering delicious tidbits about celebrities and politicians to Richard Johnson and the rest of the *Post*'s gossip mavens.

Thus, Goldberg had no hesitation about talking again to Linda Tripp when Tony Snow called late that August on Tripp's behalf. Snow had explained that Linda Tripp had some interesting new information, although he wasn't quite sure what it was. "I knew whatever it was," Goldberg later said, "it had to be anti-Clinton and pretty interesting."

*　　*　　*

From the very start of the Tripp-Goldberg conspiracy, Tripp's moralistic and judgmental side was on display. Her young friend—"who shall remain nameless for the time being"—had been promised a job back in the White House after the election, but Clinton was stalling. It was deeply upsetting to her friend, who was "very emotionally attached" and had a "deep crush."

"I mean, it just feels to me as though, enough already," Tripp said. "Personally, my opinion is it's time for her . . . She has got to move on. She's right now going through emotional hell. . . . I would very much like to see her leave and just get on with her life."

Goldberg cut straight to the main issue: "Well, have you talked to her about going public with this?"

"She refuses," said Tripp.

"Then what can you do with it?"

Tripp thought that with all the records she had kept—the dates and the times they had met, the gifts they had swapped—there might be enough to get the story out.

"Yeah, but you realize the press will destroy her," said Goldberg. The White House will destroy her too. "I mean, I love the idea, I would run with it in a second, but do you want to be the instrument of this kid really, um—"

Tripp interrupted. You need some history, she told Goldberg. The young woman comes from a "very privileged" upbringing in Beverly Hills. "She's not a naïf," Tripp said. "I mean, she's definitely sophisticated. . . . She was not a victim. When this began, she was every bit a player."

Tripp then tried again to impress Goldberg with how much "documentation" there was—even tapes of Clinton on her answering machine.

"She tapes him?" asked Goldberg, getting a bit excited.

"No," explained Tripp. "She has taped phone messages."

Goldberg was now a bit dubious. "The only way this will work, Linda, is if she is fully willing to go public," she said. "Because for you to take on the responsibility of going public with this is going to beg the question in the big world of, who is this woman?" The news media would look into Tripp's history and see that she kept popping up in one scandal after another. "They just hit the Nexis button and bang, bingo, bango . . . you would look like some kind of, uh, you know, nut case."

But Tripp was not so sure. She had been in a very unusual situation. And another thing: the Kathleen Willey matter. That hadn't begun to surface in the Paula Jones case yet. "If the depositions go forward, then it will all, in its gory detail, come tumbling out."

It was then that Goldberg had an idea. Just a thought. "Is there any way to have, uh, this Miss X that we're talking about here, have her be, um, shall we say, reached by the Paula Jones people?"

Tripp brushed Goldberg aside. "Oh, absolutely no way," she said. Tripp couldn't disclose the woman's name to anybody.

"Listen, Mike Isikoff has been on my tail about this one for months."

"He knows about it?" asked Goldberg.

"He knows it exists." But Tripp wouldn't reveal the name to Isikoff, either. Not yet, anyway. "If she ever thought . . . I mean . . . I can't even tell you."

Still, an idea had been planted.

Tripp was torn. "I respect her feelings [about protecting Clinton], but on the other hand . . . He plays to this, to the world audience as being a protector of women's rights . . ."

"Oh, I know," interjected Goldberg sympathetically.

". . . of being this sterling example of family values. And other than the fact that he's a philanderer, but I mean beyond that, he's got a daughter five years younger than that."

"Yeah."

"I have a daughter five years younger than that. I have a son her age."

"Right."

"I find it appalling, and I think parents would find it appalling."

So Goldberg wanted to know: "How do you see using this information?" Goldberg mentioned a book. Tripp replied that she actually had been working on an update of the book proposal, "a whole different spin" that played up even more her exposure to scandals in the Clinton White House. Goldberg wondered if Tripp had considered "going to Isikoff and going off the record with him."

"Oh, I could do that in a minute, but then he'd write the book. Or he'd write the whole thing."[1]

Goldberg had a solution. "Well then, we make a deal with Isikoff that here's the information that we'll give you. Here is just enough documentation for you to do the story. But the rest of it belongs to Linda because she's doing a book. He would have to honor that if he wanted the story."

"Yeah, I would think so. Believe it or not, he honored quite a bit of it in his piece [on Kathleen Willey]."

"The trick would be to get it out there, just enough of it to titillate the public."

There was more talk that night. Tripp provided additional details about the gifts the president had bought her friend and where they had been purchased (from the Black Dog at Martha's Vineyard). They talked about Tripp's search for another job. And they talked again about the deal they thought they could strike with me, a deal that, as Goldberg explained it, "protects you totally, that gets the surface of this out, and then you stand back to fill in the pieces and I get you a publisher."

Tripp agreed that this would be a good approach.

"I'm very interested in this, needless to say," said Goldberg.

"Well, I'm glad," said Tripp.

"My tabloid heart beats loud," said Goldberg.

Tripp laughed.

There would be many twists in the road. But the essential course of action had been set.

•   •   •

The highest immediate priority was documentation. Goldberg was experienced enough to know that when it came to sexual affairs involving a president, nothing would fly without solid proof. Tripp's claims to have written down what Lewinsky had told her about her many liaisons and conversations with Clinton were helpful, but hardly enough to pass the bar in the New York publishing industry— much less with *Newsweek.* About a week after their first call, the two women spoke again, and Goldberg urged Tripp to go further. "You need evidence, you need proof," Goldberg told her. "You need tapes."

Unlike the conversation on September 18, this second phone call between Tripp and Goldberg was not recorded, so Tripp's precise response is lost to history. Both women later insisted that Tripp initially balked. The notion of taping the incessant phone calls from her friend made Tripp nervous, according to Goldberg. Tripp thought it was "unfriendly," she said. To which Goldberg claimed to have responded: "Well, bubeleh, if you're going to go after the big kahuna, you better kill him."[2]

Goldberg and Tripp had a third conversation that month, on September 29, and Goldberg taped this one. Early on, there was a brief discussion of whether the proposed secret taping by Tripp of the president's friend (without her consent) would be legal. In context, it was almost an afterthought. It arose in the midst of talk about another option the two women had apparently considered: to bypass me entirely and give the story directly to the supermarket tabloids, which—unlike *Newsweek*—would pay for it.

"The tabloid stuff—I thought to myself you're right, there is a definite advantage to going that way," said Tripp. "It gets it out, it gets it out quick."

"Yeah, but the problem with that is that you've got to really rat in that you've got a tape," said Goldberg. She remembered something else. "Oh, and I checked that out," she said. "You can—

one-party taping is fine. You checked it out, too, but it's—there's no problem with that."

"I kept thinking about this," Tripp replied, not really responding to the point. "If I go buy this tape, that means that I'm committed to going with the tabloids. . . . I literally talk to this girl ten times a day."

Then Goldberg's call waiting clicked. When she returned, the conversation moved on to other subjects.

As Tripp later learned, much to her chagrin, Goldberg was wrong. Although "one-party taping" is legal under federal law, in the District of Columbia and in most states, Maryland—where Tripp lived—is one of nine states that prohibit taping of any telephone conversation without the consent of all parties. Whom Goldberg checked with—if anybody—to give Tripp this incorrect advice was never clear. Goldberg at various times has suggested it was either a lawyer friend whose name she couldn't remember or a writer, whose name she won't reveal, who looked it up on the Internet.

One intriguing subject that Tripp and Goldberg spent more time discussing that night involved Tripp's interactions with Norma Asness, an extremely wealthy socialite with homes in Georgetown, New York City and Greenwich, Connecticut. Asness was the widow of a promi-nent corporate executive who had headed a large pharmaceutical firm, Becton-Dickinson. An avid Democrat and campaign contributor, she was a friend of Hillary Clinton, who had recently asked Asness to accompany her on a trip to Africa. Tripp had first met Asness in December 1993, when, along with the rest of the White House coun-sel's staff, she was invited to a Chanukah party at Asness's home in Georgetown. Tripp had thought then that Asness seemed friendly. And Asness later showed up on one of the civilian tours of military bases Tripp arranged as part of her job at the Pentagon.

That very week, for reasons that remained a mystery but weighed heavily on Tripp's mind for many months to come, Asness had gotten back in touch with Tripp. She had invited Tripp up to Greenwich to spend Halloween weekend and attend a dinner party.

This invitation was, as Tripp said, "out of the blue"—and puz-zling. Why would a rich friend of Hillary Clinton's suddenly invite Linda Tripp to a weekend in Connecticut? Could it have anything to do with Tripp's publicly surfacing in the Kathleen Willey story? And, if so, what did Asness have in mind? Tripp and Goldberg explored the conspiratorial possibilities.

"You're being set up," Goldberg concluded.

"I just think the timing is too bizarre for words," said Tripp. "You don't think they're going to poison me, do you?"

"Uh, no," said Goldberg. "They're going to co-opt you, they're going to love-bomb you, show you this is the way you could be living . . . if you stay loyal. See they don't, they don't know where your buttons are. . . . They think this is an intoxicating thing. . . . So they're misreading you totally. They have such a tin ear about all this stuff."

"All right. Well, then I won't worry about it. I just thought, Oh good, so they're going to kill me when I'm there or something. I mean, I'm really getting paranoid."

"No, they're not going to kill you," Goldberg reassured her again. "But they're going to try to turn your head around, and they've gotten some kind of whiff of this. . . . This girl, as crazy in love as she is, um, has pillow-talked and probably dropped your name."[3]

The conversation then returned to the latest disclosures from Tripp's young friend. Tripp had just learned much more about the events of July involving the Kathleen Willey story—how her friend had been called to meet Clinton in the White House, how their conversation was interrupted by a conference call with Bob Bennett, the president's lawyer, and how after Clinton was finished talking to Bennett, he told her to have Tripp call Bruce Lindsey. And when the story finally broke and the White House learned what Tripp had told me, confirming that Willey had indeed had a sexual encounter with the president, "they went bullshit over there. I'm the enemy, I'm this, I'm that . . . ," Tripp told Goldberg.

The two women agreed the situation was serious enough to return to the original game plan and set up a meeting with me. "Tell him the three of us need to talk and try to solve this thing," said Goldberg.

"Okay. Yeah, I agree," Tripp said. "I'll call him first. . . ."

"Because this is gonna just twist you in knots for, forever."

"Well, it does twist me in knots. And every day that I have to listen to her I keep thinking the faster it should be exposed. . . . He is such a pig."

"Now what is he gonna do with—"

"Mr. Women's Rights. Mr. Women's Rights."

•   •   •

Her post–Labor Day note to Dale Young notwithstanding, Monica Lewinsky still had not accepted the idea that her relationship with Bill Clinton was finished—or that she would never make it back to work in the White House. On September 30, she sent Clinton a letter in the form of a mock memo ("Memorandum for: Handsome; Subject: The New Deal"), asking if she could see him that evening. "According to my calendar, we haven't spent any time together on the phone or in person for the past six weeks," she wrote. Lewinsky ended the memo with an allusion to an earlier presidential mistress: "Oh, and remember, FDR would never have turned down a visit from Lucy Mercer!"

She didn't get her visit. But that night, very late, Clinton called. They talked about Lewinsky's frustrations about not being able to return to the White House. Lewinsky wasn't sure, but she thought Clinton might have mentioned something that night about how he would talk to Erskine Bowles, the White House chief of staff, about the matter. Bowles later testified that Clinton did talk to him about Lewinsky, and he assigned the matter of finding a position to John Podesta, the deputy chief of staff.

According to Lewinsky's later account, their conversation that night also "possibly" included phone sex.

•   •   •

That week, Tripp stopped off at a Radio Shack near her home in Columbia and paid $100 for a voice-activated tape recorder. She taped her first conversation with Monica Lewinsky on the evening of October 3. It was a long, rambling discussion that touched on many subjects. Lewinsky was incensed because one of her supervisors, Cliff Bernath, had complained she was spending too much time making personal phone calls. Tripp and Lewinsky talked about Lewinsky's need for another job at the White House and her need (according to Tripp) for psychological counseling. Soon enough, the discussion segued into an attempt by the twenty-three-year-old Lewinsky to count the number of sexual partners she had had in her life. Lewinsky went down the list in her head—referring to a man named "Andy" and "the health-nut boy." She made it up to eight.

Tripp, undoubtedly keenly conscious of the running tape recorder, suggested she count the person she and Lewinsky frequently referred to as "the big creep."

"Not at all," replied Lewinsky indignantly. "I never even came close to sleeping with him."

"Why, because you were standing up?"

"We didn't have sex, Linda. Not—we didn't have sex."

"Well, what do you call it?"

"We fooled around. Not sex—having sex is having intercourse."

"Oh. You've been around him too long."

On the evening of October 5, Tripp taped again, this time capturing Lewinsky as she talked about phone calls she used to receive from "the big creep" from the road, a pair of sunglasses she had gotten him as a gift (a "real steal," she said, for $135, purchased to substitute for the "real dorky" pair he already had) and whether he was in fact reading a novel she had gotten him, entitled *Vox*. At one point, annoyed that "he didn't even notice" when she wore a hat pin he had given her, Lewinsky engaged in some idle and fanciful speculation.

"I've just decided that—I think he's on drugs," she said.

"That's not so farfetched, you know," replied Tripp, who then—unsuccessfully—tried to draw her friend out on the subject.

"I mean, nice people are on drugs," said Tripp. "You know how he sometimes zones out."

"Yeah."

"It's crossed my mind," said Tripp.

"Ohhh."

Tripp believed she was starting to get somewhere. But not enough, not on what really mattered. The next morning, Tripp took off from work and taped a third conversation. It would turn out to be quite important. Tripp told Lewinsky, who was at her office at the Pentagon, that she had just spoken to a friend named Kate who worked at the National Security Council at the White House. Lewinsky needed to hear what Kate had picked up about Lewinsky's prospects about getting a job at the White House, Tripp said. Lewinsky could forget it: it wasn't going to happen. "She said it doesn't matter whether your connections are, you know, huge. . . . She has heard you will not be placed over there," Tripp told Lewinsky. Tripp insisted that she told Kate "I don't believe that," but her friend was adamant: "'I promise you that if they wanted to have her [Lewinsky] placed, they would have done it by now. And the last thing on earth that they want is her in this White House."

Tripp said she felt awkward about pushing Kate further on the matter but felt Lewinsky had to know.

What happened next was key. Lewinsky was at first disbelieving. This must be something being spread by Debbie Schiff, the Oval Office secretary who she was convinced was a rival for the president's romantic affections. No, Tripp said, she pressed Kate a bit on this point, and she indicated it was coming from another source who had no connections to Schiff.

Lewinsky was now furious—and stunned. This seemed further confirmation that she was being toyed with. "This is just—I'm going to vomit," Lewinsky said.

"No, Monica, this is what we need—we needed to know this."

"No, you know what?" replied Lewinsky. "I'm going to call Betty and tell her to go fuck herself. This is what I'm going to do. . . . I don't care anymore. Because, you know what? Anyway, I stop and it's like wake up. This thing is over. It's over. It was over a long time ago."

Lewinsky was so upset that, she told Tripp, she was going to go home from work and take off the rest of the day.

Tripp tried to calm Lewinsky. She then remembered something else that she claimed Kate had told her. "Okay, she also said that you might want to consider getting a job through them elsewhere."

"Oh well."

"So let's not burn any bridges. . . . So what are you going to do?"

"I don't know. I need to go home."

It was a critical moment—a much overlooked turning point in the Clinton-Lewinsky saga. By finally persuading her that her White House job hopes were fruitless, Tripp prompted Lewinsky to adopt the alternative course "Kate" allegedly had suggested: to demand that President Clinton find her employment outside the White House. Lewinsky herself later described the news from "Kate" as "the straw that broke the camel's back." As it turns out, however, Tripp may well have been making up much, if not all, of her conversation with "Kate."

After the scandal broke, FBI agents tracked down the woman Tripp had described to Lewinsky only as "Kate of the NSC." She was Kate Friedrich, a special assistant in the office of National Security Adviser Sandy Berger. Friedrich, who started at the Bush White House in July 1992, acknowledged being friendly with Tripp and hearing her talk in the summer of 1997 about a young friend of hers who had had a sexual relationship with the president. But Friedrich said she never heard the name Monica Lewinsky until January 1998—more than three months after the alleged conversation Tripp described to Lewinsky on October 6. "Friedrich never heard about Lewinsky wanting to get a job in the White House," the FBI agents wrote in a July 20, 1998, report of their interview with Friedrich. "Friedrich never heard Lewinsky's name mentioned at the NSC and, therefore, never mentioned anything about that to Tripp."[4]

A few minutes after hanging up the phone with Monica Lewinsky on the morning of October 6, Tripp took another call, this one from Lucianne Goldberg. "Things are hitting the fan with her," Tripp told Goldberg.

Tripp then explained how Lewinsky had told her she thought Clinton was "on drugs."

"Wow," Goldberg replied. "On tape—you got it on tape?"

"Yep."

"Good for you. . . . Well, I tell you. That justifies everything. That son of a bitch."

Then Tripp told her how her young friend was in a panic over the news she had supposedly just relayed from Kate. Her friend had just left work and was "thinking of calling Betty and telling them all to [blank][5] off," Tripp said.

But Tripp was careful not to oversell. As it pertains to the core sexual relationship, there were gaps. "What I have on tape is very little," she told Goldberg, just references by Lewinsky to "dates" and phone calls with the occupant of the Oval Office. Goldberg sought to reassure her. "Well, that's enough. All you need is a snippet to—"

"Oh, I got snippets."

"Yeah."

"I'll just bring them. All right. So we are good for tonight?"

"Yeah, sure," said Goldberg.

Tripp would bring along the two tapes she had, she said. But she was still hoping she might get better material later in the day, especially given Lewinsky's highly charged emotional state about the news from Kate. "If she's flipping out," Tripp said, "I want to get that on tape."

•   •   •

What Goldberg and Tripp were "good for" that night was a rendezvous they had arranged at the Adams Morgan apartment of Goldberg's son, Jonah. Lucianne Goldberg had flown into town especially for the occasion. It was the next step in their plot—the meeting in which they were going to take their story to me.

I had gotten my invitation late the previous week. Tripp had left a message on my voice mail. I called back, identified myself to the secretary by my designated code name, "Harvey," and was put through. Tripp told me for the first time she had a friend in New York, an "adviser," to whom she had confided the information about her young friend. They were hoping to get together late Monday evening to talk about it. Was I available? Sure, I said. On Monday morning, Goldberg called, introduced herself and gave me the directions to Jonah's apartment. They wanted to meet about six P.M.

What exactly I was being invited for was hardly clear to me. The two women told me nothing about the nature of the conversations they had been having or the plans they were making "to titillate the public" by feeding bits and pieces of the story to me. They told me nothing about any book project, although I'm not sure at that point how much it would have mattered.[6] I was willing to listen to anything they had to say—if for no other reason than that I was still interested in learning the name of Tripp's friend, the alleged paramour of the president. If Tripp was now willing to be more forthcoming, and give me a way to check out her story, I wanted to hear it.

As it turned out, I was a bit pressed for time. I had been invited to appear on a CNBC talk show, *Hardball*. The subject was the latest on the campaign finance investigation—an issue that was much more on my mind at that moment. Still, by the time I arrived at Jonah Goldberg's walk-up condo, I had about an hour to spend with the two women and figured that would be more than enough to hear them out. Lucianne Goldberg graciously introduced herself and then her son, Jonah, a polite, quiet young man who said he worked for a video production company. He then stood off to the side. His presence unnerved me a bit. Both Goldbergs reassured me that I had nothing to worry about. Jonah wouldn't be sharing with anyone else what we were about to discuss.

Then, as we sat around a coffee table in Jonah's living room and I drank a beer, Tripp explained to me for the first time that she had been making secret tapes of her friend who was having the sexual relationship with the president. That's interesting, I said, thinking that this was getting a little weird. I noticed there was a bowl of pistachio nuts on the table. Goldberg had gotten them that morning from Zabar's, the posh deli on Manhattan's Upper West Side, for $13 a bag. It was late in the day, and I was hungry. I got distracted. A mildly annoyed Goldberg later remembered my helping myself—generously and repeatedly—to the pistachio nuts.

Tripp told me she was willing to play part of one of her tapes. There were no bombshells, but I would get a sense of what she was talking about. I could hear her voice.

I started to feel uncomfortable.

Wait a second, I said. I need a little more information here first. For me to do anything, I need this woman's name. You haven't even told me who she is. What good is it going to do to hear a voice if I don't know whose it is?

Tripp hesitated. She looked at Goldberg, who seemed to nod.

"Okay," said Tripp. "Her name is Monica Lewinsky."

The logjam had broken. I stopped eating the nuts and started taking notes. Tell me more about her, I said. For the first time in months—since I had been to her house back in April, in fact—Tripp proceeded to open up further. She gave me new details—when and where Lewinsky had worked at the White House and how she had been moved to a job in the Pentagon as a confidential assistant to the assistant secretary for public affairs, Ken Bacon. Tripp told me Lewinsky's mother's name, Marcia Lewis, and that her father was a doctor in Beverly Hills. She told me she had an aunt named Debra Finerman who was affiliated with a new magazine called *Capital Style.* She told me the name of the retired insurance executive and campaign contributor—Walter Kaye—who had gotten Lewinsky her White House job.

Kaye interested me. This is the kind of thing I'm talking about, I said.

Tripp told me that President Clinton had promised to find Lewinsky a job back in the White House and that her résumé had just been sent to Deputy Chief of Staff John Podesta.

What would happen if I called Podesta about this? I asked.

You can't! Tripp protested. That would get back to Monica, and it would screw up the whole thing.

Clearly, my ability to check this out was going to be severely circumscribed.

Now, with time starting to run short, Tripp returned to the subject of the tapes. Goldberg had brought a tape recorder for the occasion, and it was sitting on Jonah's coffee table. The cassette had been loaded up. Tripp asked me again if I wanted to listen to the tape, reached for the recorder and pressed the play button. I squirmed.

"Wait a second," I said. "I'm not sure I should be doing this. It probably isn't a good idea for me to listen to this."

Tripp hit the stop button.

•   •   •

Why? Some of my journalistic colleagues later expressed astonishment that I had declined the opportunity to hear Tripp's tapes. "I would have listened to those tapes in a heartbeat," Howard Kurtz, *The Washington Post*'s media critic, told me months later. It's an interesting journalistic issue. My hesitation was instinctive—but rooted in principles I had drummed into me when I first started as a young reporter at the *Post*. We don't tape without permission, the late Howard Simons, then the paper's managing editor, had decreed. Simons had overseen the paper's coverage during Watergate—when Nixon's secret tapes had shocked the world and ultimately led to the president's downfall. Taping without consent may be legal in most places, including Washington, D.C. But it was sneaky and had a bit of an odor to it. We reporters shouldn't deceive our sources, any more than we should deceive the public. Or so Simons—a wise and revered editor—had taught me.

Of course, I wasn't being asked by Tripp to tape anybody secretly. But the distinction was a bit fuzzy. Tripp's taping of Lewinsky was ongoing. If I started to listen in on her conversations as she was taping them—as opposed to when she was finished—then I inevitably would have become part of the process. Virtually any comment I made about the tape she played for me would have informed her next conversation with Lewinsky. "Gee," I could imagine myself saying, "that's interesting what I heard Lewinsky say about playing footsie with the president, but I didn't hear her say she actually massaged it." During their next conversation, Tripp would have pressed Lewinsky for the extra detail: "Did he let you massage his foot?" For all intents and purposes, I would have been writing Tripp's script. I would have become her partner in the betrayal of Lewinsky.

Did all this run through my mind in the second or two it took me to stop Tripp from playing me her tapes? Probably not. I just knew it didn't feel right. My reaction also could have been influenced by other factors: Tripp had already told me there were no "smoking gun" remarks on the tapes. (Of course, if there had been, there presumably would have been no reason for Tripp to continue to tape, thereby eliminating my fear of being drawn into an ongoing process.) And I was in a bit of a hurry to make it to *Hardball.* Although it was not quite time for me to go, listening to a long, rambling conversation between these two women struck me as a bit pointless, especially since it seemed clear to me I was still a long way away from being able to write anything.

Whatever was on the tapes, I told Tripp, I would still need much more documentation in order to write a story that even remotely touched on the idea that the president was having, or had had, a sexual affair with Monica Lewinsky. I had nothing in particular in mind when I made this point. But I noted that the job search under way for Lewinsky—the résumé on John Podesta's desk—was something that bore watching. It was reminiscent of the job Clinton had arranged for Gennifer Flowers and the inexplicable junkets to Indonesia and Denmark by Kathleen Willey. If the White House was going to arrange to get the president's girlfriend a job she didn't deserve, that might make the subject of a story in *Newsweek.*

Tripp nodded knowingly. In my mind, it was all quite vague; in

Tripp's, as events would turn out, maybe less so. I bade my farewells and agreed to keep in touch with Tripp and Goldberg. Then I rushed out the door, leaving behind (I was later told) a coffee table littered with the remains of Zabar's pistachio nuts.

●   ●   ●

That night, Tripp taped another conversation with a highly distraught Monica Lewinsky. Stewing over the news from Kate that Tripp had passed along that morning, Lewinsky said that she had spent that day repeatedly calling Betty Currie, to set up another meeting with President Clinton. She told Currie that she had switched plans and now was going to forget the White House and relocate to New York, where her mother had recently moved. She needed to see the president about arranging a job. She was going to send a letter to Clinton, laying the whole thing out, demanding that he live up to his obligations and help her.

While explaining her plans, however, she got sidetracked by one thing that was still bothering her. "I'm dying to know who told Kate," she said. "I mean, I'm trying to think of who in the NSC office—"

"I have no idea," said Tripp.

"—or who it could have been anywhere that she would deal with that—"

Tripp tried to discourage Lewinsky from pursuing this line of inquiry. "I don't know," Tripp said. "I don't know if she'll ever tell me. . . . It was not open for discussion. Let's put it that way. . . . She will respect a confidence the same way I would. I mean, you know what I mean? And does it matter?"

"Yeah, it matters," replied Lewinsky. "Yeah, it does matter." She still believed Kate's information must be coming from Schiff. "I just—I'm curious as to who it is."

After a few minutes, Tripp was finally able to steer Lewinsky off this issue and back to something she did want her friend to talk about—her job search. Lewinsky remembered a conversation with Betty Currie last July when the possibility of her wanting to move to New York had first arisen. Currie had told Lewinsky that she later mentioned this to the president and Clinton had replied: "Oh that's no problem. We can place her in the UN like that."

Over the phone that night, Lewinsky began writing a letter to Clinton, requesting that he get her a job at the United Nations. She went over it with Tripp, line by line. She would him ask to arrange "a position for me at the UN as a GS-12 or -13 beginning December 1," she read to Tripp. "I'd like to ask you to secure a position for me." She read further, composing the letter as she was going along. "Or how about 'help me secure'?"

Tripp suggested "help me obtain" might be better.

"But you know," says Lewinsky, "I don't want to have to work for this position. . . . I want it to be given to me."

"Right. You don't want to go through the whole interview process."

"Right."

A few seconds later, Tripp had another suggestion. "Now, wait. Stop. You don't have to limit yourself to the UN."

"Okay."

"All you have to say is—let me just say this. Excuse me. There are a bazillion options in New York."

By the time the two women were finished, Tripp had an important logistical question. "How are you going to send this to them?" Lewinsky said she was going to drop it off. Tripp sighed. Too dangerous, somebody would see her over there. Tripp first suggested she might be better off FedExing it, an idea that Lewinsky quickly nixed. They won't get it in time.

Then Tripp proposed another, better idea. "Hey, didn't you use a messenger service once?" she asked.

Lewinsky said yes, but that made her even more nervous. Somebody, maybe one of the messengers, could open it. "Oh, no way," replied Tripp. She knew of a good courier service, Tripp said. Speed Service in Washington. Bonded—and safe. "Courier it tomorrow morning from work," Tripp said. "What is more natural than something being couriered from the Pentagon to the White House?"

"Okay," Lewinsky replied.

The next morning, October 7, 1997, at 10:02 A.M., Lewinsky called Speed Service and said she had an envelope to be delivered to the White House. Lewinsky met the courier at the Pentagon mall entrance and paid $10 for the delivery. The designated recipient at the White House, recorded on the courier routing slip, was Betty Currie, secretary to President Clinton.

Some weeks later, Jeff Harshman, manager of Speed Service, got a call from Lucianne Goldberg in New York. Harshman knew Goldberg. She was his wife's aunt. Goldberg's brother, John Steinberger, had once owned the courier service; ownership of it had passed to Harshman's wife's family as part of a separation agreement years earlier. Goldberg, while waiting at Jonah's apartment for me to arrive that Monday evening, had suggested to Tripp that she encourage Lewinsky to use Speed Service when sending letters or packages to the president. Her original intention, she insisted, was to simply give the family company (sort of) a little extra business.

Now, Goldberg wanted Harshman to do her a favor. Would he be careful to save a copy of the delivery tickets he had written up for a pickup Speed Service had done for a woman named Monica Lewinsky at the Pentagon? Harshman remembered the pickup. His messenger who picked up the envelope thought that Lewinsky was a "hottie" and asked to be sent back if she ever phoned again.

"Hold on to this," Goldberg told him. "There may be a need."

Harshman assured her that would be no problem. He kept all the tickets anyway.

Tripp and Goldberg were making progress.

12

"We've been waiting three years to write this motion."

A rmed with the name Lewinsky and intrigued by the idea that Clinton was trying to arrange a federal job for her, I tried to check out what I could. I quickly confirmed that Monica Lewinsky did indeed work at the Pentagon as a confidential assistant to Kenneth Bacon, the assistant secretary of public affairs. (A great piece of investigative reporting, this: I looked up her name in the Federal Staff Directory, and sure enough, she was listed.) I established that she had in fact been a White House staff member in 1996. But where did that get me? Given Tripp's strong admonition that I not blow her cover and cut off the flow of information, I could hardly run around town asking a lot of questions. And the truth is, at that point, I had very little justification for doing so. Why are you asking me this? I could imagine somebody at the White House or Pentagon responding if I started pressing for information about Lewinsky. What was I supposed to say then?

On the other hand, I did spend some time looking into what Tripp had told me about Walter Kaye, the big Democratic Party donor and Lewinsky's purported patron. A retired New York insurance executive, Kaye had taken a shine to the Clintons early in 1993, and over the next four years, he had contributed more than $300,000 to the party.[1] According to Tripp, "Uncle Walter" had also become a generous patron of the First Lady, throwing a birthday party for her and showering her with gifts, including custom-made dresses.

I remembered the fuss in the early 1980s, when designers were "lending" Nancy Reagan expensive garments that stayed in the White House closet. Was Hillary guilty of a similar infraction? I asked the Office of Government Ethics for back copies of the Clintons' SF 278 forms, the public disclosures that all senior executive-branch officials are required to file each year, itemizing all gifts in excess of $100. I was fascinated by the treasures bestowed upon the president by his famous friends: a $1,200 painting from singer Carly Simon, $530 in picture frames from actor Tom Hanks, a $350 cartoon from Steven Spielberg and more than $11,000 worth of golf clubs and other equipment (including one $3,315 such present from Greg Norman). In the midst of the glitterati, I found a listing for Uncle Walter and his wife. They had given the president a scarf and sweater valued at $600 in 1994. But there were no gifts to the First Lady listed at all. Apparently, the Clintons had invoked a small provision in the disclosure form that permitted the federal officeholder not to report any gifts received by his or her spouse "that were given totally independent of the relationship to you." If she was receiving presents from Uncle Walter—or from anybody else—it was the position of the White House lawyers that such gifts had nothing to do with the fact that she happened to be married to the president of the United States.[2]

This little detour put the Lewinsky matter further on my back burner, and there it stayed until late that month, when I got a frantic call from Tripp. There had been some new developments—something I could check out, she told me. Monica would be meeting on Friday morning, October 31, at the Watergate with Bill Richardson, the U.S. ambassador to the United Nations. Tripp understood that the meeting was probably going to be downstairs at the restaurant right off the lobby. They would be talking about giving Lewinsky a job in the U.S. mission in New York. Clinton was pulling out the stops for her. Then Tripp had a suggestion for me. Why don't you get down to the Watergate that morning? Why don't you get a picture of the two of them together? You'll be able to see this for yourself. You'll have evidence.

I mulled over this for a moment—then walked down the hall to see McDaniel. She thought about it. Taking a picture was out of the question, she quickly decided. *Newsweek* was not going to stoop to the level of *Inside Edition*. But there was nothing wrong with having breakfast at a public restaurant and seeing whatever there was to see. Because I occasionally appeared on TV and might be recognizable to Lewinsky, we agreed that somebody else should do it. Dan Klaidman volunteered. His only instruction from McDaniel was that if anybody asked, he was not to misrepresent himself.

•   •   •

The meeting with Richardson was the culmination of weeks of intense developments in Lewinsky's job search that had been triggered by her October 7 letter to Clinton. The letter itself was in part the contrivance of Tripp. With her apparently phony story about Kate, Tripp had essentially tricked Lewinsky into petitioning the president for job assistance outside the White House. But if it was a trap, Clinton walked right into it. Upon receiving her letter, he called Lewinsky at two A.M. on Friday, October 10, and at first yelled at her about her seemingly presumptuous demands that he find her employment. "If I knew what kind of person you were, I never would have gotten involved with you," he said. Then, after Lewinsky burst into tears, Clinton calmed down and promised to do what he could. It was an important promise. Was this a case of humane concern for the travails of his ex-girlfriend? Was it guilt? Or was it a calculated decision that, with the Paula Jones lawsuit facing him, he could not permit Monica Lewinsky to stray too far off the reservation?

They met at the White House the next morning, and Clinton asked her to give him a list of jobs in New York that might interest her. Meanwhile, acting on Lewinsky's request in the October 7 missive that she be anointed with a position at the United Nations, Clinton asked Betty Currie to talk to John Podesta about placing the former intern there. Lewinsky, at the same time, started to have second thoughts. In a letter she sent Clinton on October 16, she listed five public relations jobs in the private sector she wanted to pursue. She had spent enough time working for the government, she wrote, and the UN held "no interest" for her. But by then it was too late. Podesta had already told UN ambassador Bill Richardson that there was a former White House intern, a friend of Betty Currie's, he wanted him to consider hiring.

This seemed to make a big impression on the ambassador. Richardson returned to New York from a presidential trip to Latin America on Sunday, October 19. Although it was a hectic time (a crisis was brewing over Iraq's restrictions on UN inspectors, and he was scheduled to leave for a trip to the Congo later in the week), the next day, he asked his staff assistant, Isabelle Watkins, to look out for the résumé of a former White House intern Podesta had spoken to him about. When it didn't arrive by Tuesday, Richardson asked Watkins to call Podesta's office. On October 21, at 3:09 P.M., Betty Currie faxed Lewinsky's résumé to Richardson's office in New York. That evening, at 7:09 P.M., Lewinsky later testified, she got a phone call at home. She was shocked. It was Bill Richardson himself, and he wanted to know if she would be available for a job interview at the Watergate—where he also had an apartment—the following Friday.[3]

Early on the evening of October 29, two days before the interview, Tripp tried to draw Lewinsky out on the upcoming meeting.

"Are you prepared?" Tripp asked. "Are you comfortable with how it's been arranged?"

"I—I—you know what? I don't like this situation at all because I can't win for losing, okay? I'm not comfortable meeting him in his hotel room."

"His hotel room?" Tripp asked with sudden alarm.

"That is how it is planned as of now," Lewinsky replied.

"Don't you dare, Monica."

"You know?"

"You go into his hotel room and—and I will never speak to you again."

"Well, I don't know what I'm supposed to do."

"Go into the—doesn't it have a place for breakfast?"

"It does, okay, and if someone sees me having breakfast with him—"

Tripp and Lewinsky discussed this issue in considerable depth. Tripp repeatedly and sternly lectured Lewinsky about the inadvisability of meeting Richardson in his room and the absolute need to meet him downstairs in the Watergate's public restaurant. ("Monica—you do not go to the ambassador of the United Nations' hotel [deleted] room. That's out of the question. Use your head.")

Even though she had her own doubts, Lewinsky didn't understand why Tripp was making such a big issue of it. Besides, meeting alone in the hotel restaurant early in the morning didn't seem so bright, either. What if somebody spotted them and got "the wrong idea?" she said again. In any case, how was she supposed to get the meeting reassigned downstairs when Richardson's staff had already scheduled it for his apartment? "I don't know what I'm supposed to say to him," she said.

Tripp was not about to let go. Lewinsky simply had to be firm with Richardson's scheduler, she advised, and explain that she would feel more "comfortable" meeting the ambassador downstairs at the restaurant. And she brushed aside Lewinsky's qualms about being seen in public having breakfast with the UN ambassador. She was "totally covered" if anybody were to suggest she was having an affair with him. She could simply say that Richardson was friendly with Walter Kaye or Peter Strauss, the former New York broadcaster who was dating Lewinsky's mother.

Every time Lewinsky expressed doubt about the wisdom of her advice, Tripp scrambled to find a new argument.

"How do you know he's not setting you up?"

"For what?" Lewinsky asked, somewhat incredulously.

"I don't know."

"A friend of John Podesta's—he's going to set me up?"

"Think about it for a minute," Tripp replied. "What if you're a problem and what if John Podesta thinks—just think about this for a minute. What if John Podesta thinks a good way to just neutralize you is to put you in a compromising situation? Then, if you ever decide to become a crazy woman, they can say, 'Oh, please, she propositioned Bill Richardson at the Watergate.' . . . I mean, you— Monica—this is big stuff."

Lewinsky struggled to follow Tripp's line of reasoning. The more she thought about it, the more baffled she became. "Why is this ever going to become an issue?" she asked Tripp. "I don't understand."

"Because what if—just what if Podesta's doing something sneaky?"

"Okay. What—what is sneaky? He's gonna come and say that— that Bill Richardson's going to come out and say, 'This girl attacked me'?"

Tripp allowed that she might be getting a bit paranoid. But, still, she didn't trust these people, she explained. Lewinsky understood. Okay, she finally said, she would raise this issue with Clinton himself and get his advice on the hotel room versus restaurant issue. In fact, she would call Betty Currie that very night and tell her she needed to speak to the president about this right away. "One, I'm going to say, 'Look, I know that he will be alone tonight. Could you please ask him to call sometime early on because I'm very nervous about this meeting tomorrow.'

"And then," Lewinsky continued, "I'm gonna say, 'Look, I really need your advice. The secretary's telling me I'm supposed to meet him in the room, and I'm really uncomfortable with that.'"

"He's not a secretary," Tripp reminded her.

"Oh yeah, I know. Ambassador. I keep forgetting that."

•   •   •

On Friday morning at 7:00 A.M., *Newsweek*'s Klaidman showed up at the Watergate's Aquarelle restaurant and requested a corner table by the rear window, giving him at once a grand view of the Potomac River and the rest of the restaurant. He brought with him a stack of five morning papers. He ordered cappuccino and smoked salmon. Then he waited, looking for some sign of UN ambassador Bill Richardson meeting with a young woman.

After a few hours, having made his way through the papers and downed half a dozen cups of cappuccino, he got impatient. He got up to wander around. He even made a few checks to see if anything was going on in the lobby. Klaidman started to worry that he might have screwed up. Then he wondered if the whole thing wasn't a bum steer. Why in the world would they be meeting in the open, anyway? he thought.

At 11:30 A.M., Klaidman gave up. He paid the tab, which came to $40, and returned to the office to report to McDaniel and me that he had seen nothing. *Newsweek*'s undercover surveillance had been a bust.

In fact, at 7:30 A.M., while Klaidman was just settling in for his vigil, Lewinsky had been yards away in the Watergate lobby, where two of Richardson's aides promptly whisked her upstairs to Richardson's apartment for a thirty-minute job interview. The UN ambassador later testified that he was impressed with the young woman, describing her as "poised" and "professional." The following Monday, without checking her employment history or interviewing any other candidates, Richardson called to offer Lewinsky a job in his public affairs office.

• • •

As it happened, developments in Little Rock were just then starting to make the job assistance to Lewinsky a potentially troublesome issue for the president. One of the first steps by Donovan Campbell and the Dallas lawyers after taking over the Jones case was to file an amended complaint on behalf of their client. It was a strategic move that served two purposes: The Dallas lawyers dropped Jones's claim that her good character and reputation had been defamed by Trooper Ferguson. By doing so, they in one stroke made it much harder for Jones's sexual past to become an issue in the lawsuit. At the same time, they recast Jones's civil rights claim, presenting their client as a victim of a much broader pattern of sexual discrimination that went far beyond the events in the Excelsior Hotel. The new theory of the case was deceptively simple: Clinton was a sexual "predator" with a well-established method of operation. While Jones had been deprived of advancements in the workplace for refusing the governor's advances, the Jones lawyers claimed, Clinton had "systematically" awarded government benefits, raises and jobs to other women who "succumbed" to his "predatory" sexual practices or who "provided him sexual favors." Under this theory, the awarding of state and federal jobs to Clinton's sexual conquests was itself a form of sexual discrimination, directly infringing upon the constitutional rights of women, like Paula Jones, who had spurned the president's advances.

This subtle revision of Jones's claims went largely unnoticed by the press when it was filed with Judge Susan Webber Wright on October 27, 1997. But it marked a dangerous turning point for the president. In any sexual harassment case, other incidents of unsolicited advances are routinely fair game for the plaintiff's lawyers—just as, to pick an example, a white corporate manager accused of discrimination against an African American employee can be confronted with testimony about racial slurs directed at other blacks. But the new Jones complaint threatened to swing wide the doors of discovery into even consensual sexual partners of Clinton—so long as there was evidence the women in question had received some form of government benefits.

If the press missed the significance of what Jones's new lawyers were up to, the president's lawyers did not. The very next day, October 28, 1997, just one week after UN Ambassador Richardson had called Lewinsky at her home to schedule a job interview, Clinton's lawyers moved aggressively to choke off the Jones team's move for broad discovery into the president's sexual history. Jones and her lawyers had "cast her discovery net far and wide to seek information relating to any rumor, innuendo, gossip or allegation of purported sexual conduct by President Clinton with anyone, at almost any time, and regardless of whether the purported conduct would constitute harassment," Clinton's lead lawyer, Robert Bennett, wrote in a motion co-signed by six other attorneys for the president. As an example, Bennett pointed to a recent list of "obnoxious" interrogatories that had been sent to the president, demanding that he admit or deny engaging in sexual relations with a host of women in Arkansas, including several who were state employees and one whom he later named to a state judgeship. The interrogatories also asked Clinton to identify all women other than his wife with whom he had "proposed having" or "sought to have" sexual relations during the time he was attorney general of Arkansas, governor or president.

The interrogatories reinforced the view among the president's legal advisers that the lawsuit was nothing less than a political assault on the Clinton presidency. As they saw it, the Jones suit was being promoted and financed by right-wing extremists bent on humiliating Clinton by spreading scurrilous rumors about his sex life. (The role of the Rutherford Institute in paying the expenses of the Dallas lawyers was looming larger in this picture.) In his motion, Bennett and the other lawyers charged that the "intrusive" questions by the Jones lawyers were being posed only "for the purpose of harassing and embarrassing the president." They urged the judge to sharply limit discovery in the case "to purported incidents, if any, of non-consensual conduct" by Clinton toward other employees at the

Arkansas Industrial Development Commission during the brief period in 1991 and 1992 that Paula Jones was employed there.

The lawyers in Dallas received a copy of Bennett's motion late one afternoon, with a demand by Judge Wright that they respond within twenty-four hours. Campbell and his partners were overwhelmed. This was perhaps the most critical issue in the case, and they had barely had a chance to research the case law. Campbell reached out for help—to the elves. He faxed a copy of Bennett's motion to Conway at Wachtell, Lipton in New York. Conway consulted with Marcus in Philadelphia. "Don't worry," Conway assured the Dallas lawyers a little while later. "We've been waiting three years to write this motion."

That night, the elves crashed. Conway and Marcus—e-mailing back and forth—prepared an outline, divided up sections, then worked all night writing their rejoinder to Bennett. When the Dallas lawyers arrived in their offices at eight A.M., they found in their computers a flawless, thirty-one-page legal brief that ripped into the president's legal arguments point by point. Interspersed with references to Clinton's "addictive, habitual sexual conduct," the Conway-Marcus brief cited a litany of prior sexual harassment cases—especially in the Eighth Circuit Court of Appeals, which oversaw the federal courts in Arkansas. The case law, they argued, was crystal clear. Not only did Paula Jones have a right to conduct unfettered discovery into the president's sexual behavior, but under prevailing appellate court rulings, it might even be "reversible error" if Judge Wright gave her anything less. As for Bennett's contention that such discovery was designed to embarrass Clinton politically, Conway and Marcus turned the argument on its head: "The Supreme Court has already explained, in the most categorical possible language, that this plaintiff is not to suffer simply because she has the misfortune to have been harassed by the President of the United States," they wrote.

When they read the brief that morning, the Dallas lawyers were blown away. It was, they thought, a tour de force—as polished and exhaustively researched a legal argument as they had ever seen. "It was like Mozart writing the overture of *Don Giovanni* overnight," one of the Dallas lawyers, Jim Fisher, later said. They filed it with Judge Wright that morning—under their own names—with barely any changes.

• • •

S ome young women, offered a prestigious position at the United Nations, might have been excited. Monica Lewinsky was mortified. She was sorry she had mentioned the idea to the president in the first place. Her doubts were reinforced when her mother, Marcia Lewis, and her aunt, Debra Finerman, paid a visit to the UN to check it out. They reported back to Lewinsky that the UN wasn't suitable: there were "a lot of Arabs" working there. "She thinks it's no place for a Jewish girl," Lewinsky told Tripp.

Lewinsky was now firmly fixated on the private sector.

In a phone conversation in late October, Lewinsky asked Clinton whether his good friend superlawyer Vernon Jordan might help in the search for her private-sector job in New York. She did so, she would later testify, after Jordan's name had come up in one of her nightly conversations with Linda Tripp. Who first raised Jordan's name—Lewinsky or Tripp—was never clear. But in Lewinsky's mind, recruiting Jordan to assist in her job search was much safer than tapping members of the White House staff like John Podesta or Chief of Staff Erskine Bowles.

"I don't think Erskine should have anything to do with this," Lewinsky told Tripp one night late in October. "I don't think anyone that works there [the White House] should."

"I don't see how that's—how that's a problem," said Tripp.

"Because look at what happened with Web Hubbell. I'm just saying—"

Tripp was dismissive. "I mean, come on. That's how networking works."[4]

In fact, Clinton was immediately receptive to the idea of bringing Jordan into the find-Monica-a-job campaign. But by the end of October, he hadn't yet called him, purportedly because the superlawyer had been out of town. "It's like, okay, Vernon, come home already," Lewinsky groused to Tripp. Then, on November 3, the same day she was offered the UN job she didn't want, Lewinsky decided to press the point. "You mentioned last week about setting up a meeting between me and . . . Vernon," she wrote Clinton in a letter. "Do you think you could do that some time soon?" The next day, Currie called Jordan's office and arranged a meeting for November 5. Jordan told her that he had already talked to the president about her and that she came "highly recommended." Lewinsky, who felt nervous during the interview and found Jordan a bit standoffish, handed Jordan the same wish list of jobs she had sent Clinton a few weeks earlier. Jordan looked down the list. "We're in business," he told her.

• • •

Lewinsky wasn't the only one getting anxious. So too were Linda Tripp and Lucianne Goldberg. From the moment their plotting began, they were hoping for something hard and tangible that could force the story of Lewinsky's relationship with the president into the open. The prospect of Clinton arranging employment for Lewinsky seemed their best shot, but that now seemed stalled. Still, they were hardly idle.

In the weeks since the October 7 letter to Clinton, Lewinsky had continued to send letters to the White House using Speed Service, the courier messenger firm Tripp had suggested, which just happened to be owned by Goldberg's brother's niece. Over the next two weeks, she tapped the courier service to send material to the White House three more times: on October 28, November 3 and November 12. For Lewinsky, the service (at a cost of $10 a delivery) was a way to bypass the White House mailroom and ensure that her missives went directly and unopened to Currie, who could then pass them right along to Clinton. But, unbeknownst to her, she was creating a paper trail.

In midmonth, Tripp left a message for me to call "New York"— her designed code name for Goldberg. I did. She had something for me, Goldberg said, something I would find interesting. I should call Jeff Harshman at Speed Service. I actually knew the number well. By coincidence, Speed Service was the same courier service regularly used by the *Newsweek* Washington bureau. Harshman and I chatted about the courier receipts he had been saving at the request of Goldberg. He didn't know who this Monica Lewinsky was. He didn't want to know.

That afternoon, one of Harshman's messengers brought me a stack of the receipts recording Lewinsky's letters to the president. The receipts showed the deliveries were called in by "Monica" at the Pentagon, with Lewinsky's office phone as the contact number. In each case, they were delivered to the White House southwest gate and a low-level West Wing staffer (in most cases, a woman named Jennifer Caroline Self) signed for them. In each case, the contact number for the designated recipient was the direct office extension at the White House of Betty Currie, the president's personal secretary.

When I inspected the receipts, I was a bit spooked. They were the first hard documentary record showing that at least some of what Linda Tripp had been telling me was actually true. They were, I thought, pretty good evidence that *something* was going on, that there was some sort of relationship between Lewinsky at the Pentagon and Currie, if not Clinton. That didn't "prove" anything—nor did it bring me or *Newsweek* any closer to a story. But I knew, from long and hard experience, that if there were ever to come a time when there was a story we wanted to write, the initial instinct from the president's aides would be to dismiss Lewinsky as an inconsequential peon—a former intern who was no more than a passing acquaintance of anybody of importance. They would deny—or, at a minimum, refuse to confirm—anything and everything that I could not absolutely document. The courier slips would give me one card I could play. Okay, I might ask them, if Lewinsky was a nobody, why was she sending all this material to Currie? If the letters were unsolicited, as they might well suggest, why did Currie on each occasion deputize a staffer to go fetch them? If they were official business, why was Lewinsky paying the charges herself? And why couldn't Lewinsky have simply sent this material with a regular thirty-two-cent stamp? I put the courier slips in a safe place in one of my file cabinets, where I was sure I wouldn't lose them.

•   •   •

A week or so later, Tripp called again. This time, in a hushed and somewhat breathless voice, she relayed a remarkable story. She had been to Lewinsky's apartment the night before and was invited to look inside the closet. There, Lewinsky showed her a navy blue dress purchased from the Gap. Lewinsky was proud of it. She had worn it when she went to see Clinton during a radio address back in

February. Then she and Clinton had gone back to the study, and . . . well, it seemed the president's semen ended up on the dress. And it was still there. In Lewinsky's closet. With the semen. She, Tripp, had seen it.

"So what do you think?" Tripp whispered over the phone.

"I think that's incredible."

Tripp paused. "Should I take it?"

"And do what with it?" I asked.

"Give it to you," she told me.

I paused. "What am I supposed to do with it?"

"Have it tested," said Tripp.

To say that nobody had ever before proposed anything along these lines would, to put it mildly, be something of an understatement.

"What in God's name are you talking about?" I said to Tripp, my voice somewhat elevated.

Well, she thought maybe there might be a way for me to test the DNA on the semen stain on the dress. Then, if it matched the president's DNA, that would be irrefutable proof.

For a moment, I thought Tripp must be out of her mind. Aside from the minor point that I was not about to become a party to theft, I tried to reason with her a bit on a rather sticky (so to speak) logistical issue.

"Where the fuck am I going to get a sample of the president's DNA?" I asked.

Tripp wasn't sure.

I told Tripp her proposal was the craziest idea I had ever heard. Then I hung up and mostly forgot about what she had just told me.

Tripp didn't, however. She thought about the dress—and thought some more. She consulted Goldberg, who—ever resourceful—had an idea. She had a consultant on hand who was an expert on precisely this sort of matter. At that very moment, in late November 1997, camping out in Goldberg's Upper West Side Manhattan apartment was Mark Fuhrman, the notorious ex–L.A. cop of O. J. Simpson fame. Goldberg had been Fuhrman's agent for his book on the O. J. Simpson case. She had arranged for him to write a second book on a two-decade-old murder case in Greenwich, Connecticut, in which two nephews of Ethel Kennedy had once been suspects, and he and his ghostwriter were racing to finish the book. Goldberg consulted Fuhrman. Was there a way to extract a DNA sample from a dress upon which semen had been deposited? she asked. Of course, said Fuhrman, who then offered a primer in forensic detective work: All that was needed was a Q-Tip, some sterile water and a plastic bag. Goldberg and Tripp talked about it some more. They discussed the possibility of Tripp's absconding with the dress during a return visit to Lewinsky's apartment, perhaps throwing her own overcoat over it and walking out. Lewinsky, much later, would remember being at her Pentagon office one day when she got a frantic call from Tripp asking if she could lend her the key to her apartment. Apparently, Tripp claimed, she had no clothes to wear for some event and she wanted to borrow something of Monica's.

Tripp never did act on what Goldberg later called their "Nancy Drew" fantasies. But she agonized over it and even raised with Lewinsky the subject of preserving the president's semen. The discussion, shortly before Thanksgiving, started off with routine talk about what Lewinsky planned to wear for some upcoming event. Lewinsky said she planned to wear *the* dress—the one she "wore to the radio address and still has the [blank] on it."

Tripp got alarmed. "Well, how, you're, what—you're gonna get it cleaned?"

"Yeah."

"Oh God."

Tripp suggested she wear a different outfit. Lewinsky said she didn't want to. The conversation continued into the next day. "I want you to think about this," Tripp told Lewinsky. "The navy blue dress. Now, all I would say to you is: I know how you feel today, and I know why you feel the way you do today, but you have a very long life ahead of you, and I don't know what's going to happen to you. Neither do you. I don't know anything, and you don't know anything. I mean, the future is a blank slate. I don't know what will happen. I would rather you had that in your possession if you need it years from now. That's all I'm gonna say."

"You think that I can hold on to a dress for ten, fifteen years with [blank] from—"

"Hey, listen. My cousin is a genetic whatchamacallit . . . and during O. J. Simpson, I questioned all the DNA, and do you know what he told me?"

"Huh?"

"I will never forget this. And he's like a Ph.D. and blah, blah, blah. And he said that on a rape victim now—they couldn't do this, you know, even five years ago. On a rape victim now, if she had pre-served a pinprick size of crusted semen, ten years from that time, if she takes a wet Q-tip and blobs on there and has a pinprick side on a Q-tip, they can match the DNA with absolutely—with certainty."

"So why can't I scratch that crap off and put it in a plastic bag?"

"You can't scratch it off. You would have to use a Q-tip.

"And I feel this is what I would tell my own daughter," Tripp con-tinued. "That's why I'm saying this to you. I would say to my own daughter, for your own ultimate protection, which mea culpa, I hope you never need it. But I don't want you to—take it away, either. I'm telling you, I would say this to my own daughter, who would tell me to fuck off, but—[sigh] . . ."

"Well, I'll think about it," Lewinsky said.

"All right."

"I'll think about it. I just—"

"I—and believe me, I know how you feel now. I just don't want to take away your options down the road, should you need them.

"And believe me, I know better than anybody probably, other than your mother, that you would never, ever use them if you didn't have to. I know this. Believe me.

"I—I just—I don't trust the people around him, and I just want you to have that for you," Tripp continued. "Put it in a baggie, put it in a Ziploc bag, and you pack it in with your treasures, for what I care. I mean, whatever. Put it in one of your little antiques."

"What for, though?" asked Lewinsky. "What do you think—"

"I don't know, Monica," replied Tripp. "It's just this nagging, awful feeling I have in the back of my head."

•   •   •

T hroughout these fall months, as Lewinsky schemed to get a new job and Tripp schemed to entrap Lewinsky and the president, the pace of the Paula Jones lawsuit steadily accelerated. Nearly every other day, the lawyers were filing new motions and taking depositions from prospective witnesses. Jones was questioned in Little Rock on November 12 and 13.[5] In Little Rock, Deborah Ballantine (on October 22) and Pamela Blackard (on October 23) testified—and stuck with their stories that Jones had told them that same day about Clinton's sexual advances. Phil Price testified that he did not believe Clinton was even at the Excelsior Hotel that afternoon—only in the morning. Danny Ferguson testified (December 10) and insisted that it was Paula who wanted to meet Clinton, not the other way around. Still, when he informed Clinton of this request from the young secretary-typist he had never before met, Ferguson testified, Clinton said: "She's got that come-hither look." Then, Ferguson said, Clinton told him to arrange to get a room upstairs and to tell the young woman to come on up. For what purpose, Ferguson couldn't say.

In Dallas, on November 14, Gennifer Flowers was deposed and testified how, after a twelve-year affair with the Arkansas governor, Clinton had arranged to get her a state job as administrative assistant of the Arkansas Appeal Tribunal, the state agency that handles disputes over unemployment claims. Flowers also was questioned closely about the grievance complaint filed by Charlotte Perry, the woman at the tribunal who wanted the same job. A key issue in that case was how Flowers had learned about the job—from a newspaper ad or some insider knowledge that was not available to Perry. In fact, she said, she had learned about the job from a member of Clinton's staff whom Clinton had told her to call. The staff member, Judy Gaddy, even helped her fill out the application.

But Flowers said that she had testified falsely in that 1991 proceeding. She told the grievance committee that she learned about it from the newspaper. "I did tell them that, because I was instructed not to be honest by Bill and Judy," Flowers said.

Clinton's lawyer, Mitch Ettinger, was caught off guard. But he thought he saw an opening. "You lied to that [grievance] committee, did you not?" he asked her, trying to discredit the witness.

Yes, Flowers said, "I did lie to the committee." But she did so only after she called Bill Clinton and asked him what she should say. "He told me to tell them I found out about it through the newspaper, and that's exactly what I did."[6]

The Jones lawyers were also seeking testimony from other women who they hoped would establish Clinton's "pattern and practice" of using state troopers to arrange sexual trysts and provide his paramours with state jobs. There were bitter fights over the testimony of Marilyn Jenkins, an employee at the Arkansas Power & Light Company; Ferguson testified he brought her to see Clinton for a final rendezvous at 5:15 in the morning before the governor left Little Rock to be inaugurated as president. The Jones lawyers also wanted the testimony of Beth Coulson, another woman identified by the troopers as one of Clinton's alleged lovers, who later was appointed to a state judgeship.

Another woman the Jones lawyers were aggressively pursuing at this time was Juanita Broaddrick, a nursing home executive who lived in the tiny town of Van Buren, Arkansas. The lawyers had been told about allegations first spread by the president's political foes in 1992—that Broaddrick had been the victim of a forced sexual encounter with Clinton after a nursing home seminar in 1978. Just the day before Gennifer Flowers's deposition in Dallas, on November 13, the Jones lawyers' private investigators—a former Dallas police officer named Rick Lambert and his wife, Beverly Lambert—approached Broaddrick at her home and tried to question her about the incident on her front porch as she was returning from a tennis game. The Lamberts were wired and secretly taped the conversation. Broaddrick emphatically told them she didn't want to talk. "I just don't want to relive that," she said. "You know, it was just a horrible horrible thing for me and I wouldn't relive that for anything."[7]

But there was one woman whose testimony the Jones lawyers desperately wanted, a woman they thought might even be critical to their case: Kathleen Willey.

In the more than three months since my original *Newsweek* story, Willey had been the subject of an intense legal battle between the lawyers for Jones and Clinton—all of it conducted behind closed doors. Even before he and Gil Davis dropped out of the case, Joe Cammarata had gone to a federal court in Richmond to enforce the Jones subpoena for Willey's testimony. Willey's lawyer, Dan Gecker, asked a federal judge, U.S. District judge Robert Merhige Jr., to toss it out. Jones's new lawyers protested. The president's lawyer, Robert

Bennett, offered to help Gecker fight the Jones subpoena. Merhige ordered a hearing in Richmond on the issue for November 19, 1997.[8]

On the day of Merhige's hearing, Bennett flew to Richmond and arranged to meet beforehand with Gecker and Willey in Gecker's downtown law office. The three gathered in the same conference room where I had first heard Willey's story eight months earlier. Bennett greeted Willey warmly and said he had a message from Washington. "The president thinks the world of you," Willey remembered him saying. Bennett recalled his greeting a little differently. "I told her she was well regarded at the White House," he said.

Then, all three present agree, Bennett gently tried to prod out of Willey exactly what she might say about her encounter with the president if she became a witness. Willey wouldn't tell the story in detail but quickly made it clear that, if forced to, she would have to say something happened. Bennett said he wanted to cut to the bottom line and find out whether Willey would say she was sexually harassed. Did Willey feel that Clinton's sexual overtures were unwanted? he asked. "Let's just say they were unexpected," Willey told him, "unexpected—and unwanted."

The lawyers and the witness proceeded to the courthouse, where Merhige gave a brief lecture on how important it was that they try to settle the Jones case. He was even willing to get on the phone to Judge Wright in Little Rock and see if he could make it happen. The Willey subpoena, he was suggesting, could be the vehicle that spared the country from the whole unfortunate case. But Merhige's attempts to play peacemaker quickly dissipated in a cloud of legal acrimony. Bennett and Campbell started shouting, accusing each other of unethical conduct. Merhige ordered the lawyers into his chambers. Later, Joe Cammarata was called to the stand and testified about the anonymous phone call he had gotten back in January. Willey was called to the stand and questioned just enough to establish that she fit the description of the woman described in the phone call. Merhige concluded there was adequate basis for the Jones lawyers to depose the witness.

When Campbell boarded his plane at the Richmond airport that night, he was in an excellent mood. At long last, he was about to get testimony from a witness he believed could crack open the case. It would give the Jones lawyers exactly what they wanted—a live and seemingly credible witness who would testify about another unsolicited sexual advance by Bill Clinton.

Campbell was also mildly optimistic about something else he had just learned was out there—something that was coming in over the transom to his colleagues back in Dallas. He had heard a bit about it before he left, and it sounded wild.

13

"Can you get me subpoenaed?"

T he week of the Willey hearing in Richmond, Linda Tripp alerted me to the latest bizarre development. Lewinsky had been to the White House the night before, she said. Betty Currie had sneaked her into the private study. Lewinsky then hid out until Clinton ducked in for a furtive rendezvous—a meeting that was rushed because the president of Mexico, Ernesto Zedillo, was waiting outside. Lewinsky was hoping for oral sex, but the president told her he didn't have time. They made out instead.

The images that leapt to mind were opéra bouffe. Or maybe French farce: Here, the Mexican president. There, the American president. And over there, the American president's comely young girl-friend crouching in the corner, waiting to please him. Could this really be happening?

Yet all the evidence so far suggested that what Tripp was telling me was essentially true. And the American voters hadn't a clue. Should they know?

That week, Tripp decided once and for all that they should. What pushed her over the line—the Zedillo escapade itself or simply the steady accumulation of Lewinsky's fantastic stories—is impossible to know. It is certainly true that Tripp—while feigning sympathy for the lovesick Lewinsky—was disgusted by what she was hearing. Clinton was supposed to have cut off the relationship, to have ended this whole tawdry affair. Yet there he was in mid-November, giving Lewinsky new encouragement, playing mind games with this emo-

229

tionally fragile young woman. (Leave aside the fact that Tripp, in her own way, was playing far more devious mind games with Lewinsky.) The day before the Zedillo incident, Lewinsky had sent Clinton an especially pathetic letter, begging to see him. "I need you right now not as president, but as a man," she wrote. That night, Clinton had called her at home, and according to Lewinsky, they had phone sex. Again. Then he invited her to the White House. From Tripp's perspective it was further proof of Clinton's callousness and arrogance—right in the middle of a lawsuit brought on by his sexual recklessness.

Motivations are ultimately unknowable. What is clear is that on the evening of November 17, 1997—four days after the Zedillo visit and two days *before* the hearing in Richmond that would determine whether Kathleen Willey would ever be a witness—Tripp again called Lucianne Goldberg. They discussed the prospect of Tripp's becoming a witness in the Paula Jones case—an idea Goldberg had raised obliquely in their conversation back in September. Tripp was tired of waiting for events to unfold. She wanted Goldberg to make it happen. "Linda wanted to be subpoenaed," Goldberg would later recall. "She asked me, 'Can you get me subpoenaed?' I wasn't egging her on."

The phone call set in motion an irrevocable chain of events. Goldberg had a wide circle of conservative friends. The next day, she called one of them—Al Regnery, the president of Regnery Books. Did he know anybody who could put her in touch with the lawyers for Paula Jones? Regnery did. He gave her the name and phone number of Peter W. Smith, the secretive Chicago investment banker Cliff Jackson had called three years earlier when he was looking for a lawyer for Paula Jones to replace the befuddled Danny Traylor.

Goldberg called Smith. Smith listened to what she had to say—then called her back with a young man on the line: Richard Porter, the ex-aide to Vice President Dan Quayle who was now a partner in the prestigious Chicago law firm of Kirkland & Ellis. It was the same firm whose most prominent member at that moment was Kenneth Starr, the Whitewater independent counsel. Porter was no stranger to the case: he was the same lawyer whom Smith had tried to recruit to represent Jones in the first place in 1994. He had been keeping in close touch with developments through his old college friend, the

Philadelphia "elf" Jerome Marcus, and George Conway, the "elf" in New York. Porter listened to what Goldberg had to say and assured the literary agent that he would make things happen.

Throughout the fall of 1997, Lucianne Goldberg kept a spiral notebook in which, amid recipes for short ribs and other culinary tips, she jotted down her contacts with all the players involved with the events Linda Tripp had brought to her attention. For the day November 18, 1997, Goldberg had noted Smith's name and phone number. Then she wrote down another phone number in Chicago—a number at the firm of Kirkland & Ellis. Richard Porter's number. Next to it, she wrote: "note: Ken Starr's partner re Linda. She will be subpoenaed." Goldberg later insisted that the reference to Starr was merely a way to identify Porter's firm; there was no discussion at that point of the Whitewater independent counsel having anything to do with the case.

That afternoon, Conway was sitting in his office at Wachtell, Lipton in New York when an e-mail popped up on his computer that practically knocked him off his chair. It was from Porter in Chicago. "There's a woman named Lewisky [*sic*]," it read. "She indulges a certain Lothario in the Casa Blanca for oral sex in the pantry." Porter's e-mail went on to mention a "Betty Curry [*sic*]" as being the woman's conduit, the existence of certain "romantic tapes" and a "certain reporter at *Newsweek*" who knows all about it. Conway immediately called Porter. Surely he had to be kidding. Porter assured him this was no joke. Conway printed out the e-mail, which had Lucianne Goldberg's phone number on it, and faxed it to Don Campbell in Dallas. Conway called Campbell and told him, "I'm faxing you something, and you should really focus on this." But Conway wasn't quite sure Campbell got it. Campbell at that moment was getting ready to leave for Richmond for the Willey hearing. So Conway called back Wes Holmes, one of Campbell's young partners, just to be sure. "Listen, you've *really* got to focus on this," he said. Holmes assured Conway he would.

The conspiracy, thoroughly right wing, may not have been that vast. But it had done its job.[1]

•   •   •

Monica Lewinsky was positively bubbly. "You want to die laughing?" she asked two nights later as soon as she picked up her phone to find Linda Tripp on the line. "Listen to this. This is so funny. This is so funny."

"What?" Tripp asked.

"Okay. So I'm taping this stupid ridiculous thing, right?"

"Yes."

"So I'm thinking to myself, Oh, that would be a funny thing. I'm going to make my phone ring. And I have this button that you can make the phone ring. So literally—okay? I'm not kidding you. In fact, here, I will play it for you."

Tripp laughed. Then Lewinsky played the "stupid ridiculous thing" she was taping: a seductive message for the big creep's listening pleasure, a tape interrupted by a fake phone call so that Lewinsky could then briefly stop her playful cooing by saying, "Oh . . . Hold on. There's my phone. Okay. I'll be right back."

"That's so cute already," Tripp told her. "I love your voice. You have a great voice."

In fact, Lewinsky had been making two tapes that night, tapes she wanted to play for Linda Tripp, who, of course, was herself secretly taping the tapes. A tape, Lewinsky figured, would be a better attention getter than the (mostly unanswered) letters she had been sending. She had made two versions, and she wanted Tripp to help her choose which would better achieve its intended purpose: to persuade Clinton to invite her over so the two of them could spend more time together.

"Hi, handsome," the first one began. "I couldn't bear the idea of sitting down to write you another note, so I thought I'd tape it." The tape contained two proposals. One called for "handsome" to "pre-plan with Betty" to leave the office one night at seven or seven-thirty so that "everyone who hates me and causes me lots of trouble goes home." Then he could "quickly sneak back, and then in the meantime, I quickly sneak over and we have a nice little visit."

The other idea is that she could arrange to accidentally run into him one night when he was going to the movies. "And I could go watch the movie with you." She reminded Clinton that he had first suggested this two years earlier. So now she wanted to take him up on it.

"You can't refuse me because I'm too cute and adorable," Lewinsky concluded. She then mentioned something about taking her clothes off.

Tripp listened to this tape and then the second version, joking and laughing, suggesting small changes, telling Lewinsky how crazy she was. "That's cute," she said. "That's cute. And so are you." Then, turning serious, she zeroed in on something. "Now here's what—here's my big concern," she says. Lewinsky couldn't just drop the tape off by the New Executive Office Building. Clinton might "freak" if he learned such tapes were being dropped off for him.

"So your only option is to courier it," Tripp continued. There were lots of advantages. "This way it doesn't go through any X-rays."

"Right," agreed Lewinsky.

"It just goes straight to whoever—"

"Right."

"—gets it. Plus, you're using a very reliable and reputable courier service, so—"

"Right."

"—it's the only way to go."

• • •

The next day, November 21, Tripp called me. There was another courier pickup from the Pentagon this morning. Only this time, it was not a letter. It was a tape—for phone sex, she told me. I called Speed Service and arranged to get the receipt. It showed once again a "Monica" at Lewinsky's extension at the Pentagon calling it in and a delivery to the White House with Betty Currie's extension as the contact number. As luck would have it, the messenger who delivered it also had to make a delivery to *Newsweek* that morning. I asked him to describe what he had delivered to the White House. It was a package, sort of like this, he said, holding up his hands, sort of like a small box. Like a tape? I asked. Yes, he told me, like a tape.

I was once more impressed with the reliability of what Tripp was telling me. And with the strangeness of the information: a sex tape couriered to the Oval Office. What would people think if they knew about this? But then I also started, for the first time really, to feel strange myself about what was going on—and what I was doing. I realized with a bit more clarity something that should have been apparent much earlier: I was in the middle of a plot to get the president.

I was only covering it, of course. Or so I told myself. But I was covering it from the inside, while it was unfolding, talking nearly every week with the conspirators as they schemed to make it happen. Tripp would at times ask *me* questions. She would seek my advice. I would, cautiously, give it: No, you shouldn't go to the tabloids with this story, it would only cheapen it, I had told her when she floated this idea. You should deal only with me. Reporters have these kinds of conversations with sources all the time. But in a situation like this, the lines between aggressive reporter and passive co-conspirator can get awfully blurry.

I had tried at every stage to adhere strictly to my role as a journalist: when I wouldn't listen to Tripp's tapes, when I rejected her harebrained scheme to steal the semen-stained dress and give it to me, when I wouldn't give Joe Cammarata the name of Kathleen Willey. But still, I was in treacherous and uncharted territory. There was a lot about Linda Tripp I didn't know—and much that even then made me distinctly uncomfortable. Her duplicity was obvious. Leave aside her tapes, which we had not talked about since that meeting back in October. She was betraying Lewinsky every time she spoke to me. She was relating in the mornings conversations she had been having with her unsuspecting young friend the night before— intensely personal conversations that Lewinsky obviously thought were taking place in confidence. On a practical level, I found it mind spinning—the cutouts, the code names, the switching on and off between sympathetic friend and devious informant. How did Tripp keep it all straight? And what were these talks between Tripp and Lewinsky really like? What was Lewinsky like? Who was she? I had no idea, really, and no effective way to find out—without tipping her off to what was going on, without betraying the woman who was betraying her. Yet it was the betrayer who was my source.

We all like to think of ourselves as ethical people, even headline-hungry reporters. But the ethics here looked a bit bewildering. I retreated to more comfortable terrain: my professional obligation as a journalist. On this score, I felt sure, I was safe. I reminded myself that neither I nor *Newsweek* had decided to publish anything. And for a good reason, too: I couldn't prove that any of this was real and that Monica Lewinsky wasn't some psychotic fantasist. I was only doing my job: listening, collecting evidence, testing what my sources were telling me to see if the information would hold up if and when *Newsweek* decided there was something here worth sharing with the public. According to Tripp, Clinton was using his office to get Lewinsky a job. That, in and of itself, was suspect. There was also a lawsuit out there in which the alleged sexual compulsiveness of the president of the United States was a central issue. This thing could well come up. I was doing only what any good reporter under the same circumstances would do, I concluded. What was I supposed to do? Tell Tripp and Goldberg to get lost? Say to them, "How dare you provide me with evidence of presidential misbehavior"?

Still, I was uneasy and told myself again I had to be extremely careful.

●   ●   ●

That night, November 21, 1997, Tripp's phone rang as expected. "Ms. Tripp," said the caller.

"Oh, Mr. Pyke," Tripp replied. "Thanks for calling."

It was David Pyke from Dallas. He was a partner of Don Campbell's, and he represented Paula Jones.

Pyke's call was the result of the Lucianne Goldberg–to–Al Regnery–to–Peter Smith–to–Richard Porter–to–George Conway–to–Don Campbell phone chain. As Pyke quickly explained, Goldberg had already "filled me in to some degree." But he had much wrong. "You're at the Treasury Department?" he asked.

"Defense," Tripp said.

Tripp wanted to establish a few things. Would the Jones lawyers get the opportunity to depose Kathleen Willey?

Pyke explained that he had to be careful, there was a gag order. But "it's safe to just say that we will get to depose Ms. Willey." (Judge Merhige had just ruled, in secret, two days earlier.)

"Okay. So that would leave you open to deposing me?"

"Right."

That was good. That meant that Tripp would have legal cover to do what she was about to do. The next thing, Tripp explained, is that it had to be done "through official channels," meaning her attorney, Kirby Behre. Tripp gave Pyke Behre's name and number. But, she emphasized, Behre should not know that Tripp and Pyke were talking. Behre was a Democrat and "feels strongly that I should not involve myself."

"Uh-huh," said Pyke a bit uneasily.

Tripp was already double-dealing Monica. Now she had added Kirby Behre to the list.

Tripp then got down to business: "I feel strongly that the behavior has to stop, um, or should at least be exposed."

"Ms. Goldberg told me about—that you've—you've talked to a woman that's having a relationship with Clinton currently. Is that correct?"

"Uh, by—by having a relationship—by—by saying that, currently, no. It's—it's in the process of ending, let's say."

"Okay."

"But it's been going for two years."

Tripp then dribbled out some of the information the Jones lawyers would need to proceed. She told Pyke how the young woman (Tripp did not use her name) had started out as an intern, then was given a White House job until a top aide responsible for "watchdogging" the president had her removed to the Pentagon. She explained how the president's secretary was posing as her "mentor" and would get the young woman in to see the president. But the secretary would lie about this to protect the president, Tripp cautioned. As a matter of fact, everybody at the White House would probably lie to protect the president.

Pyke suggested that was the way it usually was.

"I disagree," Tripp said indignantly. "I worked for George Bush directly—and I can tell you that is absolutely not true."

Pyke demurred.

"In any event," Tripp said, "just so you are aware, if I am asked the right questions, I will not lie." But, she added, "I need to look hostile."

Pyke understood. Perhaps, he suggested, a subpoena could just "drop on your doorstep out of the blue." They talked about a possible date for her deposition. By the time the conversation ended, the legal machinery was in motion to make Linda Tripp—and Monica Lewinsky—witnesses in the case of *Jones* v. *Clinton*.

•   •   •

The next week, just before Thanksgiving, Ronald Rissler, the legal affairs coordinator for the Rutherford Institute in Charlottesville, Virginia, got his second phone call from a woman who wanted him to have some information. The caller—who wouldn't give her name—had phoned a month earlier, on October 20, and claimed to know about a young woman who worked at the White House and was having a sexual relationship with the president. She thought the woman's name was "Monica." The mystery caller had suggested that the Rutherford Institute and the lawyers for Paula Jones get a list of White House employees and look it over for somebody by that name. Rissler passed this tip along to Wes Holmes in Dallas, who told him that they had already asked for a list of White House employees but hadn't gotten it yet. Nothing more came of it.

Now, just a few days before Thanksgiving, Rissler's anonymous tipster was calling back with a little more. She had "Monica's" last name, and it was Lewinsky. She was "in her early twenties with long dark hair." She had been moved from the White House "to the State Department," the woman claimed, because the "Paula Jones case had heated up." The caller had heard that Lewinsky had viewed the screening of *Air Force One* in the White House theater with the president, and it "raised eyebrows" among the White House staff. That was it, the caller said: that was all she knew.

Rissler immediately called Don Campbell to pass along this hot new information. But Campbell told him the Dallas lawyers were already on the case. They knew about Monica Lewinsky. In fact, they were going to subpoena her.

In the early months of 1998, there were many cover stories put out by all sides in the Lewinsky affair. One of them was that Jones's Dallas lawyers learned about Monica Lewinsky from the anonymous tipster to the Rutherford Institute. Another was that Linda Tripp was being forced to testify in the Paula Jones case against her will because of her knowledge of the incident involving Kathleen Willey. "I did not volunteer to become a witness in the Paula Jones lawsuit," Tripp declared in her January 29, 1998, statement to the news media. "I was subpoenaed to testify about Ms. Willey." These stories, like much else said during that period, were false. The Jones lawyers in Dallas learned about Monica Lewinsky from Linda Tripp herself with the assistance of Lucianne Goldberg and her coterie of conservative friends. And Tripp arranged for the whole thing to happen—all the while insisting, as she told Pyke that night, "I need to look hostile." In fact, before she did so, the lawyers for Paula Jones had little if any interest in Linda Tripp. "She was on the radar screen, but she probably wasn't more than a minor blip," Pyke said much later. For the Jones lawyers, Linda Tripp was at best a wild card who contradicted Kathleen Willey's story as much as she confirmed it. All things being equal, they would have been content to leave her alone. "We weren't sure she wasn't a hostile witness," Pyke said. "There was no reason to depose her."

•   •   •

I n the days after she first talked to Jones lawyer David Pyke, Tripp moved to cut off her contacts with Lewinsky. As she later described it, she couldn't take it anymore. She couldn't take the histrionics and the hysteria and the incessant late night phone calls to talk about Bill Clinton. If guilt was a factor in her actions at this point, Tripp never mentioned it.

Lewinsky got highly upset that weekend when Tripp stopped taking her phone calls. "This silence is killing me," Lewinsky wrote her on November 23 in a note that included a birthday message and gifts. "This past weekend was awful with me calling you twelve thousand times and you not answering."

On Monday, November 24, Tripp e-mailed back: "Monica: *Please* give me a break. . . . The information alone is a hefty burden and one I never asked for. The pursuant behavior concerning that information is more than I can take. I do not mean to be ungrateful, but I cannot accept gifts, Monica. Sweet as it is, I would prefer not to. LRT."

•   •   •

F or the Thanksgiving holidays, Monica Lewinsky flew to Los Angeles to see her father. While still emotionally obsessed with Bill Clinton, she was also getting antsy about her job search. She had told her superiors at the Pentagon public affairs office that she planned to quit in December and move to New York. But she still didn't have anything lined up. She had left messages for Vernon Jordan several times since their November 5 meeting. But he was again

out of town, and he hadn't returned any of her calls. (What, if anything, Lewinsky was doing to find work on her own was unclear.)
Before she left for California, Lewinsky had called Currie to complain about Jordan's lack of responsiveness. Currie promised to see
what she could do. She called Jordan. Jordan told Currie to have
Lewinsky call him again. From a pay phone at the Wilshire Courtyard Marriott in Los Angeles, Lewinsky did so. Jordan told her he
was working on her job quest. But he was about to leave for China.
She should call him when he got back in early December.

The month of November ended, and Vernon Jordan hadn't lifted
a finger on Monica Lewinsky's behalf.

14

"I feel like I'm sticking a knife in your back."

In mid-December, I flew to Dallas. The Jones case was heating up, and the risks to the president seemed to be escalating. Clinton's deposition was coming up in the next few weeks. Would there be a last-minute effort to settle the case before the president was required to answer questions under oath? I thought it worth checking in with the new Jones lawyers—whom I had never met—and learning whatever I could.

Before I did so, though, there was another witness in Dallas I was curious about: Dolly Kyle Browning. She had started showing up that fall on cable TV, touting her self-published roman à clef, *Purposes of the Heart,* which Lucianne Goldberg had once tried to market, about a decades-long love affair between a sexy blond southern girl and her high school sweetheart, who becomes governor and then president. Browning had been deposed by the Jones lawyers. What exactly had she said? Was her story for real?

Browning met me one morning on the campus of St. Mark's, a private school for the children of the Texas elite, where her current husband, Doc Browning, was a physical education teacher. She was a lawyer who worked for the Dallas chapter of Legal Services of North Texas, specializing in the housing problems of the underprivileged. She was also a likable, attractive and somewhat daffy woman of forty-nine who couldn't stop talking—although not always about the subjects I was interested in. Aside from running a Web site where she promoted her book, Browning and her husband also ran a mail-

order home-baked cookie company called "Doc's Oldtyme Cookies."
This was the holiday season—a busy period for cookie sales—so she
didn't have a lot of time, she explained. I was very understanding
and promised to order some "Oldtyme Cookies"; I had already written a $10 check for *Purposes of the Heart.*

We went to lunch at a Chinese restaurant, and I eventually got
Browning to give me her account of her long, topsy-turvy relationship with the man she called "Billy." It began when they were kids,
she told me—when she was eleven and Billy was twelve—and it continued intensely for a while, during high school and then intermit-
tently over the years. Dolly got married, got divorced, moved to
Texas, went to law school, got married again, raised four children,
got divorced, and then remarried a third time. Billy became governor, then president. They stayed in touch, and what Dolly depicted as
the embers of youthful love never completely died. Their relationship over these three decades was only occasionally sexual, Browning said. (She offered few details on this issue.) For the most part, I
surmised, it consisted of long, heartfelt talks every few years or so—
including one in May 1988, during which, according to Browning, she
and Clinton lay naked in bed all night in a Dallas hotel room. That
was the night Billy confessed to her that he suffered from a sexual
addiction.

This topic came up because Browning herself was a confessed
sex addict. In fact, she was in therapy for it at the time, attending
meetings of a sex addicts anonymous group and carrying with her a
questionnaire designed to help potential members determine if they
were similarly afflicted. (Sample question: "Do you frequently feel
compelled to have sex again and again within a short period of
time?") That night, Clinton's plane was routed through Dallas on the
way back from a trip to Washington. He called Browning and asked
her to meet him in the Hyatt Hotel near the airport for the evening.
Browning wanted to tell Clinton all about her battle to contain her
ravenous sexual appetite and began reading him the questions in
her questionnaire. Clinton at first laughed. But Browning said she
thought this was important: Billy had to hear this. Clinton settled
down and became more serious. Then she asked one that got to him.
"Have your sexual activities jeopardized your life goals?"

As Browning related the scene, Clinton grew very still, and she thought she saw tears in his eyes.

"Did you ever think *you* were a sex addict?" Dolly asked.

There was a pause. Clinton nodded. "I know I am—and I've tried to overcome it," he said. "But it's so hard. Women are everywhere, and for some reason they seem to want me."

Although she had fond memories of her times with Billy, Browning had clearly grown quite angry at him in more recent years. She dated this to the early days of the 1992 campaign, when she was being chased by one of the tabloids and she tried to alert Clinton. She didn't have any intention of cooperating at first but got upset when Clinton wouldn't return her calls. She passed word through Clinton's secretary that she didn't appreciate this. Eventually she got a call back, she said, from her brother, Walter Kyle, another lawyer who was working for the Clinton campaign. He explained that Clinton couldn't afford to call any women right now. They might, like Gennifer Flowers, tape him. Dolly was offended by the suggestion that she might do this. Her brother warned her not to talk to the tabloids and bluntly told her that if she did, she would be destroyed. This infuriated Dolly.

She next saw Clinton in the summer of 1994, when the president attended the Hot Springs High School Class of '64 thirtieth reunion. According to Browning, sometime around midnight, Clinton saw her on the dance floor, tapped her on her shoulder and asked, "How are you?"

"You are such an asshole!" Browning responded as she angrily pushed him away. "I can't believe you'd even bother to ask."

A Secret Service agent quickly came up, Browning said, but Clinton waved him away, assuring him it was all right. Then the two went off to a corner, sat on folding chairs and had a prolonged and occasionally heated talk for the next forty-five minutes. Clinton apologized for never calling her in 1992, and Browning told him about her book, which she assured the president she would tell the world was fiction, not fact. At one point, Browning said, a blond woman, apparently a member of the president's staff, came to tell him the bar was closing and the party was supposed to be over. "Tell them to keep the bar open," Clinton said brusquely, then shooed her away. Their talk, Browning said, was visible to everybody there.

Browning said she had recounted all of this in the deposition taken by the Jones lawyers. But she got quite upset when I told her that one of Clinton's lawyers publicly denied that he ever had a sexual relationship with her—and that the president was prepared to deny it, too, if he were asked about her in his own deposition. "That's crazy," Browning said indignantly. "That would be out-and-out perjury. I can't believe he will do that." But then, again, Browning made clear, her view of Billy had changed. He was still, after all these years, very much in denial about his weaknesses, she thought—and had become much more calculating about it as the stakes got higher. "Obviously, the guy will say whatever he needs to say to get whatever he wants," she said.

As fascinating as her story was, it was tempting to dismiss Browning as a bit of an embroiderer. After all, no profile of Bill Clinton or any of his biographers had ever so much as mentioned her. But with Clinton, I had long since learned, nothing could ever be dismissed. Do you have any evidence of your relationship with Clinton? I asked her. Pictures, letters, whatever? Well, as a matter of fact, she did, she told me. She had kept quite a bit. She invited me back to her apartment and unearthed a box of her Billy Clinton memorabilia—stacks of newspapers clippings, old phone books with his private numbers on it and piles of correspondence dating back to Clinton's days as attorney general. The letters in Clinton's handwriting, on his State of Arkansas stationery, were brief, a bit suggestive but ultimately ambiguous— mostly perfunctory thank-yous for gifts or birthday greetings interspersed with hints of something a bit more. But what? "Call Mon. morn—371-2006. Tell Barbara I'm expecting—Will be in El Dorado most of the day but we'll get together somehow," Clinton had jotted in a August 1977 note to her when he was attorney general. "I really enjoyed our visit. . . . Love, Bill," he scribbled on the bottom of a February 1985 letter thanking her for a note she had sent about his brother Roger's drug problems. And on it went over the years. "Dear Dolly: I'm sorry I missed you when you were here," he wrote her in August 1987. "I tried to call your mother's but there was no answer."

One exchange in particular caught my attention. It was dated June 6, 1987—a pivotal moment in Clinton's career, when he was wrestling with a decision about whether to run for president in the wake of the revelations about Donna Rice and Gary Hart. The "Dear Bill" letter Browning had written Clinton that day (she had saved a copy) suggested that she and Clinton had recently talked about it. ("I sensed when we visited last month that you're already in the race," she had written.) Browning told me that in that visit she had reminded Clinton of his troubled personal life and the inevitable toll disclosures about it would take on his family—and on him—were he to run for president.

"Now you've developed yourself well—intellectually, socially, politically—yet you know there are other parts of you that are less strong and mature," Browning wrote that day. Then there was this: "Do what you did when Chelsea was a baby: Listen to your gut. Trust it. Are you ready to be a great leader? Is your own house in order?"

Browning said the last question was a reference to the issue they had talked about in their previous meeting—Clinton's womanizing. Six days later, on June 12, 1987, Clinton wrote back. He was still "in a quandary and exhausted" over the issue, he wrote. "Your letter was on target," he added. "You know me."

Before I left Browning, I asked her for the names of some Hot Springs Class of 1964 graduates who could confirm that she and Clinton had been talking that night at the class reunion. She gave me a few, and I called them. They all said the same thing. They had no idea what it was about, but there was no question Bill Clinton and Dolly Browning were having a very intense discussion that night. One of them, Mimi Bibb, who worked for the Roman Catholic Diocese of Little Rock, seemed to laugh when I asked her whether she noticed anything along the lines of what Browning had described. "I can't believe there's a person that didn't see it," said Bibb.

Perhaps for that very reason, Browning later learned, Clinton had gone back to Washington and written his own quite different account of that evening.[1]

•   •   •

The next morning, December 17, I went to see Don Campbell. He was dry and cagey and seemed to enjoy parrying my questions about the Jones lawsuit. There was a gag order, he explained, so he really couldn't comment about very much. But it was fair to say that they'd gathered a lot of very interesting evidence in the course of discovery. What about a settlement before the president is deposed? I asked. Well, there really hadn't been any discussions along those lines of late, Campbell said. But knowing what I know, he added, "If I were president, I would want to settle this case."

I pushed him especially hard about Kathleen Willey. Were the Jones lawyers going to get an opportunity to take her testimony? Again, Campbell said, he had to be careful. The judge in Richmond had made it clear that he didn't want anybody talking about that matter. But Campbell hinted that he and his partners were not going to let the Willey matter drop. He had a copy of my *Newsweek* story about Willey on his desk. It was underlined heavily.

We went around in circles for forty minutes or so, and I wasn't getting very much. I also had to catch a plane. But before I left, I wanted to raise a delicate issue. A few days earlier, Linda Tripp had hinted to me that the Jones lawyers were seeking her testimony and they knew something about Monica Lewinsky. "They're aware of it," she had told me cryptically. I didn't push her on precisely how this happened. Perhaps I didn't want to know.

The whole situation was awkward, even eerie. I was determined not to serve as a conduit between Tripp and the Jones lawyers. That meant I couldn't tell Campbell anything he didn't already know. But I did want to find out how much he knew about a subject that stood a pretty good chance of turning his case into a nuclear explosion.

So I understand you might be aware of another situation—something a little more current? I suggested.

Campbell picked up a note on his desk and looked it over. "A situation involving a former intern?" he asked.

"That sounds like something I might be talking about."

"You can rest assured we're all over that," Campbell said, "like flies over feces." Then he sort of smiled.

• • •

Campbell and the Jones lawyers were over it more than I ever imagined. Using the information Tripp had supplied, late on the afternoon of Friday, December 5, the team had faxed to Bob Bennett a witness list that included the name of Monica Lewinsky. As it turned out, Lewinsky came to the White House the next morning to deliver her latest stash of gifts for the president (a tie, a mug, a book, an antique cigar holder). Unable to reach Betty Currie, she was kept waiting at the northwest gate guard booth. Currie finally sent word to have Lewinsky wait some more; the president had a guest in the Oval Office. One of the Secret Service officers mentioned that the guest was Eleanor Mondale. Lewinsky became "hysterical" and stormed away. She considered Mondale yet another rival for the president's affections. She went home and called Betty Currie to complain. Currie told Clinton. Clinton blew up at the Secret Service for telling Lewinsky who his guest was. Then he called Lewinsky at home and berated her for making a stink. Finally, he invited her to come back to the White House. When they met early that afternoon, he was affectionate. Lewinsky complained that Vernon Jordan had done nothing to help her get a job. "Oh, I'll talk to him," Clinton replied. "I'll get on it."

At this point, two divergent strains—Clinton's months-old promise to help get Lewinsky a job and his concern about the Jones lawyers' pursuit of her—became hopelessly intertwined. Clinton met with Bob Bennett late that same afternoon. Bennett had already checked out Lewinsky with Bruce Lindsey and was assured there was nothing to worry about. He had no reason to doubt it. Clinton had repeatedly assured his legal team and senior aides there would be no problems involving any women in the White House. ("I'm retired," he had told them on more than one occasion.) Then Clinton met with Jordan the next day, Sunday, December 7. On Monday, Jordan's secretary called Lewinsky and asked her to come over on Thursday, December 11, for a second meeting. She did so and had a turkey sandwich lunch with Jordan in his office. This time, the president's friend was far more encouraging. If she got mad at the president, he told her, take it out on me. Call me. Lewinsky thought this was odd. She didn't know Vernon Jordan's home phone number.

Jordan promised to help her and asked her to send letters to three business contacts he was going to give her. That afternoon, after Lewinsky left, he placed a series of phone calls to senior corporate executives in New York on behalf of the president's young friend. He called the chairman and chief executive officer of Young & Rubicam. He called the executive vice president of MacAndrews & Forbes Holdings (owner of Revlon). He called the executive vice president of American Express.

Later that same day, in Little Rock, Judge Susan Webber Wright ruled on Bob Bennett's motion to prohibit the Jones lawyers from demanding that Clinton identify all women (other than his wife) with whom he had had, or proposed having, sexual relations over the past twenty years. Bennett had argued the questions were overly broad, intrusive and irrelevant. Wright agreed only in part. The president was obligated to supply certain answers. She narrowed the time frame to five years before or after May 8, 1991, the date of the alleged incident with Paula Jones. And she ruled that Clinton must respond to the question by identifying anybody he had sexual relations with, or proposed to have sexual relations with, if the women at the time were state or *federal* employees. He also had to identify any and all sexual liaisons during the same time period that were procured and concealed by state troopers assigned to his security detail.

The next week, on December 15, the Jones lawyers served Clinton's lawyers with a new set of requests. They asked for the president to turn over all "communications between the President and Monica Lewisky [*sic*]." Then, early on December 17, at about two A.M., President Clinton called Monica Lewinsky at her apartment to inform her for the first time that she had become ensnared in the Paula Jones case.

The phone call had two purposes, actually. One was to tell Lewinsky that Betty Currie's brother had died in a tragic car accident. They talked about this for what Lewinsky later described as "a little bit." Then Clinton told her he had some more "bad news": her name was on the Jones witness list. Clinton said it broke his heart that she was caught up in this. He suggested that maybe Lewinsky could file an affidavit to avoid having to testify. "You can always say you were coming to see Betty or you were bringing me letters," he told her, according to Lewinsky's later recollection. Clinton told her if she got a subpoena, she should get in touch with Betty Currie. Lewinsky offered a plan whereby Clinton might settle the lawsuit.

Then Clinton told her that he had some Christmas gifts for her. He told her he would arrange for Betty Currie to come in over the weekend so he could give them to her. Lewinsky stopped him. She remembered the first reason for Clinton's call that night. She told him not to dare contacting Currie for such a purpose. Given that her brother had just died in a horrible accident, she said, it might be better if we "let Betty be."

After getting off the phone with the president, Lewinsky was quite upset. She picked up the phone and called Linda Tripp.

•   •   •

During these same weeks, another intense drama was under way. After her pre-Thanksgiving phone call with David Pyke, Linda Tripp had further conversations with the Paula Jones lawyer. "We talked about her subpoena," Pyke recalled. "She told us how to deliver it to the Pentagon—which entrance to go to, what extension to call her at." They also worked out an arrangement whereby there would be no mention of Tripp's secret tapes in the subpoena to avoid alerting Clinton's lawyers and Lewinsky to their existence.

But then a problem arose. After receiving her exquisitely orchestrated subpoena on November 24, Tripp went to see her lawyer, Kirby Behre, who was still clueless about his client's covert assistance to the Jones team. She told Behre for the first time that she had been secretly taping conversations with a woman named Monica Lewinsky. Behre, startled, told her that taping without the consent of the other person was in violation of Maryland state law. He took possession of the tapes Tripp had made to date and told her to stop making any more.

Tripp, by her own account, was stunned. It became instantly clear to her that she faced a terrible dilemma. She now couldn't turn her tapes over to the Jones lawyers without revealing her own illegal activity—something the president's lawyers would be sure to pounce on. Having schemed to nail Bill Clinton, Tripp had in effect set up herself.

Pyke was beside himself. Even more than Tripp's testimony, he and his partners wanted Tripp's tapes. "They were the Holy Grail," said Pyke. "They were clearly going to be the most explosive thing we had." Without so much as listening to a word of them, Pyke and his partner, Wes Holmes, had already plotted out how they would put the tapes to their most effective use—springing them on an unsuspecting Monica Lewinsky. As they envisioned it, they would routinely question Lewinsky at her deposition and let her, as they fully expected, deny any sexual relationship with President Clinton. Then they would take out the tape recorder and, as Holmes put it, "watch her face turn white."

But now Tripp's legal dilemma had put a big dent in their plans. At first, Pyke tried to persuade Tripp to turn over the tapes anyway, telling her she would never be criminally prosecuted for such an offense. When that didn't work, he tried to convince her to make a new legal tape of a conversation with Lewinsky that would serve the same purpose. "We just wanted one good tape," Pyke said. He and Tripp talked about several options. Tripp could call Lewinsky from her mother's house in New Jersey, or perhaps she could make a call from a hotel room in northern Virginia. They even talked about something that at first seemed wild: Tripp wiring herself and getting together with Lewinsky in person.

Ironically, during all this time, Tripp was not overly fastidious about following Behre's advice. She never unplugged the tape recorder from her phone. On December 9 and again on December 12, when Lewinsky called, Tripp picked up the phone and, she says, didn't realize that her recorder was running. During these conversations, the two women talked about Vernon Jordan and Christmas shopping and a recent fight they had had and their taste in jewelry. They talked about the Paula Jones case and whether it would settle. They talked about their own friendship and how they sometimes shouted at each other.

"The problem I have with you, frankly, is I feel entirely too maternal toward you," Tripp told Lewinsky on the evening of December 12. "And it's almost like—it's like me yelling at my kids, not that that ever has any effect. When I yell at you, it's out of love."

•   •   •

On the afternoon of Friday, December 19, Lewinsky was at her office in the Pentagon when a process server showed up to deliver a subpoena. It called for her to show up for a deposition in the Jones case on January 23—and demanded that she turn over all correspondence she had had with the president as well as "each and every gift" the president had given her, including "any and all dresses, accessories and jewelry, and/or hat pins." Lewinsky was stunned. She burst into tears. She ran to a pay phone and called Vernon Jordan. Jordan told her to come on over. As soon as she arrived, Jordan called President Clinton. Jordan told Clinton about Lewinsky's subpoena and promised to get a lawyer. He mentioned the name Francis Carter, a prominent criminal lawyer in Washington. "You think he's a good lawyer?" Clinton asked. Jordan assured him Carter was.

When Tripp learned the contents of Lewinsky's subpoena, she was furious—at David Pyke. "You put in the stuff about the hat pin!" Pyke recalls Tripp berating him over the phone. Lewinsky was going to suspect that the information came from Tripp. "You're going to turn her against me!" Pyke recalls Tripp saying. "I'm going to lose my job! You've done a stupid thing."

Actually, Lewinsky still didn't get it. On December 22, Jordan took her in his limousine to see Frank Carter. That night, Tripp called her—and taped the phone call, this time quite deliberately. The stakes had gotten too high. Vernon Jordan was now involved—big time. Lewinsky was asking her to perjure herself.

The conversation that night was emotional and rambling. Lewinsky was in tears for part of it. Tripp offered sympathy, trying to persuade Lewinsky they were in this together. She expressed alarm that the Jones lawyers had gotten Lewinsky's name and even had a "specific," like the hat pin mentioned in the subpoena. "Someone has told them something," Tripp said ominously. "Now, do we think that's a little something or a lot something? Do they have specifics to ask us? We don't know this."

Lewinsky insisted she would just deny everything and was sure there couldn't be any evidence that proved otherwise. Tripp pointed out that this would put the two of them in direct conflict. "But it doesn't have to be a conflict," Lewinsky said.

Of course it does, Tripp said. She had no choice. "If they say, 'Has Monica Lewinsky ever said to you that she is in love with the president or is having a physical relationship with the president?'—if I say no, that is fucking perjury.

"That's the bottom line. I will do everything I can to not be in that position," Tripp told Lewinsky. She was even thinking of telling the Jones lawyers that she had to have foot surgery to avoid testifying. "I will do anything," Tripp said.

"I know," Lewinsky said.

"But no, you really don't know, 'cause you don't believe me. I think you really believe—"

"I believe you."

The problem was, Tripp said, there was just one thing she could absolutely not do. And that was to lie. She just couldn't do that. It was against her principles.

"You know what, Monica?" Tripp said. "You're gonna die here, and I would do almost anything for my kids, but I don't think I would lie on the stand for them."

Lewinsky, still sobbing, said lying wasn't such a big deal for her because she was "brought up with lies all the time."

Tripp said she didn't believe that.

Lewinsky said it was true; when her parents were divorced she would make up a story to get money from her dad.

Tripp said she wasn't that way. She felt terrible.

"I know it's huge to you," she told Lewinsky. "I'm being a shitty friend, and that is the last thing I want to do, because I won't lie. Okay? How do you think that makes me feel? I could make you stop crying, and I could make your life so much easier, if I would just [blank] lie. . . ."

Tripp couldn't stop obsessing on this theme.

"How do you think this makes me feel?" Tripp said. "I feel like I'm sticking a knife in your back."

Later, she brought the conversation around to who could have possibly ratted out Lewinsky. Her old boyfriend Andy Bleiler? Did he know about that hat pin?

No, Lewinsky said, she didn't think so.

Anybody else? Anybody on the East Coast? Think.

No, Lewinsky couldn't for the life of her think of who could have been the informant for the Jones lawyers.

"There—there is no one that would do this to me," Lewinsky said, "and no one that knows anyone that would even—you know what I mean, Linda?"

•   •   •

Lucianne Goldberg's notebook records a phone call from Tripp the next day. "Linda told 'pretty girl' she would not lie," she wrote. Then, the notebook shows, she had a conference call with Richard Porter and Jerome Marcus to discuss the latest developments. Goldberg relayed to the lawyers what Tripp had said about her taped conversation with Lewinsky: "Vernon Jordan told her to lie." It was, on Tripp's part, an embellishment of what Lewinsky actually had said—at least of what was captured on tape. At one point, Lewinsky referred to Jordan—"the one that I saw today"—and said he had asked her, "You didn't tell anybody, did you?" The question seems to imply Jordan's knowledge of Lewinsky's relationship with the president and at least an implicit sanction for her to conceal it. But maybe not. That, and other references to Jordan, were ambiguous.

Still, the allegation that Vernon Jordan was coaching Monica Lewinsky to lie under oath—and that Monica Lewinsky was pressuring Linda Tripp to lie—immediately grabbed the attention of Porter and Marcus. "Holy shit!" Marcus recalled as the first words that came to his mind. This was, he and Porter thought, possibly subornation of perjury. Maybe obstruction of justice. This was criminal activity. And it was on tape. Suddenly, their thinking—as lawyers—moved into a new mode. They concentrated on one thing: They had to protect the evidence, Tripp's tapes.

Tripp by this time had grown suspicious of her lawyer, Kirby Behre. He was part of a large firm with Democratic ties and was jogging buddies with Mitch Ettinger, one of Clinton's lawyers. Goldberg that day passed these suspicions on to Porter and Marcus, who agreed that Tripp needed a new lawyer—a conservative who wouldn't leak the contents of the tapes to Clinton's lawyers. They volunteered to help find her one. There was also talk about getting the tapes into the hands of a third party—somebody who would make sure they wouldn't be destroyed. Somebody like a publisher who, among other advantages, could put the tapes under the cloak of the First Amendment.

Sometime that day, Goldberg and Tripp talked. Tripp called me. "New York thinks I should go see a publisher," she told me.

A publisher? What are you talking about?

It would be for protection, she said.

In the three months I had been talking to Tripp and Goldberg, they had never said anything about planning a book. Of course, it shouldn't have come as that big a surprise. Goldberg was, after all, a literary agent. Tripp had planned a book back in 1996—and she had showed me parts of the proposal back in April. But the idea was well off my radar screen; indeed, it seemed a bit counterintuitive. Why were they wasting their time sharing information with me, if that was their purpose? In any case, I could not have cared less about their motives or their ultimate goal. My interest in them was quite simple and fairly well focused: Was the stuff they were telling me true? Could it be corroborated? Would it make a story for *Newsweek?*

Stunned at this suggestion, I told Tripp that such a move right now, under the circumstances, was insane. It seemed to me, I said, that this was potentially serious business she was involved in here. If she started mucking this up with talk about publishers and book deals, she was only going to screw herself. She would undermine her own credibility and the credibility of her information. And though I didn't say this to her, I was thinking something else, as well: You're also going to muck up my story, you idiot.

If you get deposed, I told Tripp that day, you will have to tell them about it—that right in the middle of your conversations with Monica Lewinsky you were trying to shop a book deal. You'll get hammered.

I wrote it off as another of Tripp's wacky ideas—like stealing the dress. But then I did something that, in retrospect, I probably shouldn't have done. I called Goldberg and told her the same thing: I didn't know what the two of them were up to, I said, but I knew that trying to sell a book right now was really stupid. Linda would only have to testify about it.

Goldberg's notebook records the phone call. "Call from Isikoff saying don't see a publisher or they will ask about it in deposition."

•   •   •

My advice was right, of course. The problem was I wasn't their adviser—and had no business trying to be, even on what at the time seemed a peripheral issue. Still, when I called Goldberg and even when I shared my thinking with Tripp that day, I was trying to influence the actions of the players. As a reporter, that's not my job. But I didn't realize something else: I was at this point too involved to avoid influencing the players.[2]

In any case, that week I was under a bit of pressure from my bureau chief, McDaniel. After a year of scandal, of Whitewater and Webb Hubbell and campaign finance and Paula Jones, she wanted me to finish a story on an entirely different subject: Andrew Cuomo, the secretary of the Department of Housing and Urban Development. Cuomo was a rising political star. Washington insiders were talking about him as a possible running mate with Al Gore in the year 2000. A few months earlier, he had come to lunch at *Newsweek* and talked about a campaign to crack down on public housing developers implicated in fraud and corruption. Cuomo was subtly portraying it as an act of political courage. A lot of these developers were big Democratic contributors, and he was already getting some heat from members of his own party on Capitol Hill. McDaniel thought it might make an interesting story.

In working on it, I had gotten in touch with Cuomo's staff to seek some backup material and ran across Cuomo's new press secretary, somebody I knew from an earlier incarnation. It was Karen Hinton, the woman who in 1994 had described to me the unpleasant sexual overture Clinton had once made to her ten years earlier. Hinton was as liberal and socially committed as ever. We joked about our earlier encounter and arranged to get together for lunch, a lunch in which we talked about Cuomo and public housing and Paula Jones and Bill Clinton. Hinton wondered where it would all end.

I had been planning to file the Cuomo story the week before. Then news intervened. Cuomo's predecessor, Henry Cisneros, got indicted on charges of lying to federal investigators about how much he had paid his former mistress—lying, as it were, about sex. *Newsweek* was not going to run two stories about HUD secretaries in the same issue, so Cuomo got bumped into the new year. But McDaniel wanted me to finish it before I flew off to California with my family for a few days the week after Christmas.

As I rushed to finish the story, I stopped by McDaniel's office to give her an update on the latest developments on the women front. Things were really heating up, I explained. Both woman number two and woman number three had gotten subpoenas. This might yet actually become a story, I told her. McDaniel listened with fascination, but I'm not sure either one of us believed it would really happen.

•   •   •

The march of events in the Jones lawsuit proceeded. On December 23, President Clinton answered the interrogatories the Jones lawyers had sent him back in October—the questions Judge Wright had ordered him to answer two weeks earlier. In response to the question demanding he identify all state or federal employees with whom he had had sexual relations between 1986 and 1996, Clinton answered: "None." The answer was signed "under penalty of perjury" and filed with the court in Little Rock.

Other women from Clinton's past kept getting caught up in the case. On Christmas Eve, Rick Lambert, the private investigator for the Jones lawyers, called the Russellville, Arkansas, home of the parents of Elizabeth Ward Gracen. An actress and former Miss America, Gracen, according to the testimony of a friend, had been the victim of an unwanted sexual encounter with Clinton in 1983. That night, a man answered the phone.

"Hey, man, Merry Christmas," Lambert said. "Is Liz around?"

No, the man said, I think she's down at the dance studio.

"Well, listen, just tell her Rick called," said Lambert, suggesting he was some sort of old friend. He then left his phone number in his chummiest voice.

Ten minutes later, a woman called him back. "I'm a friend of Liz's, and she wanted to know why you're calling." Lambert explained that he was an investigator for the Paula Jones legal team.

The woman hesitated. "She's in Paris," she answered.

Lambert didn't buy it. "Come on, Liz, I know that's you." Gracen hung up.

According to Gracen's boyfriend, an investment banker named Pat Augustus, Gracen, fearing a subpoena, then quickly left Arkansas—flying first to Las Vegas, then to the Caribbean, where she went island-hopping for the next few months. She had no interest in being drawn into the case. She had already lied for Clinton once—in 1992. The tabloids were after her then, too. There had been anxiety among some of Clinton's aides. It was the eve of the New York primary and some of them feared that, on top of Gennifer Flowers, Gracen could really hurt if she were to come forward and acknowledge illicit sexual relations with the candidate. She was, after all, a former Miss America—a bit harder to smear than Gennifer Flowers. Around that time, Gracen's agent, Miles Levy, got a call from Mickey Kantor, Clinton's campaign chairman. They arranged to have breakfast. Hollywood producer Harry Thomason, a close friend of the Clintons', tagged along. Kantor and Thomason agreed it was terrible how the tabloids were chasing Elizabeth and suggested that perhaps they could help. Within days, Hollywood producer Michael Viner offered Gracen a part in a TV miniseries that was about to start filming in Croatia. Levy, who later confirmed the series of events, including the breakfast with Kantor and Thomason, insisted that Gracen was "very qualified" for the part. Before she left the country, however, she agreed to issue a press statement, prepared by the Clinton campaign, denying she had ever had sexual relations with Bill Clinton.

It wasn't true. Nine years earlier, when she was twenty-one and still serving as Miss America, Gracen had been doing a public service announcement in Hot Springs, Arkansas, when Clinton offered her a ride in his state limousine. According to Gracen's later account, Clinton flirted with her—then invited her to the apartment of one of his friends at the Quapaw Towers. They had sex that night. It was rough sex. Clinton got so carried away that he bit her lip, Gracen later told friends. But it was consensual. The governor of Arkansas didn't force himself upon her. Afterward, Gracen felt terrible about it. She was married at the time—as was Clinton. Clinton later called her at the apartment in New York that Gracen shared with her husband. He wanted to get together again. She cut him off. "I just said, 'You have the wrong number,'" Gracen said in 1998. "I didn't want any more to do with him."

•　•　•

After Christmas, Porter and Marcus wrestled over what to do next. Marcus began an immediate effort to locate a new lawyer for Tripp, calling in rapid succession a string of prominent Republican attorneys in Washington. He called two former Justice Department officials during the Reagan administration—Ted Olson and Victoria Toensing—and neither could take it. A third former Reagan administration lawyer, Charles Cooper, promised to get back to him but never did. In the meantime, Marcus was focused on what was going to happen to Tripp's tapes. He had a gnawing fear that Tripp would get spooked by the Maryland statute and even destroy them. "I was worried that they might end up in a Dumpster," he said.

For days, Marcus ruminated about what to do. He thought about another civil case that had been much in the news that year: a case involving Texaco. It had started out as a race discrimination suit, a civil case, in which the plaintiff's lawyers learned of secret tapes on which corporate executives allegedly could be heard using racial slurs and discussing the destruction of documents. There were charges that the tapes had been doctored—and federal prosecutors in New York had opened a criminal probe. This was like that, Marcus thought. "It was a direct analogy." That would mean taking the information about Tripp's tapes to the U.S. Attorney's Office. Or maybe the Justice Department. But you can't do that here: the alleged beneficiary—and possible participant in the crimes—was the same president who appointed those people.

At home over the Christmas holidays, Marcus continued to wrestle with the issue: "All I kept thinking was, What does one do with this information? *Who do you call?*"

Book Four

KEN STARR

December 1997-January 1998

15

"One of your friends is in imminent danger."

The holidays were an intense and in some ways heady period for Monica Lewinsky. The subpoena at her office had been terrifying. But it was also transforming. Only weeks earlier, Lewinsky had felt marginalized and ignored. Now, she was more important to Bill Clinton than ever before.

Her last day at the Pentagon was December 24; the day before, her colleagues gave her a little send-off in Ken Bacon's office. Then on December 28, after getting a call from Betty Currie, she went to the White House to pick up her Christmas gifts from the president—the gifts Clinton had first mentioned eleven days earlier when he woke her at 2 A.M. to tell her she was on the Paula Jones witness list.

A little after 8:30 A.M., Lewinsky was ushered into the Oval Office and found Clinton playing with Buddy, the dog. She had brought a present for Buddy. Then Clinton and Lewinsky went into the private study. Clinton got out a big bag from the Black Dog in Martha's Vineyard and presented Lewinsky with her gifts. There was a marble bear's-head carving and a Rockettes blanket. There was a stuffed animal and a box of cherry chocolates. There was a pair of joke sunglasses and a pin with a New York skyline on it.

They talked about the Jones case and how Lewinsky had ended up on the witness list. Clinton thought it might be "that woman from the summer"—he meant Linda Tripp—or maybe the Secret Service. Lewinsky expressed anxiety about the reference to the hat pin in the subpoena. Clinton said that bothered him, too. Lewinsky wondered if she shouldn't get the gifts away from her house—giving them to somebody, "maybe Betty." Clinton, Lewinsky testified, pondered. Then he said, "I don't know," or, "Let me think about that."

They were alone in the private study for about forty-five minutes. They spent some time, according to Lewinsky, "goofing off." They took turns putting on the "really funny" sunglasses Clinton had gotten for her. They also kissed. The kiss was "passionate," she later testified. It was "physically intimate." "I don't call it a brief kiss," she said. But it wasn't fully satisfactory, either. As they kissed, standing in the doorway by the study, Lewinsky opened her eyes and got upset. Clinton's eyes were open, too—and he was looking out the window. "I got mad," Lewinsky said. This wasn't very romantic. Clinton explained. "Well, I was just looking to see to make sure no one was out there," he said.

As she was leaving, Lewinsky noticed that Clinton hesitated before picking up all the gifts for her to take home. It was, she thought, as if he were wondering whether he really should be giving them to her.

Lewinsky went home. According to her, later that day Betty Currie called from a cell phone. She said either "I understand you have something to give me" or "The president said you have something to give me." Then, Lewinsky said, she packed up many—but not all—of the gifts she had received from the president over the past two years. Currie swung by her apartment, and Lewinsky gave her the box.

Currie's account was different. She testified that she thought it was Lewinsky who had called her and asked her to come by her apartment to pick up the gifts. She didn't remember Clinton saying anything at all about picking up the gifts.

Later, there would be much debate about whose memory was more reliable. It was an important debate: if Clinton had told Currie to get the gifts, then the president was arguably complicit in a scheme to conceal evidence in a legal case. Currie's cell phone records were checked. They showed that at 3:21 P.M. on December 28, 1997, Currie called Lewinsky. The president's lawyers said that didn't prove anything. Currie and Lewinsky talked all the time.

But there was something else that raises questions about the reliability of Currie's memory. It was the one thing about the exchange that Currie did remember, something Lewinsky supposedly had said about why she wanted Currie to have the gifts. It actually was something Lewinsky couldn't possibly have said.

Something about me.[1]

•   •   •

On December 31, Lewinsky later said, she had breakfast with Vernon Jordan. She was worried about what to do about Linda Tripp, she explained, and wanted to consult the president's best friend. Jordan met her at his usual corner table at the Park Hyatt Hotel. Lewinsky told him about Tripp, about how she had been her friend, but she didn't trust her anymore. She told Jordan that Tripp had spent the night at her apartment a few times and might have seen some notes lying around.

"Notes from the president to you?" Jordan asked.

"No," Lewinsky said. "Notes from me to the president."

"Go home," Jordan told her, "and make sure they're not there."

During the breakfast, Lewinsky remembered, she ordered cereal with yogurt and Jordan had an egg-white omelet. Afterward, Jordan gave her a ride in his car, and Lewinsky asked him if he thought Clinton would always be married to his wife. Jordan said, "Yes, as he should be," and then volunteered—a minute or so later—"Well, maybe you two will have an affair after he leaves office." Lewinsky was shocked. She had assumed Jordan already knew. "Well, we already had an affair," she told him, explaining they had done "everything but sex." Jordan's reaction, she said, was: "Mmmmph." She figured she should drop the subject.

But she took Jordan's advice about the notes, she later testified, and discarded about fifty draft love notes to Bill Clinton that might have been seen by Linda Tripp.

In March 1998, Jordan was asked about his breakfast with Lewinsky. He didn't say he couldn't remember it. He didn't say the conversation covered different subjects. He said, flatly and unequivocally, "I've never had breakfast with Monica Lewinsky."

Then in August, Lewinsky testified and provided minute detail about the breakfast. The records of the Park Hyatt Hotel were reviewed. They showed that on the morning of December 31, 1997, there was a breakfast receipt signed by Vernon Jordan for an egg-white omelet and a cereal with yogurt.

On February 4, 1999, during the Senate impeachment trial, Jordan was asked again about the breakfast. "My recollection has subsequently been refreshed," he said. They did have breakfast that morning, he conceded. But the notion that he instructed Lewinsky to go home and destroy notes to the president was "ridiculous," he said. "I'm a loyal friend," Jordan said, "but I'm not a fool."

*　*　*

In early January, Bill, Hillary and Chelsea Clinton flew to St. Thomas in the U.S. Virgin Islands for a brief vacation. All things considered, it had been a pretty good year for the First Family. Chelsea had started college at Stanford. Bill Clinton had weathered the political storms over his campaign fundraising, most Washington pundits believed, relatively unscathed. The economy was good. His approval ratings were high. It was time to be thinking about his legacy. What kind of president would history judge him?

Hillary Clinton, after a year of foreign travels and largely ceremonial events, was refocusing her energies on public policy initiatives. She had hosted a White House conference on child care in October. It was an issue that had always engaged her—even more than health care—and the First Lady was gearing up to launch an ambitious administration initiative to expand access to child care for working parents.

While the Clintons were on vacation, a small controversy erupted. On Sunday, January 4, the president and First Lady, wearing bathing suits, went for a stroll on a secluded beach that had been sealed off by the Secret Service. A photographer for Agence France-Presse, hiding behind some trees, snapped a photograph as the two embraced during what looked like a playful slow dance. The picture of a seemingly loving First Couple ran the next day in papers across the United States. At first, the White House berated the press for invading the Clintons' privacy. But many commentators were skeptical.[2] They wondered if the Clintons had not been well aware of the photographer's presence. Could this, the cynics speculated, have anything to do with the Paula Jones lawsuit—and the upcoming deposition of the president?

Clinton himself brushed off the controversy when he returned to Washington. "Actually, I liked [the picture] quite a lot," the president told reporters. "But I didn't think I was being photographed."

•   •   •

By the time the president returned from the Caribbean, he had every reason to believe that Monica Lewinsky would be kept out of the Paula Jones case. That very day, she met with her new lawyer, Francis Carter, to go over the wording of an affidavit that would avoid the need for her to testify. She later called Clinton to tell him about it. She was a bit curt, she later said, because she was "peeved" and "annoyed" about the romantic picture of the Clintons.[3] The next day, she picked up a copy of the affidavit at Carter's office, then called Jordan to discuss it. She tinkered with the wording. On Wednesday morning, January 7, she signed it—and took it to Jordan. It asserted: "I have never had a sexual relationship with the president." Although she had seen him after leaving the White House in April 1996, it was only at official receptions and formal functions, and "there were other people present on all of these occasions," the affidavit said.

Then Lewinsky flew to New York. On Thursday, January 8, she had an interview with a senior vice president of MacAndrews & Forbes Holdings, Inc., the parent company of Revlon—an interview arranged by Vernon Jordan, who sat on the Revlon board of directors. The interview didn't go well. Lewinsky called Jordan to complain. Jordan called Ronald Perelman, the chairman and chief executive officer of MacAndrews & Forbes. Lewinsky was invited back for a second interview. The next day, another senior vice president offered Lewinsky a $40,000-a-year job in Revlon's public relations office. She called to thank Jordan but complained that she thought the salary was too low. Jordan told her to "quit whining."

Then Jordan called Betty Currie to relay word to the president: "Mission accomplished." Clinton called Jordan. "Thank you very much," he said.

That same day, Friday, January 9, Lewinsky returned a phone call to Linda Tripp. It was an odd call. Tripp asked Lewinsky what was going on with her job search. Lewinsky said she didn't have one yet—and she hadn't seen Clinton or Jordan or Currie since they'd last talked. Tripp told her not to sign her affidavit until she got her job. Lewinsky promised she wouldn't.

The two women were now lying to each other with almost every sentence they spoke.

Tripp said she had been thinking, and maybe she wouldn't confirm Kathleen Willey's story to the Paula Jones lawyers after all. She didn't really know anything. Maybe she wouldn't even say anything about Monica Lewinsky if the Jones lawyers were to ask her.

According to Lewinsky, Tripp also said she had been to New York over Christmas and gone shopping with Norma Asness, Hillary Clinton's friend. Asness told Tripp she should move to New York and she would help her get a PR job there.

A PR job in New York? Lewinsky thought. That's what I'm doing. Lewinsky concluded that Tripp was jealous.

Then the really odd part: Tripp told Lewinsky about an Indian friend with whom she worked out at the gym. The friend recently had gone to see a psychic, who had relayed a warning: One of your friends is "in imminent danger." The danger had to do "with the words she would speak."

Lewinsky and Tripp agreed they would meet the following Tuesday to talk some more.

• • •

It was not clear who first had the idea. It may have been Marcus, who was mulling the question at home over the Christmas holidays. It also could have been Goldberg, who was talking quite a bit to Marcus and Richard Porter during this period. Or it may well have been Tripp herself, who was frequently on the phone with Goldberg. But to all of the conspirators, it made perfect sense: Linda Tripp's tapes, and her allegations that Bill Clinton and Vernon Jordan were coaching Monica Lewinsky to lie, should be taken to the one prosecutor in the United States who had no reason to protect the president. It was a prosecutor who had spent the last three and a half years in an exceedingly frustrating and expensive effort to catch Clinton and his closest aides in criminal wrongdoing: Whitewater independent counsel Kenneth Starr.

The idea surfaced the first week in January. But would Starr want it? And more important, would he give Tripp immunity for her precious but illegally recorded tapes? As it happened, Marcus knew just how to find out. In an arrangement he insisted was pure serendipity, Marcus was due to have dinner in Philadelphia on Thursday evening, January 8, with another University of Chicago Law School classmate, Paul Rosenzweig. In fact, the elves were having an impromptu convention that night. Porter, another member of Marcus and Rosenzweig's law school class, had a business closing in Philadelphia the next day so he agreed to fly in from Chicago that night to join his old buddies for dinner. Conway, largely for the hell of it, decided to take the train down from New York.

Rosenzweig was no stranger to the Jones case. In the spring of 1994, Marcus had sought to recruit him to work on it. He even had a brief conversation with Cammarata about joining the secret legal team, but nothing came of it. A former environmental crimes prosecutor in the Bush Justice Department, Rosenzweig had since joined Starr's staff where he was assigned some mop-up work on the White House travel office—a case nobody really thought was going anywhere. He took the train to Philadelphia after work that day and arrived at the townhouse that housed Marcus's law firm barely two hours after Vernon Jordan had called Ronald Perelman in New York City. Marcus had made reservations at an expensive French restaurant, Deux Cheminees. But he wanted to get this matter taken care of first. He told Rosenzweig, very briefly, about a witness in the Paula Jones case whom Vernon Jordan was trying to line up with a job—and of tape recordings in which the woman described a sexual relationship with the president. "I haven't listened to this stuff," Marcus said he told Rosenzweig. "I don't know if it's real or not. But do you think this is something that your office would be interested in?" Rosenzweig was always careful when talking about anything to do with Starr's office. "I don't know," he said. "I'll find out."

Then they started to leave for dinner and ran into Conway. The elf from New York needed to drop his briefcase off so they went back to Marcus's office. Marcus pulled him aside and whispered: "I told him about Lewinsky." He told Conway he had asked Rosenzweig to find out if Starr would take the case. Conway was stunned.

"My jaw dropped," he recalled much later. They'll never do it, he thought.

That rainy and cold night, in a private room with a fireplace at Deux Cheminees, Marcus and Conway sat down for dinner with their guest from Ken Starr's office. Marcus and Rosenzweig did most of the talking, catching up on old times and talking about their families. Conway said little, drinking large quantities of wine. It was a little awkward given Rosenzweig's position and the message he had been asked to relay. So the lawyers largely avoided any direct mention of the subject on everybody's mind although every now and then one of them would make comments like "Aren't these people [meaning Clinton and his crowd] unbelievable?"

Porter's plane was late. He got there three hours late and shortly after he did Rosenzweig had to leave to catch the train back to Washington. As soon as Rosenzweig left, Conway couldn't contain himself. "You won't believe it," he told Porter. "Jerome told him." Marcus filled in Porter with a few more details—how Vernon Jordan had given Lewinsky a ride in his limo and supposedly told her to lie. Now, it all might be in the hands of the independent counsel.

As they sat around the flickering fireplace at Deux Cheminees, the potential enormity of what they had just done suddenly dawned on all of them. Porter thought it was like the opening chapter of a John Grisham novel. Holy Jesus, he thought, this is really turning into something.

•   •   •

The elves had other pressing business that week. Linda Tripp still needed a new lawyer. Marcus's efforts to recruit a high-profile conservative had gone nowhere. Meanwhile, the urgency seemed to be increasing. In a front-page story on Wednesday, the *Washington Times* had reported that the date for Clinton's long expected deposition had been set. It would be in Washington at the end of the following week, Saturday, January 17.

The Jones lawyers were increasingly anxious: they wanted Tripp's tapes as soon as possible. They wanted to be able to question Clinton about some of what they had been told the tapes contained. But Tripp was dodging David Pyke's calls. As she would later testify, she was terrified that if the tapes ever surfaced, she could be criminally prosecuted. She was hanging out there, a sitting duck for the president's lawyers.

The issue came to a head at the end of the week. Tripp went to see her lawyer, Kirby Behre, and brought him a copy of the December 22 tape—the one that mentioned Vernon Jordan. "I am scared for my life," Tripp later testified she told Behre.

Behre was furious. "What have you done?" he asked. "That tape is illegal. I told you that was illegal."

Tripp said she made Behre listen to the tape. His reaction, she testified, was: "Oh, my God, we have to call Bob Bennett." Behre was suggesting that he call Bennett only to find out if the Jones case was likely to be settled any time soon. If so, there would be no reason for the Jones lawyers to subpoena Tripp's tapes, no reason for his client's potentially criminal conduct to become known to the world.

But Tripp was horrified at the thought of any contact with the president's lawyer and rejected it.

Well, what do you want to do, then? Behre asked.

She needed to make a new tape, she said, a legal tape, a tape that would permit her to back up the story she planned to tell the Jones lawyers.

"I want a body wire," Tripp told Behre.

Behre told Tripp he would see what he could do. His law firm had a relationship with a private investigator; Behre promised to see what they could work out.

But Tripp had her doubts—and they were being fanned by Goldberg, who was convinced that Behre couldn't be trusted. Goldberg was getting bombarded by calls—from Tripp, from Porter, from the Jones lawyers Pyke and Wes Holmes, all of them recorded in her notebook. She was working on the problem of getting her a new lawyer, she told Tripp. On Friday, January 9, Holmes—now desperate—called Conway and pleaded for help.

"Can you help us find Tripp a new lawyer immediately—like over the weekend?" Holmes asked him. "Do you know of anybody—anybody at all?"

Conway thought for a second—then called his buddy Ann Coulter in Washington. Coulter knew just the person, she said, a fellow conservative who wasn't a member of a big law firm that would likely have untrustworthy Democrats.

Who's that? Conway wanted to know.

Jim Moody, Coulter told Conway.

"That's a great idea," Conway said—and called him.

• • •

So Moody became the newest recruit in the confederacy of elves. Moody was a big lumbering man from Kansas City, a perpetually cheerful, solo practitioner of decidedly libertarian sympathies who liked to represent whistleblowers doing battle with the federal government. He was something of a mystery even to his friends. A techno-geek who, as a student at MIT, once hatched plots to blow up the Harvard football field, Moody after college had gone to work for a U.S. intelligence agency. He was always fuzzy about which one. His friends credited him with helping to design the cruise missile system.

Moody had met Coulter at a dinner party and quickly formed a fast friendship held together by a common passion: the Grateful Dead. (They sometimes joked that they were the only two right-wing Deadheads in Washington.) They would fly off to Dead concerts at a moment's notice—a habit they indulged when band leader Jerry Garcia died in 1995 and a memorial concert was held in his honor in San Francisco. They also took ski vacations together, including one the year before in Vail (Conway tagged along). But skiing with Moody could be frightening: Moody wore very thick glasses—a thin disguise for the fact that he was legally blind.

Moody told Conway on Friday that he was interested in representing this woman with the tapes problem. He and Tripp talked for several hours. (Tripp gave Moody a code name to use when calling her: Col. Rose.) Then Moody spent much of Saturday lining up the equipment necessary to put a body wire on Tripp for her upcoming meeting with Lewinsky. Tripp by now was fed up with Behre, who had called Tripp at home that day and told her he didn't think he was going to have her wired after all. "You need to be a truth-teller, not a fact-finder," he told her.

For Tripp, that clinched it. "That's completely ludicrous," she later testified she told Behre. "How do you become a truth-teller when you're walking into a perjury trap against the president of the United States? I know what they're capable of. The gloves are off. I am going to protect myself, with or without your help."

• • •

L ate that week, I called Bob Bennett. I wanted to bounce off the president's lawyer a theory I had been mulling over the past few days. The smart money in Washington said the Jones case would never really go to trial—that in the end, after all the bluster and posturing, Clinton and Jones would have to settle. The spectacle of the president of the United States actually sitting through a trial on the issues Jones had raised seemed impossible to imagine.

I told Bennett my theory was he would settle the case the next week.

Why do you think that? Bennett asked.

The president's deposition is the following Saturday, I explained. If you're going to end up settling this anyway, you'll do it in the next few days. You'll never allow him to be deposed under oath if you can avoid it. Bennett was too shrewd to show his hand, even if there was something to what I was saying. But there wasn't. In this lawsuit, the feelings were too bitter, the antagonisms too deep, for anyone to act in his or her own self-interest.[4]

Bennett couldn't have sounded more confident. I can tell you that there's no plan to settle this case, he said. The president has nothing to worry about. He couldn't foresee any reason the deposition would not take place just as scheduled.

• • •

O n Saturday, January 10, Don Campbell and Bob Bennett arrived in Richmond, Virginia, for the long postponed deposition of Kathleen Willey. It was supposed to have taken place a month earlier, but at the last second, Willey had gone in for back surgery and begged off. The Jones lawyers had been furious. Willey was going to weasel out of it, they feared. She would balk at fingering the president. Maybe somebody had gotten to her. Bennett was on edge as well. How far would she go? When she was actually under oath, what exactly would she say Bill Clinton had done?

The proceeding was slated to start in the morning. But Judge Mehrige decided to make one last stab at settling the case. The lawyers bickered, as they always did, and the talks soon collapsed. But the deposition was put off until afternoon. During the lunch break,

Bennett—still trying to act chummy—went to lunch with Dan Gecker. Afterward, they swung by Gecker's office. Bennett's pager went off. He told Gecker he needed to use a phone—in private: it was his client. Bennett called a private line into the Oval Office. (The number later showed up on Gecker's phone bill.) Clinton, believing Willey's testimony had already taken place, wanted to know: What did she say?

When the questioning finally began that afternoon, it went slowly. Willey was still ducking and dodging, giving monosyllabic answers to Don Campbell's incessant questions. She was, she later said, very scared.[5] Campbell finally built up to the climactic moment—the events of November 29, 1993, when, Willey confirmed, she had gone to see the president about getting a paying job.

Yes, the president had hugged her during this meeting, Willey said.

Yes, the president had attempted to kiss her, Willey said.

"Did Mr. Clinton ever seek to take either of your hands and place it on his body anyplace?" Campbell asked.

"Yes," Willey said.

"Please describe that," said Campbell.

Gecker watched his client, saw her hesitation, and asked for a break. Willey huddled with Gecker in a jury room. "Are you ready for this?" Gecker asked her.

"I might as well be," she replied.

Willey then returned to the stand.

"He put his hands—he put my hands on his genitals," Willey testified.

Campbell was ecstatic. He had a second witness to crude and unsolicited sexual advances by Clinton—this time in a private office of the White House while he was president of the United States.

•　　•　　•

On Monday, from her home on the Upper West Side of Manhattan, Lucianne Goldberg called Linda Tripp. Goldberg had just heard from Porter in Chicago, who had spoken to Marcus in Philadelphia, who had just heard back from their friend Rosenzweig in Washington. Tripp should call Jackie Bennett, Goldberg told Tripp. He was the deputy Whitewater independent counsel, and his telephone number was 202-514-8688.

16

"In Watergate . . . you had tapes."

I nside the perpetually locked fourth-floor suite of offices at 1001 Pennsylvania Avenue NW, there was a recurring line—half historical analogy, half prosecutorial lament—voiced by veterans of the operation of Whitewater independent counsel Kenneth Starr. It was heard more and more through the months of 1997, when it looked as if the office's work might well be stymied. The lawyer most likely to be invoking it—a big, brawling bulldog of a prosecutor who had been through nearly every one of the controversies that had swirled around Starr's office—was the chief Washington deputy, Jackie Bennett.

"In Watergate, you had John Dean, you had tapes," Bennett liked to point out to the nodding assent of his colleagues. "We've never had that. We've never had the insider."

As Bennett saw it, that difference better than anything else explained the investigative setbacks that had beset Starr's operation. Contrary to the image cultivated by presidential allies like James Carville, the record of the Whitewater independent counsel during its three-and-a-half-year, $40 million investigation was not one of unremitting failure. In its early days, Starr's office had racked up nearly a dozen guilty pleas from Arkansas political and business figures caught up in the tangled business dealings of Madison Guaranty Savings and Loan, the fast and loose thrift run into the ground by James and Susan McDougal, Bill and Hillary Clinton's partners in the Whitewater Development Corp. Then, in May 1996, after a three-month trial, Starr's prosecutors won stunning felony convictions of both McDougals and of Jim Guy Tucker, the sitting governor of Arkansas. The convictions rattled the White House. Tucker, Clinton's successor, resigned. The erratic Jim McDougal turned state's evidence. Bennett, one of the office hawks, had served on the prosecution team that won the McDougal-Tucker case, and he joined in the initial excitement. There had been a rush of prosecutorial adrenaline, made even more potent by a sense of real progress in unraveling a highly complex conspiracy that could lead straight to the First Family.

Then, in the summer of 1996, it fell apart. Starr's office brought another case—against two small-time Arkansas bankers who had helped fund Clinton's 1990 gubernatorial campaign. Much to the prosecutors' surprise, they lost. Susan McDougal refused to cooperate like her ex-husband and went to jail instead. It was another unexpected blow.[1] Another key defendant who had initially promised to tell all, Webster Hubbell, clammed up and insisted that he remembered very little—certainly nothing that was the least bit incriminating—about Hillary Clinton's legal work for McDougal's thrift.

All this made Jackie Bennett, a career prosecutor, more determined than ever to forge ahead. Other members of Starr's team had returned to more satisfying legal careers, concluding that the ceaseless pursuit of the Clintons was probably futile. In fact, Starr himself had tried to jump ship in early 1997 to become dean of the Pepperdine Law School in Malibu—only to scrap his plans when his colleagues and newspaper editorial writers raised a ruckus. But Bennett and a handful of other true believers had stayed behind, committed to seeing Starr's probe through to the end.

Most of the lawyers who passed through Starr's office tended to like Bennett. An imposing ex-tackle on the Hanover College football team who had spent years with the Justice Department's public integrity section, the forty-one-year-old Bennett displayed a refreshing "who gives a shit?" attitude toward the sometimes stinging press criticism of the office. And inside the courtroom, he was a sight to behold—a ball-busting interrogator with an intimidating swagger who hurled rapid-fire questions that rattled even the most recalcitrant of witnesses.

Bennett's colleagues did sometimes worry about his judgment.

Convinced to the core of his own rectitude, Bennett would often play hardball when a tad of finesse might do. Perpetually suspicious of the forces aligned against him, he had a tendency to view the world in conspiratorial terms and was often hot to chase after new tips and leads—pursuits that more often than not led only to more dry holes.

In the early weeks of January 1998, the case of Web Hubbell was beginning to look like just such a dry hole. After pleading guilty to bilking the Rose firm and pledging his "full cooperation" in the Whitewater inquiry, Hubbell had stiffed Bennett and company at every turn. Much later, just as Hubbell was getting ready to leave prison, the Starr team learned of some curious financial transactions that would have piqued the interest of any self-respecting prosecutor. In the year before he entered federal prison, Hubbell had received $700,000 in legal retainers—payments arranged by people with very close ties to the Clintons. In June 1994, Hubbell had gotten his biggest payment—$100,000 wired from a Hong Kong bank account controlled by the Lippo Group, an Indonesian financial conglomerate headed by billionaire and Clinton friend James Riady. That month, Riady had attended a series of meetings at the White House. On June 23, he breakfasted with Hubbell. Then he showed up, along with his chief U.S. executive, John Huang, for a private Oval Office meeting with the president (a "social visit," the White House called it). Then Riady went to lunch—again with Hubbell. Four days later, the funds for Hubbell were wired from Hong Kong.

Another lucrative retainer for Hubbell had come from Revlon. It had been arranged by board member Vernon Jordan. In March 1994, just as Hubbell was resigning his post at Justice, White House Chief of Staff Thomas F. (Mack) McLarty made notes of people who should be contacted to help Hubbell find employment. Jordan's name was on the list. The following month, Jordan had personally escorted Hubbell to New York to be introduced to top officials of the international cosmetics firm. The retainer had netted Hubbell $62,775.

Bennett and some of Starr's deputies were convinced that the Clintons must somehow have sanctioned these payments and that they were tantamount to "hush money"—an implicit reward to ensure that the highly vulnerable Hubbell continued to protect the Clintons' interests. But they couldn't prove it. (Clinton himself insisted he was unaware of Hubbell's Lippo retainer until he read about it in the newspapers.) Starr's office had no tapes of Clinton's Oval Office meeting with James Riady just before the $100,000 materialized from Hong Kong. It had no insider witness who could say Clinton had talked to Vernon Jordan about lining up work for Hubbell at Revlon. The nearly year-long investigation had turned up instances of possible tax fraud by Hubbell for failing to report some of these payments to the Internal Revenue Service. But by early 1998, after hearing countless hours of grand jury testimony and poring over thousands of pages of documents, Jackie Bennett had little to show for his efforts other than a string of suspicious circumstances.

All this explains why Bennett was tantalized when Paul Rosenzweig walked into his office on the morning of Friday, January 9, and told him what he had learned the night before in Philadelphia from his friend Jerome Marcus. Rosenzweig mentioned the existence of a woman with tapes. He mentioned an alleged girlfriend of the president who was supposedly being asked to lie. He mentioned Vernon Jordan—and the effort to find the alleged girlfriend a job at Revlon.

Bennett was smart enough to give Rosenzweig a cautious response. Yes, the office might be interested in hearing more about this, he said. Vernon Jordan and Revlon could give them a basis for being involved. But they were not going to chase rumors and hearsay. If this woman who made the tapes had some information, she would have to give it to the Starr team directly. "It needs to come in the front door," Bennett later said he told Rosenzweig.

For all his reputation as a prosecutorial cowboy, Bennett was a bit troubled. He knew this was dicey, and he wanted to consult with somebody about what to do. But who? Starr had left town a few days earlier to attend an American Bar Association conference. This was not the kind of subject he wanted to discuss on the phone. There were no other seasoned veterans around the office whom he really trusted. So Bennett called an old colleague, John Bates. A sober-minded and widely respected civil lawyer, Bates had been Bennett's predecessor as chief of Starr's Washington office. He was also close to Eric Holder, the rising young star of the Clinton Justice Department who was now serving as Janet Reno's number two.

Bennett and Bates met for coffee that Friday afternoon. Bennett relayed what he had been told by Rosenzweig. Bates listened—and agreed with Bennett that the pattern with Jordan and Revlon was similar to what they had seen in the Hubbell case. But he also saw all sorts of red flags. The subject of sex and the president had burned the office before. Bates also understood Bennett to be telling him that the information had come to the office from lawyers associated with the Paula Jones case. Bennett told him, "It came directly or indirectly from people connected to the Jones legal team," Bates said in an interview much later. This bothered Bates. "I remember the warning light of the Jones legal team went off," he said. Bennett later insisted that he thought the information came from lawyers working with Linda Tripp, not Paula Jones. Bates told Bennett to be careful. His main advice, he would later recall, was: "Watch it."

●   ●   ●

Starr was back in the office on Monday, January 12, and Bennett had Rosenzweig brief the boss. Starr, a former federal appellate judge and solicitor general, was an innately cautious man, but also a collegial one. He liked to operate by consensus. He did not like to overrule his deputies. It was partly Starr's sometimes eerily cheerful personality, which shied away from personal conflict. But it may also have been a deep-seated insecurity on the independent counsel's part: for all his abundant legal experience, Starr had never been a prosecutor. He had never tried a criminal case. His general inclination, he often said, was to defer to "the professionals," the "career prosecutors" who worked for him, prosecutors like Jackie Bennett.

Starr listened that morning and agreed that Bennett had taken the right course. Let the witness contact the office directly and we'll see what she has to say. Rosenzweig relayed word to Marcus, and Bennett was told to expect a phone call later in the day.

The call didn't come until after nine P.M. At first, Linda Tripp did not give her name. She wanted to speak in hypotheticals. "Let's say I have a friend," Tripp told Bennett. It didn't take long for Bennett to pierce through this fiction, to realize that the "friend" was really the caller. But he agreed to play along. Tripp told Bennett about her friend's tapes, about how her friend was being asked to lie under oath, about Vernon Jordan. Then she got to the nub. If the friend gave the tapes to Starr's office, could the friend get immunity from prosecution?

Bennett indicated that would not be a problem. Taping wasn't illegal under federal law anyway, so it was not exactly a concession on his part. Soon enough, Tripp dropped the "friend" fiction and identified herself. The name at first didn't mean anything to Bennett. But a bit into the conversation, Tripp said something that grabbed his attention. She had been a witness for Starr's office before—on the Vince Foster case and on the travel office investigation. She had been represented by a lawyer suggested to her by the White House. On certain matters, under the advice of counsel, Tripp said, when she had testified before their grand juries, "I didn't tell you everything. You didn't ask all the right questions."

At this point, Bennett got excited. "In my mind, that absolutely established our justification in talking to her," he said later.

Just about this time, Steve Irons, one of the top FBI agents assigned to Starr's office, wandered by, and Bennett waved him to his office to listen to his half of the conversation. Tripp told Bennett about a lunch she was planning the next day with the woman who was Clinton's girlfriend, the woman who had asked her to lie. Bennett told her to hold on—they needed to speak to her first. He took down directions to her home in Columbia, a forty-minute ride from downtown Washington.

Bennett and Irons cased the office. There were a couple of prosecutors still around. Sol Wisenberg, a relatively new member of Starr's team who had come from the U.S. Attorney's Office in San Antonio, was preparing for a grand jury appearance the next day. Another prosecutor, Steve Binhak, was also still there. "Come on," Bennett ordered as he bounded down the halls. "We've got to go to work." The four—Bennett, Irons, Binhak and Wisenberg—piled into Wisenberg's rental van and headed out to Linda Tripp's house.

They didn't get there until after 11:00 P.M. They were ushered into Tripp's antiques-filled living room and stayed for nearly two hours. Tripp told her visitors a more detailed version of the entire story, starting with the day back in March 1997 when a *Newsweek* reporter named Michael Isikoff had showed up at her office and asked her a bunch of questions about Kathleen Willey. Shortly into the story, Tripp's teenage son, Ryan, came bounding down the stairs. "Mom, I don't think they're coming," he shouted.

"Who?" Tripp asked.

"The feds." At that point, Ryan Tripp saw the four visitors in the living room. "Oh," he said, embarrassed—and went running back up the stairs.

As the meeting went on into the early hours of the morning, Tripp told the visitors quite a bit—about Monica Lewinsky's subpoena in the Paula Jones case, about Tripp's own subpoena, about the pressure she felt to lie and her fear that she might lose her job. But she didn't tell them everything. She made no mention of the fact that she was in touch with a New York literary agent named Lucianne Goldberg to whom she had once tried to pitch a book about the Clinton White House. She didn't tell them how, through Goldberg, she had gotten in touch with the lawyers for Paula Jones and told them all about Monica Lewinsky so they would know to subpoena her. Tripp didn't tell them that she had even arranged for her own subpoena, essentially setting up the predicament from which she was now trying to extricate herself. Finally, she didn't tell them that she and her literary agent had been in repeated touch with Isikoff in hopes he would ultimately expose the Clinton-Lewinsky relationship to the world.

The more she talked that night, the more Tripp pressed upon her visitors the urgency of the situation. She was supposed to meet with Lewinsky for lunch—tomorrow. It was scheduled. She had talked to her lawyer about recording the conversation herself—arranging to wear a body wire so she would have a legally obtained tape of Lewinsky's efforts to get her to perjure herself. As soon as Bennett heard Tripp talking about applying her own body wire, he stopped her.

"You're not going to be making any more tape recordings on your own," Bennett told her. "If this is going to be done, we'll do it."

It was, Bennett would later say, a "judgment call," made right there on the spot by a midlevel federal prosecutor. It was also arguably the single most audacious and consequential U.S. law enforcement decision in decades: Bennett had pretty much just committed the office to wiring a witness in order to "sting" a young woman alleged to be the girlfriend of the president of the United States. Big decisions by government agencies are normally the product of cumbersome bureaucracies. Committees review them, decision makers debate them. Memos get written. Questions—lots of them—get asked. Sometimes the decisions don't get made at all because of the sheer weight of the process. But that night, as Bennett and his three colleagues saw it, there wasn't time for any of that. They had to act—and they had to act quickly if they wanted to catch the crimes, or the possible crimes, or the possible potential crimes, Linda Tripp had told them about.

Linda Tripp and Monica Lewinsky were having lunch.[2]

"It was the only thing to do," Bennett would later say about the decision to wire Tripp for her lunch the next day. "Those were the cards we had been dealt."

The cards had been dealt by Linda Tripp.

*   *   *

Bennett and the rest of the Starr team stayed at Tripp's house until about 1:30 A.M. When they got back to Starr's office in Washington, Irons went upstairs to call the night supervisor on duty at the command center of the J. Edgar Hoover Building—headquarters of the Federal Bureau of Investigation—two blocks away. He needed some help from the Bureau's information resources division, Irons told the supervisor. He needed electronic equipment for a "consensual recording" of suspected criminal activity the next day. He needed a team of agents to install and monitor the recordings. It involved a sensitive and urgent matter related to the Whitewater investigation of independent counsel Ken Starr.

Irons's request quickly moved up the FBI chain of command.

17

"Terror."

On Tuesday, January 13, Linda Tripp made a flurry of phone calls from her office in the Pentagon. She called Lucianne Goldberg and gave her a briefing on her meeting with the FBI the night before. She called Lewinsky and arranged to meet her at 2:45 P.M. at the Ritz-Carlton Hotel at the Pentagon City mall in Virginia. Then she called Starr's office and left a message. A few minutes later, the secretary at Tripp's office told her "Fred Bennett" was on the line. It was the code name she and prosecutor Steve Binhak had arranged the night before. Binhak told her to come to the hotel early and meet him in room 908.

That afternoon—the day she set up her young friend for the benefit of federal agents—Tripp made copious notes of everything that happened when she met with the FBI. The notes are a remarkable document. They contain an almost minute-by-minute diary of events leading up to the sting—as well as Tripp's inner thoughts at the very moment that her months of plotting and scheming were coming to their inevitable conclusion. They are, at times, evocative—as though Tripp had become a character in an Alfred Hitchcock movie or perhaps a novel by Dostoevski.

When she spoke to Lewinsky at 10:20 that morning, Tripp wrote: *She sounds "normal": Maybe this will work.* Then, right after, there was this:

Feeling low—guilt—fear—overriding emotion fear, however.

Tripp left her office a little after one P.M. and took the Metro one stop to Pentagon City. She walked through the mall entrance into

281

the Ritz-Carlton lobby and headed for the elevators. *Is everyone look-ing?* she wrote in her notes. *Does anyone know?* When she arrived at room 908 she was greeted by a swarm of agents who briefed her on what was about to happen. Tripp got distracted. She noticed one man off in the corner, a younger "clean-cut" man in a sweater, who hadn't said anything. "What do you do?" she asked.

"I watch," he said.

She looked at a slim, casually dressed woman agent, noticing there was a camera lens visible in her Dooney & Bourke purse. Tripp expressed shock that it was so obvious. She was told not to worry; the lens would be turned away until it was time to snap shots of the subject.

Tripp gave the FBI agents some photos of Monica Lewinsky—including one of the two of them arm in arm—that had been taken at Lewinsky's going-away party on December 23. She was wired by one of the female agents. A microphone was strapped onto her thigh. Another small radio transmitter was clipped to the inside of her blouse. *I am drenched w/perspiration,* Tripp wrote. *A Grisham-like experience—horrifying.* She was read a statement—which she was asked to sign—that said she had agreed to be wired by the FBI and to allow the contents of the recording to be used in court testimony. Tripp looked it over. It said nothing about immunity. They had promised her the night before that she was going to get immunity. It wasn't there.

Well, it is still the right thing to do, Tripp wrote in her notes. *Terror.*

•   •   •

That morning, Lewinsky stopped by Vernon Jordan's office to thank him for his help getting her a job with Revlon. She came with gifts, of course—a tie and a pocket square. She also brought a copy of the affidavit she had signed denying a sexual relationship with Bill Clinton.

By now, the Washington superlawyer may well have been getting uncomfortable about this little favor for his friend the president. A job, a court affidavit. This was cutting it a bit close.

"I don't need to see it," Jordan said.

Lewinsky left within five minutes.

She was getting worried about references. Revlon's manager had called that morning and formally reaffirmed the job offer but mentioned that the company would need to see references. Lewinsky panicked. What would happen when they called the White House? What would the guy in legislative affairs say? The director of the office, John Hilley, had been there when she got booted out. Could she put his name down? Lewinsky called Betty Currie. She needed her to check with the president about this.

Currie did. Clinton spoke to Erskine Bowles, the White House chief of staff. Bowles spoke to John Podesta, the deputy chief of staff. Podesta spoke to Hilley. There was no problem: Hilley didn't even remember Lewinsky. The office would give Lewinsky a standard reference confirming her dates of employment. Nobody would say anything negative.

*   *   *

Tripp went down to the piano bar at the Ritz-Carlton about 2:30 P.M. and negotiated for a quiet table in a corner where she could smoke. She spotted the hotel sales manager—someone she dealt with when she arranged for conference rooms for her Pentagon program. Tripp was chatting with him when Lewinsky arrived. Tripp introduced them. "Hi, nice to meet you. Monica Lewinsky," she said, extending her hand. The sales manager left, and the two women sat down.

"Oh, my God. Happy New Year," said Lewinsky.

"Oh, my God. How are you?" asked Tripp.

A waitress approached. "Would you ladies like coffee?"

*   *   *

Inside room 908, where the technicians and agents from the FBI had assembled, it didn't take long to realize there was a problem. FBI undercover surveillance is designed with built-in redundancy. The microphone strapped around Tripp's thigh that day was supposed to record on microcassette tape every word she and her luncheon guest uttered. The radio transmitter clipped into her blouse was supposed to beam the same words up to room 908 so the agents could make a backup recording and listen in while the conversation was taking place. This is particularly important in organized crime and drug cases—the usual scenario for undercover surveillance—when one of the parties might suddenly get threatened with bodily harm and it becomes necessary for the listening agents to intervene.

But that afternoon, the radio transmitter in Tripp's blouse wasn't working. Tripp later testified it kept slipping down into her bra. When Lewinsky and Tripp started talking, the FBI agents monitoring this event had no idea what was being said. They were flying blind.

Across the river, back in Ken Starr's office, Jackie Bennett grew anxious. He called room 908 to speak to Steve Irons, the supervising FBI agent. How's it going? he asked.

"Don't know," Irons replied. "The transmitter isn't working."

Bennett couldn't believe it. It's Murphy's law, he thought. Everything in this damn investigation always goes wrong.

• • •

Lewinsky and Tripp were soon deep in conversation. It was a continuation of their talk the previous Friday—the phone conversation when they both lied about everything. Lewinsky, trying to lure Tripp into thinking she was following her advice, said she hadn't signed her affidavit and hadn't gotten a job. She had gotten in touch with "the black woman," she said, referring to Betty Currie, and told her, "Look, I'm supposed to sign something . . . and I'm not signing it until I have a job."

Tripp, thinking of the federal agents she assumed were listening in, talked about how tormented she was by the prospect of having to lie under oath. Then she repeatedly tried to steer the conversation around to Vernon Jordan.

"This is with Vernon's help?" Tripp asked after Lewinsky told her about her interviews in New York.

"But you have Vernon Jordan behind you," Tripp said after Lewinsky told her she had "no fear" about lying in her affidavit.

"Maybe I'm placing too much emphasis on Vernon's involvement in this," Tripp said when the two were talking about the consequences of perjury, "but I see that as a huge, huge, huge umbrella of safety."

It worked. Lewinsky started to say much that sounded incrimi-nating. She said that she would never cross the president and testify against him. She urged Tripp—repeatedly—to pull back from and "spin" what she had told *Newsweek* about Kathleen Willey. "You were not under oath in what Michael Isikoff printed," she said. As for Vernon Jordan, Lewinsky said: "You think he took me to that lawyer to be nice to me? No, I think he took me to make sure . . . I said what I was supposed to say."

When Tripp insisted again that she couldn't perjure herself and would have to testify truthfully about Lewinsky's relationship with the president, the younger woman grew exasperated. She tried dif-ferent tacks. She begged. Then she offered what sounded like a bribe. "I would be indebted to you for life," Lewinsky said. "I would do anything." She would even write her a check, she said, giving her an interest in an Australian condominium of which Lewinsky was part owner.

By this point, FBI supervisor Irons in room 908 had dispatched a team of undercover agents to take a table next to Lewinsky and Tripp and try to overhear what they were saying. They reported back—and Irons immediately called Jackie Bennett to tell him not to worry. "You're going to like this," Irons told Bennett.

After an hour or so, Tripp excused herself to go to the bathroom. She met with one of the women FBI agents. "Um, I think she's got at least forty-five minutes left or something like that," she told her.

Lewinsky, as she later testified, was by now suspicious. She quickly rummaged through Tripp's handbag, looking for a tape recorder.

•   •   •

E arly that afternoon, in the offices of *Newsweek*'s Washington bureau, I was at my desk, scrolling through the Associated Press wires. It was Tuesday—a relatively slow day in the newsmagazine cycle. Deadlines aren't until Saturday. This week, I imagined, I would be working on my first story having anything to do with the Paula Jones case since the Willey piece back in August. The story, I thought, would revolve around the president's deposition on Saturday—an extraordinary event, perhaps unique in the annals of the presidency. I knew there would never be time to get anything Clinton actually said into the magazine even if we miraculously could find out what it was. (The deposition, like all others in the Jones case, was going to be nonpublic.) Still, I thought I might get a little break on the competition if I could nail down some of what Kathleen Willey had said the previous Saturday. I assumed she would at least have confirmed under oath what she had told me back in March of 1997.

Then I got a phone call.[1] There's a little event about to start at the Ritz-Carlton Hotel right now that you might be interested in, the caller told me. You know that woman you quoted last summer in the Kathleen Willey piece? FBI agents working for Ken Starr have wired her for a lunch with a former White House staffer named Monica Lewinsky. How this had come to pass, the caller claimed not to know.

I immediately called Lucianne Goldberg.

Do you know anything about this?'

So you heard? she said, sounding surprised.

My first reaction was visceral. This is nuts, I thought. What in God's name is Starr doing? Then I thought for a moment and suddenly felt as if I had been kicked in the stomach.

Everything that had happened up until this moment—my conversations with Tripp and Goldberg, the courier slips, the dress, all of it—always had a playacting quality. I had felt at times as if I had wandered into one of those murder-mystery weekends in which I was acting out the role of a reporter in a written-for-modern-day-Washington Agatha Christie play. Having the chance to peer into Linda Tripp's world was seductive, there was no question about that. It offered an eerie and fascinating, if tinted and very blurry view of what purported to be seedy conduct inside the White House. But it had been hard to connect it with any objective reality, no way to be sure the whole thing wasn't some gigantic, psychotically induced mirage.

But Starr: that was real. If I could confirm what I had just been told, that was a goddamn story. An unbelievably big story, in fact. I quickly realized that while I always more or less believed Tripp's story about the Lewinsky-Clinton relationship, it really didn't matter anymore if I could "prove" it. It also didn't matter if I or *Newsweek* could make a case for its relevance to public business. This was not about sex, or even about the Paula Jones case. This was about a special prosecutor launching a secret criminal investigation of the president—and targeting his supposed girlfriend in an effort to nail him. It was breathtaking news.

●　　●　　●

I felt a little dizzy and weak. I went out for some fresh air and walked two and a half blocks to Au Bon Pain on 20th Street and Pennsylvania Avenue. It was unseasonably warm, so I sat outside, eating a sandwich, trying to think through what I should do next. I briefly thought about rushing over to the Ritz-Carlton to see if the event was still going on. Then I realized that could be a disaster. I could wander into the middle of an FBI "sting" and blow the whole thing wide open. Tripp would see me and freak. Lewinsky might recognize me and throw up. My picture would end up next to front-page headlines: REPORTER DISRUPTS CRIMINAL PROBE OF PRESIDENT.

No, I just needed to report this out the traditional way, working sources, checking and rechecking my facts, confirming everything as solidly as I could.

I needed to talk to somebody. I headed back to *Newsweek,* walked into Klaidman's office and shut the door.

"You're not going to believe what has just happened," I told him.

I explained how the story involving "woman number three" and the president had taken a rather unexpected turn. Starr was involved. A sting was under way—as we spoke. The story was about to blow up.

That's unbelievable, Klaidman said. Astonishing.

Then, for the first time, he asked me her name. I felt uneasy. I had never told anybody. But, I figured, he's going to learn soon enough.

"Monica," I said reluctantly.

His face went ashen.

"What's her last name?" he asked with some alarm.

Why do you need to know? I asked.

He had just started dating this new woman, someone he had been pursuing for some time.

Her name was Monica.

"Lewinsky," I said.

Klaidman breathed easy, relieved to know that the current object of his affections was not on the rebound from a messy love affair with the president of the United States.

• • •

When Linda Tripp finished talking to her FBI handler in the bathroom, she and Lewinsky decided they were hungry. They ordered a cheeseburger with extra-crispy French fries. The order didn't come quickly. "Jesus, how hard is this?" Tripp snapped. The burger and fries arrived, and as the two women started munching, they resumed their long, rambling discussion about perjury and truth, reviewing the same issues over and over again.

The longer it went, the more incriminating Lewinsky's comments got.

"You know the truth, Linda?" Lewinsky said. "What's the truth? The truth is you're either an FOB [Friend of Bill's] or not."

"This is gonna sound really stupid," Lewinsky said a bit later, "but other than how you feel yourself, like inside, what is the advantage of telling the truth? What advantage do you see for yourself? Where will that put you? What does that do for you?"

On the subject of Bill Clinton, Lewinsky said: "I don't think the way the man thinks, I don't think he thinks of lying under oath. . . . If—if—if I said, if somebody said to him, 'Is Monica lying under oath?' he would say yes. But when he on his own thinks about it, he doesn't think of it in those terms. Okay?"

Finally, on the subject of Vernon Jordan, Lewinsky quoted him as telling her: "It doesn't matter what anybody says, you just deny it." She said she asked Jordan, "What if someone's been tapping my phone?" and said he replied: "Well, as long as you say it didn't happen, it didn't happen." Then, a bit later, when Tripp asked whether Jordan had addressed the consequence of perjury, Lewinsky quoted him as reassuring her: "You're not gonna go to jail, you're not gonna go to jail."

Lewinsky, questioned months later about these comments, said she made them up. Jordan never said them at all, she said. She had told Tripp that Jordan had told her these things because she was trying to get Tripp to realize that she wouldn't have to worry if she just kept her mouth shut about Lewinsky's relationship with the president.

• • •

The luncheon finally ended nearly four hours later. Tripp and Lewinsky agreed to talk again, soon, but not on the phone. It was too risky, they agreed. Lewinsky went home—and was tailed by the FBI. Tripp went upstairs for her debriefing. Back at Starr's office, Jackie Bennett was anxious. He drove over to the Ritz-Carlton to talk with the agents. With the failure of the radio transmitter, he still didn't know if he had a reliable recording of what had been said. Everything depended on the microphone and the microcassette on Tripp's leg. If those hadn't worked, Bennett later recalled thinking, "I'm going to have somebody's ass."

That night, Bennett and Irons drove to an FBI annex where the tape was being processed. Irons went inside. Bennett waited in the car. When Irons returned, he told Bennett he could rest easy: "I think it works fine."

At long last, Bennett had a tape. Now, if only he could flip this woman Lewinsky, he might actually have an insider.

18

"You walk in off the street and expect me to give you case files?"

I got to work early on Wednesday. I had briefed McDaniel the night before, and she'd told me to start crashing. That meant I needed to start learning a lot more about Monica Lewinsky—and find some sources other than Linda Tripp who knew her. It was still a little touchy. I would have a hard time explaining why I was asking questions without tipping my hand. But my earlier caution had to give way to the imperatives of a looming deadline.

Willie Blacklow had recently retired as deputy director of the Pentagon public affairs office. He had worked on Capitol Hill for years, and I had dealt with him from time to time. That morning, I reached him at his home in the Maryland suburbs. How well did he know Ken Bacon's former assistant, Monica Lewinsky?

Monica? Sure, I know Monica. A sweet young kid. Very nice girl. Why are you asking?

I didn't want to lie. Well, I'd appreciate it if you could keep this between us, but it seems like she's been named as a possible witness in the Paula Jones case.

You're kidding, Blacklow said. Why would they possibly be interested in Monica?

I'm not sure, I said.

Blacklow said Lewinsky had done a fine job as Ken Bacon's assistant. When I pressed him, a couple of things stood out. He found her a little young and naive to have been in that job—a position that required a security clearance higher than top-secret and took her on

290

trips around the globe. It was always a "mystery" to him how that came about, he said.

Then there was something else. Lewinsky had a habit of implying she was pals with all sorts of high-level people in the White House. Blacklow knew she had been an intern there but always assumed she was something of a name-dropper and probably exaggerating. Then he happened to go with her to the White House Christmas party in December 1996. Lewinsky was "dressed to the hilt, with a semi-low-cut red dress," he recalled. They went through the receiving line together and got to the Clintons. The president gave her a big enthusiastic greeting—"Hi, Monica!" he said—then "hugged" her. Hillary Clinton shook her hand. Clinton's hug wasn't anything sexual, Blacklow said. But still, he said, "I was kind of stunned. There was no question that she was something more than just another gofer."

Blacklow did have one suggestion for me. Do you know who you should talk to? he said. There's a woman she was pretty friendly with. They always used to take coffee breaks together. She worked downstairs.

Who's that? I asked.

Linda Tripp, Blacklow said. Have you tried Linda?

•   •   •

I called Goldberg. She had talked to Tripp the previous night. The sting had gone down without a hitch, she told me. Tripp was firing her lawyer, Kirby Behre, today and replacing him with this new guy, Jim Moody. Moody was going to go over to Behre's office and retrieve the tapes and then give them to Starr.

Wait a second, I said—I need to hear those tapes.

Back in October, I had refused to listen. But now, everything had changed. The stakes were ten times higher. The tapes were critical evidence in Starr's investigation. Listening to them was the only way to establish whether Lewinsky's claims of a relationship with the president sounded credible. More important, in order to evaluate whether Starr's investigation was legitimate, I needed to know whether the tapes really contained evidence that Lewinsky was being pressured to lie to the Paula Jones lawyers.[1]

I explained this to Goldberg. She said she would talk to Moody and see what she could do to help. In the meantime, I should call him myself. I did—and left a message on his answering machine.

Goldberg, the consummate mischief maker and agent provocateur, was in high spirits that day. Her Manhattan apartment was conspiracy central. Tripp, the elves, Moody—everybody was calling her. Later that afternoon, Tripp called from a phone booth. *Hasn't heard from Feds,* Goldberg wrote in her notebook. *Monica still calling her. Moody on the way.*

Then, a bit later: *Call from Linda—Moody is in Kirby's office trying to get the tapes back and Kirby is throwing a fit. . . .*

•   •   •

He was. Moody had walked in unannounced to the Washington law firm of Paul, Hastings, Janofksy & Walker and asked to see Kirby Behre. Behre came out, saw the big, hulking Moody and wondered what was going on. They went into a conference room. Moody handed him a retainer letter Tripp had signed, appointing him her new lawyer. He told Behre he was there to pick up the case files—and the tapes.

"You walk in off the street and expect me to give you case files?" Behre said.

Yes, Moody said, and he was prepared to wait for them. He sat down. "I will wait for as long as is necessary," he said.

Behre questioned Moody about his background. He called Tripp, asking if she realized Moody was not a criminal defense lawyer. Tripp called Goldberg. Goldberg wrote down what Tripp told her. Something got lost in the translation: Behre, she wrote, *is asking how does Linda know Moody isn't a criminal.*

•   •   •

I had called Jackie Bennett midmorning and left a routine message. That afternoon, I called again and left a more urgent one. Bennett got the message and got a sinking feeling in his stomach.

That afternoon, the day after the "sting," the lawyers of the Whitewater independent counsel were engaged in a vigorous debate over whether they even had the legal authority to conduct this new investigation.[2] It had been Jackie Bennett's position that they did—

that the probe of alleged perjury and obstruction of justice in the Paula Jones case was a matter "related" to the office's ongoing, if not greatly promising, inquiry into the legal retainers arranged for Webster Hubbell. Vernon Jordan was the nexus. The alleged conduct—jobs for silence—was similar. But others were not sure. They thought Starr needed to consult with the Justice Department before proceeding—and probably needed an expanded mandate from the panel of three senior federal judges who oversee the operations of all independent counsels.

Some of the prosecutors were worried that if they consulted with the Justice Department, news of the undercover sting of Lewinsky might leak. Secrecy at this point was essential. They were just starting to review the "sting" tape, and while it was good, they could use more before they moved in on Lewinsky.

Bennett, who had left to pick up his messages, walked back into the conference room. I've got a message here from Isikoff at *Newsweek,* he told one of his colleagues. I think he may already know.

The decision was made that they should consult Justice—that Bennett should call Eric Holder, the deputy attorney general. But it was now after 9:30 P.M., and Holder had gone to a basketball game: the Washington Wizards versus the San Antonio Spurs. Bennett paged him. Holder ignored the beeper. Bennett paged him again at 10:18 P.M., adding the word "urgent." It was the fourth quarter. Holder waited until the game was over.

Holder and a friend were on the way to the Spurs locker room to meet star center David Robinson when the deputy attorney general figured he'd better call Bennett. In the bowels of the MCI center, near a training room, Holder found a pay phone. "We are sort of into a sensitive matter," Bennett told him. "We need to meet with you in person." Holder said he would see him the next day.

• • •

That afternoon, Linda Tripp later said, Monica Lewinsky called her incessantly from pay phones. Tripp at first ducked the calls. But Lewinsky persisted and had Tripp interrupted during a meeting in Ken Bacon's office. Then Lewinsky swung by the Pentagon and gave Tripp a ride home.

During the ride, Tripp said, Lewinsky was extremely upset. Lewinsky told her she was "in danger," Tripp said. "The president expects you to be a team player," Lewinsky told her. "He feels you screwed him in the *Newsweek* article." Lewinsky handed Tripp a three-page document that had some "new ideas" on how she could word an affidavit on the Willey incident that would keep her out of trouble. "Points to make in affidavit," it said on top of the front page. The document repeated and amplified some of the suggestions Lewinsky had offered the day before about how Tripp could undercut her own seemingly damning description of Kathleen Willey's flustered and disheveled appearance in the *Newsweek* story.[3]

When she got home, Tripp had another visit from the FBI. She told the agents about her conversations with Lewinsky that afternoon and gave them the three-page document. They tried to wire her telephone but had trouble hooking up their equipment. So they authorized Tripp to continue using her own tape recorder to record any more conversations with Monica Lewinsky. They also told her to keep her blinds closed.

While the agents were still there, Tripp peered through the blinds. She fixated on an unfamiliar car parked on the street. There was a woman inside—just sitting there. Tripp, alarmed, called the agents to the window. They were just about to check the car when the woman finally got out. Tripp knew her. It was okay after all.

After the agents left, Tripp got out her notebook. *I'm paranoid,* she wrote. *Why is this so terrifying?*

•   •   •

The next day, Thursday, January 15, I was more than a little anxious. I knew I was sitting on something enormous. But I still had a lot to do. And there wasn't a whole lot of time.

I placed the safest call first. It was to Kirby Behre, the lawyer Tripp had fired. I ran through what I'd learned in the past few days: how his former client had gone to work as an undercover informant for Ken Starr; how there had been a "sting" at the Ritz-Carlton Hotel aimed at ensnaring Monica Lewinsky; how Tripp's new lawyer, Jim Moody, had been by Behre's office to pick up secret tape recordings that Tripp had made with Lewinsky, purportedly talking about Lewinsky's sexual relationship with the president.

Behre listened politely and sounded genuinely surprised at how much I knew. But, he explained, he just couldn't talk about any of this. It was all covered by attorney-client privilege.

Then again, he didn't wave me off anything.

I now, for the longest time, stared at the telephone on my desk. The lot of a reporter is not normally filled with moments of dramatic tension. Nor is it especially tormented by bouts of mental anguish. But it occurred to me, as I looked at my phone that morning, that almost anything I did was going to dramatically change the events I was trying to cover.

I got out the Speed Service courier slips. Then I picked up the phone and called Betty Currie.

19

"I've never had a conversation with a reporter like this in my life."

She picked up the phone right away. I had her direct White House extension. It was on the courier slips. "Is this Betty Currie?" I asked.

"Yes it is," replied the president's secretary, sounding very much as if anyone who called on this number deserved her most immediate and helpful attention.

I told her who I was. Currie would later testify that when she heard my name that morning it was as if a "thud" went off in her head. Clearing my throat, I explained what I was calling about. The thud must have gotten louder.

I was hoping she could help me, I said: I have some courier slips here showing there is a woman named Monica Lewinsky at the Pentagon public affairs office who has been sending a series of letters and packages to the White House to be delivered to you. There's a woman named J. Caroline Self who seems to have been dispatched by you to pick up these letters and packages at the White House southwest gate. It seems like there was one of these letters on October 7—and I then proceeded to read the dates of some of the others. They all have your extension down as the contact number.

I was wondering: Can you tell me what they are about?

"I'm not quite sure," Currie said calmly. "But I'll be happy to look into it and get back to you."

I wonder what's happening right now, I thought after I had hung up.

If only I had known. After getting off the phone with me, Currie picked it up again—and beeped Monica Lewinsky. Lewinsky called back immediately. Currie told her about my inquiry. Lewinsky felt "very strange," she later said, "like somehow this was closing in."

The two women talked about how I possibly could have gotten such information. Lewinsky thought—hardly for the first time—that maybe Linda Tripp was ratting on her. But she didn't know for sure. There was this other guy at the Pentagon public affairs office who hated Clinton. Maybe it was he. Currie and Lewinsky talked about what they should do now. Clinton was out of town. Currie called Vernon Jordan and left a message. The message was from "Betty/POTUS" and it read: "Kind of important."

In the meantime, I had called Jackie Bennett again. This time, I told his secretary it was extremely urgent and absolutely essential that I talk to him right away.

He came to the phone.

"I know what you guys have been doing," I told him. "I know everything. We need to talk. Right away."

Bennett, anxious and extremely upset, told me to come over. I rushed out the door.

● ● ●

There was no disguising the irritation on Bennett's face. "Let's face it," he said as I sat in the austere conference room in suite 410, Office of the Independent Counsel. "You've got us over the barrel."

The probe by Starr's office at that point hinged on secrecy—and surprise. The game plan was straight from the standard prosecutor's play book. Starr's agents wanted to gather overwhelming evidence against Lewinsky as quickly as possible—to capture her on tape committing federal crimes, coaching and encouraging Tripp to lie and talking about her own perjuries. Then, the plan went, they would suddenly confront Lewinsky and offer her a bleak choice: Cooperate or go to prison. If Lewinsky would go to work for Starr, if she herself would wear a body wire and allow the FBI to tape her phone calls, they believed, there was no telling where this investigation would go.

Now here was a reporter, threatening to blow the entire operation by writing about it. It briefly occurred to Bennett that maybe that was the plan from the start. Maybe it was Isikoff who sent Tripp to his office in order to manufacture a big story. "I thought we might have been set up," he later said. "I was furious."

Bennett was accompanied by two of his deputies, Mike Emmick and Steve Bates. They sat around the conference table looking glum and worried, saying nothing. Bennett wanted to strike a bargain. Was there any way *Newsweek* could be persuaded to hold off on the story?

Well, I don't know, I said. I doubt it.

What if I could be assured of an even better story down the road—a story that would include hard evidence of a conspiracy to get Tripp to lie in the Paula Jones case? It was a lie about something Tripp told you, Bennett emphasized, and it would only benefit one person.

That was obviously Clinton.

What is this hard evidence? I asked. It sounded as if he were referring to a document of some kind. The idea of something hard, something tangible, intrigued me.

Bennett waved his hand, backing off. Not now, he said.

"We need to know everything you know," Bennett said. Even more important, they wanted to know everything I had done: whom I'd interviewed, whom I'd called. From Bennett's perspective, the questions—and the grounds for the meeting itself—were entirely legitimate. He needed to know if his investigation had already been compromised. He was trying to plot strategy, and he couldn't do so in the dark. He had to know who might already have his or her guard up.

But his very questions were for me an implicit confirmation that my information was solid. I played along. I repeated the incredible details I had learned: Tripp's surreptitious tapes, her contacts with Starr, the decision to open a criminal probe, the sting at the Ritz-Carlton Hotel.

Bennett wanted to know to whom I had talked about all this. It was important, he said. Their investigation might already be exposed. I couldn't tell him sources. But I could tell him some things. I told him I had called Kirby Behre, a lawyer Tripp had fired just a few days earlier, to see what he knew about what was going on. Behre had told me nothing. Bennett looked disgusted. He had by now heard about Tripp's fears that Behre had secret White House sympathies. He was a member of a prominent Washington law firm with Democratic ties. Somebody at the firm was probably going to leak this to Clinton's team, Bennett predicted. The investigation might already be blown.

I told him about the call to Betty Currie asking about the courier receipts. Bennett shot a glance at Mike Emmick.

What had she said? Bennett asked. Nothing, I said. She said she would look into it and get back to me.

Now I made my pitch. Look, you guys are the ones that need to cooperate with me, I said. You need to lay out your evidence, or at least your basis for starting this investigation in the first place. I reminded them that Starr was already under attack for letting his probe drag on too long and straying too far afield from the original mandate; for them to be involved in the Paula Jones case without adequate justification would only reinforce the critics' worst suspicions that they were out of control.

"Unless you show me what you've got and establish the predicate for this, you're going to get roasted," I told Bennett.

It was, in a way, a form of blackmail. I was threatening to make him look really bad if he didn't give me information.

He professed to be unmoved. "We can take the heat," he said. "I'm 100 percent comfortable that we have adequate justification for getting involved in this."

About twenty minutes into this session, one of Bennett's colleagues, Bruce Udolf, entered the room. "What have I missed?" he said, asking to be briefed. I knew Udolf from his days as a federal prosecutor in Miami—a small, wiry, intense man who had brought a string of cases against corrupt politicians in southern Florida. He was also, as far as I was concerned, a prosecutor of integrity: he had been one of the leaders of a small band of dissidents in his Miami office who, in the late 1980s, had rebelled against a controversial Republican U.S. attorney who was allegedly misusing the office.

I explained to Udolf that I knew all about the office's Lewinsky investigation—and planned to move ahead with a story on it. Udolf looked at me aghast. "You can't do that," he said. Udolf and his colleagues needed time to work on this.

I brought up the wiring of Tripp at the Ritz-Carlton. How hard was the evidence on the tapes? Did you hear evidence of federal crimes? I asked. It was, to me, a vitally important question. I respected Udolf's judgment and figured his answer would be a good reality check.

He paused for a few seconds and looked pained. His body language told me that this case was no lark.

"I can't believe I'm having this conversation," Udolf finally said. "I've never had a conversation with a reporter like this in my life."

At any rate, Udolf said, the situation was clear: If I were to publish a story, the case could go up in smoke.

We bargained. I don't come out until Sunday, I told them. You've got time.

What are you waiting for? Why don't you move on Lewinsky now? I asked, half-joking.

There were things I didn't understand, Udolf explained. That wasn't possible—they couldn't do anything until Friday at the earliest. Bennett was concerned about who else I might call in the meantime; I explained that there was no way I could write my story without calling Vernon Jordan and Lewinsky—and I would have to start doing that soon.

How long could I hold off making those calls? they wanted to know. Not long, I explained. How about until Friday afternoon? We struck a deal—I gave them until four P.M. on Friday. In effect, I had just set Starr's deadline—a deadline they would never be able to meet.

It was tricky, what I had just done. They wanted me to not publish my story at all or, at a minimum, to delay it until they could complete the undercover side of the investigation. There was no way I would agree to that. It wasn't my job to help Starr sting the president. Starr's office had made an awesome decision to get involved in this. That was news, and I was going to report it.

But by the same token, it wasn't my job to get in the middle of their investigation. Whatever the merits of their probe at that point, the only role I had here was as reporter—the guy who tells the public what's going on. If I had to screw up Starr's probe in order to do my job—to ask Lewinsky and Clinton's inner circle about the allegations and hear what they had to say—then so be it. But that was my only ground for doing anything. Within the context of my needs, calling Vernon Jordan and Monica Lewinsky on Friday, rather than Thursday, seemed a relatively modest concession—especially if the price of doing otherwise would inevitably be to transform the event I was trying to write about.

As the meeting broke up, I felt I had accomplished what I needed to. I really hadn't learned any new details. But I felt more confident that my information was solid and that I had an unbelievably explosive story. It occurred to me that this might be bigger than I first thought, that Starr might have more serious evidence of felonies by Clinton and Jordan than I realized. But maybe he didn't. Maybe his cup was empty. In that case, the independent counsel's office had just committed a monumental blunder that would discredit Clinton's enemies once and for all.

Maybe it was both. Either way, it was a pretty damn good story.

As I walked out of Starr's office, I went down the hall toward the bathroom. There, much to my amazement, I saw Starr himself, washing his hands in the sink. Starr saw me out of the corner of his eye and turned as he dried his hands. His white shirt, I noticed, was stained with ink. He greeted me amiably, as though he didn't have a care in the world.

"Mr. Isikoff, good to see you," he said.

For the next thirty seconds or so, we exchanged awkward pleasantries. I struggled to find something useful to say.

"So I see you were at the White House yesterday," I noted, referring to the brief and ultimately meaningless deposition he and his deputies had taken from Hillary Clinton about the Filegate matter, which had been reported in the morning papers.

"Now, Mike, you know I can't talk about that," he said.

I mumbled something about just having come from an interesting meeting with his staff. He smiled—and said nothing. If Starr had the slightest idea that he was about to plunge the country into a political crisis, he didn't show it. The affable prosecutor seemed oblivious.

• • •

That Thursday afternoon, when I got back to the office, I briefed McDaniel. The entire situation was surreal; the prosecutors were pleading with us for time so they could nail the president on sex and perjury. The potential fallout, we were starting to realize, could be huge. I mentioned to McDaniel my impression that they were monitoring Lewinsky.

McDaniel, usually the coolest head at the magazine, was temporarily overwhelmed. She threw up her hands and screamed.

Down the hallway, my *Newsweek* colleagues, almost all of them in the dark about this, wondered what was going on.

•   •   •

At 4:30 P.M., Moody showed up once again at Kirby Behre's office. After Moody's impromptu sit-in the day before, they had reached an accommodation. Behre had asked for a day to catalog the items he was handing over. Now, on Thursday, Moody had come to pick everything up—the case files and Linda Tripp's precious tapes.

Moody stuffed them in the briefcase. As he walked onto the street, it was dark and overcast. It suddenly occurred to Moody that somebody might be following him—perhaps a private investigator working for Behre's law firm, perhaps an agent of the White House. So he didn't go straight back to his office about thirteen blocks away. Instead, Moody, the ex-spook, grabbed a cab and took it to Capitol Hill. He had the taxi stop in front of the Hart Senate Office Building—a building you can enter and exit using different doors. He walked briskly through the building, his heart pounding, and left from the other side. Then he hailed another cab and took it across town to the upscale Georgetown Park shopping mall. He wandered around the shops for a half hour, clutching his briefcase with the tapes, furtively looking over his shoulder every now and then to detect with his imperfect eyes his imagined pursuers. Finally, he took a third cab back to his office at 24th and N Street, NW, across the street from the offices of *U.S. News & World Report.*

By this time, I was back in my office and had been calling him repeatedly, leaving messages nearly every hour. I also tried to reach Tripp, but her number had been changed. I called Lucianne Goldberg in New York and also George Conway, trying to get them to intercede on my behalf.

You've got to get Moody to let me listen to those tapes, I shouted at Goldberg. You've got to get Tripp to give him the go-ahead. You don't understand how important this is. Without that, if I can't write that there is compelling evidence backing up Tripp's allegations, this is going to blow up in your face—and Tripp's. Starr would look stupid and, I told Goldberg, Tripp would look worse. She was going to be front and center in this story. She had triggered the whole thing, and only the tapes could establish whether she had been telling the truth.

That, at any rate, was what I was telling them. It is the way reporters operate: We threaten, we cajole, we feign sympathy. But the truth for me was slightly different: Whatever was on those tapes, listening to them, and quoting them, would make this a much more compelling and dramatic story for *Newsweek.*

I was not the only person desperate for the tapes that day. The night before, Wesley Holmes, one of the lawyers for Paula Jones, had checked into the Hyatt Regency Hotel in Washington. The president's deposition was coming up on Saturday. Questions about Monica Lewinsky—detailed, specific questions about Monica Lewinsky— were going to be the Jones lawyers' little surprise for the president. But in order to pull it off, Holmes and the rest of the Jones lawyers wanted the tapes.

Holmes, like me, was calling Goldberg and George Conway. Where is this guy Moody? he wanted to know. Why can't I get through to him? Holmes spent the day pacing in his hotel room, waiting for Moody to call.

Like the Maltese falcon in the Humphrey Bogart movie, the tapes had assumed mystical status: whoever acquired them, it was imagined, would acquire strange power over the Clinton presidency.

•   •   •

About six P.M., Lewinsky picked up Currie outside the White House, and they drove to Vernon Jordan's office in Dupont Circle. Currie went inside. Lewinsky parked the car and waited across the street in a bar. (It was called the Front Page, named for the famous play about newspaper reporters in Chicago in the 1920s.) Currie told Jordan about the call from me about the courier slips. Jordan suggested she raise this with Mike McCurry, the press secretary, and with Bruce Lindsey.

Currie never did bring it up with McCurry. But she did talk to

Lindsey, asking him how she should respond to my inquiry. As Currie later recalled, Lindsey told her not to respond at all. "Make Isikoff work for his story," Lindsey told her.

•   •   •

At seven-thirty P.M., Goldberg called Tripp's new number and left a message with her son, Ryan: "The shit is about to hit the fan." Tripp got home and immediately called back. Goldberg told her: "Isikoff is outing you tomorrow." Tripp had just set off a criminal investigation of the president. She had volunteered to become the prosecutors' key informant. But she expressed shock that I would now use her name in a news story. *So much for journalistic integrity,* she wrote in her notebook.

•   •   •

Early in the evening, Jackie Bennett and three of his deputies— Udolf, Bates, and Emmick—walked across Pennsylvania to meet with Eric Holder and one of his deputies, Monty Wilkinson, at the Justice Department. With a tone of gravity and seeming sorrow in his voice, Bennett explained how his office had "unhappily" come across a serious matter that seems "to go back to the president and a close associate of his, Vernon Jordan." Bennett then explained the whole story of Linda Tripp and Monica Lewinsky, the visit to Tripp's home on Monday and the event at the Ritz-Carlton on Tuesday.

As if this wasn't enough to stun Holder, Bennett then mentioned something else: "A seriously complicating factor came to our attention this evening," he said, according to one of his deputy's notes of the meeting. "Mike Isikoff is on to this. He has been receiving information from a friend of Tripp's. We met with him and he is disturbingly far along. So we have a very short window of opportunity to try to move this along."

"His article will come out next week?" Holder asked.

"Yes," Bennett told him.

Bennett stressed the need to act quickly. "This is real," Bennett said. "There is inchoate criminality." Starr's office wanted the Justice Department's blessing.

"I'm sorry to leave you with this," Bennett said.

"I never anticipated this," Holder said.

The meeting broke up and Holder agreed he had to contact Attorney General Janet Reno—right away.[1]

• • •

That night, Ann Coulter went to dinner with some TV producer friends at the Daily Grill, a hip new restaurant off Connecticut Avenue. George Conway had arrived in town and tagged along. But he was distracted, constantly stepping outside to talk on his cell phone. He was talking cryptically. Coulter knew something was up. "I've got to go see Moody," Conway finally said.

When he got to Moody's office that night, Conway was horrified. Moody was trying to play the Tripp tapes. As Tripp's lawyer, he wanted to make a record of what was on them. He needed to know the evidence his client was going to be questioned about. But there was a problem. He couldn't get his tape recorder to work. Conway looked at Moody's recorder. It was a twenty-five-year-old Dicta-phone—so old, the lettering on the play and record buttons was no longer even visible. This was too much, Conway thought. Moody was supposed to be the techno-geek. One of the reasons they had come to him in the first place was that they figured he'd know how to wire Tripp. And he didn't even have a working tape recorder? For a few moments, Conway watched the legally blind Moody fumbling over the recorder.

"You can't use this," he said finally. "You have no idea how to work this thing."

"No, it's okay, really," Moody replied.

Then Conway was struck with a sudden, awful fear. What if he hit the wrong button? Oh, my God, he thought. He's going to erase the tapes.

For six years, right-wingers had frantically tried to find the killer evidence that would bring down Bill Clinton. Now, it was finally in hand—Conway was looking at it—and it was in imminent danger of being destroyed by a blind man.

Maybe we better call Coulter, Conway suggested. He did. Moody needed a tape recorder, he told her. One that worked. She invited them over.

They arrived at her place in the elegant New Deal–era Kennedy-Warren apartments about one A.M., the cache of tapes in tow. Coulter had an elaborate, high-tech stereo system she used to listen to her Grateful Dead CDs and tapes. She turned it over to Moody and Conway for the elves' first screening of the Tripp-Lewinsky tapes. Marcus and Porter were patched in by speakerphone. The five of them listened well into the morning.

As they did so, Coulter was ecstatic. Her first thought was that these were dynamite. A hoot, in fact. Monica wasn't boasting of a sexual relationship with the president on the tape they listened to that night. She was all emotion—a clear sign she was genuine and the relationship with Clinton was real. "The weeping and the crying—I thought it was unbelievable," Coulter later recalled. She was pumped.

But Moody and Conway weren't. They were listening more carefully, paying attention to nuances and precise language. They had been told Monica had been recorded saying the president told her to lie—and that Vernon Jordan told her to lie. But as they listened to the December 22 conversation, the one that had been billed as the "smoking gun," she never said those things. At one point, Coulter looked over at Conway and Moody. "They were crestfallen," she said.

●　　●　　●

They talked again by phone late that night. It was the same conversation, that endless debate about Bill Clinton and sex and telling the truth. Monica Lewinsky told Tripp it was very important that she meet with Bob Bennett. She was telling her that "as a friend." Lewinsky herself wasn't worried anymore, she said. "I feel like I've done what a political appointee should do." She didn't have to fear the fact that she was going to sign a false affidavit to the Paula Jones lawyers. "I'm not going to get in trouble," she said. "I will not get in trouble because you know what? The story I've signed—under oath—is what someone else is saying under oath."

She meant Clinton.

"And you're positive, 100 percent without doubt positive, he's not going to slip up when he gives his deposition?" Tripp asked.

"Hah, him?"

Tripp said—again—it was all too difficult for her. "The bottom line is the only person you have to be truth—truth—truthful to in your life is essentially yourself," Tripp said. She had a new attorney, she told Lewinsky. She was going to be meeting with him tomorrow. She didn't know what she was going to do. She was "scared to death."

Lewinsky explained why it was not the same way for her. "It is not as black and white for me as it is for you. . . . This is not a murder case. This is not even a criminal case." If she really thought Paula Jones had been "damaged for life because of this," then she would have a "harder time" doing what she was doing. But she didn't think that.

And on it went. Tripp's call waiting beeped. "Do you know what I get worried about?" Lewinsky asked. "You don't think Isikoff would call you this late, do you?" Tripp said not to worry. If it were Isikoff, she'd just hang up. She took the other call. It was Jim Moody. "I'm still on the phone with her," Tripp told him. Moody gave her his number, telling Tripp to call back.

Tripp clicked her phone and got back on with Lewinsky. The conversation then veered, as it always did. They talked about all the nights they had stayed up late talking, about all the times Lewinsky had cried over the phone over the way "he" had treated her. Tripp said she could never forget that, it was like "steel" in her mind.

"He could have been decent," Tripp said.

Lewinsky said she knew that, but now, "I—I want this to be behind me. In the least intrusive way possible."

They talked about Tripp's job. They talked—for a change—about Tripp's love life, or lack thereof. "We gotta get you laid," Lewinsky said.

"Oh God, wouldn't that be something different," Tripp said. "I don't know. After seven years, do you really think there's a possibility I'd remember how?" They talked, of course, about Clinton's love life. "He has a problem, Monica, he does," Tripp said.

"He does," agreed Lewinsky. "And you know what? . . . He has a problem, and we, the American people, elected him, so let him do his stupid job. You know?"

Then finally, they were talked out. For now.

"So I'll talk to you tomorrow," Lewinsky said.

"All right, bye," Tripp said.

"Sweet dreams," Lewinsky said. "Bye."

Tripp got out her notebook and wrote:

This is no longer a friend, but a manipulator. I feel the same way— we are on opposite sides. Guilt is still there, but lessening. Her decision to lie is hers alone.

20

"I don't recall."

At *Newsweek* headquarters in midtown Manhattan, the senior brass had been briefed Thursday morning. Richard Smith, the editor in chief, had come down to the sixteenth-floor office of managing editor Mark Whitaker. There, as they looked out on the spectacular view of Central Park, Ann McDaniel laid out everything the magazine knew. This had the potential to be big, Smith and Whitaker quickly agreed. It sounded as if Clinton had really gotten himself into trouble this time. But as they listened to McDaniel run through the strange story of Bill Clinton, Monica Lewinsky and Kenneth Starr, yellow lights started to go off. We need to know more about this, they concluded. A lot more.

It was a natural reaction, only in this case the caution was perhaps even greater than usual. At *Newsweek,* the starting quarterback was Maynard Parker, the magazine's editor, a man legendary for making gutsy calls. Sometimes they succeeded brilliantly, other times not so. But Parker had nothing to do with this one. In November, he had been diagnosed with leukemia. He had gone into the hospital earlier that week for a round of chemotherapy. That left the decision about the Lewinsky story to a committee of senior editors headed by Smith and Whitaker. Both had dedicated their professional careers to the magazine. Smith, a veteran foreign correspondent who had covered the Vietnam War, was now not just editor in chief, but the magazine's president as well—a position that gave him responsibility for *Newsweek*'s business operations. Whitaker,

309

forty, was Parker's number two and heir apparent, an employee of *Newsweek* since the late 1970s, when he signed on as an intern while still an undergraduate at Harvard. Both Whitaker and McDaniel were keenly aware that they were stewards for the magazine in Parker's absence—and needed the more experienced Smith's help.

What if *Newsweek* went big with this and Monica Lewinsky turned out to be a fruitcake? What if Starr announced next Monday that there was nothing to the charges against the president or Vernon Jordan? *Newsweek* would look terrible. The magazine would have been used. Whitaker would later recall thinking he had a "fiduciary responsibility" that week. "The credibility of the magazine was at stake," he said.

In their discussion on Thursday, the editors had focused on one issue early on: If we could hear Linda Tripp's tapes, we could at least make our own assessment of Lewinsky's credibility. There might be more leads on the tapes—references to documents or dates or *something*—that could be independently checked. We would also presumably be able to hear if there really was, as advertised, evidence that Clinton or Vernon Jordan had pressured Lewinsky to lie. Getting the tapes was very important. Isikoff should do everything he could to get his hands on them.

In the meantime, though, Whitaker and McDaniel had practical concerns. There was a magazine to put out. Jon Meacham, the national affairs editor, had a section to fill. They quickly decided we had to have something ready to run in the event that the Lewinsky story wasn't nailed down in time.

When I got to the office on Friday morning and briefed McDaniel on where we stood, we talked about the tapes. I told her I still hoped I would have a chance to listen to them. Great, she said. But in the meantime, we needed a backup story about Clinton's deposition in the Paula Jones case.

A backup? I asked. What do you mean? They're not going to run this?

No, no, McDaniel told me. It's just in case. We'll see where everything stands tomorrow.

Fine, I told her. I had plenty of stuff for a story on Clinton's deposition and the Jones case—including a detail nobody else had reported: Willey had finally testified about Clinton's sexual advances in her secret deposition the previous Saturday.

Sounds great, she said as I walked out.

I had my first clue: New York was nervous.

•   •   •

That morning, Moody finally called back. I nearly jumped out of my chair.

Where the hell have you been? I shouted. Don't you realize how important it is that I hear those tapes? Don't you realize Linda is going to get clobbered if I can't prove how serious all this is?

"Oh," Moody said, "you're calling about that. I thought you were calling me about this great computer fraud case I've been working on out in California."

I am not in the mood for this, I told him.

"No, really, I'm representing a whistleblower, and it could lead to millions of dollars in savings for the government," he said.

I was now starting to feel homicidal.

Cut it out, I snapped. I'm not bullshitting here.

Okay, Moody said. He agreed that it would be in the public interest if I heard the tapes. But there were some things he had to work out. He would be back in touch.

"When?" I asked. "My deadline is tonight. I've got to hear these tapes tonight."

I understand, Moody said. I'll be back in touch.

•   •   •

This will be another rough day, Linda Tripp wrote in her notebook Friday morning. It was January 16, 1998. It was the day Starr's office planned to swoop in, the last day they could do so before *Newsweek* started calling the principals, asking them to comment. Tripp beeped Lewinsky and arranged to get together at the Food Court at the Pentagon City Mall. It was another chance to have lunch—and one last chance to go over everything, Tripp said, explaining that she was meeting with her new lawyer that afternoon and might sign an affidavit. They should talk about it. Lewinsky said she'd be there.

Then Tripp called Starr's office to let them know it was all arranged for 11:30 A.M.

No good, one of the prosecutors told her. It's not enough time. Move it back. *Christ. I'm not a pro, I'm losing it,* Tripp scribbled in the notebook. She called Lewinsky back and moved the meeting to 12:30 P.M.

Tripp mulled over her situation. She thought again about the dress. She had remembered it the day before and told one of Starr's prosecutors about it. The prosecutor seemed surprised when he heard there might be a garment with the president's semen on it. Now, on Friday, waiting at home all alone, Tripp recalled that she had once had the opportunity to swipe it. Why hadn't she? She had asked Kirby Behre about that at the time, and he had *gone ballistic & claimed I would look like a nut.* Tripp wished she'd never listened to him and had taken the dress after all. *A nut?* she wrote. *A vindicated nut.*

Now look where she was. *My integrity is on the line and I have no proof.*

•   •   •

S hortly after nine A.M., in the office of the independent counsel, Jackie Bennett and Lee Radek from the Department of Justice placed a conference call to the home of U.S. judge David Sentelle. A crusty and conservative North Carolinian appointed to the bench by President Ronald Reagan, Sentelle oversaw the three-member panel that governed the operations of all independent counsels. Radek did most of the talking. There was a new matter that had come up relating to the Paula Jones lawsuit, he explained. Starr's office had requested, and the Justice Department was supporting, a formal expansion in Starr's legal authority to investigate it.

The participation of Radek was crucial—and surprising. As chief of Justice's public integrity section, he had a deep-seated hostility to the operations of independent counsels. In large part, this was a matter of institutional turf—and pride. Any case ceded to an independent counsel was a case that wouldn't be worked by Radek's unit at Justice. But in this case, the process that began Wednesday night when Jackie Bennett beeped Eric Holder at the Wizards game had borne fruit.

After the meeting in Eric Holder's office on Thursday night, the deputy general and his deputies would later say they felt boxed in. If they refused to move quickly, they could be accused of dragging their feet in order to protect Clinton. That night, Holder briefed Attorney General Janet Reno (she had gone to the theater at the Kennedy Center and, like Holder himself the night before, didn't immediately return his page). Meanwhile, one of Radek's deputies, Josh Hochberg, was dispatched to Starr's office to carefully review the transcript of the "sting" tape of Tripp and Lewinsky's conversation at the Ritz-Carlton.

Early Friday morning, Hochberg briefed Radek, Holder and Reno. They all agreed that they had no choice. The statements made on the FBI tape warranted further investigation. Justice couldn't do it—the alleged crimes directly involved Clinton, a clear conflict of interest under the independent counsel law. Appointing a new special prosecutor would take too much time. The only alternative, Reno concluded, was to back Starr's request.[1]

Starr's office had by then drafted language for an order that could be filed with the three-judge panel. It called for Starr to investigate Lewinsky, Vernon Jordan and others for subornation of perjury and other crimes in the Paula Jones lawsuit. When he arrived at Starr's office after his meeting with Reno, Radek said that Justice didn't think Jordan's name had to be mentioned; the words "and others" would cover it. (It would also cover the president, of course.) Starr's office didn't object.

When he heard Radek lay out the case that morning, Sentelle asked a few questions and then said he would get back to them. A few hours later, after checking with the other two judges on the panel, he did. By early afternoon, the judges had approved an order—which was placed under seal at the U.S. Federal Courthouse in Washington—formally granting an expanded mandate to the office of the Whitewater independent counsel. The order identified only one individual as the target of this new federal criminal investigation, an individual whose existence was unknown to the world at large. Monica Lewinsky.

•   •   •

L ewinsky was on time, waiting at the Food Court in the Pentagon City mall at 12:30 P.M. Tripp got there late. It was 12:45 P.M. when the older woman started down the escalator. Lewinsky went to greet her. Then Tripp made a swift motion, and before Lewinsky could figure out what was happening, two men briskly stepped forward and flashed their badges.

They were Steve Irons and Patrick F. Fallon Jr., special agents of the Federal Bureau of Investigation. Irons and Fallon told Lewinsky she was the subject of a criminal investigation. There were some people who wanted to speak to her upstairs, they explained. They suggested she come with them. Lewinsky was bewildered. She didn't understand what was going on. "I was so scared," she later said.

Lewinsky followed Irons and Fallon into the elevator. Tripp came along. The two women were ushered into a tenth-floor suite, where FBI agents and federal prosecutors from Starr's office had assembled. It was now about one P.M. Mike Emmick introduced himself to Lewinsky. Emmick had come from the U.S. Attorney's Office in Los Angeles. A veteran white-collar prosecutor, he was also handsome and single and known as something of a ladies' man—the best choice, Starr's team figured, to handle this somewhat delicate assignment. Emmick tried to put Lewinsky at ease. But his words were terrifying. The attorney general, Janet Reno, had authorized Starr's office to investigate federal crimes related to the Paula Jones case, he told her. She had been recorded on tape saying she was going to lie under oath, and they knew she had signed a false affidavit. The FBI agents showed her pictures of her lunch with Tripp on Tuesday. She could be charged with a number of federal crimes, Emmick said: perjury, subornation of perjury, obstruction of justice, witness tampering. They were all felonies, and she could go to jail for twenty-seven years.

Lewinsky finally figured it out. "This is the best thing for you," Tripp told her. Soon, the agents hustled Tripp into the next room. Emmick and the two FBI agents tried to resume the conversation. But it was impossible. Lewinsky was "nearly hysterical with tears," Emmick later said in a court affidavit. "She would sob, then cry out, then stare into space, then cry for long periods." Emmick and the two FBI agents tried unsuccessfully to calm her down, bringing her water and tissues and coffee.

By about two P.M., Lewinsky seemed to collect herself. Emmick resumed his pitch. They wanted Lewinsky to cooperate, he explained. If she did, the prosecutors would take that into account in deciding whether or not to indict her. Lewinsky wanted to know what Emmick meant by cooperate. He said she, like Linda Tripp, would have to agree to be wired—to place a phone call or have a microphone placed on her while she had conversations with others.[2]

One of Lewinsky's first questions was what if she agreed to do that and then "messed up"? What if she were wired for a meeting with Vernon Jordan and then started signaling to him that something was "wrong"? One of the FBI agents jumped in. They would be watching, the agent explained, to make sure she didn't do that.

The discussions went slowly. Lewinsky, according to Emmick's account, would sob and continued to stare out into space. About three P.M., Emmick recalled Lewinsky asking, "What if I want to call my attorney?" Emmick and Bruce Udolf had talked about this. It would be a disaster for the investigation if she did so. As the lawyer hand-picked by Vernon Jordan, Carter was at that point a potential suspect. But Emmick knew he had to be careful. She was free to call, of course, he said. But Emmick asked her to hold off and listen to more of what they had to say. Informing Frank Carter of what was happening, he said, might make her less useful if she agreed to become an undercover informant.[3]

By late afternoon, it was increasingly clear that Lewinsky was not coming around. Emmick tried another gambit: She could get full immunity from prosecution if she would cooperate. They would also not prosecute her mother, even though they knew that she had participated in some of the discussions about concealing the relationship with Clinton. As Lewinsky saw it, however, they were actually threatening to prosecute her mother if she *didn't* cooperate. Lewinsky wanted to call her. She was "extremely close" to her mother, she told Emmick, and could not possibly make such a decision without consulting her.

Jackie Bennett had been back in his office, calling over to the hotel for updates. About this time, Udolf suggested to him perhaps a little "gray hair" would help. Bennett came over—the room was quite crowded at this point—and sat down in front of Lewinsky. As Lewinsky later recalled it, Bennett said: "You're twenty-four years old, you're smart, you're old enough, you don't need to call your mommy." Bennett would later remember it differently. He didn't say "mommy." He said "mother." Whatever the word he used, it didn't break the witness.

"Well, I'm letting you know I'm leaning toward not cooperating," she said.

Lewinsky still wanted to speak to her mother. But from where? Starr's men offered her the use of any of the phones in the suite. She made a brief call, telling her mother that "something had come up." Emmick suggested she find a pay phone in the mall on her own to speak longer. Lewinsky suggested those phones might be bugged as well. Emmick and the FBI agents assured her they were not.

So Lewinsky left to call her mother. As she did, walking among the bustle of shoppers in the Pentagon City Mall late on a Friday afternoon, she ran into somebody she knew.

Linda Tripp.

Tripp had been asked by the FBI to hang around while Lewinsky was debriefed. She had gone shopping. But just a little while earlier, she had checked with Starr's prosecutors and been told she was free to leave. She was on her way to do just that, about to take the subway home.

Lewinsky and Tripp passed right by each other. Their eyes met.

They had their last conversation.

"Thanks a lot!" Lewinsky said.

"They did it to me, too," Tripp said. It was, she later conceded, a lie, her final one. She got onto the escalator and slowly disappeared underground into the Metro.

•   •   •

Wes Holmes was more impatient than ever. He was still pacing back and forth at his room at the Hyatt Regency Thursday afternoon, waiting to get his hands on the Tripp tapes. By now, he knew something heavy was going on. Everybody he was calling—Goldberg, Conway, Moody—was being cryptic. There had been a mention of some law enforcement involvement in matters relating to Tripp, but nobody would give him any details. Holmes didn't care. The clock was ticking. He needed the tapes. He needed to get more from Tripp. The president's deposition was now less than twenty-four hours away.

On Thursday, Holmes had gotten through to Moody. They'd arranged to meet—first at two P.M., then at four P.M., then again at six P.M. Moody cancelled every time. Then, late on Friday afternoon, just as Linda Tripp was on her way home,[4] Moody told Holmes to meet him in his office—at six P.M. Then they would drive out to Tripp's house.

Holmes, wearing blue jeans and a cowboy shirt, arrived at Moody's office in downtown Washington and they headed out to Maryland. Holmes had a rental car. He had no idea where he was going. He was relying on Moody, who had never been there, either. Moody had the directions and was holding them up right in front of his thick eyeglasses. Suddenly, Holmes realized the problem. Moody couldn't see a thing. They missed several turnoffs and ended up in a shopping mall. They were lost.

• • •

At the White House, President Clinton sat down with his lawyer Bob Bennett for one last prep session before his deposition in the case of *Jones* vs. *Clinton.* The meeting stretched on late into the evening. Among other items, they reviewed the names of all the women the Jones lawyers would be asking about and how the president would respond. There would be questions about Gennifer Flowers, of course, and Kathleen Willey, Dolly Kyle Browning and a handful of other "Jane Does" who had been deposed during the course of discovery. (The true identity of the Jane Does had been deleted from all public filings to protect their privacy.) One of them—Jane Doe #6—was Monica Lewinsky. But there was no reason to take up much of the president's time on this one. Earlier that day, Francis Carter had faxed over to one of Bennett's colleagues, Katherine Sexton, a copy of the affidavit Lewinsky had signed the previous week, stating flatly, "I have never had a sexual relationship with the president." As far as Bennett was concerned, on this one, he and Bill Clinton were covered.

• • •

The first sign of trouble came mid–Friday afternoon. Deborah Orin, Washington bureau chief of the *New York Post,* called, saying she heard I had a blockbuster in the next issue. She just wanted to see if she could get an advance copy late Saturday so she could write about it for her Sunday paper—with full credit, of course. I put her off, telling her nothing. Then I slammed down the phone, quite agitated. What the hell was going on? I wondered.

In fact, Orin had been tipped off through a circuitous route that had started, appropriately enough, with Lucianne Goldberg. By now, Goldberg was in a sour mood. When Starr's office two days earlier had learned of Tripp's contacts with Goldberg, they immediately assumed (incorrectly) that it was the literary agent who had tipped me off to the "sting" at the Ritz-Carlton. They forced Tripp to change her phone number and stop talking to Goldberg. Goldberg wrote in her notes that she was *not amused* by this. *Pissed that they have cut me off from Linda,* Goldberg wrote, she called her friend Marc Kalech, managing editor of the *New York Post* (the paper with whom she was on retainer), and let him know *Newsweek* had a hot one coming.

After Orin, I heard from Bruce Udolf. Starr's office wanted me to hold off even longer before making my calls to Jordan and Lewinsky—until Saturday morning, he told me. Under normal circumstances, I would have told him to take a hike. Saturday is the last deadline day, and it would be cutting it way too tight to hold off that long before contacting a principal in a sensitive story like this. But the fact was, my hands were tied. I had been told to sit tight. I would get to hear the tapes that evening. But I still didn't have my hands on them, and I knew the story was never going to be a sure thing unless I did. It was also hard to know precisely what to ask Jordan until I heard exactly what Lewinsky had said on tape about him.

I checked with McDaniel. Don't worry, we'll be able to track Jordan down on a Saturday if we need to, she told me. There are ways to retrieve Jordan's phone numbers from the right Rolodexes, she said. Extremely reluctantly, I told Udolf we'd wait.

The reason Starr's prosecutors needed extra time was that events at the Ritz-Carlton had by then gone from horrific to wacky. Lewinsky had reached her mother, Marcia Lewis, in New York. Then Lewinsky came back to the tenth floor and told Starr's prosecutors that she really needed to talk to her mother in person. It was soon agreed that Lewis would come to Washington—by train. Emmick got on the phone and assured Marcia Lewis that nothing would happen until she arrived.

In the meantime, Lewinsky had decided she was tired of sitting around in the hotel room. "I thought maybe I should try and make these people like me," she later explained. "So I tried to be nice, and I told jokes." She suggested they all go out for a walk. Before long, Emmick, FBI agent Fallon and Lewinsky were taking a leisurely stroll around the mall, mixing in with all the rest of the weekend shoppers.

The prosecutor, the FBI agent and the suspected perjurer window-shopped. They chatted. They went to dinner.

They went back to the hotel. Lewinsky read a Bible—Psalm 21. She and the prosecutors watched movies on cable. *The Godfather* came on, then an Ethel Merman musical, *There's No Business Like Show Business.*

•   •   •

Holmes and Moody finally did make it to Linda Tripp's house on Friday night. As soon as they walked in about eight P.M., Holmes was ushered into the living room and Tripp gave him some pictures of Lewinsky. Then she and Moody went into another room. "You can talk to Linda, and she'll tell you whatever you want to know," Moody said when they came back. All Holmes could think was, Yeah, that's great. But what about the tapes?

Still, Holmes thought he'd ease into it, maybe establish some rapport. In the meantime, he'd take what he could get. He got out his notebook. But Tripp was a mess. That day, she had implemented the final betrayal of her friend and set off a secret criminal investigation of the president. She was, Holmes thought, "very agitated." For more than an hour, Tripp paced back and forth, chain-smoked and rambled on, offering everything she could think of about the relationship between Monica Lewinsky and Bill Clinton. Holmes quickly got frustrated. Tripp kept bouncing from one subject to another, going down "rabbit trails," talking about one thing and then another without ever finishing her point.

"What I need are specifics," Holmes told her, "specific facts about Monica Lewinsky that we can use to question the president with." Gradually, he started to get somewhere. Tripp told Holmes about the T-shirts Clinton had brought Lewinsky from the Black Dog at Martha's Vineyard. She told about a book that Clinton had given Lewinsky. She remembered the name—*Leaves of Grass,* by Walt Whitman. She told him about Clinton's love of phone sex and the book on phone sex Lewinsky had bought. Holmes scribbled furiously away and started to feel better. This was good, he thought. This was helpful.

But what Holmes really wanted was the tapes. Moody hadn't offered them. What about the tapes? he asked. They didn't give him a straight answer. Look, he said, I've got a subpoena for those tapes in my briefcase. I don't want to have to serve this on you, Linda. If I do that, then I have to give Bennett a copy of it and he'll know all about the tapes.

At that point, Moody jumped in. "I can't give you the tapes because I don't have them."

What do you mean? Holmes said, now quite agitated. How about copies?

Nope, Moody said, no copies either.

Holmes remembered Moody saying more, telling him the tapes were now evidence in a criminal case being supervised by Ken Starr. Moody denies saying this. Either way, it didn't matter. Holmes wasn't going to get them.

Goddammit, Holmes thought, we've been screwed again. Campbell was going to hit the roof.

• • •

Sometime after ten P.M., Marcia Lewis made it to the Ritz-Carlton. Starr's prosecutors still harbored hopes that somehow they could turn things around and get Lewinsky to place a few monitored calls—perhaps to Betty Currie, maybe to Vernon Jordan. They knew they didn't have much time. Clinton would be deposed in just a few hours. Then, by Sunday morning, they assumed, *Newsweek* would blow the whole case wide open.

But Marcia Lewis wasn't about to rush into anything. After hearing Emmick out, she told him she had to talk to Monica's father, Bernard Lewinsky. Then Bernard Lewinsky wanted to talk to Emmick. So the prosecutor got on the phone and explained it all to him. Lewinsky suggested it might be better if his daughter talked to a lawyer before she decided anything. Emmick's court affidavit suggests considerable impatience on the part of the prosecutors at this point. "I said that was fine, but we needed a decision quite soon, and I wasn't sure if an attorney could be contacted that soon," he said.

Bernard Lewinsky said, don't worry, he would find one.

About fifteen minutes later, Emmick got a call from a man who identified himself as William Ginsburg.

He was a medical malpractice lawyer in Los Angeles and an old friend of Bernard Lewinsky's. He had known Monica since she was a baby. This was just a courtesy call, Ginsburg explained to Emmick. He was taking a plane to Washington that night and would see him when he arrived on Saturday.

• • •

The tapes were now in the midst of a circuitous chain of custody. During the afternoon, Moody had delivered all seventeen of them to Starr's office and received in exchange a letter from Jackie Bennett granting what he thought was the immunity his client so desperately wanted. Then, late that evening, after he returned from his meeting with Wes Holmes at Tripp's house, Moody reunited with Conway. The two of them then taxied over to a Howard Johnson's restaurant, across the street from Lewinsky's apartment at the Watergate hotel, where they met with Bennett and Udolf from Starr's office.[5] The purpose of the meeting would not become public until nearly two years later. It wasn't flattering for Starr's deputies. Moody wanted one of the tapes—the December 22 conversation—back. At least one reason for this request was that he hadn't made a copy—and needed to know more precisely what his client had recorded herself saying. Another reason apparently was the badgering phone messages from me, and my threats to make Tripp, and perhaps more important, Starr, look bad if there wasn't convincing evidence that would justify the extraordinary events of the last few days. Moody "had received many messages from Michael Isikoff of *Newsweek*, who said that Mr. Moody ought to call him because he was preparing an article highly damaging to Ms. Tripp," another Starr deputy, Steve Bates, later stated in an affidavit given to Maryland state prosecutors investigating Tripp's taping. The tape was turned over. It was about midnight.

As Linda Tripp later testified, Jim Moody brought the tape to *Newsweek*'s Washington bureau. It was 12:30 A.M. It was, we were told, the most important tape. I had been planning on listening to it myself. But too much was riding on this. McDaniel wanted to hear at least part of the tape herself. She had assured Smith and Whitaker that she would personally listen and verify that the tape sounded real. I didn't object. Danny Klaidman was still in the office. So was Evan Thomas. The four of us gathered in McDaniel's office. Somebody—either Thomas or Klaidman—took one look at our source and instantly dubbed him "Lurch," from the character in *The Addams Family.*

We loaded up the recorder, and the four of us listened intently—scribbling notes as fast as we could.

Thomas and McDaniel had started out as natural skeptics. Until now, they had no way of independently verifying anything Tripp had been reporting for months. But within minutes, the doubts started to fade. The conversation sounded real—and McDaniel quickly concluded that Tripp basically had been telling the truth about what Lewinsky had been saying to her. But what about Lewinsky? Had she been telling Tripp the truth?

I thought so. One question on all our minds was whether Lewinsky seemed to be boasting of a sexual relationship with a president—a sign, perhaps, that she might have invented or at least embroidered much of it simply to get attention. In fact, Lewinsky's voice sounded genuine. Sweet, young, engaging, but also spoiled and whiny at times. And scared. It was the December 22 tape, the one Tripp had made illegally, the one that—based on Tripp's accounts—prompted Jerome Marcus to think about going to Ken Starr in the first place.

The talk turned to the Paula Jones case and whether Lewinsky should inform "the big creep" that she had told her friend Tripp all about their relationship.

Lewinsky: "Look, maybe I should just tell the creep. Maybe I should just say, 'Don't ever talk to me again. If I fucked you over, so now you have this information, do whatever you want with it.'"

Tripp: "Well, if you want to do that, that's what I would do. But I don't know that you're comfortable with that. I think he should know."

Lewinsky (with a sigh): "He won't settle. He's in denial."

Tripp: "I think if he fucking knew, he would settle."

They talked, too, about whether the Jones lawyers would have hard evidence that she was having a relationship with Clinton.

Lewinsky: "Whatever they have, if they have anything, has to be inadmissible. Nobody saw him give me any of those things, and nobody saw anything happen between us."

Tripp: "Are you positive that nobody saw you in the study?"

Lewinsky: "I'm absolutely positive."

I was listening closely—and just as intently watching the faces of McDaniel and Thomas. Within moments, I thought, they had become believers. I may have misread them. McDaniel was still wondering about Lewinsky, still thinking that she might have slowly invented for Tripp an elaborate fictional world from which she could no longer escape. There was no explicit mention of sex with Clinton. But the conversation proceeded as though the two of them assumed it to be true.

At one point, on the tape, we heard Lewinsky's call waiting beep. Tripp and Lewinsky had just been talking about their plan to have Tripp fake a "foot accident" to get out of her scheduled deposition. Lewinsky then got back on the line and told Tripp her mother thought the plan was "brilliant."

McDaniel couldn't get over it. She's told her *mother?*

The most important issue, of course, was whether there was evidence of obstruction. Did Lewinsky in fact say that she had been told to lie? On this point, the conversation seemed to skirt around the edges.

Tripp: "He knows you're going to lie. You've told him, haven't you?"

Lewinsky: "No."

Tripp: "I thought that night when he called you established that much."

Lewinsky: "Well, I mean, I don't know."

Tripp: "Jesus. Well, does he think you're going to tell the truth?"

Lewinsky: "No . . . Oh, Jesus."

Tripp: "So he's at least feeling somewhat safe that this is not going to go any further right now, right?"

Lewinsky: "Yeah."

I stayed at the office until four A.M., typing my notes into the computer.

• • •

In his room at the Hyatt Regency that night, Jim Fisher never slept. A slight, soft-spoken, bookish man with a choirboy face, Fisher had been the consensus choice of the Dallas lawyers to conduct the questioning of Bill Clinton. If anybody's appearance would surprise Clinton, it was Fisher's, they figured. If anyone could lull the president into complacency, it was he. But for Fisher, the pressure was almost unbearable. Alone in his room that night, Fisher studied up for hours, poring over hundreds of pages of documents and deposition transcripts, then rehearsing his questions. When he finished studying, he did the only other thing he could do: he prayed.

Before he left for Washington, Fisher's wife had given him a note with verses from the Scriptures she wanted him to read before going into battle with Bill Clinton. Late that night, Fisher got out the Bible he had brought in his briefcase. He read the verses his wife had chosen. Then he turned out the lights, lay down on his bed and, for the rest of the evening, sought the Lord's guidance.

About seven A.M., Holmes knocked on Fisher's door and quickly briefed him on everything he had learned from Tripp the previous evening. Holmes told Fisher about the semen-stained dress, the *Leaves of Grass* and the phone sex. Then, after breakfast downstairs, the Dallas lawyers hopped into cabs and took them to the offices of Skadden, Arps. By the time Fisher walked into the conference room that morning, his evening of prayer had paid off. He no longer felt nervous.

"I had a strange sense of calm," Fisher recalled months later. "I get nervous a lot, but I was as calm and peaceful for this as anything I've ever done. I didn't feel intimidated. I felt I was where I was supposed to be, and He was not going to let me fail."

• • •

I arrived at the offices of *Newsweek* early that morning, just as the Clinton deposition was about to start, and immediately marched into McDaniel's office. It was, for me and *Newsweek*, D-Day. Either the magazine was going to go to press with the most explosive political story Washington had seen in years—or it would take an amazing pass. I needed a decision soon—like in the next few hours, I told

McDaniel. If we are going with this story, I absolutely have to call Lewinsky and Vernon Jordan to get fair comment. But if we're not going to publish it, then I shouldn't be making those calls. We would only be interfering with a criminal investigation by tipping off two of the prime targets. She agreed and said we would decide fairly soon—that morning.

When I got back to my desk, I found a message from John Podesta, deputy White House chief of staff. This was odd, I thought. I called him. We chatted. I knew Podesta and had always gotten along with him. The previous summer, he had even asked me to speak as a guest lecturer at a Georgetown University law class he had been teaching on media coverage of White House scandals.

"So I hear you got quite a story coming," he said.

Oh, really, I said.

Something about tapes and obstruction of justice and Ken Starr, he told me. My competitors at *Time* had been calling all over the White House asking about this. So, Podesta wanted to know, what's going on?

I was in a bind. I could hardly tell him. I didn't even know if I had a story at that point. (If I didn't, I wasn't going to fill him in—especially after he told me he'd been talking to my competitors.) I dodged, mumbling something about not working on anything relating to Whitewater. He took my response as a no.

But I was reluctant to get off. Podesta was also a potential source for one of the elements of the story: Lewinsky's interview with Bill Richardson back in October. It had been supposedly set up at Podesta's behest.

By the way, I asked him as casually as I could, do you know somebody named Monica Lewinsky?

Not really, he said. He had met her only once—at a funeral. He wouldn't tell me whose. He sounded vague and a bit evasive. I told him I understood her name had come up in the Paula Jones case, and I had some questions about her. Bennett was the only person who could handle this, he said, and he was tied up in Clinton's deposition. He'd see what he could do about getting him back to me later.

After the call, Podesta later testified, he went to see Cheryl Mills in the White House counsel's office. "I talked to Isikoff," Podesta told Mills. "He said he wasn't working on a matter having to do with the grand jury and Ken Starr . . . he was working on a Paula Jones matter that involved Monica Lewinsky."

•   •   •

Three long blocks away, in the offices of Skadden, Arps, around a large, oval mahogany table, the lawyers assembled. The men from Dallas were on one side, with an exceedingly nervous Paula Jones next to them. Clinton's lawyers were on the other, facing them. Judge Susan Webber Wright and her clerk, Barry Word, had flown in from Little Rock and were seated toward the far end of the table on the side where Clinton's lawyers sat. A videocamera had been set up on the south end of the table facing the north, where the president was to sit.

The lawyers and judge had gotten there on time at nine-thirty A.M., shook hands and awkwardly waited in silence for the president. Finally, Clinton walked in with Bob Bennett by his side. The president headed straight to Judge Wright and gave her a hearty greeting, shaking her hand, asking about her family, asking about mutual friends in Arkansas and joking a bit about the time the judge had been a law student of his when he taught at the University of Arkansas.

It was, the Dallas lawyers thought, vintage Bill Clinton, the consummate politician even when he was being deposed.

Then Clinton sat down. He never greeted Jones or her lawyers. He never even looked at them. Fisher hadn't known what to expect. But, he thought, this was extraordinary. He had been at scores of depositions in his eighteen-year legal career, and every time it was the same. The lawyers and litigants always observed the formalities, shaking hands and greeting each other before something like this began. As Fisher viewed it, it was part of the "code of civility" that participants in legal proceedings always observed—at least in Texas they did. But Washington is a different place, he thought. It is a different world.

This wasn't law. This was war.

Clinton took the oath. There was some early skirmishing about how the questioning would be handled. There was the issue of questions about sexual relations. It was at the core of the case. Had Clinton done to others what he did to Jones? Was there a pattern and practice? The Jones lawyers had a definition. It was taken from a 1994 crime control act, a law signed by President Clinton. They thought it covered everything they wanted to ask about. "This will eliminate confusion," Fisher said.

Bennett objected. It was too complicated, too hard to remember. "We acknowledge that some embarrassing questions will be asked . . . but I do not want my client answering questions not understanding exactly what these folks are talking about."

The judge ruled. They hadn't used definitions in the past. She was reluctant to start now. In this instance, she agreed to use Fisher's definition but wanted it modified so it was less confusing. Fisher and the Jones lawyers were satisfied. As they saw it, even with the modification, the definition covered what they wanted to ask about, which first and foremost was oral sex. It was the form of sexual relations most directly relevant to the allegations of their client.[6]

This was, in fact, a case about oral sex.

The first questions were about Kathleen Willey. Clinton was well prepared. Yes, he knew her. She and her husband had contributed to his campaign. He did indeed meet with Willey just before her husband's death. "She was very upset that day," Clinton testified, and was looking for a "paying job" because she was having "financial difficulties."

Fisher: "Are you aware that she has testified that you kissed her in the hallway between the Oval Office and the private kitchen?"

Clinton: "I am aware of that."

Fisher: "And you're aware that she testified that you took her hand and put it on your penis?"

Clinton: "I'm aware of that."

Fisher: "All right, and you deny that testimony?"

Clinton: "I emphatically deny it."

Why, Fisher wanted to know, would she tell such a story? Clinton said he didn't know, but she had "been through a lot." He talked about the death of her husband and the financial problems she had faced.

"All I can tell you is . . . when she came to see me she was clearly upset," Clinton testified. "I did to her what I have done to scores and scores of men and women who have worked for me or been my friends over the years. I embraced her, I put my arms around her, I may have even kissed her on the forehead. There was nothing sexual about it."

That, and that alone, is what happened, Clinton testified. He was quite sure of that. "I remember this very well," he said at one point. A bit later, he added: "I remember this conversation very vividly because she was so agitated and she seemed to be in very difficult straits."

In so doing, Clinton contradicted what Bennett had told me six months earlier, on the night we were crashing on the Willey story that started it all. That night, Bennett had said, the president had "no specific recollection" of meeting with Willey in the Oval Office.

After Willey, Fisher moved on to another subject.

"Now, do you know a woman named Monica Lewinsky?"

•   •   •

About ten-thirty A.M., Klaidman, Thomas and I gathered in McDaniel's office for a conference call. Smith, Whitaker and Jon Meacham were on the other end in New York. I was apprehensive. McDaniel started to explain what we knew. We had confirmed that Starr had launched a criminal investigation into Clinton's efforts to conceal his relationship with Lewinsky and his recruitment of Vernon Jordan to help find her a job in New York. We had confirmed that Starr's prosecutors conducted a sting of Lewinsky while she was having lunch with her pal Linda Tripp on Tuesday. And we had listened to one of the tapes. The tape appeared to support the notion that what Tripp had been telling us was true—that Lewinsky had indeed been talking about having a sexual relationship with Clinton.

But it was clear within minutes that Smith and Whitaker were not sold. Smith took the lead. What about Vernon Jordan? How much did we really know about his involvement?

A lot, I said, overstating things. There were references to Jordan on the tapes, and we knew this was one of the central issues in Starr's investigation. It was what had drawn Starr into this in the first place. Smith and Whitaker seemed concerned, however, that we might be unfair to him. I thought of Jordan's many connections in Washington—and the fact that he is a sometime dinner guest at the home of Katharine Graham. Smith, in fact, knew Jordan. He had once played golf with him at the Robert Trent Jones golf club, where Jordan was the president. But that, he told me much later, had nothing to do with his thinking that day.

McDaniel conceded that there was no direct reference on the tape we heard to Jordan asking Lewinsky to lie. This bothered Smith. A few days ago, he said, when this story was first sold, I heard there was evidence that Vernon Jordan and the president had asked Lewinsky to lie, to commit perjury. Now I hear that isn't on the tape. What else are we going to learn that might not be true?

McDaniel spoke up. I might have oversold the story a bit, she said. Mike never said we had clear evidence of that.

Still, Smith wanted to know: "Can we really accuse Jordan of suborning perjury without something harder? Can we really accuse Clinton of committing an impeachable offense?"

"Impeachable?" What does this have to do with impeachment? I thought. Who's thinking about that? I glanced at Klaidman, and we both rolled our eyes.

But then, Klaidman later recalled, "I started to get a funny feeling." Maybe this was going to play even bigger than we thought.

Smith was now wondering about Lewinsky. What do we really know about her? We've never even talked to her, we've never laid eyes on her. She's a private person—and we were about to thrust her into a media maelstrom.

Look, I argued, this is as much a Ken Starr story as it is a Clinton story. What Starr is doing here is extraordinary. It is news by any definition. It is potentially a bombshell. Washington will go nuts over the fact that Starr has done this. We can't ignore it.

Smith objected. You can talk all you want about Starr and obstruction of justice. But at the end of the day, people are going to look at this as a sex story. That's what they're going to think this is—a story about Clinton having sex with a young woman.

The idea that Starr's involvement would be big news inside the Washington Beltway didn't move Whitaker much, either. He asked how our readers would be served if we couldn't resolve the underlying facts of what had really happened.

"Then it just becomes another 'Ken Starr is investigating' story," he said.

I was quite agitated. Come on, I thought. This is *the ultimate* "Ken Starr is investigating" story.

As the debate droned on into its second hour, I noted that Meacham, the boy-wonder nation editor (he was only twenty-nine), had said nothing. In fact, Meacham later said, he was lost in the practical issues. What would this story actually look like? he was thinking. How would it read? Newsmagazine stories don't just impart hard news. They look behind the news, they analyze, they focus on the personalities involved. Readers would hear the name Monica Lewinsky for the first time and want to know: Who is she? What is she like? "I kept thinking," Meacham said much later, "what will the second paragraph look like?"

McDaniel was playing broker. She was fully engaged in the discussion—but had offered no opinion on whether we should publish the story or not. Neither, at that point, had Evan Thomas. The only person supporting my view that we should go with this was Danny Klaidman.

●   ●   ●

C linton started out fine with the questions on Lewinsky. After all, they were hardly a surprise. He had known to expect them for more than five weeks, ever since he first learned that her name was on the witness list. Yes, he knew Monica Lewinsky, he told Fisher. She had worked in the White House for a while, "first as an intern, and then in, as the, in the legislative affairs office."

Then Fisher very quickly threw a curveball. But Clinton ducked deftly and seemed to throw off his interrogator.

Fisher: "Did you ever talk to anyone about finding a job for Monica Lewinsky?"

Clinton: "When she got the job in the legislative affairs office? No."

Fisher: "Before she got that job."

Clinton: "No."

Fisher: "Did you ever talk to anyone about the possibility of her obtaining a job in the White House?"

Clinton: "She, she came there as an intern. . . . I was not involved in her moving from being an intern to being a full-time employee. I had no involvement in it whatever."

Fisher had gone down the wrong path. Clinton's primary involvement in helping Lewinsky find a job had been much more recent. It had been in the fall of 1997, when he recruited Vernon Jordan to help her, not in early 1996, when she went to the White House legislative affairs office.[7] But for the moment, Clinton had escaped unscathed—simply by answering a question other than the one Fisher had asked.

After a while, though, it became clear that Fisher planned to dwell on the subject. He asked if it were true that when Lewinsky worked at the White House "she met with you several times."

Clinton once again dodged it. "I don't know about several times," he said, then mentioned that he recalled seeing her "on two or three occasions" during the 1995 government shutdown and later when she worked at the White House. "I think there was one or two other times when she brought some documents to me," he said. Clinton's responses, narrowly speaking, may well have been right. What Clinton omitted was the (according to Lewinsky's count) twelve other private meetings they had while she worked in the White House— ten of which involved oral sex or other physically intimate contact— not to mention the twelve additional private meetings they had inside the White House after she stopped working there.

Finally, after about fifteen minutes of warm-ups and a ten-minute break, Fisher picked up his pace.

Fisher: "Mr. President, before the break, we were talking about Monica Lewinsky. At any time were you and Monica Lewinsky together alone in the Oval Office?"

Clinton: "I don't recall, but as I said, when she worked at the legislative affairs office, they always had somebody there on the weekends. I typically worked some on the weekends. She—it seems to me she brought things to me once or twice on the weekends. . . ."

Fisher tried to pin Clinton down. So he was saying that "it was possible" that he had been alone with Lewinsky, but he had "no specific recollection of that ever happening?"

Clinton said that was correct. Fisher asked if he and Lewinsky "ever went down the hallway from the Oval Office to the private kitchen?"

Bennett had had enough of this.

"Your Honor, excuse me, Mr. President, I need some guidance

from the Court at this point," said the president's lawyer. "I'm going
to object to the innuendo, I'm afraid, as I say, that this will leak. I
question the good faith of Counsel, the innuendo in the question.
Counsel is fully aware that Ms. Lewinsky has filed, has an affidavit
which they are in possession of saying that there is absolutely no sex
of any kind in any manner, shape or form, with President Clinton,
and yet listening to the innuendo in the questions—"

While Clinton stared at his lawyer, the judge interrupted. Fisher
was "an officer of the Court," and she assumed that he had a "good
faith" basis for these questions.

Bennett said that in light of Lewinsky's affidavit, he would like
to know what it was.

Fisher said he would "welcome the opportunity" to inform the
judge what it was *in camera.* He could tell the court he was "very
confident" there was a "substantial basis" for these questions.

Wright finally concluded that Fisher's assurances were good
enough for her. "Go ahead," she said.

Fisher marched relentlessly onward.

"Do you recall ever walking with Monica Lewinsky down the
hallway from the Oval Office to your private kitchen there in the
White House?"

"At any time were you and Monica Lewinsky alone in the hallway between the Oval Office and this kitchen area?"

"At any time have you and Monica Lewinsky ever been alone
together in any room in the White House?"

Clinton zigged and zagged. He talked about the topography of
the Oval Office. ("There are no curtains on my private office.") He
talked about the naval aides in the White House. (They "come and
go at will," he said.) He launched into a soliloquy about his political
enemies and what they had done to his mental state.

"I was, after I went through a presidential campaign in which
the far Right tried to convince the American people I had committed murder, run drugs, slept in my mother's bed with four prostitutes
and done numerous other things, I had a high level of paranoia,"
Clinton said.

Fisher watched Clinton closely. He was floundering, he thought.
But he still hadn't pinned him down. The president hadn't answered

anything directly. Maybe Lewinsky had been in the private office, he said, maybe he had been with her in the hallway when she was delivering a pizza once. "I just, I don't remember," he said.

Fisher asked Clinton to identify the last time he spoke to Lewinsky. Probably sometime before Christmas, he said, when she was there to see his secretary, Betty Currie, "and I stuck my head out, said hello to her." Fisher asked if he had ever talked to her about the possibility that she might have to testify in this lawsuit. "I'm not sure," Clinton said, and then launched into another long response, talking about how, that time before Christmas, he and Betty Currie and Lewinsky were joking how "you all, with the help of the Rutherford Institute, were going to call every woman I'd ever talked to."

Fisher asked about Betty Currie, about Vernon Jordan, about Bill Richardson at the United Nations. Clinton slipped through all of them. It was Betty who told him that Vernon Jordan had been helping to find Lewinsky a job, the president said. It was Betty who helped set up the interview for Lewinsky at the UN.

Then, more than an hour into this, Fisher asked a simple, straightforward question that seemed to stop the president cold.

"Have you ever given any gifts to Monica Lewinsky?"

Clinton paused. It was a long pause, more than ten seconds, and the president's eyes rolled upward, as if he were thinking. Gifts were something that could be retrieved. Gifts could be a problem. Fisher watched Clinton closely. His demeanor was changing. His body was stiffening, Fisher thought. His jaw was clenched. His face started to redden.

"I don't recall," Clinton finally said. Then a slight, sheepish grin crept across the president's face. "Do you know what they were?"

Fisher: "A hat pin?"

Clinton: "I don't, I don't remember. But I certainly, I could have."

Fisher: "A book about Walt Whitman?"

Clinton: "I give—let me just say, I give people a lot of gifts, and when people are around I give a lot of things I have at the White House away, so I could have given her a gift, but I don't remember a specific gift."

Fisher sensed that Clinton felt he was in a bind. If he described Monica as a nobody—as just another face in the crowd—might she turn on him? Was she already talking? He imagined Clinton's mind racing through the possibilities.

And then, finally:

Fisher: "Did you have an extramarital sexual affair with Monica Lewinsky?"

Clinton: "No."

Fisher: "I think I used the term 'sexual affair.' And so the record is completely clear, have you ever had sexual relations with Monica Lewinsky, as that term is defined in Deposition Exhibit One, as modified by the Court?"

Fisher thought the question left no wiggle room at all. So did Bennett, Clinton's lawyer.

Clinton: "I have never had sexual relations with Monica Lewinsky. I've never had an affair with her."

• • •

The debate at *Newsweek* over whether to publish the Lewinsky story moved into its third hour. It was clear that none of the brass wanted to go with this—and they were looking for a way out.

Jackie Bennett's concern that our story would disrupt his investigation had not been a major topic. But for McDaniel in particular, it was a real factor. She wondered about the ethical issues of interfering with an ongoing law enforcement operation. In the course of the conversation, somebody got the idea: Perhaps we should hear directly from Kenneth Starr on this. If he wanted us to hold off, let him make his case.

To me, it was a dodge. Still, I went along. We adjourned. I was told to have Jackie Bennett get Starr to phone McDaniel.

I called Bennett at home. Bennett called Starr. But Starr wouldn't call McDaniel. He was angry that his office had gotten itself into a situation like this. A prosecutor's office shouldn't be begging a news organization. It was unseemly—wrong. "Ken was disgusted by the whole thing," Bennett later recalled.

Early that afternoon, Danny Klaidman called a source at the Justice Department. A few minutes later, he ran into McDaniel's office. Another astonishing development: Starr had gone to Janet Reno, and the attorney general had gone to the three-judge panel, authorizing an expanded mandate for Starr. They had filed the papers in court on Friday under seal. This thing was even more real than we already knew.

This made a big impact on Evan Thomas. It pushed him over the edge. Now, the Starr investigation was a matter of official record. There was another conference with New York. We reviewed the bidding. "If we were *The Washington Post* or *The New York Times,* we would print," Thomas said.

But his remarks didn't draw any discernible reaction from Smith or Whitaker. Meanwhile, Thomas got out a legal pad. I had on Friday written a memo outlining the main points that would be included in the story. But now Thomas began drafting a new version that could actually go into the magazine.

I was by now close to exhaustion. I was convinced the editors were making a big mistake, that we were going to blow an enormous exclusive. I tried one more time. "You know, this is not the Bay of Pigs," I said. "Human lives are not at stake here. The national security isn't hanging in the balance. Why the hell shouldn't we publish this?"

The analogy, in my mind, actually had a historical context. In 1961, a *New York Times* reporter, Tad Szulc, had the story of the planned CIA-sponsored invasion of Cuba. Kennedy administration officials expressed concerns to top *Times* executives. Szulc's story was toned down. References to the CIA were taken out. In retrospect, *Times* executives acknowledged that they had made the wrong decision. Had they run the story, the Kennedy administration might have avoided a major foreign policy disaster.

My argument was that this was exactly the opposite. The *Times* really did have a tough journalistic call that justified the kind of agonizing we now were engaged in. We did not. This was not that kind of story.

Thomas was now in agreement. "This is a pretty dipshit investigation," he said. Starr had been flailing around for years and hadn't come up with anything on Clinton. Now, he was trying to nail him on sex. So what if we blew this investigation? It wasn't as if they were about to catch a terrorist or something.

McDaniel was unpersuaded. She has sound news judgment. But she is, by nature, cautious and respectful of authority. She was once again thinking through the journalistic issues, wondering if we had considered them hard enough. Did we really have enough to print? Can we really be confident we've got this right?

McDaniel was looking off into the distance, staring at the Washington Monument, deep in thought and for the longest time quiet.

"There are times it's just not worth being first," she finally said.

Oh Christ, I thought. What is this?

"Sometimes, it's just not the right thing to do," she said.

What is going through her mind? I wondered. Scoops are what it's all about. It's what we strive for every week. It's what you pay me for.

• • •

C linton's deposition finally ended a little after four P.M. In the final hours, the president once again denied that he had ever met with Paula Jones or had any recollection of even seeing her.[8]

He also denied sexual relations with the other Jane Does.

There was, however, one answer that caught the Jones lawyers off guard.

"Did you ever have sexual relations with Gennifer Flowers?" Fisher asked.

Bill Bristow, the lawyer for Danny Ferguson, objected. Wright overruled him. Clinton then referred to the definition of sexual relations that had been handed to him hours earlier and replied: "Yes."

On how many occasions? Fisher wanted to know.

"Once," Clinton said.

In what year? Fisher asked.

"Nineteen seventy-seven," Clinton said.[9]

After the deposition was over, the Jones lawyers were ebullient. They felt they had scored some significant points and laid the groundwork for some useful trial testimony. David Pyke actually thought Clinton's concession on Flowers was the biggest coup. Contrasted with his 1992 denials of a sexual relationship between him and Flowers, he thought it conclusively established Clinton as a liar on matters relating to his relations with women. They could do a lot with that if this case ever came before a jury, he thought.

After they filed out of the room, the Jones lawyers assembled in a small holding room and started congratulating Fisher. It had been a good day, they agreed, laughing and smiling. Did you see his face when you asked about the gifts? Can you believe he admitted Flowers?

Then one of them noticed off in the corner their client, Paula Jones. She was sobbing. They went over to her. Paula, what's the matter? one of the lawyers asked.

"That chickenshit," she said, trying to hold back the tears. "He wouldn't even look me in the eye. He lied. He just lied."

The lawyers reassured her. This went well, they told her. This was good for us. Soon enough, they got their client composed and ready to go out and put on a triumphant face to the media horde.

But Pyke, watching the scene, was struck. That was real, he thought. That was real emotion. She didn't make this up.

For their part, the president's lawyers thought it had gone well enough. Clinton didn't seem rattled. Still, Bennett wondered about all those Lewinsky questions. "They were just fishing—don't you think?" he said to one of his colleagues.

•   •   •

Back at *Newsweek,* time was ticking away, and I had pretty much given up all hope. Still, they hadn't said no for sure. I went back to my office and sulked. About five-thirty P.M., McDaniel asked me to come back to her office. Smith wanted to speak to me directly. He felt strongly that I shouldn't have to hear the news from somebody else.

I want you to know this is no reflection on your reporting, Smith told me over the speakerphone from New York. We think you've done a great job, and we appreciate it. He wished the magazine had more time. If we were a daily newspaper, we could take another day or so to resolve some of the issues, to make more checks. But we were stuck with the deadline. We've decided to hold the story.

I told him I understood it was a tough call and left the room, utterly defeated.

I had asked Moody to be on standby, in case we had any questions. I called and told him the story was not going to run after all. The editors, after a lot of debate, had decided the obstruction stuff about Jordan wasn't hard enough, I explained. I called Goldberg and told her the same thing. These calls were, under normal circumstances, a common courtesy you would extend to sources. Goldberg and Moody had helped me get what I asked them for, the tapes, and they deserved to know that at least for now, the story wasn't going to run. It wouldn't take long for me to wish I hadn't made those calls. But it wouldn't have made any difference in the end. The magazine would be out on Sunday, and they would know that the story of Bill Clinton and Monica Lewinsky wasn't in it.

I also called Podesta and told him the story we had talked about earlier in the day wasn't going to run. Podesta was later asked about this before the grand jury and suggested that he was puzzled I bothered to tell him this. He didn't know what the story was anyway.

That night, Paula Jones—now persuaded that she had in fact had a good day—went out to the Old Ebbitt Grill with her lawyers, her husband, Steve Jones, her adviser, Susan Carpenter-McMillan, and her hairdresser. They broke out bottles of champagne and celebrated late into the night.

Clinton went back to the White House and cancelled his dinner plans. He had a meeting with Bruce Lindsey. He called Vernon Jordan. At 7:13 P.M., he called Betty Currie at home. He asked if Currie could come to the White House the next day—Sunday. There was something he wanted to talk to her about.

Time magazine closed its own story that night. Under the headline THE BIG FACE-OFF, about the Clinton deposition, the magazine tapped its sources at the White House to report these nuggets of news in the second paragraph: "All the same, at the end of six hours of questioning by Jones's attorneys, Clinton departed in what sources close to him say was an ecstatic mood. The president felt the deposition had gone smashingly for him. Describing the mood Saturday night at the White House, one person close to the president said: "Everyone is going to sleep well tonight."

I went home, barely conscious, and ate dinner. My in-laws were visiting, and I had no energy left to speak. I apologized and went upstairs to bed. A few hours later, about eleven P.M., when I was fast asleep, the phone rang. My wife, the journalist Lisa Stein, took the call.

It was Matt Drudge.

He's sleeping, Stein told Drudge—and she was not going to wake him up.

Not for you, she said as she hung up the phone.

21

"Well, we'll just have to win, then."

NEWSWEEK KILLS STORY ON WHITE HOUSE INTERN
BLOCKBUSTER REPORT: 23-YEAR-OLD, FORMER WHITE HOUSE INTERN,
SEX RELATIONSHIP WITH PRESIDENT
★★ WORLD EXCLUSIVE★★
★★Must Credit the Drudge Report★★

At the last minute, at 6 p.m. on Saturday evening, NEWSWEEK *killed a story that was destined to shake official Washington to its foundation: A White House intern carried on a sexual affair with the President of the United States!*

The DRUDGE REPORT *has learned that reporter Michael Isikoff developed the story of his career, only to have it spiked by top* NEWSWEEK *suits hours before publication. A young woman, 23, sexually involved with the love of her life, the President of the United States, since she was a 21 year old intern at the White House. She was a frequent visitor to a small study just off the Oval Office where she claims to have indulged the president's sexual preference. Reports of the relations spread in White House quarters and she was moved to a job at the Pentagon, where she worked until last month . . .*

The DRUDGE REPORT *has learned that tapes of intimate phone conversations exist . . .*

NEWSWEEK *and Isikoff were planning to name the woman. Word of the story's impending release caused blind chaos in media circles;* TIME *magazine spent Saturday scrambling for its own version of the story, the* DRUDGE REPORT *has learned. The* NEW YORK POST *on Sunday*

*was set to front the young intern's affair but was forced to fall back
on the dated* ABC NEWS *Kathleen Willey break. . . .*

*Ironically, several years ago, it was Isikoff that found himself in
a shouting match with editors who were refusing to publish even a
portion of his meticulously researched investigative report that was
to break Paula Jones. Isikoff worked for the* WASHINGTON POST *at the
time, and left shortly after the incident to build them for the
paper's sister magazine,* NEWSWEEK.

Michael Isikoff was not available for comment late Saturday.
NEWSWEEK *was on voice mail.*

•   •   •

I t moved at 2:32 A.M. Sunday morning. About seven hours later,
a friend, David Tell, editorial writer for the *Weekly Standard,*
called me at home. Look, he said, he didn't mean to pry. But his
boss, Bill Kristol, asked him to make this call. There was an item on
the Drudge Report saying that *Newsweek* had spiked a story that
was about to expose a sexual relationship between Clinton and a
young former intern. Kristol, along with Stephanopoulos, is a regular on ABC-TV's Sunday morning talk show *This Week.* He was
thinking about mentioning this on the air. What, Tell asked, should
I tell Kristol? Would it cause me any problem?

Oh God, I thought. This is going to be ugly. I had told Moody and
Goldberg the story wasn't going to run. I never imagined they were
going to do this. Then again, how could I have thought they would do
anything different?

What does it say? I asked Tell. He read it to me. Drudge didn't
have Lewinsky's name. More important, there was no mention of Ken
Starr, no mention of the "sting" at the Ritz-Carlton, nothing about
the secret criminal investigation of the president, authorized by the
attorney general, that was the principal reason for doing the story.
That's odd, I thought. All the conspirators knew about Starr. Why
would they hold back?

I said nothing. Look, if Kristol wants to go with something based
on Drudge, that's his problem, I said. How could he rely on anything
that guy writes? Tell was apologetic. Of course, he said. He'd pass
that along to Kristol.

Kristol ignored him. He had talked to Richard Porter and Conway, who had talked to Moody. It was the usual loop.

"The story in Washington this morning," said Kristol that morning on national television, "is that *Newsweek* magazine was going to go with a big story based on tape-recorded conversations in which a woman who was a summer intern at the White House, an intern of Leon Panetta's—"

"And Bill, where did it come from?" Stephanopoulos interjected. "The Drudge Report. We've all seen how discredited that's been."

"No, no. There were screaming arguments at *Newsweek* magazine yesterday. They finally didn't go with the story. There's going to be a question of whether the media [are] now going to report what are pretty well-validated charges of presidential behavior in the White House."

Barely an hour later, I got a call from Karen Wheeler, the chief of *Newsweek*'s publicity department. Her phone was ringing off the hook, she told me, ever since Kristol started talking on *This Week*. I liked Wheeler. She and I occasionally gossiped about the assorted lunacies of the *Newsweek* brass. Michael, what can you tell me about all this? she asked. I need to know.

Nothing, I told her curtly. I can't say anything. You'll have to call McDaniel.

There was a pause. Okay, fine, she said, slamming down the phone.

Will the story break out into the mainstream? I wondered. It was clear that much of Washington would be buzzing about this after Kristol's plug. But I took some refuge in thinking that, as with the Willey story last July, it couldn't immediately go anywhere. Nobody knew anything, and the most important part—Starr's criminal investigation—was unknown to Drudge. There would be no obvious source to confirm what Drudge had written. Maybe it could be contained, I thought—but I doubted it.

•   •   •

In fact, Clinton that afternoon took steps to insure that when it finally did break, the story would be much bigger. Currie came to the White House at five P.M. Clinton was outside with Buddy on

the putting green. "I'll be with you in a minute," Clinton told her.
Currie went to her desk. Clinton came in and sat down next to her.
He'd gotten some questions about Monica Lewinsky in his deposi-
tion on Saturday, he said. He sounded concerned, Currie thought.
Clinton then made a series of statements, "in a very quick manner,
one right after the other":

"I was never alone with Monica, right?"

"Monica came on to me and I never touched her, right?"

"Monica wanted to have sex with me and I cannot do that."

When first questioned about this meeting, Currie said she
answered, "Right," to each of these questions. But she didn't feel the
president was trying to get her to agree with him, she testified. She
didn't feel intimidated. Clinton told a federal grand jury he was only
trying to "refresh" his memory—an explanation that many found difficult to follow given that Currie couldn't possibly know whether he
ever touched her. Currie said the president might have asked her to
try to get in touch with Lewinsky. The rest of the afternoon and into
the night, she did.

Some idea of the urgency of the president's request—and the
level of his concern—might be gleaned from Currie's phone records.
Right after talking to Clinton, she paged Lewinsky at 5:12 P.M.
("Please call Kay at home," the page said, using the code name she
usually used with Lewinsky.) She paged her again at 6:22 P.M., and
again at 7:06 P.M. Then a fourth time at 8:28 P.M. Finally, at 10:15 P.M.,
Lewinsky called and, as she later said, tried to send Currie a cryptic
signal that something was up. She made a reference to "Hoover," hoping that Currie would figure out that the FBI was involved. But Currie
didn't get it. She was, by that time, "sound asleep" and told Lewinsky
she'd talk to her first thing in the morning.

Then, at 11:02 P.M., Clinton called. No, the sleeping secretary told
the president, she hadn't talked to Lewinsky yet. "I was almost too
tired to talk to him," she said later.

In fact, Lewinsky had by then consulted with her new lawyer,
William Ginsburg, who had arrived in Washington on Saturday morning. That Sunday, Ginsburg was in the offices of Kenneth Starr, trying to negotiate an immunity agreement for his client. He had told
Lewinsky not to respond to any of Currie's pages.

So when Currie resumed her attempts to reach Lewinsky on Monday morning, there was no response at all. At 7:02 A.M., Currie left her first page: "Please call Kay at home at 8:00 A.M. this morning." At 8:08 A.M., she left her second. Her third page was at 8:29 A.M. and her fourth at 8:33 A.M. Four minutes later, at 8:37 A.M., Currie left her fifth page with a slightly amended message: "Please call Kay at home. It's a social call. Thank you." Then, at 8:41 A.M., a sixth page. One minute later, she called the president to tell him she wasn't getting through.

At 8:44 A.M., Currie placed her seventh page with a new message: "Please call Kay regarding family emergency." Then at 8:50 A.M., Clinton called Currie again. No, Currie told him, Lewinsky still hadn't responded. Then there was another Currie page to Lewinsky, the eighth of the day: "Message from Kay. Please call. Have good news." It was 8:51 A.M. There was no response.

Not long after, Vernon Jordan joined the search. Clinton and Jordan had talked at 8:55 A.M. for ten minutes. Jordan called the White House again at 10:29 A.M. Then, at 10:33 A.M., he paged Monica Lewinsky. At 11:16 A.M., he paged her a second time. "Please call Mr. Jordan," read the page. That afternoon, Jordan had lunch with Frank Carter and showed him a copy of the Drudge Report. "You need to talk to your client about that," Jordan said. A few hours later, Carter called Jordan with an update. It wasn't good. He was no longer her lawyer.

●　　●　　●

The dam burst on Tuesday. *The Washington Post*'s Sue Schmidt and Chris Vlasto of ABC News confirmed the Starr investigation. That night, at 10:00 P.M., Vlasto—a fearless reporter—called me at home. "We're about to scoop you on your story," he said. He was going with it on *Nightline,* he told me. The *Post* had it, too. I waited, feeling profoundly depressed and cursing my fainthearted editors. Then *Nightline* killed it. Ted Koppel was in Cuba with the pope and didn't feel ready to make the decision to put this story on the air. The *Post* posted it on its Web page at 12:32 A.M. Vlasto's cohort, Jackie Judd, reported it on ABC radio at 12:38 A.M. Some ninety minutes later, the *Los Angeles Times* weighed in.

That night, there was alarm at the White House. The vast White House damage-control machinery—the lawyers, the spin doctors, the political aides—were learning for the first time about the existence of a woman named Monica Lewinsky. At 12:08 A.M., the president called Bob Bennett. "This story seems ridiculous, and frankly, I smell a rat," Bennett then told the *Post*. It was the same smell-a-rat line Bennett had used with me about Willey. Right after that, Clinton called Bruce Lindsey and spoke with him for about half an hour. Then, at 1:16 A.M., the president called Betty Currie. Once again, she was fast asleep. "Have you heard the latest thing that's happened?" Currie recalled the president saying to her. He told her there was going to be a story in *The Washington Post* in the morning mentioning Monica Lewinsky, and Currie's name was going to be in it. Clinton kept talking. Currie would later remember what was going through her mind as she listened to the president. "God, will he please shut up so I can go back to bed."

But Clinton didn't stop. "I think he just went on and on about that," Currie said. "I got the impression that I think he just wanted to vent or whatever. He just talked."

•   •   •

The next morning I read the *Post* as soon as I retrieved it from the front lawn. The Schmidt-Baker piece carried a banner headline across the front page: CLINTON ACCUSED OF URGING AIDE TO LIE; STARR PROBES WHETHER PRESIDENT TOLD WOMAN TO DENY ALLEGED AFFAIR TO JONES LAWYERS. For those learning all this for the first time, it was a shock. Most surprising to me, though, was the fifth paragraph. Quoting unidentified "sources," it described the evidence that gave rise to the investigation in the first place: the surreptitious tapes of Tripp's conversations with Lewinsky. "In some of the conversations— including one in recent days—Lewinsky described Clinton and Jordan directing her to testify falsely in the Paula Jones sexual harassment case against the president, according to sources."

That's odd, I thought. That wasn't on the tape we heard—and that was supposed to be the most important tape, the tape that most raised the issues of obstruction of justice and suborning perjury. That tape had been much more ambiguous, much fuzzier. A bit later, I called Conway. He had listened to the same tape six nights earlier at Coulter's apartment. It was the tape that, according to Coulter, had caused

Conway and Moody to look "crestfallen." Yeah, he noticed that, too, Conway told me: it sounded like the *Post* got oversold a bit.

By the morning talk shows, Washington had already gone crazy. "Look, if the president of the United States asked this young woman to lie under oath . . . that's a federal felony, that's a crime," said Sam Donaldson from the White House lawn on *Good Morning America.* "And if sufficient evidence exists to really prove that, well, clearly an impeachment investigation will begin on Capitol Hill of a very serious nature."

There it was. *Impeachment.* Rick Smith had used the term during the debate at *Newsweek* on Saturday. Klaidman and I had both wondered then what he was talking about.

A few moments later, Stephanopoulos provided an even bigger jolt to Washington's nervous system. He, too, was on *Good Morning America.* "These are probably the most serious allegations yet leveled against the president," said the president's onetime spin-doctor-in-chief. "There's no question that . . . if they're true . . . it could lead to impeachment proceedings."

Meanwhile, Clinton was making things worse. When Betty Currie arrived at work that morning, he called her into the Oval Office and made the same series of false statements—"I was never alone with Monica, right?"—that he had posed on Sunday. Only this time, when Clinton said these things, it was more serious. A federal criminal investigation was under way, and although she hadn't yet been served, Currie had already been subpoenaed as a witness before Ken Starr's grand jury.[1]

*   *   *

At 11:25 A.M., Clinton paged his old consultant Dick Morris. Morris called the Oval Office as soon as he got to a phone. Betty Currie put Morris through. "You poor son of a bitch," Morris said. "I know just what you're going through." Morris did. He had been booted off Clinton's campaign in the summer of 1996 over a far tamer sex scandal.

"Oh God," Clinton said, "this is just awful."

According to Morris, the president said: "I didn't do what they said I did, but I did do something." Morris suggested that it was going to be a "he said, she said" thing. But Clinton corrected him.

There was evidence. "There may be gifts," Clinton said. "I gave her gifts, but only after she gave them to me. And there may be messages on her phone answering machine."

They then discussed Clinton's options. Morris suggested that Clinton "play this thing outside the foul lines," go over Starr's head and "go to the public and ask their forgiveness." But what about "the legal thing?" Clinton asked. "You know—Starr and perjury and all that?"

He was the president, Morris reminded him, and at the end of the day it was still more a "political process," not legal. The public will forgive you.

"You think so?" Clinton asked.

"Why don't we poll it?" Morris suggested.

Clinton liked the idea. "Call me late tonight with the numbers," he said.

•　　•　　•

I got to the office early and went in to see McDaniel. "I feel like shit," she said. So do I, I told her. But she had a plan. She had already talked to New York about the idea of posting our story on *Newsweek*'s America Online Web site. It was unusual, but made perfect sense: we had a ton of exclusive material. We were in the middle of this story. The public was starving for details. We should tell them what we know. All that day, Thomas and I crashed. As we did, the story was gaining speed—and getting better.

The White House had already scheduled a series of interviews for that day—warm-ups to the next week's State of the Union address. They couldn't cancel them without feeding the sense of panic that seemed to be engulfing the building. So Clinton went through with them. The first was with PBS's Jim Lehrer. The president looked dazed. Lehrer referred to the reports that Starr was investigating to determine whether he had asked a former White House intern to lie about having had an affair with him.

"Is that true?" Lehrer wanted to know.

"That is not true," said Clinton. "I did not ask anyone to tell anything other than the truth. There is no improper relationship."

Is?

Inside the White House press room, where the audio feed was

being pumped, the response was electric. "We went wild," recalled Mara Liasson, the veteran White House correspondent of National Public Radio. "It was, like, 'Aaaaagghh!'" The White House press corps—and all the other journalists and politicos who had followed the man for years, who had watched his word games and his zigzags, his all-too-clever evasions and denials that sounded like one thing and turned out to be another—all knew right away: This thing was real. It was the Bill Clinton who didn't inhale. The Bill Clinton who forgot his draft notice. The president was not now, as we spoke, having an improper relationship. Clinton did another interview with Mort Kondracke of *Roll Call* and tried to blur the issue. "It is not an improper relationship," he said. "The relationship was not sexual, and I know what you mean, and the answer is no." At 4:40 P.M., Liasson and Robert Siegel of NPR were ushered into the Oval Office for a third interview. They would be broadcasting live. Clinton's jaw was bulging, a clear sign of tension. But he seemed eerily calm, Liasson thought, almost disengaged. "It was like he was having an out-of-body experience," she later said. She started right out asking about Lewinsky. She was waiting to see what tense he would use, ready to pounce if "is" resurfaced. But Clinton by now had realized his blunder. His loyal aide Paul Begala had talked to him about it. "I think it's more important for me to tell the American people that there wasn't improper relations," he said.

The tense was amended. But for Washington insiders, and perhaps for much of the public, it was too late.

I did more reporting—and learned new "details" about the sting at the Ritz-Carlton and Lewinsky's descriptions of her conversations with Vernon Jordan. I obtained a copy of the "talking points" Lewinsky had given Tripp the previous Wednesday, suggesting ways she could alter her testimony about Kathleen Willey. In the excitement, I forgot to go back to read the Tripp letter to *Newsweek* four months earlier. In the middle of a media feeding frenzy, it looked bigger than it really was.

Then, over the fax machine at 6:43 P.M., as we were racing to finish the piece, came a press release from Revlon. "Monica Lewinsky was referred to MacAndrews & Forbes by Vernon Jordan, a member of the board of directors of Revlon, a MacAndrews affiliate, for a possible entry-level public relations position," it read. The company acknowledged it had offered Monica Lewinsky a job—an offer it was now rescinding.

My stomach had been in knots all day. When I saw the Revlon press release, they disappeared. What do you know? I thought. It's true. It really is all true.

Newsweek posted the story, headlined DIARY OF A SCANDAL, early that evening and faxed out copies to every news organization it could think of. The story provided a wealth of details that for months, nobody else came close to matching. It described the secret taping of Lewinsky by Tripp and included the first and only direct quotes from the tapes. "Look, I will deny it so he will not get screwed in the case, but I'm going to get screwed personally," Lewinsky was quoted as saying. It described the Ritz-Carlton "sting" and Starr's subsequent efforts to flip Lewinsky. It cited the courier message slips showing that Lewinsky was sending letters and packages to the White House and Vernon Jordan. It revealed the existence of and quoted from the "talking points." The story was more nuanced than the accounts of the *Post* and ABC about the core obstruction charge. "There was no clear evidence on the tape that would confirm or deny Tripp's allegation that Clinton or Vernon Jordan had coached Lewinsky to lie," we wrote. But it didn't matter. Most people missed it. The Lewinsky affair was by now proclaimed as the most stunning political scandal in a quarter century, and—for better or worse—that night, and for weeks and even months to come, *Newsweek* owned it.

•   •   •

About 11:15 P.M., Morris called Clinton with the results of the poll. It had been conducted by Action Research, a company in Melbourne, Florida, that Morris regularly uses to do polls for his newspaper column. Morris went through the switchboard operator—Nancy Hernreich had told him not to use the private number he had for Clinton in the residence so as not to wake Hillary up. Clinton came on. "Let me take this phone in another room," he said.

A moment later, Clinton called him back. As Morris later remembered it, the conversation went this way: "Well, I'm wrong," he told

Clinton. "You can't tell them about it—they'll kill you." Clinton didn't respond. "They're just too shocked by this," Morris said. "It's just too new, too raw." Then Morris went through the poll results, reading each question and giving the breakdown on the numbers. Clinton listened, interjecting at times, asking Morris to repeat some of the numbers, making comments like "What did you say, thirty-five?" or "Read me that again." It seemed to Morris that Clinton was taking notes.

The results confirmed Morris's prediction that the public would be willing to forgive Clinton the adultery. But the numbers against him moved up when the questions got more specific and were placed in a legal context. If Clinton had lied and encouraged Monica Lewinsky to lie, 48 percent said he should be removed from office. "If President Clinton lied, he committed the crime of perjury," the poll question read. "If he encouraged Monica to lie he committed the crime of obstruction of justice. In view of these facts, do you think President Clinton should be removed from office?" On this one, 60 percent said yes.

"So you just can't do this," Morris said.

"It just won't fly," Clinton said. Then he repeated it. "It just won't fly."

Clinton knew what he had to do. His strategy was set. He would get those numbers up.

"Well, we'll just have to win, then," Clinton said.

"You bet your ass," said Morris.

EPILOGUE

"We are scum."

For Bill Clinton, the furor over Monica Lewinsky must have seemed somewhat familiar. He had faced these sorts of allegations many times before. In 1987, Betsey Wright confronted him with a list of women and demanded the truth. It was only then, according to Clinton biographer David Marannis, that he dropped out of the presidential race. The whispers resurfaced during the 1990 gubernatorial campaign. Then they broke out in public when he started running for president in 1991. How could it be otherwise? Back in Arkansas, he told Lewinsky, he had had "hundreds of affairs."

Each time, the sheer energy needed to conceal the problem was staggering. "We have to destroy her story," Hillary Clinton decreed to George Stephanopoulos back in 1991, when she first heard the allegations of rock groupie Connie Hamzy. Gennifer Flowers had been trickier. There were tapes. There was the state job he got for her ("If they ever asked if you'd talked to me about it, you can say no," Clinton told Flowers). The Clintons went on *60 Minutes* after the Super Bowl. "The allegation is false," Clinton said when asked about Flowers's claim of a twelve-year affair. Cynical reporters may have wondered exactly which allegation was false. It didn't matter. This wasn't about his character, Clinton declared: "This will test the character of the press."

On January 26, 1998, Clinton appeared in the Roosevelt Room. It was, remarkably, six years to the day after the *60 Minutes* interview, in which he had "absolutely leveled with the American people." The

350

president's advisers were worried. The State of the Union was that evening and the Lewinsky affair threatened to overshadow everything. Events had taken a serious turn. Betty Currie, hounded by the press, was due to appear before the grand jury the next day. Lewinsky was being threatened with indictment—for lying to protect the president. Harry Thomason—producer of the *The Man from Hope,* the slick 1992 documentary that dwelled on the Clintons' loving home life—had moved into the White House. You need to be more forceful, he had told the president. You need to explain it "so there's no doubt in anybody's mind that nothing happened."

Clinton did what he had to—even if it meant, as he must have known it would, prolonging the agony for Currie, for Lewinsky, for everybody.

"I want you to listen to me," he said from the podium in the Roosevelt Room, wagging his finger at the American public. "I'm going to say this again: I did not have sexual relations with that woman, Miss Lewinsky. I never told anyone to lie, not a single time. Never. These allegations are false."

●   ●   ●

The rules of this game—a decade after Gary Hart—were still something of a blur. *The Wall Street Journal*'s Al Hunt, sympathetic to Clinton, had tried to straighten them out in early 1992. The flap over Flowers was a disgrace, he wrote in a January 26 column. L'AFFAIR CLINTON: A PRESS SCANDAL, NOT A SEX SCANDAL, read the headline. There were only a few conditions, Hunt argued, that would make more information about a candidate's private life relevant to the public. "One, if the candidate lies," he wrote. "Two, if it's a contemporaneous situation."

L'Affair Lewinsky met both criteria—and involved not just a candidate, but a sitting president of the United States. Clinton, however, had always instinctively understood one thing: Trying to catch him would bring more discredit to his foes than he would face if he actually got caught. "I just wanted to see his asshole pucker," Clinton chortled to Gennifer Flowers after he nailed a Republican enemy trying to collect affidavits from the women prisoners of Arkansas. "People will think you're scum," Stephanopoulos told the caller in *The War Room.* To prove his lies, Clinton knew, his foes would be forced into the gutter—or to go to such extraordinary lengths that, in the end, they would look worse than he. It was his coldest and most cynical calculation—the mutual assured destruction at the core of his political survival.

So it played out—on a much grander scale—in 1998. Clinton played the hand he knew best. Privileges were invoked: more and bigger lies were told. "She had come on to me and I didn't have sex with her," he told Sidney Blumenthal, who then repeated it to the grand jury. Even when Clinton finally confessed—after seven maddening months—he lied. "I regret that what began as a friendship came to include this conduct," he told the grand jury in August 1998. "Friendship" was an odd choice of words. According to Lewinsky, they had met just two hours before their first sexual encounter, on November 15, 1995, when he invited her back to his private study and she went down on him while he took a call from a member of Congress. Six weeks and two episodes later, she still feared he didn't know her name.

So Starr's agents played the hands they knew. They wound up using the awesome powers of the prosecutor in ways that looked disproportionate and even frightening. Starr's probe, it can be said with the benefit of hindsight, was flawed from the start. It began on a moment's notice, instigated by a scared but devious woman who had gotten ensnared in her own plotting. My initial instincts had been right: "That's nuts," I said, when I learned on the afternoon of January 13, 1998, of the impending "sting" in the Ritz-Carlton. The phrases "obstruction of justice" and "subornation of perjury" seemed out of place when applied to the angst-ridden babble of two lonely women.

To catch Clinton in his lies, Starr's prosecutors hauled Lewinsky's mother before the grand jury. Secret Service agents were forced to testify. Lewinsky herself was asked the most intimate questions about where she was touched on what parts of her body.

After Starr completed his investigation in September 1998, I was talking with Brett Kavanaugh, one of the young lawyers who had helped write the portion of the 449-page report arguing the grounds for Clinton's impeachment. A clean-cut and clear-headed

Yale Law graduate and former Supreme Court clerk, Kavanaugh believed in the essential justice of Starr's probe. The president had toyed with a duly authorized federal law enforcement body. He had abused the solemn powers of his office, invoking executive privilege—created to protect important public policy discussions—for the cheap purpose of concealing his misconduct. Still, Kavanaugh was troubled. The tawdriness of the case ate at him. "Sometimes, I wake up in the middle of the night and wonder to myself, what am I doing?" he told me. "There are a lot of mixed emotions about this."

There had been much anxiety within Starr's office about the level of sexual detail in the report. The prosecutors, led by Starr himself, were convinced the details were necessary to prove Clinton's lies. But others were uneasy and feared a potential backlash. Nobody knew what would happen when the report got to Capitol Hill. On the morning of September 11, 1998, the prosecutors got word that Congress was about to publicly release the report and put it on the Internet. Suddenly, there was alarm among Starr's deputies. Did the House leaders realize what was in it? Kavanaugh hastily drafted a letter to House Speaker Newt Gingrich, urging him to withhold it from the public until the members at least had a chance to read it. The report included "highly explicit" material that is "almost certainly inappropriate for wide public dissemination," Kavanaugh wrote. But Starr wouldn't send the letter. It wasn't the office's job to intrude into the House impeachment process, he concluded.

Starr later came to regret that decision. It was one of his many bad calls. Within hours, the Starr report was posted on the Internet. It was reprinted in all the major newspapers. Editors struggled with how to handle the references to oral and anal sex, presidential ejaculations and the cigar. Democrats expressed horror at the "pornography" the Republicans had unleashed upon the country. Just when the public tide had seemed to be turning against Clinton, it began to ebb back the other way—and never stopped.

●   ●   ●

But there were quite a few bumps on the road. On April 1, 1998, Judge Wright had dismissed the Jones lawsuit, concluding there was insufficient evidence to conclude that Jones's claims—even if true—constituted a violation of her civil rights. Then, after Clinton's confession, the president's lawyers got concerned Wright would be reversed. On November 13, 1998, Clinton settled the case by agreeing to pay Jones $850,000.

Jones never got her apology—or even a recognition by Clinton that he had indeed had her brought up to the hotel room that day. It was not clear she would ever get much of the money either. As soon as the president cut the check in January, the Rader, Campbell firm quickly got into a dispute with Davis and Cammarata over how to divvy up the proceeds. Among the lawyers who had worked on the case and didn't weigh in asking for some of the booty were Danny Traylor, Jerome Marcus and George Conway—not to mention Richard Porter, who insists his main role was that of "switchboard operator."

Meanwhile, the impeachment engine sputtered forward, and with little popular support from the country, proved a disaster for the Republicans. On October 8, 1998, the House voted 258 to 176 to hold an open-ended inquiry into the president's conduct. Then came the November elections and the GOP's stunning loss of five seats. Gingrich resigned. The Republicans on the Judiciary Committee held abbreviated hearings without calling any witnesses to the events in question, including Monica Lewinsky. On December 19, 1998, by a near party line vote, the House narrowly voted two articles of impeachment of the president—one for perjury before the grand jury about his relationship with Lewinsky and another for obstruction of justice in the Jones lawsuit.

On February 13, 1999, Clinton was acquitted by the U.S. Senate. Neither of the two articles commanded a majority.

For me, these events—the long drawn-out saga of impeachment and trial—were something of an anti-climax. My role in the soap opera was over. Still, I would watch on television as my name was invoked repeatedly—and cringe. In December, White House counsel Chuck Ruff defended Betty Currie's account of the exchange of gifts. Currie didn't retrieve the box of gifts from Lewinsky because Clinton was worried about the subpoena from Jones's lawyers, he said. Ruff then cited Currie's much overlooked testimony: She got the gifts, she claimed, because Lewinsky told her a reporter, Michael Isikoff, was asking questions about them.

It was, of course, patently false testimony. I had never asked any such questions. I mentioned this to a journalist friend. How can you not say anything? he asked. You've got to let them—the House Republicans—know. I don't think so, I said. I've had enough involvement in this story. One afternoon in January 1999, one of the House managers, Lindsey Graham of South Carolina, called. He was on the prowl. Did I know something more? Did I have anything on Elizabeth Ward Gracen? About jobs or intimidation? I'm sorry, I can't help you, I said. I can't tell you anything I haven't already published.

In the end, uncovering Clinton was no morality play. This was not Watergate—nor did I ever imagine that it was. But that doesn't mean it wasn't right to undertake the enterprise. Presidents ought not be permitted to deceive the public. Clinton did so repeatedly and brazenly. Paula Jones's core claims had more credibility than was commonly recognized. Willey's story still strikes me as true—even if her state of mind about it is subject to question. I have thought quite a bit about the woman who reached me in early August 1997 and described how humiliated she felt walking out of the Oval Office—and how scared she was to come forward and talk about it. Clinton's recklessness and arrogance deserved to be uncovered. But exposure—not impeachment—was the only remedy that interested me.

•   •   •

In January 1999, Kathleen Willey got a phone call in Richmond. It was Juanita Broaddrick, the nursing home operator who rebuffed Paula Jones's investigators when they approached her at her home in Van Buren, Arkansas, in November 1997. Broaddrick was reaching out for help. Lisa Myers of NBC News, a tenacious reporter, was trying to persuade Broaddrick to finally go public with the story she had told close friends and family members and eventually the FBI: the story of how Bill Clinton had forced her to have sex in a room in the old Camelot Hotel in Little Rock after a nursing home conference in 1978.

Broaddrick wanted to know what Willey's experiences had been after she told her story on *60 Minutes.* If she finally came forward after all these years, would anybody believe her? What would it be like for her family? Would they malign her for letting Clinton come up to her room in the first place? Willey listened. She said it had been difficult—her time of "troubles," she called it. Still, the women bonded. Broaddrick finally gave the interview to Myers, a long cathartic account of how she felt aggrieved by the man who would later become president.

Then NBC balked, worried about how to document such a sensational allegation. A week after Clinton's acquittal, *The Wall Street Journal*'s editorial page ran its own interview with Broaddrick. Then *The Washington Post*—one of whose reporters also had been talking to the nursing home operator—put the story on the front page. It was a remarkable signal right there. The story listed two authors, Lois Romano and White House correspondent Peter Baker, and nine other reporters and researchers as contributors: Broaddrick's current husband and a friend, Norma Rogers, a nurse, were cited as corroborating portions of Broaddrick's account. Still, the paper hedged its bets. "With no witnesses and the passage of so much time, Broaddrick's story is difficult if not impossible to verify," the paper wrote. David Kendall, the president's lawyer, was quoted as saying that "any allegation that the president assaulted Ms. Broaddrick more than 20 years ago is absolutely false." On February 24, 1999, NBC broadcast Lisa Myers's interview with Broaddrick.

*   *   *

However right I believed my reporting was on Clinton, legitimate journalistic issues linger. What do you do when you find yourself sucked into the story? What happens when you become beholden to sources with an agenda? There are no easy answers here. When I went to see Linda Tripp at the Pentagon in March 1997, I had no idea what I was going to learn—and no inkling of the anger and resentment that stirred inside her tortured soul. There were warning signals, of course. What sort of woman tapes her friend? But for me, back then, Bill Clinton was a more interesting and important subject of journalistic inquiry than the embittered psyche of a Pentagon bureaucrat. Tripp at the time seemed incidental—a means to an end. It is a blunt truth of journalism: We use our sources just as, in this case, she and Lucianne Goldberg tried to use me.

Much that I learned later cast a somewhat different light on events. I was stunned to learn, upon reading the transcripts of the Tripp-Lewinsky tapes that fall, that Tripp had tried to persuade Lewinsky to have breakfast with U.N. Ambassador Bill Richardson downstairs at the Aquarelle restaurant—even as she was urging *Newsweek* to stake the place out and take pictures. I was amazed to discover, buried in Starr's volumes of evidence, the FBI interview of Kate Friedrich, then of the National Security Council. It was Tripp's claims about what "Kate of the NSC" was saying about Lewinsky that caused Lewinsky to flip—and demand that the president find her a job in New York. But, according to Friedrich's account, it was all made up: Friedrich at the time had never heard of Monica Lewinsky.

I was chagrined to discover, while reading the transcripts of the Tripp-Goldberg conversation on the evening of September 18, 1997, that they had been talking about a book deal from the start. I had relied on the elves for information at critical junctures—even while they concealed from me their role in bringing the Lewinsky allegations to the Jones lawyers and later to Ken Starr.

None of this changes the essential facts. Clinton did what he did quite apart from the machinations of Tripp and Goldberg—or the plotting of any right-wing cabals. As a general rule, we don't give our sources moral litmus tests—nor should we. Sometimes the best stuff comes from the most unpleasant people. Motives are often complicated, the high-minded hopelessly intertwined with the political and the pecuniary. What's important is what is true—although the public has every right to know how you learned it and from whom.

It is a journalistic problem much larger than my case. After Sidney Blumenthal appeared before the grand jury in June 1998, Anthony Lewis wrote a column in *The New York Times* bashing Starr's prosecutors for asking the presidential aide degrading questions such as "Have you ever discussed with Mrs. Clinton whether the president has a sex addiction?" and "Does the president's religion include sexual intercourse?" Blumenthal was Lewis's source. Only it wasn't really true. Starr's prosecutors never asked those questions— not that way. The subjects had come up in different contexts than Lewis implied—and in responses to statements that Blumenthal had made.[1] Was Lewis manipulated by Blumenthal to make a political point that benefited the president? Of course. It is the way, unfortunately, the world works and certainly the way the journalism in this story worked all too frequently.

The best we can ever do is what I have tried to do here—figure out, as best we can, what really happened and report it thoroughly, fairly and accurately.

• • •

In early September 1998, just days before the release of Starr's report, I was talking to Goldberg. It was a long, rambling conversation in which the literary agent told me about the latest idea she had to market Tripp's tapes via the Internet—one of her many brainstorms that never actually went anyplace. The main topic, though, was Clinton's fate. At that point, the situation looked bleak. His August 18, 1998, statement confessing the relationship he had denied in January had not gone over well. Newspaper editorial pages were calling for his resignation. Democratic senators like Joe Lieberman of Connecticut and Bob Kerrey of Nebraska had expressed their dismay and even anger at his conduct. It was not the affair itself. It was the recklessness, the stupidity, the lapse in judgment—and the drawn-out prosecutorial nightmare that his lies had made inevitable.

But Clinton was never going to resign, I was sure. He would never do a Richard Nixon. I had a theory about it—and I shared it with Goldberg that day. Nixon and Clinton had one thing in common: They both hated their enemies. But in another respect, they were fundamentally different. Nixon, deep down, suspected his enemies might be right—that they were better than he.

With Clinton, I said, it was totally different. He believes, deep down, that his enemies are scum. "He thinks you're scum," I told Goldberg. "He'll never give you the satisfaction of resigning."

For all her diabolical mischief-making, Goldberg has her virtues—and one of them is sudden bursts of candor that, like a summer squall, come without warning.

"Well, we are scum," she said. "If anybody ever did to me what we did to him, I would hate them too."

I grabbed my notebook. When that happens, I thought as I scribbled down the quote, I will plan to be there, watching, listening—and taking notes.

AFTERWORD

In the matters of Julie Hiatt Steele, James Riady, and Linda Tripp

No sooner was the writing of *Uncovering Clinton* complete in March 1999 than the journalistic dilemmas I faced during my reporting on the president's conduct returned—this time in new, and in some ways more vexing, forms. By then the impeachment saga was over, and much of the country had made clear its desire to "move on"—a message politicians in Washington heard loud and clear. But as Dickens instructed, the law operates according to its own illogic. The vast legal machinery spawned by *Jones* v. *Clinton* was still churning—and threatening to drag me back into arenas that, as a reporter, I was more than anxious to avoid.

The first and most problematic case was that of Julie Hiatt Steele, Kathleen Willey's ex-friend in Richmond. Steele had been a perplexing figure in the unfolding of the Clinton-Lewinsky story. As is explained in Chapter 6 and Chapter 8, Steele—a divorced mother with a young adopted child—had at first confirmed to me Willey's story that a distraught Willey had come to her home on the evening of November 29, 1993, and described an unwanted sexual advance by Clinton outside the Oval Office earlier that day. Then, almost five months after my first interview with her, Steele retracted her account and claimed that her friend Willey had asked her to "lie" about it. There was, as shall be seen, some grounds to be skeptical of Steele's version of events. Among other things, the details of her story kept changing at critical junctures. Yet her evolving recantation proved invaluable to the Clinton defense: By casting doubt on

Willey's claims, it permitted the president's defenders to deflect and muddy charges that he was a serial sexual harasser and perjurer. (Clinton, in his grand jury testimony, had denied any sexual overtures *at all* during his meeting with Willey that day.) For that reason, and because they suspected the president's agents had somehow "gotten" to her, Starr's prosecutors pursued Steele relentlessly—too relentlessly, as it turned out.

Wiser heads within Starr's office advised not to bring a case against Steele. She might have dissembled, they argued, but—absent clear evidence of a conspiracy to intimidate her by agents of the president (which Starr's agents never had)—she was too peripheral a player for an independent counsel to spend his time prosecuting. Starr, purist to the core and with his usual tin ear for the politics of the moment, didn't listen. In January 1999, he secured a grand jury indictment of Steele on charges of false statements and obstruction of justice. Thus, the only criminal case that would arise out of the entire Lewinsky investigation—*United States* v. *Julie Hiatt Steele*—was scheduled for trial in federal court in Alexandria that spring.

Throughout the investigation, Starr's prosecutors very much wanted my cooperation. I had, after all, first heard Steele confirm Willey's story—an account she appeared to provide spontaneously and with at least some particulars when I went to see her in March 1997. Steele's later claim that she first learned of the Willey-Clinton encounter while I was on the way to her home seemed inconsistent with some of the nuanced texture and level of detail she provided to me that day.[1] But *Newsweek* and I refused the entreaties of Starr's deputies to assist them in their investigation. They had their job, we had ours. Other than one small and innocuous discussion—in which a *Newsweek* lawyer confirmed to Starr's prosecutors that pertinent portions of our accounts in the magazine were accurate renditions of the facts as we understood them—the independent counsel built his case against Steele without any help from me.

●   ●   ●

There the matter stood until one unseasonably warm evening in February, the book in its final stages, when I was home on my back porch grilling some hamburgers and my doorbell rang. I was expecting my *Newsweek* colleague Dan Klaidman, whom I had invited to stop by and join my family and me for dinner. Instead of Klaidman, I opened the door to discover the smiling face of a process server. "I've got something for you," he said as he slapped an envelope into my hand. I opened it—and found a subpoena signed by Steele's lawyer, the insufferable Nancy Luque. I read it quickly. Luque was demanding I turn over my phone records for the past year, my book in all its draft forms and all of my notes with just about everybody in the Clinton saga—Lucianne Goldberg, Linda Tripp, etc.—whether or not they had anything to do with the relatively narrow charges against Julie Hiatt Steele. Irritated at this audacious invasion of my First Amendment rights, I quickly got on the phone and tried to reach a *Newsweek* lawyer. It took about forty minutes before I was able to track down *Newsweek*'s outside counsel, Stu Gold, who told me to calm down. In all likelihood, he assured me, such a fishing expedition would never be upheld by the judge. By then, Klaidman had arrived—and the dinner I was grilling had been charred to a crisp. Klaidman and I spent much of the rest of the evening plotting a counterclaim against Luque, seeking compensatory damages for the by-then-inedible burned burgers.

Over the next few weeks, there was much legal jockeying back and forth. In pretrial proceedings, the presiding judge, Claude Hilton, tossed out Luque's subpoena. Then Luque came up with a more narrowly focused one—demanding my testimony at Steele's trial along with my notes of my conversations with Steele and Willey. Her pretrial motions suggested she was prepared to put on an O. J. Simpson–like defense, in which she would portray the charges against Steele as the product of a giant conspiracy of Clinton enemies that encompassed everyone from Kathleen Willey and Lucianne Goldberg to Kenneth Starr and that somehow began with . . . me.

As nonsensical as all this was,[2] the prospect of a court order to produce my notes was very real and Gold warned me could well be upheld by the judge. This caused me to launch an exhaustive search of my cluttered office for anything that might be covered by the contours of the subpoena. It seemed a Herculean task. But one afternoon, rummaging through a box of old materials on the 1997 Senate campaign finance investigation, I came across a surprise discovery: a misfiled notebook with contents I had all but forgotten, notes that sorely tested my determination to stay off the witness stand and out of the limelight.[3]

•   •   •

At this point, it is useful to examine the precise nature of the criminal case Starr was seeking to make against Steele. She was charged not with lying to me, of course, but with lying before a federal grand jury when she flatly and unequivocally asserted that Willey had never told her *anything* about a sexual encounter with the president until the afternoon of March 19, 1997, when I was on the way to her home. "I had never heard of any allegations of improper conduct by President Clinton until she called to tell me her story in 1997, as Mr. Isikoff was en route to my home," Steele had stated in February 1998, in a sworn affidavit that was originally prepared by one of President Clinton's lawyers. Asked later by one of Starr's prosecutors before the grand jury if she had ever told anyone (other than me) that Willey had related to her an account of sexual advances by Clinton, Steele responded, "No." Then she stated: "She [Willey] did not tell me these things happened. . . . She [Willey] hadn't told me anything like that."

The problem was Steele apparently *had* told several of her close friends—all of whom later described to Starr's agents hearing Steele talk independently about the Willey-Clinton encounter at various times over the years. One of them, Bill Poveromo, a Richmond television producer who had briefly dated Steele, testified about having dinner with Steele one evening in April 1997 and hearing her recount how Clinton had "fondled and groped her [Kathleen Willey] when she worked at the White House." (According to Poveromo, Steele never mentioned anything about Willey asking her to make this up.) Another witness, Mary Highsmith, who described herself as Steele's former best friend, recounted how Steele first told her about the incident in January 1994—more than three years before I ever arrived on the scene—and then she had lunch with Willey and Steele in the summer of 1996, when the subject came up again. Another longtime Steele friend, Amy Horan, testified that she thought she first heard Steele describe the Willey-Clinton encounter as early as 1993 but was "pretty positive" she and Steele had discussed it by September 1996.

Even my initial August 1997 story on the Willey incident—the story in which I reported Steele's recantation—contained a sentence that caused potential problems for Steele. After citing Steele's claims that Willey had asked her to lie about coming to her home and relating the details of the encounter that night, I had gone on to write that the apologetic Steele had still acknowledged to me being told *something* about the incident. "In fact," I had written in the August 1997 story, "Willey had told her [Steele] about the incident weeks after it happened, saying only that the president had made a pass at her." I then added: "To Steele, Willey had not appeared upset by it at the time." If this *second* amended version of Steele's account was correct, then Starr's narrow charges in the indictment were true: Steele had lied in what became the *third* and final amended version of her story when she stated in her affidavit and before the grand jury that she knew *nothing* about the Clinton-Willey encounter prior to my arrival on the scene.

But could I prove my story? When I had first collected my notes to write *Uncovering Clinton* in the spring of 1998, I couldn't find the notebook in which I had recorded all my conversations with Steele that frantic week the previous summer. In the meantime, the media-chummy Luque—Steele's lawyer who, among other clients, represented the Clinton-Gore campaign committee—was freely suggesting to reporters all over town that I had simply gotten it wrong. Steele had never said anything like what I reported her saying, Luque claimed (as though she would know). At best, Luque suggested, when I wrote about Steele knowing something about "the incident," I had simply misunderstood a reference Steele was making to something else—the so-called chicken soup conversation, in the fall of 1992 (see Chapter 6, pages 117–118).

As the Steele trial began, this was pretty much the Steele defense strategy with all of Starr's witnesses: They were all either misremembering or confused about what they testified Steele had told them. But my missing notebook, I soon discovered, told a very different story. As I reviewed it, I realized it backed up what I had

written completely—and more so. There was no question that—in
our second series of discussions in the summer of 1997—Steele was
still affirming that there had been a sexual encounter between Clinton and Willey outside the Oval Office in November 1993. *"I do
believe it happened,"* my notes showed Steele had said to me on July
31, 1997. In a later conversation that day, I pressed Steele yet again
for details of precisely what Willey had told her about the incident—
and when she had told her about it. *"She told me weeks later,"* Steele
replied, according to my notes. *"I do believe it happened that day. . . .
She told me he had made passes on* [sic] *her. . . . She had gone and told
only one person—Linda at the WH. . . . He took her in the other room
and made a pass at her, and she just about died. . . . She was embarrassed. . . . I can't lie. . . . I do think she was flattered. . . . I think she
thought a job would come out of this."* Then, in words that apparently
refer to how Willey described the incident to her, I had written
down: *"You won't ever believe what happened."*

Not to put too fine a point on it, but my notebook was direct evidence relating to the very issue that was central to the Steele trial.
Even when she was apologizing for her earlier lie about Willey coming to her home that night, Steele was still affirming the essential
truth of Willey's story. The notes, my lawyers and I quickly realized,
could be powerful evidence supporting Starr's case. What now was I
supposed to do?

It would be disingenuous to suggest that I wasn't tempted to let
the prosecutors know. After all, Steele was still suing me in federal
court (see page 385, footnote 1, Chapter 8). As bogus as *Newsweek*
and we believed her claims to be, making her a felon would surely
strengthen the magazine's hands in winning a dismissal of those
claims. But we stuck to our guns—and sat silently back as the trial
proceeded. Meanwhile, Luque and her cocounsel, Eric Dubelier,
never followed through on their threat to call me as a witness—and
risk having my damaging notes (which they also knew nothing
about) entered into evidence. After two days of deliberations, the
jury pronounced itself hopelessly deadlocked. A mistrial was
declared. The jury foreman later told the Associated Press that the
jury had voted nine to three for conviction on all counts. But Starr—
having been pummeled in the press for bringing such a marginal

case—elected not to retry. It was the final courtroom setback for his five-year investigation. Neither the prosecutors nor the jurors would ever see the notes that could have made the difference.

Some public-spirited readers might at this point object: By what right did *Newsweek* and I withhold pertinent evidence in a criminal trial? Hard as it might be for the cynics to believe, this really was a matter of principle. As journalists, we are not agents of the government. When we knock on people's doors or call them up on the phone and ask them to share information with us, it is vital that they believe we are acting in good faith—as independent news gatherers, and not as backdoor investigators for some federal agency. To turn over our notebooks willy-nilly to prosecutors would radically transform the nature of what we do, making us partners of power and authority rather than the watchdogs we are supposed to be.[4]

Of course, no privilege is absolute. There are cases where the courts would surely rule—and the press might well agree—that reporters should yield their notes for the greater public good. But this was not one of them. Steele was no terrorist. Nobody's life was at stake. (As Monica Lewinsky herself pointed out to Linda Tripp, in a different context, "this is not a murder case.") Steele's "transgressions," such as they were, were small and petty and stupid—the unfortunate by-product of a maddening prosecutorial quest for "truth" that had gone on too long and lost its way.

●　　●　　●

W hat finally then to make of the whole Willey-Steele fandango— the shadowy Richmond sideshow that led me to the Monica Lewinsky story in the first place? In the criminal trial, the reputation of both women took hits. In much of the press, and in repeated appearances on *Rivera Live* and *Larry King Live,* Steele had portrayed herself as a martyr—an innocent bystander swept up in the Clinton drama very much against her will. In fact, as her trial established conclusively, Steele had aggressively sought to cash in on her association with Willey from the start. Even before my initial Willey story was ever published, Steele had contacted the tabloid *National Enquirer* and sold them a photograph of Willey and the president, earning herself $9,000 plus an all-expenses-paid vacation for her family and her to Palm Beach, Florida. Steele later tried to profit again, using an agent to try to sell a story about Willey to the *Star* tabloid and then (after the Lewinsky story broke) reselling the Willey-Clinton picture a second time to *Time* magazine in January 1998 for another $5,000. Steele then resold the same photo to CNN a third time in March 1998 for $3,500. Steele's motives for such dubious behavior—enriching herself from the misfortunes of her erstwhile friend—are hard to discern. But it is worth keeping in mind Willey's claim that—in the months before the storm over her claims erupted in the summer of 1997—Steele had come to her house with a stack of tabloids, urging the two of them to sell a version of the Clinton sex story and split the take. According to Willey, she rejected the scheme. Whatever the truth of this claim, the facts remain ironic in the extreme: In a lawsuit that was initially branded by Bob Bennett, Bill Clinton's lawyer, as "tabloid trash with a legal caption on it," the one witness who actually went running to the tabloids for profit was Julie Hiatt Steele, the witness most favorable to the interests of Bennett's client, the president of the United States.

Of course, Willey was no choir girl. Although Tripp's original account of a romantic vixen intent on ensnaring the president appears overblown and motivated by jealousy (see Chapter 6)—there seems little doubt that Willey and Clinton did have a flirtation going on in the weeks and months prior to their encounter. Her reaction to his crass sexual overtures that day was probably more a jumble of contradictory emotions than the immediate indignation she later professed. At Steele's trial, Willey was forced to make a number of damaging admissions: that she had asked Steele to lie on an earlier occasion (telling an ex-boyfriend who had jilted her that she was pregnant with the man's child); that she, too, through her lawyer, had toyed with selling her story to the supermarket tabloid *Star* for a whopping six-figure payment; that during a decidedly unpleasant grocery store encounter after the story had broken, she had exploded at Steele and—according to the somewhat delicate court testimony on the matter—called her a four-letter word that describes a part of the female anatomy and begins with the letter *c*.

And yet, almost completely overlooked by the press at the time, corroboration of Willey's core story actually grew stronger as a result of the Steele trial. Two new witnesses, never before heard from, came forward to take the stand. Friends of Willey, they testified that—long before there was any talk of tabloids or television appearances or even any lawsuit—they, too, had heard her contemporaneously recount the story of her sexual encounter with Clinton. Contrary to the claims of Tripp, they didn't say Willey sounded "thrilled" by what happened. One of these witnesses was Ruth Eisen, a demure retired schoolteacher and former Clinton White House volunteer who had no interest in publicity or personal enrichment (she had resolutely refused to talk to reporters for over a year). She testified that Willey had called her that very day, November 29, 1993, and told her that Clinton had taken her into his private office, "kissed her on the lips" and "gotten aroused." As Eisen recounted it, Willey described Clinton as telling her "he had wanted to do that for a long time." Eisen said Willey's principal reaction was that she was "caught off guard" by the president's behavior. Another witness, Diane Martin, also remembered getting a call from Willey that day and hearing the story of the Clinton encounter. She described Willey as "shocked" by the incident. "She couldn't believe what had happened and didn't know what it meant," she said from the witness stand.[5]

In these sorts of matters, it appears, most witnesses tell some version of a more complicated and elusive truth. In this case, those versions might ultimately mesh something like this: After I first interviewed Willey in her lawyer's office that day in March 1997, she probably did call her friend Steele and ask her to embellish the story by lying about certain details. Trying to impress the visiting reporter (i.e., me) with the verisimilitude of her account, and fearing contradiction when my own demand for details yielded the name of the ever-resentful Linda Tripp, Willey stupidly asked Steele to say she came to her house that night and expressed distress and anger about the president's behavior. Then, five months later, Steele saw her friend's story become the focus of national publicity. Steele confessed to me, perhaps from a streak of conscience—and then hastily (and just as stupidly) tried to cash in on her own. Once one of Clinton's lawyers arrived on the scene in late January, after Willey's deposition and news of the Lewinsky affair had broken, Steele said something she never actually had said before—that she knew nothing at all about the encounter. It was the only version of events the president's lawyers wanted to hear or could possibly accept. Once having signed the unequivocal, if false, sworn affidavit, Steele was stuck with it—and maintained her dubious story through the grand jury investigation, her trial and her many television appearances.

That is, at any rate, my best guess of how to resolve what is otherwise a hopelessly muddled mess of contradictions. But as for the central event, the only one that matters, the cumulative weight of the evidence is reasonably strong. All witnesses agree that Willey was in financial and emotional distress in late November 1993 and went to see Clinton about getting a job. Common sense suggests that—at that point, at any rate—her interests were not exactly romantic. Clinton listened with sympathy—and then for whatever reason (lust, loneliness, who knows?) got physical. "She goes to see him about a job and he hits on her?" I had said to Willey's lawyer, Dan Gecker, after I first heard the story in his office. At the end of the day, it still looks like that is pretty much what happened.

•   •   •

I t was a much-echoed debating point during the cable talkathons that dominated 1998 that if any corporate CEO or law firm managing partner had done what Clinton was accused of doing he would probably lose *his* job—or at least have his career shattered by embarrassment and shame. But by the time all the evidence on Clinton had come in—Jones, Lewinsky, Willey, Juanita Broaddrick—the president was home free. By early April 1999, U.S. military warplanes were bombing Serbia to stop the atrocities in Kosovo, and the president's personal faults suddenly seemed quite small. In such an environment, Clinton could casually dismiss the significance of the impeachment trial—and all the travails through which he had dragged the country. "I do not regard this impeachment vote as some great badge of shame," he told Dan Rather that spring in an interview that revealed much about his own inner thought process. He was asked if he had ever considered resigning. "Never, not a second, never, never," he said. "I wouldn't do that to the Constitution. I wouldn't do that to the presidency. . . . I would never have legitimized what I believe is horribly wrong with what has occurred here over the last four or five years." Now here was spin with gusto: Clinton as Horatius at the Tiber bridge guarding the Constitution from the marauding Etruscans of the Republican right.

And yet, there was still the small matter of the rule of law to deal with. On April 12, 1999, U.S. Judge Susan Webber Wright weighed in on that subject. Wright was, in some ways, the unsung hero of the Jones case. A crisp, no-nonsense jurist, she had been tossed the case from hell by the Supreme Court and then presided over the distasteful task with the air of a stern, impatient governess charged with managing a bunch of unruly schoolchildren. She had warned the Jones lawyers back in January 1998—just before the Lewinsky story broke—that they would have difficulty proving their claims, and then she summarily tossed the suit out a few months later. (It was only when the U.S. Court of Appeals in St. Louis was set to hear the matter that Clinton was moved to settle.) But Wright had also personally presided over the January 16, 1998, deposition in the Jones case, swearing Clinton in as a witness, directing him to raise his right hand and place his left on a Bible. After hearing objections from his lawyer, she had directed him to answer Jim Fisher's questions about Monica Lewinsky, judging them to be within the legitimate scope of civil discovery. "There simply is no escaping the fact that the president deliberately violated this court's discovery orders," wrote Wright in a scathing thirty-two-page ruling that spring, "and thereby undermined the integrity of the judicial system." After all the many months in which the president's lawyers made their tortured arguments to the Congress as to why Clinton had not really lied, Wright cut right through them with swift efficiency. The evidence, she said, was "clear and convincing," she wrote. Clinton gave "false, misleading and evasive answers that were designed to obstruct the judicial process." In order "to deter others who might themselves consider emulating the President of the United States," Wright found Clinton in contempt of court and ordered him to pay the legal fees and expenses incurred by Jones's lawyers, which were caused by his falsehoods.

Clinton's lawyers chose not to appeal, and in September 1999, the president cut a $89,000 check to the Jones legal team he so despised. Under the judge's orders, he signed another for $1,202 made out to the U.S. government—reimbursement for the cost of Wright's plane trip to Washington, so she could listen to the president's lies.

•   •   •

That Wright's finding barely caused a ripple with the public was in large part a reflection of the national exhaustion with the topic. But the extraordinary fact of its existence—a president in contempt—also underscored the enduring paradox of Clinton's presidency. On more levels than his enemies would ever give him credit for, Clinton had, by the end of 1999, racked up a record of successes in office. The economy was still booming, the crime rate low, even national poverty levels had fallen. After the brief interlude of the intervention in Yugoslavia, the country was at peace. How much of all this could be directly attributed to particular Clinton policies can and will be debated for decades to come. But presidents inevitably get the blame when things go wrong. They should be indulged their efforts to take the credit when matters for the most part go right.

On other fronts, Clinton's record was decidedly mixed. The excitement he engendered among many progressive Democrats in 1992 was never rewarded. Clinton's promises of sweeping changes—of universal health care, for example, or ambitious initiatives to attack the ills of the inner city—were by the end of his term all but forgotten. Instead, the country got "triangulation" and a host of timid, poll-driven proposals designed to offend the smallest group of voters. Many in his party will forever be grateful to Clinton for his political skills in outmaneuvering Newt Gingrich and the House Republicans during the critical budget battles of 1995. At a time when the armies of a reenergized right wing seemed on the verge of seizing control of the government, Clinton thwarted them, wielding his veto pen and boxing his adversaries into a political corner from which they never recovered. But for what higher purpose Clinton used his success was never clear.

In the end, the legacy of Clinton's deceit is not likely to be erased, either—it will stand as a black mark that will forever taint his achievements. Even as memories of the year-long Lewinsky trauma faded ("It's almost as though it never happened," one of the

lawyers in the case said wistfully to me in the summer of 1999), lin-
gering distaste for the president and his conduct still registered in
the polls. Time and again, Vice President Al Gore felt the need to distance himself from the president he had so loyally served. In many
other quarters of the U.S. government, among the ranks of the military and the front-line troops of federal law enforcement, disdain for,
and even disgust with, the president was unusually strong. "It's fair
to say that most FBI agents think Clinton is a criminal," one longtime and now retired FBI official confided to me months after the
impeachment trial had ended. Occasionally, these thinly disguised
feelings would bubble to the surface. In October 1999, just after Ken
Starr resigned, FBI director Louis Freeh wrote the much-maligned
independent counsel a remarkable letter that lavishly praised him
for the "persistence" with which he had pursued his five-year probe
of the president. Freeh was a one-time altar boy, street agent, prosecutor and federal judge—a man who exuded moral purity. Clinton
had appointed him in the fall of 1993, hailing him in a public cere-
mony as a "law enforcement legend." Now, six years later, the FBI
director openly mocked the president—even as he heaped kudos
upon Clinton's tormentor. "You have never engaged in any false or
misleading conduct or practice," Freeh wrote Starr, mimicking the
language Wright had used to describe the president.

Much of Freeh's and the bureau's animosity toward the president
sprung from what they widely believed to be his continuing cover-up
of other improper conduct, especially the unorthodox financing of
his political campaigns. This was a matter I always viewed as closely
intertwined with Clinton's personal recklessness. Clinton's hunger
for campaign cash, like his lust for women, were of a piece: They
were powerful, all-consuming passions, resulting in shabby behavior
that forever needed to be concealed. In the fall of 1999, new details
of just how much Clinton had to cover up once more began to
emerge. A House committee obtained copies of hundreds of pages of
previously secret FBI debriefings of John Huang, the secretive
Democratic Party fund-raiser at the center of the scandal over Clinton's reelection campaign. In these talks, Huang for the first time
laid out the origins of the so-called Asian connection to the White
House—a story that actually began four years before the widely pub-

licized abuses of the 1996 election. In August 1992, during a cam-
paign trip to California, Clinton had taken a limousine ride with
Huang's employer, James Riady, the billionaire chief of the Lippo
Group, a banking and trading conglomerate based in Jakarta,
Indonesia. Clinton had known Riady for years. In the early 1980s,
Lippo had invested heavily in an Arkansas bank and the Indonesian
businessman had for a while made Little Rock his home. Now, during their car ride reunion, Riady offered to pump $1 million into
Clinton's presidential campaign. (An internal memo prepared for
Clinton that day states that Riady had "flown all the way from
Indonesia" and wanted to "talk to [Clinton] about banking issues
and international business.") Over the next several weeks, Riady
made good on his pledge. Massive wire transfers began. As ultimately documented by federal investigators, hundreds of thousands
of dollars from Lippo's bank accounts in Asia flowed to Lippo
employees and Lippo-owned corporations in the United States.
These employees and companies in turn then wrote contribution
checks recommended by Clinton's campaign operatives in Little
Rock. The contributions were in most cases doubly illegal: Not only
did they come from a foreign source, but they were also funneled
through "conduits" to disguise the true identity of the giver. Meanwhile, Riady and his wife also wrote large "soft money" checks
under their own names—but they were distributed to state parties
around the country where the national press never noticed them. By
the time election day came around, James Riady's Lippo Group—a
foreign corporation whose existence was virtually unknown in official Washington, much less to the American public—had become the
largest single financier of Clinton's campaign against President
George Bush, dwarfing the donations of trial lawyers, labor unions
and other traditional Democratic Party "soft money" givers.[6]

As Huang also described to the FBI, Lippo was at that time
deeply enmeshed in business dealings with the Chinese government.
(An entity called China Resource Holdings, an arm of the Chinese
Ministry of Trade and Investment, had already bought up a stake in
Lippo's Hong Kong bank.) What impact Lippo money later had on
Clinton's policies as president is ultimately unknowable. But even
still, in retrospect, the full impact of the Lippo-Clinton-Riady story

seems staggering. Clinton, in the fall of 1992, was running as the candidate of political reform. "On streets where statesmen once strolled, a never-ending stream of money changes hands," decried *Putting People First,* the Clinton-Gore campaign manifesto of that summer. In a chapter on campaign finances, the Clinton-Gore book even pledged to "end the unlimited soft money contributions that are funneled through national, state and local parties to presidential candidates"—an especially striking plank since at that very moment Clinton was secretly accepting precisely such donations (from a foreign source, no less) on a scale never before seen. Clinton was also running on a foreign policy platform that railed against Bush's capitulation to the "butchers of Beijing"—a formulation he quickly dropped after taking office, while his administration moved toward supporting renewal of Most Favored Nation for China. Historical what-ifs are great parlor games. One well worth playing is to imagine what might have been the political impact on the country had it suddenly been disclosed in the fall of 1992 that Clinton's biggest financial backer was a mysterious Indonesian billionaire with extensive ties to the Chinese government. That Clinton and his entourage kept all this hidden from the public for years is, at a minimum, an impressive testament to their ability to conceal from the public that which is politically awkward. For such a man, waving his finger at the public and denying an illicit sexual relationship with a young intern must have seemed small beer—and nothing to cause undue anguish.

●   ●   ●

A nd still, the legal process wasn't over. In Maryland, state prosecutors had spent much of 1998 investigating whether Linda Tripp had violated a state statute that prohibits taping phone calls without the consent of the other party. It is an anomalous law: In forty-one of the fifty states, including Virginia, where Tripp worked, and the District of Columbia, one party taping is legal. For that reason, the Maryland law had almost never been enforced—and its courts had established a high bar for prosecution, requiring the state to prove that the taper knew the particularities of the Maryland statute. The political dimension of the Tripp inquiry were clear from the start. In February 1998, forty-nine Democratic state legislators had signed a letter demanding that Tripp be prosecuted. The case was bucked to Stephen Montanarelli, the special state prosecutor charged with handling public corruption cases. The state legislature funds Montanarelli's budget. Montanarelli did as the lawmakers asked.

It didn't take too long for Montanarelli's crew to track me down. One day, in the spring of 1998, I got a phone call at home from one of his prosecutors. He asked if I would meet him. I asked him if he wanted to grant me an exclusive interview about the progress of his investigation. He said no, that was not why he was calling. He wanted to interview *me*. I told him I would have to talk to my lawyers about that. Then I hung up, having no intention of ever conversing with him again.

Newsweek and I took the same position with Montanarelli's office as we did with Starr's in the Steele case. We are not in the business of assisting prosecutors. But before long, the threat of a subpoena was being dangled before us. To avoid a confrontation, *Newsweek* offered Montanarelli a simple and (we thought) relatively innocuous affidavit, signed by the Washington bureau's Ann McDaniel. It affirmed that she had heard a tape in the offices of *Newsweek* early on the morning of January 17, 1998. We had published that we had listened to the tape that night in the pages of *Newsweek*. McDaniel and I had also said the same thing during television appearances when we talked about our coverage. It seemed a bit of a stretch to mount a major court battle to avoid taking the witness stand before the grand jury if the issue could be resolved by a simple declaration that what we had reported was true.

The matter went away for a while. Still, I was a bit nervous. As a matter of principle, I didn't like the idea that we had given the prosecutors anything. As it turned out, I had reason to be concerned. On July 30, 1999, Montanarelli announced that a Howard County, Maryland, grand jury had indicted Tripp on two counts of breaking Maryland's wiretapping law. The first count—of taping Lewinsky without her permission—was not a surprise. The second count stunned me: Tripp was charged not just with making the tape but also with illegally "disseminating" the December 22 tape by allegedly authorizing Moody to play it for me. The act of playing the tape for *Newsweek* had been judged by the special state prosecutor and a Maryland grand jury to be a felony—for which Tripp was facing an additional five years in a state prison.

Anybody who reads *Uncovering Clinton* will find a portrait of Linda Tripp that can hardly be described as flattering. She was unquestionably my source for much of my early reporting on the president's relationship with Lewinsky. But she was also—in ways I never imagined when I first started talking to her—a manipulative and deceptive woman, who was given to bizarre flights of paranoia and embellishment. It is fair to say she was not the ideal guide one would want for these sorts of events. That said, I was struck by how many commentators of all stripes found her indictment a mean-spirited and pointless exercise that raised deeply troubling constitutional issues. Tripp had given the tapes to Starr's office—setting off the events that put them into the public arena—only after obtaining what she was led to believe was an iron-clad promise of immunity for any criminal charges that she might face for making them. If I know anything about Linda Tripp, I know this much: She was always most concerned about saving her own skin. Had it not been for Starr deputy Jackie Bennett's promise that she would be given immunity on the evening of January 12, 1998, Tripp probably would have burned the incriminating tapes before she turned them over to anyone. In this sense, the Maryland indictment represents an end run around one of Tripp's core constitutional rights: her Fifth Amendment right not to incriminate herself.

But the second count—the one involving me—is much worse than that. Read again the pages of *Uncovering Clinton* and my account of those crazed days in mid-January 1998. One thing ought to be absolutely clear: Linda Tripp was not beating down the doors of *Newsweek* and forcing us to listen to the tape of her conversation with Monica Lewinsky. We anxiously wanted to listen to the tape, and I did everything I could to make it happen. Here the moral ambiguity that is often at the heart of much that we as journalists do comes into sharp relief. Tripp's taping was unquestionably an egregious violation of Lewinsky's privacy. Yet for *Newsweek* and me, listening to that tape early that Saturday morning, January 17, 1998, was entirely justified for compelling journalistic reasons. Once Starr launched his secret criminal probe, we were sitting on a political and legal earthquake.

The public had every right to know what it was all about and what the prime evidence—i.e., Tripp's tapes—contained. By listening to the tape, we were the only news organization that could independently assess the central evidence that prompted Starr to launch the most audacious and controversial criminal investigation in many years. Because we did so, we were able to provide the most detailed, accurate and nuanced account of what Lewinsky was saying about her conversations with the president (and, just as important, what she wasn't saying). Because we did so, *Newsweek* won a National Magazine Award, the highest honor in magazine journalism.

As I write (in January 2000), Tripp's case is still awaiting trial. My *Newsweek* colleagues and I could yet be pulled into it—a step we will almost certainly resist to the maximum extent the law allows. (Maryland's unusually strong "shield" law protects reporters from having to testify about their dealings with sources even if some of the information at issue has already been published.) Beyond that, however, the manifest injustice of criminally prosecuting Tripp for allowing the tape to be played for *Newsweek*—an act that redounded to the greater glory of *Newsweek*—couldn't be clearer. Of course, there have been many injustices throughout this long saga: injustices to Monica Lewinsky and to her family, injustices to Paula Jones and her friends, injustices perhaps even to Bill Clinton—even if he did bring it all upon himself and everybody else. At this late date it seems—to me, at any rate—to make little sense to add one more injustice to the mix. Far better to let the whole business fade away, off the public horizon and into the pages of history.

NOTES ON SOURCES AND METHODS

Whenever a journalist writes a book, questions inevitably arise about where his material comes from. This book is an amalgam. Much of the Paula Jones and Kathleen Willey stories derive from my own interviews with the principals combined with my recollections of events within *The Washington Post* newsroom and inside the *Newsweek* Washington bureau.

In the later portions of the book involving Monica Lewinsky and Ken Starr, the sourcing gets both easier in some parts and more complicated in others. The easy parts involve the conversations between Lucianne Goldberg and Linda Tripp in September 1997 and extensive conversations starting in October 1997 and ending in December 1997 between Tripp and Monica Lewinsky. They were all tape-recorded, the first set by Goldberg, the second by Tripp. I have relied on the transcripts of those recordings to reconstruct the conversations exactly as they occurred. The scenes involving Lewinsky and President Clinton come from Lewinsky's grand jury testimony, which is remarkably detailed and precise on many points—certainly far more so than Clinton's. There are certain events in which the testimonies of principals obviously differ. If it is important, such as the exchange of gifts between Lewinsky and Betty Currie, I note the difference.

When I was reporting in 1997, many of the people I talked to did not then want to be publicly identified. Then events changed and they became more accommodating. To pick one example, Kathleen

Willey in 1998 permitted me to quote from my interview with her in 1997—an interview she was unwilling to permit me to quote from at the time. My interviews with various of the "elves" in 1997 and 1998 were done during a period when they would not permit me to quote or even refer to them. But eventually, they agreed that I would be able to use what they told me for a book that would come out when "the story was over." Whether they have told me everything is another question.

My January 15 meeting with Ken Starr's prosecutors took place with an understanding that I would not quote them. But Starr's chief deputy, Jackie Bennett, agreed to place it on the record for the book, largely because, as I argued to him, the actual conversation was far less damning to the prosecutors than has been suggested by some of Starr's critics. Jim Moody was publicly identified as the person who brought the December 22 tape to *Newsweek* by his client Linda Tripp.

A word about Tripp: My conversations with her in 1997 were conducted on background, meaning I could use the information she was giving me, but I couldn't identify her as the source. Tripp went on the record briefly on the morning of August 1, 1997, to give me the quote she did about Willey, then retreated to background again. Then, in the summer of 1998, Tripp identified herself as my source on matters relating to Willey and Lewinsky before Starr's grand jury. She testified at great length about her conversations with me. That grand jury testimony got placed on the public record and has been quoted by other journalists. In most cases, Tripp's rendition of events is not quite how I remembered them and, in a few cases, her account conflicts substantially with my own. (Certainly, that is the case on how she came to be quoted for the Kathleen Willey story.) In any event, after thinking it through and discussing the matter with a number of veteran journalists, I concluded that Tripp's dealings with me were fair material to write about in this book. Tripp outed herself as my source. She talked about what she said to me and what I said to her. In 1999, I sought to recontact her and offer her the chance to comment about my account of those conversations—or anything else in this book. She declined to do so except for two narrow responses—both of which are incorporated into a note to the passage in Chapter 14 where Tripp consulted me on taking her information about Lewinsky to a publisher.

That doesn't quite cover everything. There are still a few other sources whose existence I cannot reveal. But I have identified as many of the players, and told as much of the story, as I possibly can.

NOTES

CHAPTER TWO

1. Patterson described this in an unpublished March 7, 1994, interview with *Post* reporters Sharon LaFraniere and Charles Shepard.
2. Max Brantley, an unabashed liberal and veteran Clinton watcher who was editor of the *Arkansas Times,* later told me about seeing Clinton when he got home that night. Brantley's daughter was in the same softball league as Chelsea Clinton, and both girls had games that evening. With Hillary out of town, Clinton headed straight from the airport to the ball field. Brantley had never seen Clinton so pumped up. In the bleachers, he regaled Brantley and other parents with accounts of his rousing success in Cleveland—and joked about how another prospective candidate, Jay Rockefeller, had bombed. When Chelsea came to bat, Clinton cheered loudly and ragged on the umpire. "He was flushed, he was ebullient," said Brantley. "He was wired."

CHAPTER THREE

1. I assumed, mistakenly, that Blackard was skittish about the graphic details of Jones's claim that Clinton exposed himself. In fact, in 1997, Blackard testi-fied that Jones did not tell her until later that Clinton dropped his pants—although she did indicate that afternoon that "there was more" to the story.
2. "Goodness, how time flies," her supervisor, Clydine Pennington, wrote in a chatty August 28, 1991, review, barely three months after the Quality Man-agement Conference. "Seems just yesterday you came in for an interview. . . . Throughout this review time, I have been excited about your willingness to learn. . . . This probationary period is really only the beginning of your career in State Government."
3. Years later, Hamzy wrote an angry rant to the office of independent counsel Kenneth Starr about the injustice of it all. Hamzy thought Starr might be interested because of something she had just learned about Gaines: A lawyer who had served as Clinton's attorney for state pardons, he had just been nominated by the White House to serve as the new chairman of the U.S. Board of Paroles. Hamzy charged it was a payoff for Gaines's assistance in falsely discrediting her. Starr never followed up. Gaines got the job.

4. Price later testified that he had personally talked to Clinton almost immediately after the Jones press conference in February. Who called whom is unclear. But despite my initial anger about being misled, there is no reason to doubt Price's testimony that he had been at the Quality Management Conference with Clinton in the morning and saw nothing suspicious while he was there. The most likely possibility is that Clinton returned to the hotel after his luncheon without telling Price. An exhaustive search by lawyers for both Jones and Clinton found no evidence of any other activities for Clinton that afternoon.

5. Traylor's initial involvement with Clinton enemy Cliff Jackson is critical to the theory floated by the president's defenders: that Jones was a tool of the president's political foes from the start. I questioned Traylor and Jackson intensely at the time, and the accounts they independently gave point toward an innocent explanation. Traylor first called Jackson thinking, wrongly, that he represented Ferguson, the trooper who had allegedly slandered his client. When Jackson learned the nature of Traylor's grievance, he hit upon the idea of inviting Traylor and Jones to Washington for the Conservative Political Action Conference. Traylor, who had been rebuffed in his efforts to negotiate an out-of-court settlement for his client, accepted the offer, having no idea—he insisted—what CPAC actually was. Having Jones speak at the right-wing parlay, he later told me, was the worst mistake he made while representing her.

6. While I had been in Little Rock, Downie had lunch with Stephanopoulos. The White House aide made the case against the *Post* running anything about the Paula Jones allegations. Downie rarely tips his hand on such occasions. Stephanopoulos much later told me about the lunch and said the *Post* editor did little more than sit there sphinx-like and hear him out. Downie told me and others at the *Post* about the lunch at the time. I had no reason to believe he was especially influenced by it.

CHAPTER FOUR

1. At least two newspapers, *Newsday* (Feb. 6, 1992) and *USA Today* (Feb. 7, 1992), did publish stories about the Charlotte Perry grievance. And in a deposition in the Paula Jones case in November 1998, Flowers testified that Clinton had advised her to falsely testify in the grievance procedure that she had learned about the state job from a newspaper advertisement, rather than from Clinton himself.

2. Barely a month later, after Flowers aired her allegations, Clinton's office acknowledged the existence of correspondence showing that Clinton and Flowers had talked about finding her state employment. A January 28, 1992, statement from Clinton's office says that Clinton returned a Flowers phone call in February 1990 seeking assistance in finding a state job. Clinton then assigned a member of his staff to help her. The statement described Clinton's aid to Flowers as a "routine" exercise performed for many other constituents.

3. Thompson laid out the evidence in the Thurmond case in her book, *Ol' Strom: The Unauthorized Biography of Strom Thurmond,* coauthored with Jack Bass and published in 1998 by Longstreet Press.

4. When Peretz killed Lessard's piece, Michael Kinsley, *TNR*'s editor at the time, quit in protest. A few weeks later, he returned to work and wrote a piece—"Yes, We Have No Bananas"—lambasting the media Sanhedrins and, by implication, his boss. Kinsley was especially caustic on the privacy issue. When philandering politicians demanded privacy from journalists, he argued, what they were really trying to shield from the public was their own hypocrisy: "If a man running for office ever declined the campaign services of his wife, if he refused to let photographers near his kids and household pets, if he told reporters that his church volunteer activities were none of their business, I could listen without snickering to pleas that any interest in his relations with other women was an unfair invasion of his privacy. But of course this never happens. Instead, great effort goes into arranging, or even fabricating, elaborate family tableaux for the benefit of the press and the public."

   Kinsley's words are especially noteworthy given that they were written thirteen years before the 1992 Democratic Convention, which featured the unusually smarmy film biography, *The Man from Hope.* The work of Hollywood producer Harry Thomason, the film extolled the loving marriage of Bill and Hillary Clinton. Clinton himself can be heard in the film quoting Chelsea, then thirteen, saying how proud she was to be his daughter after he responded to the Gennifer Flowers allegations on *60 Minutes.* It then cut to an idyllic scene of the three Clintons embracing in a gently swaying hammock.

   When Clinton, almost exactly six years later, demanded "privacy" after confessing to his "inappropriate" relationship with Monica Lewinsky, few commentators recalled that it was the president himself who permitted the purported strength of his family life to be publicly advertised to the country in the movie of his life made by his Hollywood friend.

5. Hinton, who later served as press secretary for Andrew Cuomo, Clinton's secretary of the Department of Housing and Urban Development, agreed to be quoted by name for this book.

6. In the spring of 1998, Zercher gave an interview to the *Star* tabloid that provided a considerably enhanced account of her experiences on the Clinton campaign plane. In the *Star* account, Zercher was quoted as saying that, among other things, Clinton had fondled her breasts for over an hour one night. Zercher was also quoted as saying that she viewed Clinton's actions as harassment—something she specifically denied to me. Zercher's explanation of the discrepancy was that she was reluctant to tell me the full story in 1994. But it is also true that the *Star* paid Zercher about $50,000 for its interview in addition to thousands of dollars more for her photographs. That she accepted money does not necessarily discredit Zercher's more recent version of events. But given the discrepancies with the older, lamer and uncompensated version she had given me four years earlier, Zercher's sale of her story to the *Star* makes it much harder to accept her as an entirely credible witness.

   One other point should be noted. In May 1998, Zercher's friend McKay was sentenced to one year in federal prison after pleading guilty to securities fraud.

CHAPTER FIVE

1. Marcus actually also contacted another University of Chicago alumnus to try to get him to work on the case: a former Justice Department lawyer named Paul Rosenzweig. "I need help," Marcus recalled telling his friend when he called him that spring. Rosenzweig at first expressed interest and later got in touch with Cammarata about possibly aiding the Jones legal team. But for reasons that remain unclear, Rosenzweig never participated. Four years later, he would reappear in the story in a new capacity as a lawyer on the staff of Whitewater independent counsel Kenneth Starr's office.

2. Another factor that resulted in the Jackson settlement was, ironically, research conducted by private investigator Jack Palladino. This time, Palladino played a role exactly opposite the one he played for the Clinton campaign in 1992. Instead of flying around the country to dig up derogatory information on other accusers, Palladino and his ex-wife/business partner, Sandra Sutherland, were retained by the parents of the fourteen-year-old to develop information about other boys allegedly harassed by Jackson. The detective was later quoted as saying they had gone "across the country and back in time" to talk with nearly one hundred people. In the process, he said, he had learned of "a significant number" of other boys, some as young as seven, who claimed to have been sexually abused by Jackson. None of these, however, ever agreed to step forward to accuse Jackson of any wrongdoing. Palladino and his wife said the boys were "too frightened to go public" and face the "incredible publicity" that would result from accusing a world-famous entertainer of sexual misconduct. (See the *San Francisco Examiner* of Jan. 30, 1994, and *People* magazine of Feb. 7, 1994.)

3. Jones's later lawyers were extremely critical of Cammarata and Davis for introducing this claim. They believed that Jones's brief observation could have been explained by a number of scenarios other than a congenital or permanent deformity. And even if Clinton had suffered from a medical condition known to cause such curvatures (see chapter 10), the new lawyers were aghast to learn that the condition, Peyronie's disease, was episodic and curable. That meant that whatever Jones saw in 1991 might no longer have been present in 1998. The allegation, they concluded, was as likely to backfire as it was to vindicate their client's claims. David Pyke, one of Jones's later lawyers, said he and his partners were greatly relieved in late 1998, when Judge Susan Webber Wright blocked the Jones lawyers from obtaining the president's medical records. The ruling freed them of the burden of having to prove the truth of the allegation written into the complaint by Cammarata and Davis.

4. It was also false. As my inspection of Jones's personnel records had already established, she had in fact received at least one merit increase after the incident. Davis and Cammarata, in their rush to get out the complaint in time to beat the statute of limitations, had apparently missed this fact—a mistake that would come back to haunt them.

CHAPTER SIX

1. In a July 1996 *Vanity Fair* article ("The Doomsday Man," by William Prochnau and Laura Parker), Robertson was quoted as follows: "The man named Mike

Isikoff . . . is one of the most vicious anti-Christian bigots in the entire world. He is absolutely unbalanced and he is, uh, emotionally in my opinion uh, uh, stunted." Robertson's remarks were made in a telephone conversation secretly recorded by the wife of the former president of a Robertson-owned company who was suing the televangelist for defamation.

2. After Taylor wrote his piece, the president's lawyers circulated affidavits they had collected from other colleagues of Jones who insisted she had a different reaction to her encounter with Bill Clinton that day than was remembered by Jones's friends Blackard and Ballantine. One in particular stood out. Carole Phillips, a former secretary of Clinton's in the governor's office who came to Washington when he was elected president and landed a position at the Department of Agriculture, had said she remembered having lunch with Jones the day after the Quality Management Conference. Phillips recalled Jones was excited about her meeting with the governor and said she described him as "gentle" and "kind" during their meeting.

It is impossible for the mere journalist to say whose accounts—Phillips's and Danny Ferguson's on the one hand or Blackard's and Ballantine's on the other—are a more reliable guide to Jones's state of mind in the hours and days after her encounter with Bill Clinton. But in evaluating the competing recollections, it is worth keeping in mind several points.

One is that if Jones really did fear for her job, as she insisted she did, she would have had a motive for telling those she perceived as close to Clinton that she enjoyed the experience even if she really didn't. A very similar conflict can be found in the controversy over the Hill-Thomas allegations: those close to Thomas said they remembered talking to Anita Hill at the time she was working for him and insisted she never displayed the slightest hint of disapproval toward his conduct. Those close to Hill said different things, although none could relate anything similar to the vivid and precise recollections of Jones's friends.

Partisans of the president will no doubt insist that Blackard and Ballantine are impeachable on the grounds that they were close friends of Paula Jones, therefore could be expected to cover her made-up story. Partisans of Jones can argue that Phillips's and other accounts friendly to Clinton are coming from individuals who remain beholden to him (Phillips was an employee of the Clinton administration at the time she signed the affidavit) and therefore can be expected to try to protect him.

In the end, there is no reasonable way for further journalistic inquiry to resolve the question of Paula Jones's state of mind after she left the hotel room that day. The person who would know best—Paula Jones—insists she was horrified. I must, in the end, stand by my evaluation that Blackard and Ballantine—who back Jones up—seemed like credible witnesses to me. But only a trial, in which all the witnesses testified, could have ultimately settled the matter. It is a trial that, mercifully for all concerned, will never take place.

CHAPTER SEVEN

1. The most sensational claim in Aldrich's book, *Unlimited Access,* was that Clinton was sneaking out of the White House for late night trysts at a Marriott

Hotel. In August 1996, the *Washington Times*—having obtained an advance copy of the book—trumpeted this allegation in a banner headline. I interviewed Aldrich that morning. I pressed for his source. In his book, he had cited "an independent investigator." Okay, don't tell me the name, I said. But can you tell me if this investigator was with a law enforcement agency? No, he said. Might this investigator be a journalist? I asked. It might, he said. He refused to go any further.

After the interview, I surveyed the list of possible suspects and quickly hit on a likely candidate: David Brock, the *American Spectator* writer of Troopergate fame. I called Brock at home. "Can we go off the record?" Brock asked. Sure, I said. Yeah, he told me sheepishly. He had passed this information to Aldrich over lunch months earlier. But it was only a rumor that he, Brock, couldn't possibly verify. He never imagined that Aldrich would actually run with it and was somewhat chagrined. I told Brock he couldn't remain off the record. The president was being smeared with a bogus sex charge. He had an obligation to set the record straight. Brock agreed to come forward, and I wrote a story for the next week's *Newsweek* about the highly questionable origins of Aldrich's charge. As it happened, Brock stole my thunder a bit. Upon learning that Aldrich was to appear that Sunday on ABC's *This Week*, he called one of the show's regulars, conservative commentator George Will, and gave him a heads-up about his own role. As a result, Will was able to sandbag Aldrich that morning before most of the country had an opportunity to read my story. Still, I got my share of credit—at least from the Clinton White House. Later that Sunday morning, I was invited to appear on the CNN talk show *Reliable Sources* to discuss the Aldrich-Brock affair and ran into an ecstatic George Stephanopoulos. "Congratulations, Mike," Stephanopoulos said as he shook my hand. "You have exposed Gary Aldrich's lies and David Brock's sleaze."

CHAPTER EIGHT

1. In June 1998, Julie Hiatt Steele filed a lawsuit in U.S. District Court in the District of Columbia charging me and *Newsweek* with breach of contract. The suit charged that Steele's conversations with me—in March and July of 1997—were off the record and that I violated that promise by publishing her name in the August 11, 1997, edition. *Newsweek*'s lawyers have described Steele's claims as "fantasy" and moved to dismiss the complaint. The notes of my conversations with Steele do not reflect any request that her comments be considered off the record, and no such assurances were ever given her. (In retrospect, it seems to me possible that Willey told Steele she had spoken to me off the record, and Steele assumed that the same ground rules would apply when I met with her in March.) In any case, Steele voiced no objections to her name appearing in the magazine at the time and continued to call me to chat after the story ran. She even apologized for failing to give the picture of Willey and the president to *Newsweek;* instead, she acknowledged, she had sold the photo to the tabloid *National Enquirer* before the *Newsweek* story appeared.

On January 7, 1999, Steele was indicted by a federal grand jury on three counts of obstruction of justice and one count of making false statements to the FBI. The indictment, brought by Kenneth Starr's prosecutors, charged, among other things, that Steele lied when she signed an affidavit in the Paula Jones case in February 1998 stating that Willey had never told her the story of her encounter with Bill Clinton until the day in March 1997 when I was on my way to her house to see if she backed up her friend's story.

In May 1999, a mistrial was declared when the jury was unable to reach a verdict. For a fuller discussion of Steele's case and my role in it, see the Afterword, page 359.

CHAPTER NINE

1. For the first fourteen months of this period, according to Lewinsky, Clinton would not ejaculate while Lewinsky was performing the act. On one occasion, after a December 31, 1995, encounter in which she performed oral sex after Clinton fondled and kissed her breasts, Lewinsky described watching the president turn away and masturbate in the bathroom near the sink. It is a staple of the detective game to look for the signature acts of the subject. When I read Lewinsky's depiction of this episode in Ken Starr's report in September 1998, I was immediately reminded of the account provided to me by the anguished and anonymous caller to *Newsweek* in August 1997 (see pp. 161–163).

2. When the report by independent counsel Ken Starr revealed that this was the date that, according to Lewinsky, Clinton had cut off their sexual relationship, there was some speculation that the president might have acted because he had somehow been tipped off, or at a minimum was expecting, the adverse Supreme Court ruling in the Jones case. But there may have been another factor on Clinton's mind that prompted him to seek to sever his ties to Lewinsky that weekend.

   In the weeks prior to his Saturday, May 24, meeting with Lewinsky, national media attention had focused on the case of U.S. Air Force first lieutenant Kelly Flinn, the bomber pilot who was facing a court-martial over charges that she had conducted an adulterous relationship with the husband of an enlisted woman and lied about it to air force investigators. The prospect that the twenty-six-year-old Flinn could be imprisoned over issues growing out of an illicit sexual relationship provoked considerable criticism from members of Congress; it also prompted military officials to defend their policy of forbidding adultery on the ground that it was potentially disruptive to morale. On May 22, the controversy was effectively ended when U.S. Air Force secretary Sheila Widnall accepted Flinn's resignation from the air force. In so doing, Widnall rejected Flinn's request for an honorable discharge, granting her instead a general discharge—a move that barred Flinn from ever flying in the air force reserves and forced her to surrender all pension and veterans benefits. In explaining her decision, Widnall said that while the charges of adultery were less serious, Flinn's "lack of integrity" in denying the affair required her to face some form of punishment. It is, of course, impossible to know whether the commander in chief was influenced in his dealings with Monica Lewinsky by concern that his own conduct could be equated with that of the publicly humiliated and officially sanctioned Kelly Flinn.

3. Much later, Tripp's letter to *Newsweek* turned out to be a somewhat significant document. The sentiments expressed in the second paragraph (questioning whether anything actually happened between Willey and the
president) were similar to those in the three-page "talking points" Lewinsky handed Tripp on the afternoon of January 14, 1998—which Ken Starr's
investigators initially thought might have been drafted by someone in the
White House. Questions were then raised as to why *Newsweek* didn't publish
Tripp's letter when she wrote it. But at the time, Tripp's letter seemed quib-
bling at best. She didn't dispute any of the factual assertions in the article—nor did she challenge the accuracy of any quotes (Starr's September
1998 report to Congress wrongly characterizes the letter as charging that
she had been "misquoted," an assertion not borne out by the full text published here).

CHAPTER TEN

1. When the contents of this letter were disclosed in the spring of 1998, there
was much attention to the proposed selling of this sealed court document.
Some critics suggested it exposed Jones's sleazy motives. But there is dis-
agreement about who first suggested the idea—and none of those involved
attribute it to the client. Cammarata said Davis thought of it while they were
writing the letter, and they never discussed it with Jones. Carpenter-
McMillan insisted it was Cammarata who proposed the idea and that when
she and Jones first heard it they had the same reaction: "We thought it was
disgusting."

2. Another reason for Davis and Cammarata's urgency was that in early September they would have to respond to a motion filed by Kathleen Willey's
attorney, Dan Gecker, to quash the subpoena they had issued for her testimony. Cammarata would have to lay out in court papers what he understood
Willey's allegations to be, based on the anonymous telephone call he had
received in January. Bennett had made it clear to Cammarata that any such
move to file new allegations about the president would kill the settlement
offer on the table.

3. Bennett's direct role in the Kirkland saga was documented when Judge
Susan Webber Wright released portions of Kirkland's deposition, taken on
October 23, 1997, in Little Rock. The deposition was nominally conducted by
Bill Bristow, who had signed the subpoena for Kirkland's appearance. This
maintained the fiction that it was Ferguson's lawyer, not Bill Clinton's, who
was "dragging out Paula Jones's prior sex life." But Bennett was present and
started passing notes to Bristow to prompt him on questions to ask the witness—a process Jones lawyer Jim Fisher quickly moved to put on the
record:

Fisher: Sir, did you see Mr. Bennett, the man sitting to Mr. Bristow's right,
passing notes to him a few minutes ago? . . . Did you see him write some
notes and set them right here?

Kirkland: Yes.

Bennett: Yes, I wrote notes to my co-counsel. I'll stipulate to that. . . . Is
there something wrong with that, Counsel? If you are going to make innuen-
dos about me, let's put it on the record. . . .

Kirkland: Yes, I did see a note set over there, yes.

Fisher: And then Mr. Bristow asked you some more questions?

Kirkland: Yes.

Fisher: Nothing further.

Kirkland acknowledged that day that while he had talked with members of the president's legal team in the past, he had never met Bristow before the deposition began. And there were other potential problems with his story. He got key dates wrong, testifying, for example, that he had first discussed the incident with Clinton's lawyers in either 1991 or 1992—at least two years before Jones had gone public. He also acknowledged that at the party in question, he had been drinking heavily and smoking marijuana.

Jones herself adamantly denied Kirkland's account, insisting that she did not even remember meeting him. That does not mean, of course, that there wasn't some truth to it, or that Jones didn't have a lively sexual past. She acknowledged to her lawyers having five or six sexual partners before she married, though she said none were one-night stands. Clinton's lawyers later located someone who claimed he had met Jones at a bar a few months before the incident at the Excelsior Hotel and that she performed oral sex on him. Managers at an Arkansas trucking company also testified they had fired Jones in 1987 in part for violating the company's dress code. (One witness was quoted as saying the young Paula Corbin had been "walking around the place and flirting with men" but the then personnel director of the company insisted that this was not the grounds for her dismissal.) But Jones's new lawyers believed they had effectively blunted this line of attack when Kirkland imploded as a witness. In sealed court papers, they expressed outrage at the "smear campaign," especially given Bennett's public vows never to use such tactics on behalf of a client who was such a valiant defender of women's rights. "It gave us all a sense of righteous indignation," said Fisher. Bennett, for his part, later argued that evidence of Jones's sexual history was ultimately made necessary to raise questions about her claims that she was emotionally traumatized by the events in the Excelsior Hotel that day. In addition, Ferguson's lawyer, Bristow, had advised the president's legal team that such testimony plays well with Arkansas juries.

CHAPTER ELEVEN

1. Tripp also claimed in this conversation that I was "working on a book deal. He's doing an all-the-president's-women kind of thing." Actually, at the time Tripp made this comment she was wrong. But it is worth spelling out what Tripp may have been referring to.

   In the late spring of 1997, Glenn Simpson of *The Wall Street Journal* and I had explored the idea of collaborating on a book about the many scandals that had afflicted the Clinton presidency. We wrote up a rough outline of a proposal that included a brief, anonymous allusion to the Kathleen Willey incident. I did not disclose Willey's identity to Simpson for the same reason I did not disclose it to Ann McDaniel, my editor, or for that matter, to Joe Cammarata. At the time, Willey was off the record and I was honor-bound to protect that. The proposal contained no reference whatsoever to Monica Lewinsky, whose name I still did not know. In any case, the idea never got much beyond a lunch Simpson and I had with my agent, Gail Ross, in the early summer of 1997. The proposal was never completed; no material was circulated to any New York publishers. Like hundreds of Washington journalists, we were two writers entertaining a book idea that never got off the ground.

In July, in one of his items about Kathleen Willey, Matt Drudge charged that I had been holding back the story, saving it for a book. That was nonsense. As chapters 6 through 8 make clear, until Cammarata's subpoena, there was no story to write, especially given Willey's refusal to go public with her charge of sexual misconduct against the president. But Drudge's bogus allegations were a jolting reminder that it can be dangerous to try to mix book proposals with the obligations of daily or weekly journalism. Simpson and I agreed to forget the entire project. All the reporting that I did about Willey, Linda Tripp and Monica Lewinsky in 1997 was done strictly for *Newsweek*. Ann McDaniel was regularly briefed. The discussions that led to this volume did not start until late January 1998, after the Lewinsky story broke. My negotiations with Crown over this book and my decision to take a leave of absence from the magazine in late 1998 to complete it were made with the full consent of McDaniel and other senior editors at the magazine.

2. Whether Goldberg used this line in talking about the taping is open to doubt. The tape of the September 18, 1997, phone call shows that she did say something similar to Tripp, but in a different context. Tripp was talking about her hopes of finding another job and mentioned that she had an application pending to become director of special events for the army. Because this was a career position, Tripp thought it would protect her from dismissal if her role in outing the president's relationship with Lewinsky became public. Goldberg replied: "Yeah, but bubeleh, you blow the whistle on the big kahuna and you ain't gonna be working for the government."

3. Goldberg was certainly right, in one sense: The time with Asness was intoxicating for Tripp. A few weeks later, Tripp gave Lewinsky a full report on the weekend. Asness's house, Tripp said, was "incredible"—with a swimming pool and tennis courts, "ten or twelve" bedrooms, "like ten bathrooms," and a crew of servants who provided the guests with slippers and robes and turned down the beds at night. Asness never directly brought up Tripp's comments about Kathleen Willey. But she did engage Tripp in conversation about other women rumored to have had romantic liaisons with the president, raising further questions about her ultimate purpose in cultivating Tripp.

In particular, Tripp told Lewinsky, Asness had "asked me a lot about Debbie Schiff and Marsha Scott"—two White House aides whose relations with the president had been the subject of periodic gossip. According to Tripp, Asness explained that she and two others close to the First Lady had been recruited to "get rid of" Schiff, the attractive blonde from the campaign plane who became an Oval Office secretary. The recruitment failed, and Asness had concluded that Mrs. Clinton no longer thought Schiff was a threat "because she is still there." Asness also told Tripp how she had deployed her "absolutely stunning" daughter-in-law to test the president's willpower. At a holiday party, Asness asked her to approach the president. Asness planned to snap a photograph to record Clinton's reaction and then another, a few seconds later, after he learned the identity of the temptress. According to Tripp, Asness said her daughter-in-law obliged, and Clinton, in a photograph recorded for posterity, was "instant lech."

Tripp told Lewinsky that Asness had asked her to "commit to coming up once every eight weeks." Later, she invited Tripp on a cruise—and offered to help her find lucrative employment in the private sector. Why was she so interested in Tripp? Was she on a secret mission for the First Lady, who perhaps saw Tripp as a useful source of intelligence? Or had she been deputized by the president himself to, in Goldberg's phrase, "love-bomb" Tripp back into the fold?

Tripp quoted Asness as saying, "You know, Linda, I like to be mentally stimulated. I like to enjoy the people I'm with. I like them to be articulate, bright and mentally stimulating. . . . That's why I like you so much."

Asness herself has refused to talk to the press about her cultivation of Tripp. And perhaps because Asness never made any direct reference to Tripp's upcoming testimony in the Paula Jones case, the Asness matter was never pursued as part of Ken Starr's investigation of the president.

4. The importance of Kate in the Lewinsky saga went largely unnoticed after the release of independent counsel Kenneth Starr's report in September 1998. The sole exception was an admirable article by Byron York in the December 1998 *American Spectator,* which focused on the role of UN ambassador Bill Richardson in the Lewinsky job search. York was the first to describe the October 6 conversation about Kate as a "turning point in the scandal," a formulation I have adopted here. But York appeared to have missed the July 20, 1998, report of Kate Friedrich's interview with the FBI, which raises serious questions about Tripp's claims to have learned anything about Lewinsky from Kate.

5. Portions of the transcripts of these tapes were deleted by congressional redactors before they were released to the public.

6. In their September 29, 1997, conversation, secretly taped by Goldberg, Tripp invented a conversation with me in which I am supposed to have encouraged her to write a book. "Let me tell you what else Mike said the last time I spoke to him . . . ," Tripp told Goldberg that day. "He said, 'Based on your notes, I think you must plan to do a book.'"

The only "notes" Tripp shared with me were excerpts from the book proposal she showed me at her home in April—a book proposal that, as readers of chapter 7 will recall, had been prepared more than a year earlier by Maggie Gallagher. Tripp also claimed I'd told her that, while I doubted she'd find a publisher "in the present climate," she should work with me to "allow some of this to get out into the mainstream media" in order to create a more favorable environment. This, too, is ridiculous. As a reporter, the one thing I would never have settled for is part of the story. The entire purported conversation with me that Tripp related to Goldberg that day is reminiscent of the apparently bogus conversation with "Kate of the NSC" Tripp recounted to Lewinsky a few days later. Tripp's Machiavellian mind seems to have been working in overdrive that week.

CHAPTER TWELVE

1. His most valuable contribution, I soon learned from a Democratic Party source, had gone unrecorded. According to my source, Kaye had boasted to party fundraisers that he recommended that the First Family check their insurance policies to see if they would pay the cost of defending the president in the Paula Jones lawsuit. When it was first reported in *The Wall Street Journal* that Chubb and State Farm were paying the president's legal bills, Bennett had taken the public credit for this discovery.

2. After the Lewinsky scandal broke, the First Lady's office and Kaye denied to my colleague Mark Hosenball that Kaye ever purchased dresses for Mrs. Clinton. However, there is some evidence to suggest Kaye's beneficence for the First Family went beyond what was publicly reported. In an angry (and unsent) letter to Clinton she wrote in September 1997, retrieved from her computer by Ken Starr's investigators, Lewinsky vented about the treatment she was receiving compared to the "golden" treatment afforded Oval Office secretary Debbie Schiff, who, she wrote, "can prance around in your shoes or stand in front of fifty people gathered for dinner bragging about just how she obtained your shirt for Walter to have bespoke shirts made for you."

   In her May 7, 1998, grand jury testimony, White House secretary Betty Currie was questioned about the contents of this letter. The following exchange took place between prosecutor Robert Bittman and Currie:

   Q. Okay. Do you know whether he [Walter Kaye] in fact has actually purchased custom-made shirts for the president? Had custom-made shirts made because Mr. Kaye is from New York, is that right?

   A. Correct.

   Currie was then asked if she was aware that Kaye was a "very wealthy man." She professed not to know.

   Q. Okay. Did you know that he had custom-made shirts—

   A. Correct. I did know that.

   Q. Okay. And that appears to be what this is relating, that Debbie had shirts taken from the president to get his size, sent them to Walter Kaye, who had custom-made shirts then made for the president and then gave them as a gift to the president.

   A. Correct.

3. As an example of how President Clinton's allies sought to downplay the level of attention given Lewinsky's job search, the phone call to Lewinsky's apartment that night is a fascinating case study. Richardson, under oath, denied to Kenneth Starr's investigators that he personally talked to Monica Lewinsky that night and insisted that his assistant, Isabelle Watkins, made the call. Lewinsky swore that it was Richardson himself who got on the phone and recalled being "shocked" that he had done so. In a contemporaneous conversation with Tripp, Lewinsky referred to talking directly to Richardson. Starr's investigators later found phone records showing that a call to Lewinsky's apartment that evening was placed from Richardson's direct office extension at the UN Mission.

4. The two women at this point had an extended discussion about the political implications of having Jordan help Lewinsky with her job search. Lewinsky said that it was much better if Jordan, rather than a member of the White

House staff, coordinated the networking. Tripp said she couldn't remember; during the controversy over Hubbell, was Vernon mentioned? In asking the question, Tripp may well have been disingenuous. There had been many press reports that Whitewater independent counsel Kenneth Starr had been investigating the extensive efforts by White House aides and allies to arrange consulting work for Hubbell after he was forced to resign from the Justice Department over charges that he had bilked his old law firm. Jordan's name had come up in several of those reports, including an item I wrote for *Newsweek*'s Periscope section that spring.

Yes, Lewinsky told Tripp, Jordan's name had come up in the Hubbell affair. Still, she said, there's a big difference. If Bowles were involved, Lewinsky explained, somebody could say, "Well, they gave her a job to shut her up. They made her happy. . . . And he works for the government and shouldn't have done that."

"With the other one," Lewinsky continued, referring to Jordan, "you can't say that."

5. In this deposition Jones added a few new details to her story of her encounter with Clinton that she hadn't mentioned to me when I interviewed her in February 1994. Most significantly, Jones claimed that as she proceeded to leave the room that day, Clinton rushed up behind her and "put his hand on the door to where I could not open it up any further." She added that Clinton "stopped me and he says, 'You're a smart girl, let's keep this between ourselves.'" Jones also claimed that when Clinton slipped his hands up her culottes, he was "going up to my middle pelvic area."

Jones's lawyers insisted that these new details—never before mentioned—were small variations that are inevitable in recounting the events of long ago. And, it is worth noting that the essential details—including Jones's claim that Clinton exposed himself—remained consistent. Still, the new wrinkles appear to have been designed to shore up holes in Jones's legal case. Any hint that Clinton physically restrained Jones from leaving the room, even momentarily, would make her claims far more damaging.

But Jones's overall case was weakened in any event during the deposition when Clinton lawyer Bob Bennett repeatedly hammered her for any evidence that she suffered at the workplace after her encounter with Clinton. Jones, who had never complained about workplace retaliation when I interviewed her in February 1994, was hard-pressed to come up with any tangible examples beyond her recollection that she did not receive flowers on "secretary's day"—a complaint the president's lawyer would later shrewdly use to his advantage to ridicule the plaintiff.

6. There is support for Flowers's claim in an October 1991 conversation secretly tape-recorded by Flowers. In it, she expresses concern because "they were questioning me about how I found out about the job." Flowers says she responded that she learned from the personnel office that it would be "advertised in the newspaper. . . . And I pursued it from there." Clinton responds: "Good for you."

This apparently shows Flowers volunteering the newspaper ad defense before she talked to Clinton. But later in the conversation, Flowers and Clinton revisit the issue in the context of media inquiries:

Flowers: "Well, the only thing that concerns me where I'm, where I'm concerned, at this point, is the state job."

Clinton: "Yeah, I never thought about that, but as long as you say you've just been looking for one, you'd, uh, check on it. If they ever asked if you'd talked to me about it, you can say no."

A few seconds later, Clinton raises the Perry case: "Has the grievance committee ruled yet?"

"Uh, no, not that I know of."

Flowers then provides Clinton with a more detailed explanation of the questioning. The conversation moves on to other subjects—and then once again Clinton returns to the grievance procedure: "All right. I'm gonna nose around. If I find out anything, I'll call you."

In the conversation that follows, Flowers says that even if the committee rules Perry should have Flowers's job, the Clinton appointee who oversees the agency—Don Barnes, the husband of Judy Gaddy—"can always say, 'No, I won't,' and period, that's it." Clinton agrees. He then expresses a small concern that Perry could file a lawsuit if that happens and asks Flowers if she was represented by a lawyer. One appointed by the tribunal, Flowers replies.

The conversation in its entirety is open to two interpretations. The first, more sympathetic to Clinton, is that when he told Flowers to deny ever talking to him about her state job—an apparent falsehood since they were talking about it, at a minimum, in that very conversation—he was thinking only about media inquiries. The other is that Clinton was instructing Flowers to lie in an official state proceeding. That interpretation might be supported by the fact that Clinton learned a moment later that the grievance procedure might still be ongoing. It is also worth noting that Flowers's suggestion that Clinton appointee Don Barnes overrule any adverse recommendation is precisely what subsequently happened.

7. Broaddrick was later subpoenaed by the Jones lawyers and filed an affidavit denying that she had ever had an unwanted sexual encounter with Clinton. But when questioned by Starr's investigators in early 1999, and granted immunity, Broaddrick asserted that her affidavit in the civil suit was false. Her chilling account to Starr's FBI agents of what she alleges happened to her was later turned over to the House Judiciary Committee and, although never made public, was credited as being a factor in persuading wavering House Republicans to vote articles of impeachment against Clinton. In February 1999, Broaddrick provided her own public accounting in interviews with, among others, *The Wall Street Journal*'s Dorothy Rabinowitz and *The Washington Post*'s Lois Romano. (She first gave an interview to NBC's Lisa Myers, but NBC executives held it up until after the *Post*'s account ran.)

Years later, in the summer of 1991, as he was preparing to run for president, Broaddrick claimed Clinton had her summoned to another nursing home seminar in north Little Rock and talked to her by the stairwell. "I'm so sorry for what happened," Clinton said to her, according to Broaddrick's account. "I'm not the man I used to be. How can I make it up to you?" Broaddrick said she told Clinton to "go to hell" and walked off.

Starr's deputies decided not to pursue the Broaddrick matter in large part because she made no claim that she had been pressured to conceal her story during the course of the Paula Jones lawsuit—the only legal basis for them to investigate the matter. They also noted that her claims were clouded by the fact that Broaddrick was having an extramarital affair at the time of the encounter with a man who later became her husband. A nurse and friend of Broaddrick's, Norma Rogers, told my *Newsweek* colleague Mark Hosenball that she met Broaddrick in the hotel immediately after the incident. Broaddrick had badly swollen lips and described them as having been caused by forced sex with Bill Clinton. The president's lawyers have dismissed the Broaddrick allegations as a scurrilous story that has been fanned for years by Clinton's bitter political foe, Sheffield Nelson. Publicly, Clinton's lawyer, David Kendall, called the claim "absolutely false." Privately, Clinton's lawyers have conceded that Clinton may have had consensual sex with Broaddrick but insist that he would have never forced himself upon an unwilling participant.

8. At this time, Willey later said, she was getting advice on what to do about all this from a wealthy businessman named Nathan Landow. Landow was the father of Harolyn Cardozo, the woman she had worked with in the White House social office. He also was a powerhouse Democratic contributor with friends in high places, especially in the office of Vice President Al Gore. He had met Willey three years earlier, when his daughter invited the recently bereaved widow to the family estate in Easton, Maryland. (That estate seemed to have an eerie connection to suicides. Cardozo had extended a similar invitation the previous July to Vince Foster, having learned that he was feeling stressed out. Two days after returning from a weekend at the Landow home, Foster killed himself.) They had struck up an on-again, off-again relationship that seemed to become on again in the summer of 1997, right about the time Willey's name was surfacing on Drudge and then in *Newsweek*. In October, Landow again invited Willey to Easton. He chartered a plane and flew her down, at a cost of more than $1,000. While there, Willey said, Landow questioned her about the legal fight over her testimony in the Jones case. According to Willey, her host suggested that she could simply keep her mouth shut about the whole thing.

CHAPTER THIRTEEN

1. It was right about this time that the president's legal team got the first whiff of the cabal of elves behind the Jones legal team. In late November, Clinton lawyer Bob Bennett got a phone call from a woman in Chicago. The woman had been at a meeting with a young lawyer named Richard Porter and his wife. The woman relayed how Porter stepped away to take a call on his cell phone. Porter's wife then explained: It was about the Paula Jones case. "He's always working on that case," Porter's wife allegedly said. "It's driving me crazy."

   For Bennett, it suddenly clicked. For years, he had been suspicious about the briefs filed in the Jones case. They were too polished and professional to have been written by the lawyers whose names were on them and figured that somebody had to be helping out. But he had no inkling who. When he got the tip about Porter, Bennett thought he had it figured out. Porter was with Kirkland & Ellis. That was Kenneth Starr's firm. On December 3, he served a subpoena on the law firm demanding that it turn over all documents in its possession related to the Jones case.

Kirkland & Ellis later informed one of Bennett's partners they had no such documents. Bennett's tip had been right as far as it went, but he was off on his subpoena. Porter actually wasn't doing any of the legal work on the Jones case. As he later described it, he was more of a schmoozer—the "switchboard operator" who put parties together, but never wrote any briefs.

Bennett, in short, had gone after the wrong elf.

CHAPTER FOURTEEN

1. In Clinton's version—an account he wrote out by hand and then stored under his desk at the White House—Browning was "angry and sulking" and said "something hateful" when he approached her. He agreed that the two went off to a corner to talk, but according to Clinton, Browning complained that she "didn't have much money to live on" and that she "loved me for years since she was very young" but that he "had never really been there for her because it wasn't my friendship that she wanted." She agreed that she would describe her book as "fantasy," but "she needed the money and she didn't care if it hurt me or the presidency, that others had made money and she felt abandoned." Because Browning was in such an "agitated state," Clinton wrote, he asked his aide Marsha Scott to listen in. Scott then wrote her own account underneath Clinton's: "I stood by the president the entire conversation and heard and watched [Browning] the entire time. The conversation lasted over thirty minutes . . . and at times she was very animated and threatening acting. . . . It was a bizarre conversation because she repeatedly said her story was not true but that she was angry and needed money. She would throw out an accusation and then say it was a lie. It was this erratic behavior that made me stay so attentive. . . ."

   In January 1998, Clinton's lawyers introduced these notes as evidence in the Jones case to impeach Browning's testimony that Clinton had acknowledged a sexual addiction. On March 6, 1998, Browning filed her own affidavit challenging the accuracy of Clinton's account and stating that the notes attributed to Scott were false. "She did not stand by Billy Clinton during my conversation with him. Neither she nor anyone other than possibly the two male Secret Service agents were in a position to hear our conversation." In December 1998, investigators for the House Judiciary Committee flew to Hot Springs to talk to others who attended the reunion. They came back with three affidavits from eyewitnesses to the Clinton-Browning encounter. None claimed to know what the two said to each other, but all supported Browning on one point: They did not recall seeing Marsha Scott, or anyone else, listening in.

   On September 14, 1998, Browning filed a lawsuit against Clinton alleging, among other things, that he and his agents engaged in a pattern of threats and intimidation to prevent her from publicly revealing their relationship through her novel *Purposes of the Heart*. The president's lawyers have moved to dismiss the complaint as groundless.

2. In February 1999, I posed a series of questions to Linda Tripp. Most of them revolved around the issue: Did she think anything I said or did during this

period influenced her course of action? Tripp declined to answer almost all of them. But one she chose to respond to, through her spokesman Phil Coughter, was whether my comments to her that day about not taking her material to a publisher influenced her decision not to do so. Tripp's terse response on this score was, according to Coughter, the only reason she raised with me the idea of going to a publisher was "because of the importance to her of getting the truth out." In the end, as Coughter noted, she chose another way to do that. (The only other comment Tripp offered was that, when she showed me a portion of her earlier book proposal at her home in April 1997, it was not to seek my advice, but simply demonstrate that she had already written about the Kathleen Willey incident before I asked her about it.)

CHAPTER FIFTEEN

1. To understand why Currie's account of the gift exchange is suspect, it is useful to review how few details about it she actually claimed to remember— and how even those details shifted each time she testified. Consider the simplest of issues: Where did Lewinsky give Currie the gifts? When first questioned by the FBI on January 24, 1998, Currie couldn't remember. "Currie is not sure where Lewinsky gave Currie the box, but it was not in the White House," reads the FBI report. (By May, she did remember going by Lewinsky's apartment to pick them up.) But when? This proved especially elusive. Questioned by the FBI on January 24, she said "sometime in December." When she testified before the grand jury three days later, Currie retreated. "I don't know when she gave them to me," she told prosecutor Robert Bittman. Bittman tried to pin her down:

Bittman: Was it within the last several months?
Currie: Can we use the six again?
Bittman: You want to use "within the last six months"?
Currie: Yeah.

By the time Currie testified before the grand jury in May, she had yet a third time frame. The exchange, she said, was "a couple weeks" after she had set up the December 28, 1997, meeting, when Clinton gave Lewinsky her gifts. That meant it took place in January 1998—just days before the Lewinsky story broke. But even that, Currie said, was "a guess again."

Compared to this fuzziness, there is one detail about the exchange Currie claimed in her May grand jury testimony that she did remember with great specificity: that when Lewinsky gave her the box of gifts, she said she was doing so because Michael Isikoff of *Newsweek* was asking questions about them. Here is an excerpt of Currie's testimony before the federal grand jury on May 6, 1998:

Currie: My recollection—the best I remember is Monica calling me and asking if I'd hold some gifts for her. I said I would. . . .
Bittman: What exactly did Monica say when—
Currie: The best I remember, she said that she wanted me to hold these gifts—hold this—she may have said gifts. I'm sure she said gifts, box of gifts—I don't remember—because people were asking questions. And I said, "Fine." . . .

Bittman: And these questions that were being asked, what were the questions? What was the nature of the questions?

Currie: The best I remember, she said that Mr. Isikoff was making inquiries about the gifts.

Bittman: Anyone else?

Currie: That's the only name she mentioned. It's the only name I remember.

There is one important problem with this account: It could not possibly have been true. I had never posed any questions to Monica Lewinsky, or to anyone associated with her, about gifts from the president. Lewinsky's own grand jury testimony confirmed that: "Do you recall any calls from Michael Isikoff that you would have told Betty about, calling about gifts from the president?" Lewinsky was asked on August 6, 1998. "No. Absolutely not," she replied. In fact, if the exchange took place when Lewinsky said it did, on December 28, 1997, Lewinsky had no reason to suspect I was even aware of her existence. Indeed, during the relevant time frame, I wasn't reporting on her or anyone else. December 28 was a Sunday. The week before, I, along with the rest of *Newsweek*'s employees, had been on vacation, and I took personal time off the following week and went to California. Nothing I could have said or done during those weeks could have prompted the conversation Currie claims to have had with Lewinsky. (Leave aside the logical implication of Currie's account: What did these women think I was going to do? Break into Lewinsky's apartment?)

It is equally implausible that any talks I had with Linda Tripp could have led to the conversation Currie purports to remember. My notes of my interviews with Tripp show no references to any gifts Clinton gave Lewinsky. And even if the subject had somehow come up, and I neglected to scribble it down, it stretches credulity to imagine that Tripp would have mentioned to Lewinsky that she was having any contacts with me at all during this time period.

Why, then, would Currie have invoked my name? The simplest explanation is that she confused the gifts with the separate inquiry I made more than two weeks later, on January 15, about the courier message slips showing Lewinsky's letters and packages to the White House (see chapter 19). I called Currie directly about the slips, and she later remembered the call quite well. But if Currie's memory was simply confused, it is useful to keep in mind that the White House lawyers who debriefed her before and after her grand jury appearances had a vested interest in maximizing that confusion. The debriefings were conducted primarily by associate White House counsel Cheryl Mills, who gave such a spirited defense of the president during his impeachment trial. The cornerstone of the defense efforts by Mills and other White House lawyers was to link all actions by the president, Betty Currie and Vernon Jordan to concerns about news media inquiries—mainly by me—rather than to any developments in the Paula Jones lawsuit. The reasons are rather simple: Whereas it was potentially illegal to conceal evidence in a lawsuit, it is not at all illegal to conceal evidence from and lie to the news media. Therefore, Currie's testimony that Lewinsky told her she was trying to hide the gifts from Michael Isikoff of *Newsweek* was an exceedingly convenient explanation for the White House—much more convenient than acknowledging what seems far more likely to have been the truth: that Currie (as Lewinsky testified) was acting at the direction of Bill Clinton, who was in fact trying to conceal the gifts from the Paula Jones lawyers who had subpoenaed them.

2. Among the skeptics was Bill Kovach, former Washington bureau chief of *The New York Times* and now curator of the Nieman Foundation at Harvard University. "I'm skeptical how candid it was," Kovach told the *Los Angeles Times* about the loving beach scene. "I have difficulty believing that we have, in that photograph, been witness to something deep and meaningful in the relationship between the president and the First Lady."

3. On August 6, 1998, Lewinsky described her feelings to the grand jury: "I was jealous, and it just seemed sort of something he had never—an aspect of their relationship that he had never really revealed to me, and it made it me feel bad."

4. Who was chiefly responsible for the stalemate is hard to tell. Lawyers for Jones believed that even at this late date Clinton's team was open to a settlement along the lines of the $700,000 offer negotiated back in August 1997—a deal, of course, that would not include any apology from the president. It was Jones and, perhaps more important, her husband, Steve, who were holding out for considerably more. In late November, under court pressure to make an effort to find a deal, the Dallas lawyers had met with the Joneses and urged them to permit them to make a reasonable counteroffer. But once again the couple held fast. Steve Jones talked once more about the indignities his family had suffered from the president's agents and about how, under the kind of deal the lawyers were discussing, Clinton wouldn't suffer at all. The Joneses then informed the lawyers they should counter with a demand for $2.6 million—a proposal that was forwarded to Judge Mehrige on December 3. Shortly thereafter, Jones lawyer David Pyke was talking on the phone with Mitch Ettinger, the Clinton lawyer who usually acted as liaison during settlement discussions. Referring to the $2.6 million proposal, Ettinger said: "You just blew it."

5. Only two days earlier, Willey later told the FBI, she had been out jogging early in the morning when a strange man, wearing a baseball cap and sweat pants, approached and started asking her a bunch of questions. The stranger knew the name of her lawyer, the names of her children. He even knew about her missing cat, "Bullseye," who had disappeared two months earlier. Willey told federal agents she ran away from the mystery jogger as fast as she could.

Ken Starr's agents later intensively investigated to determine whether Willey was the target of a White House–linked effort to intimidate her. Their initial theory—that the mystery jogger was ex-Clinton campaign detective Jack Palladino—was proven false when Palladino was able to provide evidence that he was elsewhere on the day in question. Starr's agents did find evidence that a lawyer for Maryland businessman and Democratic fundraiser Nathan Landow—who had substantial contacts with Willey in the months leading up to her testimony—had hired private investigators to research Willey's background. When called before a federal grand jury, Landow invoked his Fifth Amendment rights, and his lawyers refused to turn over documents relating to the private investigators on the ground that it was covered by the attorney-client privilege.

In February 1999, the case took another twist when Jared Stern, a private investigator in Rockville, Maryland, said he had been personally asked to conduct an undercover investigation of Willey that included checking her phone records, finding out what medication she took, and poring through her trash. Stern said he felt uncomfortable by the request and never did most of what he was asked. In interviews with various members of the news media, Stern described a bizarre scene in the winter of 1998 in which a man named Robert Miller, the then head of the private investigative firm Prudential Associates, which had done work in the past for Saul Schwartzbach, Landow's attorney, met him late one night in a parking garage to pass along the assignment. When Stern asked where this was coming from, Miller purportedly replied: "The White House."

It is hard to know what to make of Stern's account. In 1998 Miller died from cancer. Schwartzbach and Landow have denied any connection with the assignment described by Stern. Stern himself places the request in March, 1998, or at least two months after the alleged jogging incident related by Willey. Still, Stern says he was provided information by Miller that caused him to conclude the incident described by Willey actually took place. The matter was intensively investigated by Starr's office, but no charges were ever filed.

CHAPTER SIXTEEN

1. On September 2, 1996, Jane Sherburne, the special White House counsel overseeing Whitewater matters, got a surprising report about Susan McDougal's motivations. The day before, another White House lawyer, Mark Fabiani, had been called by Harvard University law professor Alan Dershowitz, who told him Susan McDougal had just called, seeking advice about how to handle Starr's threats to incarcerate her for refusing to testify before the Whitewater grand jury. McDougal had said she feared having to testify because she would have to acknowledge a sexual relationship with Clinton. Dershowitz told her she was right; there would be no way to avoid such subjects if she testified. He thought the White House should be aware of her concerns. Sherburne took no action on Fabiani's report, and on September 4, McDougal was held in contempt of court for refusing to testify. She was jailed the following week. In 1998, she was indicted for a second time on criminal contempt charges for failing to say what she knew about Whitewater.

   Starr's office heard about a relationship between Susan McDougal and Bill Clinton in debriefings of James McDougal. As McDougal later wrote in his book, *Arkansas Mischief* (co-written with *Boston Globe* journalist Curtis Willkie), he discovered the relationship when he picked up the phone in his house and heard Susan and the Arkansas governor having an "intimate" conversation.

   Susan McDougal has publicly denied any sexual relationship with Bill Clinton. Dershowitz declined to discuss their conversation with me, on the ground that it was protected by attorney-client privilege even though he never actually represented her.

The reports of a McDougal-Clinton relationship are of more than prurient interest. They provide a plausible motive for the allegation that triggered Starr's probe: David Hale's claim that in 1986, Clinton pressured him to make an illegal $300,000 loan to a sham company owned by Susan McDougal. Jim McDougal later said Hale's story was true. Only Clinton persisted in denying it. His defenders have argued that there was no reason for him to intercede on Susan McDougal's behalf. Starr's prosecutors showed that some of the loan money was briefly routed through the accounts of Whitewater to pay for an unrelated purchase of property. But no evidence ever surfaced that Clinton took an active interest in Jim McDougal's Byzantine dealings—or that he personally benefited. A far more likely scenario is that Clinton interceded with Hale as a favor for a woman with whom he was having a fling. If true, this may be the best single example of how Clinton's sexual recklessness was behind virtually all the problems that beset his presidency.

One more note of historical interest on this matter: In 1997, before any of the prosecutors had ever heard of Monica Lewinsky, Starr's office secretly drafted a proposed impeachment report to Congress alleging that Clinton committed perjury at the McDougals' trial in Little Rock when he denied under oath ever talking to David Hale about the loan to Susan McDougal or ever receiving a loan from Jim McDougal's Madison Guaranty Savings and Loan. The impeachment report was written by Steven Bates, the Starr prosecutor who ultimately became one of the principal authors of the report on Lewinsky. In the end, however, Starr's prosecutors concluded that—in light of Susan McDougal's continued refusal to testify—they had insufficient evidence to sustain an impeachment charge against Clinton based largely on the testimony of two convicted felons, Hale and Jim McDougal.

2. Precisely who asked for the lunch later emerged as a matter of dispute. Tripp testified before the federal grand jury on July 29, 1998, that it was Lewinsky who had pressed her to have lunch that day. "She was calling me from pay phones repeatedly," Tripp said, "and she had asked if I would meet with her on the thirteenth." But in her own grand jury testimony on August 6, 1998, Lewinsky suggested that it was really Tripp who asked for the lunch, saying during the phone call on January 9, "I agreed to meet with Linda on the thirteenth of January."

CHAPTER SEVENTEEN

1. In this book, I have tried as much as possible to identify all of my sources. I thought it especially important to do so because in this story the sources—including their motivations, backgrounds and connections—are as much a part of the saga as almost any other detail. But at the end of the day, I am bound by the ethics of my craft. The caller who tipped me off to the Lewinsky-Tripp sting continues to insist on anonymity; "I don't exist," the caller has said. Therefore, I can report only this: I got the phone call. The person who made it doesn't exist.

CHAPTER EIGHTEEN

1. For the ethically scrupulous, as well as those searching for inconsistency on my part, it is worth recalling that my primary objection to listening to the

tapes in October was that I would become part of the ongoing taping by Tripp of Lewinsky. But at this point, I assumed Tripp's taping was complete. In light of Starr's inquiry, the contents of the tapes were now a matter of public interest—and a far more reliable indicator of Lewinsky's description of her relationship with the president than the subjective impressions of Linda Tripp or anybody else the former intern may have talked to. This more than outweighed my reservations of three months earlier.

2. It had been an unusually busy day for Starr's office. That morning, the independent counsel and several deputies had briefly questioned Hillary Clinton at the White House. The interrogation of the First Lady, reported to have lasted no more than ten minutes, related to the office's investigation of allegations that the Clinton White House had improperly obtained hundreds of FBI files of past administration officials in an effort to find political dirt on prominent Republicans. Starr's inquiry found no credible evidence that the First Lady or any other White House officials had ordered the acquisition of the FBI files for any improper purpose.

3. The most damning paragraph of the "talking points" document notes the "dissimilar" nature between Willey's account to Tripp of what happened that day and Willey's subsequent claim in 1997 to have been sexually harassed. It also makes oblique reference to the claims of Julie Hiatt Steele that Willey had asked her to lie to corroborate her story:

"As a result of your [Tripp's] conversation with her [Willey] and subsequent reports that showed that she had tried to enlist the help of someone else in her lie that the president sexually harassed her, you now do not believe that what she claimed happened really happened. You now find it completely plausible that she herself smeared her lipstick, untucked her blouse, etc."

This does indeed seem to contain some "new ideas" about what Tripp should say. But the underlying sentiments and fundamental goal of distancing Tripp from Willey's claims parallel those in the unpublished letter to *Newsweek* that Tripp had faxed to me the previous August, which is quoted in full in chapter 9. In that letter, it will be recalled, Tripp also noted the alleged discrepancies between Willey's account of events in 1993 as Tripp recalled them and as Willey portrayed them to me in 1997. "One must wonder how such disparate allegations spanning a period of four years could have much, *if any*, credibility," the letter stated (emphasis added).

In the weeks and months that followed, there was considerable speculation—among Starr's prosecutors and in the press—that the "talking points" must have been written by a lawyer associated with President Clinton's defense.

Regrettably, my own early reporting helped feed this speculation: *Newsweek*'s original account on its America Online Web site on the evening of January 21, 1998, first disclosed the existence of the "talking points" and reported—perfectly accurately—that Starr's prosecutors were investigating to determine if they had been written by anybody associated with Clinton's legal team. In the excitement of the moment, I simply forgot about Tripp's August 1997 letter and the underlying similarities to the "talking points." A few weeks later, when I learned that Lewinsky's lawyer William Ginsburg was looking for a copy of the Tripp letter, I dug out a copy and immediately spotted the similarities. I pressed my editors for full disclosure as quickly as possible and *Newsweek,* in three separate issues over the ensuing months, cited the August 1997 Tripp letter as possibly casting doubt on the theory of secret White House authorship of the talking points. It is always possible, of course, that somebody associated with Clinton's defense, or even the president himself, encouraged the "talking points" to be written and even suggested some of the lawyerly language. But Lewinsky seemed to lay the controversy to rest in August 1998 when she testified that she herself wrote the document based on conversations she had had with Linda Tripp.

CHAPTER NINETEEN

1. On at least one point in this meeting, Bennett's comments appear to have been misleading. "No contacts w Paula Jones attorneys by C office," read the notes of one of Starr's deputies. Bennett clearly was omitting any mention of the meeting in Philadelphia the previous Thursday when Paul Rosenzweig was asked by his law school friend Jerome Marcus whether the independent counsel's office would be interested in pursuing the allegations of Linda Tripp. There is no question that Rosenzweig for starters knew of Marcus's work for the Jones legal team. How much he communicated this to Bennett is unclear. Yet Bennett's statement at the meeting also conflicts with the recollections of John Bates who, during his coffee with Jackie Bennett on Monday, was left with the clear impression that the information was coming "directly or indirectly" from lawyers associated with the "Jones legal team." Starr's office has since argued that the meeting in Philadelphia between Rosenzweig and his friends was relatively inconsequential. In February 1999, Jackie Bennett also told me that he thought that Rosenzweig's friends were associated with Linda Tripp, not Paula Jones, and when he made the statement about "no contacts" with the Jones team he was thinking about Jones's public lawyers in Dallas.

   Still, the failure to inform Justice about the Marcus-Rosenzweig meeting was one of a number of omissions that, taken together, later played into the hands of those building a case that Starr's office had misled the Justice Department in getting approval for the Lewinsky investigation. In addition, for example, none of Starr's deputies mentioned that Starr himself had been consulted in 1994 by Jones's previous lawyer, Gil Davis, about fashioning a constitutional case in opposition to the president's motion that he was immune from private litigation while in office. Grilled on this issue by Clinton lawyer David Kendall in his November 1998 appearance before the House Judiciary Committee, Starr noted that there had been public references to these conversations (by one newspaper, the *Washington Times*) and that they didn't constitute a conflict in any case because he had taken no position on the merits of Jones's claim.

   Finally, and perhaps most intriguing to the White House lawyers, there was the involvement of one of Starr's law partners, Richard Porter, in providing legal assistance and encouragement to the Jones team and in helping to steer Tripp to Starr's staff. There is no evidence that Starr had any knowledge of Porter's activities. Kirkland & Ellis has hundreds of partners. Porter was in Chicago, Starr in Washington. Still, there is some reason to believe Porter himself was worried that his activities might create a problem. Lucianne Goldberg's notebook records that on the critical day of Wednesday, January 14, she had five phone conversations with Porter. In her notations for the last contact, she wrote: "Call from Richard on mobile phone worried that Ken Starr might be hurt."

These matters were later investigated by the Justice Department, but as of this writing, no charges have been brought against any member of Starr's staff.

CHAPTER TWENTY

1. Actually, Starr's position, urged upon him by Jackie Bennett, was that the Lewinsky allegations were "related" to his office's ongoing investigation into the Hubbell payments and therefore he did not need the Justice Department's approval. The case for this was spelled out by Starr in a letter to Reno written late Thursday night, January 15, after the briefing Bennett gave Holder. (In that letter, Starr cites the tape of the Ritz-Carlton event, writing "on the tape, Ms. Lewinsky recounts the conversation in which Mr. Jordan urged her to lie." This was, of course, slightly more than the transcript actually shows.) Justice officials disagreed with Starr's position, concluding that the Lewinsky matter was too attenuated from the core of the Hubbell investigation. Rather than fight over this legal point, Starr's deputies agreed with Justice's conclusion that there needed to be a formal court-approved expansion of the independent counsel's authority.

2. Lewinsky later recalled Emmick's mentioning Betty Currie, or Vernon Jordan, or "possibly" the president as a candidate for a "sting" by Lewinsky. Starr himself would later deny that any of his men ever got that specific, saying they spoke with Lewinsky only in "generality" about those they wanted her to speak to while she was wired.

3. Did Starr's prosecutors violate Lewinsky's right to counsel by refusing her permission to talk to Frank Carter? In an affidavit filed with U.S. judge Norma Holloway Johnson on March 12, 1998, Lewinsky flatly asserted that Starr's prosecutors told her that "I could contact any other attorney, but I could not contact Mr. Carter." But Starr's prosecutors and the FBI agents— in their own affidavits—disputed Lewinsky's account. FBI agent Fallon said he even called Carter's office late that afternoon on Lewinsky's behalf. A hotel phone record, which Starr's office placed into the court record, shows a phone call from the hotel room to Carter's office at 5:23 P.M. According to Fallon's affidavit, Carter had left for the day and the person answering the phone declined to provide a forwarding number. Judge Johnson ultimately rejected Lewinsky's claim that she had been deprived the right to counsel. Still, it is hard to argue that the circumstances Lewinsky was facing that day were truly conducive to her exercising her constitutional right to call any lawyer she saw fit to call.

4. There were a number of media reports during this period stating that Starr's prosecutors drove Tripp home that night for a meeting with the Jones lawyers. This account fed White House conspiracy theories that the Jones lawyers colluded with Starr's office to set a perjury trap for the president. But these reports appear to be overblown. While Starr's agents did drive

Tripp home after the Tuesday "sting" at the Ritz-Carlton, the independent counsel's office denies that any of its employees drove Tripp home on Friday night when she met with Jones lawyer Wes Holmes. There is no evidence to contradict them. According to Moody, Tripp's lawyer at the time, Tripp took the subway to Federal Triangle that afternoon and then hopped on an express bus that took her home to Maryland.

In a television interview that aired February 12, 1999, Tripp did say she had casually mentioned to one of the FBI agents at the Ritz-Carlton that Friday that she planned to meet with one of Paula Jones's lawyers when she got home that evening. But how specific Tripp was, and whether the agent passed word along to one of Starr's prosecutors, is unclear. Starr's prosecutors have repeatedly insisted they had no prior knowledge of the Tripp meeting with Jones's lawyer Wes Holmes, although Starr has acknowledged that his office could have exercised tighter control over Tripp, their prime cooperating witness, during that period.

5. The Howard Johnson's meeting involving Moody, Conway, Bennett and Udolf didn't become public until the Steve Bates affidavit was entered into evidence as part of a pretrial hearing on Tripp's indictment in December 1999. Immediately, it raised legitimate questions as to whether Starr's deputies had been party to the "leaking" of the December 22 tape to *Newsweek*. I should point out here that we at *Newsweek* were unaware of the Howard Johnson's rendezvous at the time it took place. It is also not entirely clear precisely what Bennett or Udolf knew Moody was going to do with the tape after they gave it back to him. In her grand jury testimony, Tripp suggests that Moody told her Starr's deputies believed acquiescing in permitting *Newsweek* to listen to the tape would buy additional time for their investigation. They also might have thought it would fend off a potential critical article suggesting that Starr had plunged his office into a sex investigation without an adequate predicate. Certainly, I pursued that argument with everybody I spoke to that day, although we at *Newsweek* were mercifully kept in the dark about the precise mechanics by which the tape finally made it to our offices.

I should also add that my ability to report on the precise circumstances of the delivery of the tape to *Newsweek* was circumscribed by pledges of confidentiality made that evening. *Newsweek* did not at first identify who brought the tape because it was an explicit part of the bargain I entered into that evening. That, for those who wonder about such matters, is precisely how journalism works. We get stories, and obtain sensitive materials of public interest, by protecting sources. Fourteen months later, I felt compelled to name Moody in *Uncovering Clinton* because Tripp had testified he brought the tape to *Newsweek*—and Tripp's testimony at that point was a matter of public record. (Unfortunately, an editing error in the hardcover edition of *Uncovering Clinton* wrongly placed the time of the delivery as "later that afternoon." It is here corrected to 12:30 A.M., exactly the time *Newsweek* originally reported it obtained access to the tape in its February 2, 1998, issue. No deception was intended.) In the pretrial hearing on Tripp's wiretapping case, one of the prosecutors referred to an affidavit submitted by Conway stating that he accompanied Moody that night—both to the meeting at the Howard Johnson's and later to the offices of *Newsweek*. (For a fuller discussion on the Tripp case, see the Afterword, page 359.)

6. The full definition that Fisher proposed to use read as follows:

"For the purposes of this deposition, a person engages in 'sexual relations' when the person knowingly engaged in or causes—

1) contact with the genitalia, anus, groin, breast, inner thigh, or buttocks of any person with an intent to arouse or gratify the sexual desire of any person.

2) contact between any part of the person's body or an object and the genitals or anus of another person; or

3) contact between the genitals or anus of the person and any part of another person's body.

Contact means intentional touching, either directly or through clothing."

Wright at the deposition that day struck subsections 2 and 3, leaving only 1. Clinton's lawyers argued that a literal reading of the words excludes oral sex on the recipient's part: Clinton when receiving oral sex was not having contact with the "genitalia, anus, groin, breast, inner thigh or buttocks" of the other person. Therefore, it was argued Clinton did not commit perjury when he, a few moments later, denied having sexual relations under the modified definition with Monica Lewinsky.

Much overlooked, however, when Clinton's lawyers made that somewhat strained argument was Judge Wright's reasoning when she removed subsections 2 and 3. Bennett had just objected that sections 2 and 3 could be construed as encompassing wholly incidental contacts between two people. "[I]f the president patted me and said I had to lose ten pounds off my bottom, you could be arguing that I had sexual relations with him," the president's lawyer argued.

It was at that point that Wright agreed to restrict the definition because, she said, subsections 2 and 3 could be construed as encompassing *"nonconsensual contact"* between two people. What Wright was interested in was *"contact that is consensual."* She then reminded the parties: *"And the Court has ruled that consenting consensual contact is relevant in this case."*

Therefore, she said, she was restricting the definition of sexual relations to subsection 1 because it "encompasses intent." The plain meaning of this exchange was that Wright's purpose in narrowing the definition was not to exclude oral sex, but rather to insure that Clinton knew he was being asked about *"consensual"* sexual contact in all its forms. It was largely because of this exchange that Bob Bennett and other Clinton lawyers were stunned to learn in August 1998 that the president was going to argue he did not commit perjury at the deposition because he understood the definition to exclude oral sex. At the time, neither Bennett nor other Clinton lawyers imagined that the definition had any loopholes.

7. Even so, Clinton was skating on exceedingly thin ice. In later testimony before the federal grand jury, Betty Currie said that sometime in 1997 Clinton had in fact talked to her about finding Lewinsky a White House job. Erskine Bowles, the chief of staff, testified that in the late summer of 1997 Clinton had spoken to him about finding Lewinsky a White House job. Lewinsky herself contended that in the spring of that year, Clinton had told her to talk to Marsha Scott about finding a position in the White House. And, of course, Lewinsky also contended that Clinton had promised as early as the spring of 1996 that he would bring her back to the White House after the

presidential election that fall. So in order to respond truthfully to the question Fisher had asked ("Did you ever talk to anybody about the possibility of her obtaining a job in the White House?"), Clinton would have had to respond in the affirmative. He talked to Currie, Bowles, Lewinsky and quite possibly Scott about the possibility of finding Lewinsky a job. Instead, Clinton did what he would do repeatedly that day. In his own mind, he reformulated and then substantially narrowed the question to his liking and then answered only that small sliver of a question with a truthful response when he said: "I was not involved in her moving from being an intern to being a full-time employee. I had no involvement in it whatever."

8. Fisher: Now, seated to my right, two chairs down, is Ms. Paula Jones. Do you recall ever having met her before today?

   Clinton: No, I've said that many times. I don't.

   Fisher: Do you recall ever having seen her before early 1994, when she first made public her accusations against you?

   Clinton: No, I—I actually saw her on television then, just by accident. I just happened to be walking by a television in the office, and I remember I asked Bruce Lindsey to come there. I said, "Bruce, do we know this lady—who is this person?" That was my first surprised reaction.

9. There later was considerable debate about why Clinton responded the way he did. He had seemed to deny any sexual relationship with Flowers in 1992, when the former lounge singer first came forward with her story. So what made him change?

   A reasonable hypothesis would go as follows:

   Clinton knew when he walked into the Jones deposition that nobody really believed his 1992 denials. Therefore, if he simply answered "no" when Fisher asked the question, it was inevitable that some press commentators would accuse the president of perjury. So he gave the least damaging answer he could possibly give without reviving the Flowers issue all over again. Surely, he might have thought, nobody was going to make a fuss over how many *times* he had sex with her.

   As to why Clinton chose to date their supposedly single sexual contact when he did, it is useful to remember that 1977 was the earliest possible time that Clinton could choose. That is the year Flowers says the two of them met. Clinton was then attorney general, not governor. Chelsea Clinton wasn't born until February 1979. Had Clinton acknowledged sexual relations with Flowers any time later than 1977, he was vulnerable to accusations of either cheating on his pregnant wife or philandering while the father of a young child. Of course, according to Flowers's account, their sexual relationship was active and passionate throughout Hillary Clinton's pregnancy and continued right through Chelsea Clinton's childhood until she was ten years old.

CHAPTER TWENTY-ONE

1. There was later much confusion about this second meeting between the president and his secretary, but it was arguably the most serious act of wrongdoing by Clinton in the entire Lewinsky affair. The president's lawyers argued that the first time Clinton met with Currie on Sunday, to "refresh my memory" with patently false statements, it was not a case of witness tamper-

ing because the secretary was not a witness in the Paula Jones lawsuit. To be sure, Clinton had virtually invited the Jones lawyers to call her as a witness the day before, when he repeatedly invoked her name on all matters that appeared suspicious relating to Lewinsky. ("She came by to see Betty," Clinton said about Lewinsky's Christmas week visit to the White House. "I think Betty suggested he meet with her," he said about how Lewinsky came to get job help from Vernon Jordan.) Indeed, by the time they headed back to Dallas, according to Jones lawyer Wes Holmes, he and his colleagues were already planning to subpoena Currie.

But by the time of this second session on Wednesday morning, there could have been no question in Clinton's mind that Currie was going to be a crucial witness in a federal grand jury investigation. (Although Currie's subpoena was dated January 20, it wasn't served until the evening of January 21.) Clinton's flurry of false statements to her that day—"I was never alone with Monica, right?"—could therefore have constituted a far stronger case of witness tampering on a far more consequential matter: a federal criminal inquiry, not a mere civil lawsuit. Why, then, didn't Ken Starr or the House Republicans who impeached Clinton make more of this?

The answer, it appears, is rooted in a critical blunder by one of Starr's deputies, Robert Bittman, first discovered in January 1999 by David Tell of the *Weekly Standard.* During her initial interrogation by the FBI on January 24, 1998, Currie placed the timing of the second session with Clinton as the "next time" she saw Clinton after the late night phone call informing her about the *Washington Post* story, "whenever Clinton was next in the White House." That was unquestionably Wednesday morning, January 21, when Clinton knew about Starr's investigation. But when Currie testified before the grand jury on January 27, she got confused about the night she got the phone call from the president about the *Post* story when Bittman got his own timing mixed up. When she described Clinton's calling her about "whatever story that broke on Wednesday," Bittman, who was doing the questioning, quickly interrupted her with the wrong information: "The story broke on Tuesday morning in *The Washington Post.*" There then followed this exchange:

Currie: "It was Tuesday morning?"

Bittman: "It was Tuesday morning that the story broke in the print media. It was on Monday that it broke in a report called the Drudge Report."

Currie: "Then he may have called me Monday night."

Incredibly, Starr, in his report to the Congress, perpetuated this confusion by saying that the second witness-coaching session between Clinton and Currie took place on Tuesday, January 20, or Wednesday, January 21, 1998. No small matter. In so doing, the independent counsel lost the best opportunity it had to build a case that Clinton tampered with a witness and obstructed justice in a grand jury proceeding.

EPILOGUE

1. A transcript of Blumenthal's June 4 grand jury testimony shows that the supposed question about the president's religion actually arose after Blumenthal had just finished relaying his conversation with Clinton on January 21, 1998, in which he cited to him the First Lady's comments earlier in the

day that he "ministers to troubled people all the time." Blumenthal said he told the president that he should not "minister" in such a way anymore. Shortly after that, Starr deputy Sol Wisenberg, with perhaps excessive sarcasm, asked Blumenthal the question: "Did the president . . . tell you that part of his ministry with Ms. Lewinsky in any way, shape or form was in engaging in any kind of sexual activity with her?"

The question about whether Blumenthal ever asked Mrs. Clinton about whether her husband has a "sex addiction" arose in the context of questions about his meetings with the Clintons to discuss articles being prepared by the news media. Noting that when the Lewinsky story broke there had been articles in the media speculating about whether the president suffered from sexual addiction, Starr deputy Karin Immergut asked Blumenthal, "Did you prepare the president and/or First Lady for responding to any questions that might arise because of the nature of the Lewinsky case about sexual addiction?"

A perhaps even more questionable case of Blumenthal's manipulation of the news media came after his first grand jury appearance on February 26, 1998, when he appeared on the courthouse steps and made a ringing denunciation of Starr's inquisitorial tactics. "Today, I was forced to answer questions about my conversations, as part of my job, with, and I wrote this down, *The New York Times,* CNN, CBS, *Time* magazine, *US News,* the *New York Daily News,* the *Chicago Tribune,* the *New York Observer* and there may have been a few others I don't remember right now. Ken Starr's prosecutors demanded to know what I had told reporters and what reporters had told me about Ken Starr's prosecutors."

Blumenthal's speech was carried prominently on news broadcasts that day. But it was misleading. When the transcript of the February 26 grand jury session was released months later, it showed Blumenthal had been asked if he had been privy to any "talking points" that had been prepared about the Lewinsky matter. Blumenthal responded: "If reporters called me or I spoke with reporters, I would tell them to call the DNC to get those talking points. And those included news organizations ranging from CNN, CBS, ABC, *New York Times, New York Daily News, Chicago Tribune, New York Observer, LA Times.*"

In other words, it was Blumenthal in his answer who mentioned specific news organizations, not any of Starr's prosecutors in their questions. Blumenthal's public statements, misrepresenting what actually went on in secret grand jury sessions, was disturbing enough that at the end of his final June 25, 1998, appearance he was upbraided by the grand jury foreperson. "We are very concerned about the fact that during your last visit that an inaccurate representation of the events that happened were retold on the steps of the courthouse," the foreperson told him. "We would hope that you will understand the seriousness of our work, and not in any way use it for any purpose other than the purpose that is intended, and that you would really represent us the way that events happened in this room."

Other than the conscientious James Bennet of *The New York Times,* so far as I am aware, neither Anthony Lewis nor any of the other journalists that relied on Blumenthal as a key source on matters relating to the Lewinsky investigation (including the media watchdog Steve Brill) brought to the public's attention the ways that he had sought to manipulate them.

AFTERWORD

1. Steele's version of events also seemed inconsistent with the one piece of hard evidence in the case: Willey's cell phone records. Steele had claimed everything she knew about Willey's sexual encounter with Clinton was imparted to her that afternoon during a phone call from Willey while I was on the way there. Steele thought Willey had made the call from her car cell phone. Then, she contended, Willey called her again—and in this second phone call, Steele reported to Willey she had done as requested.

   The phone records show there was indeed a phone call from Willey's cell phone to Steele's home that day. It came at 4:21 P.M. It lasted one minute— the smallest possible increment by which calls are recorded. There was then, just as Steele suggested, a follow-up. It came at 5:31 P.M. and was billed for two minutes. Readers can review all the details Steele provided me that afternoon on pages 122 and 123 and judge for themselves whether it is likely Willey told her all of this for the first time—and then managed to persuade her to falsely corroborate it to a reporter for *Newsweek*—during the course of a single cell phone call that lasted no longer than sixty seconds.

2. I used the word "nonsensical" here, but there is, it appears, a continuing public market for this sort of thing. In January 2000, Luque's fanciful theories about my role in these events resurfaced in an unusually unreliable book, *A Vast Conspiracy,* by Jeffrey Toobin of *The New Yorker.* Toobin had spent many hours huddled with Luque and other lawyers associated with the president's defense. His book, more or less, mimicked the legal arguments they invoked during the impeachment debate. At the same time, *A Vast Conspiracy* shamelessly passed along uncorroborated sexual gossip about Clinton's foes and stitched together far-fetched innuendo about me: I was, Toobin argued, one of Clinton's longtime "enemies," who was supposedly motivated in my reporting by my "greed" for a book contract. Aside from the fact that it bore no relation to reality, Toobin's account was—as several commentators pointedly noted— almost freakishly hypocritical. Some years earlier, Toobin had burst onto the journalistic scene as a veritable poster child for ethically dubious book deals. Although the broad outlines of the story were dimly known, the precise details were actually quite astounding: As a young federal prosecutor in 1991, Toobin was caught having absconded with large loads of classified and grand jury–related documents from the office of Iran-contra independent counsel Lawrence Walsh. Toobin, it turned out, had been using his tenure in Walsh's office to secretly prepare a tell-all book about the Iran-contra case; the privileged documents, along with a meticulously kept private diary (in which the young Toobin, a sort of proto–Linda Tripp, had been documenting private conversations with his unsuspecting colleagues) were to become his prime bait to snare a book deal. Toobin's conduct enraged his fellow lawyers in Walsh's office, many of whom viewed his actions as an indefensible betrayal of his public trust. Walsh at one point even considered pressing for Toobin's indictment. ("I was petrified," Toobin confided at the time, "that criminal charges were going to be brought against me.") The matter also triggered an internal

disciplinary inquiry by the Justice Department. Whether he feared dismissal and disgrace, or simply wanted to move on, target Toobin soon resigned from the U.S. Attorney's office in Brooklyn (where he had gone to work after Walsh) and abandoned the practice of law.

Toobin's journalism turned out to be scarcely more admirable. *A Vast Conspiracy* was riddled with errors, grotesque distortions, and even a few fabricated quotes. *Newsweek*'s managing editor, Ann McDaniel, later filed a formal protest with Toobin's publisher, Random House, questioning the author's "integrity and credibility as a journalist." Upon receipt of McDaniel's letter, Random House took the unusual step of retracting and agreeing to delete from all future editions at least one of Toobin's bogus claims: that on the day of President Clinton's deposition in the Paula Jones case, I was "protecting" Ken Starr's investigation into the Lewinsky matter.

3. Skeptics will inevitably raise questions about how it is I could misfile—and then suddenly rediscover—a notebook containing important notes with one of the players in this story. For anybody who has worked with me, the greater surprise is that it didn't happen more often. Whatever my strengths as a reporter, tidiness is not among them. (Throughout the many months of the Starr investigation, the running joke inside the *Newsweek* Washington bureau was if I only would clean out my office we would find buried in the detritus of my reporting Lewinsky's semen-stained dress.) It is also worth emphasizing that the Willey story erupted smack in the middle of my work on the campaign finance case. In context, it is not that odd that I would have haphazardly deposited the Steele notebook in a file with my other notes from that summer, especially in light of the fact that, at the time, I had no particular reason to believe that the subject of Steele and Willey would ever return on my radar screen anytime soon.

4. It is also worth pointing out that, as a practical matter, *Newsweek* had already done its job: We had accurately published the relevant information about what Steele had told me in our original 1997 story, even if the public relations efforts of her defense lawyer had succeeded in casting an unnecessary cloud over the account.

5. It is not surprising that Eisen and Martin's public testimony got little media attention. By the time it was offered, the press had been so successfully spun by Steele's handlers that all evidence that tended to cut in Willey's favor was being routinely twisted against her. Consider the question of FBI polygraphs given to Willey. I am no great believer in the infallibility of such techniques. But nothing is more damaging to a person's public credibility than the claim that he or she has "flunked" a lie detector. In stories that relied almost exclusively on leaks from the Steele defense lawyers, it was widely reported that Willey had "flunked" a lie detector. Even Steele herself repeated this claim in later testimony before Congress.

Actually, Willey's polygraph examinations—entered into the court record after Steele's trial was over—were, while confusing and hardly dispositive, ultimately closer to the opposite of what had been reported about them. The reports show that Willey voluntarily took two polygraphs administered by the FBI. (Steele, for her part, refused to take any.) The first was on September 9, 1998, and the examiner found the results "inconclusive" when Willey was asked whether she had lied about what she was saying happened with Clinton. One of Willey's responses, however, dealing with the timing of when she provided details to Steele about the incident, was deemed to be "consistent with deception."

Dissatisfied with this muddled result, the FBI asked Willey to take another polygraph six days later. The exam was administered by James K. Murphy Jr., chief of the FBI's polygraph unit. Murphy asked more direct and specific questions about Willey's account of the 1993 meeting with Clinton. The two key questions were: Did the president in 1993 "place his hand on your breast"? Did the president "place your hand on his groin"? Willey answered "yes" to both. Murphy concluded her responses were "truthful."

6. In 1998, congressional investigators calculated Lippo-related contributions to Clinton and related Democratic causes in 1992 at $786,000, including $286,000 to Clinton's presidential inaugural committee. An even larger chunk of the total came in the form of twelve "soft money" checks written by James and Aileen Riady to various Democratic Party entities during a two-month period between August 13, 1992, and October 15, 1992. Among these, for example, were checks of $75,000 apiece to the Michigan, Ohio, Arkansas and Louisiana Democratic Parties signed by James Riady. His wife, Aileen, wrote her own soft money checks of $50,000 apiece to the North Carolina and Georgia Democratic Parties as well as another one for $15,000 to the Democratic National Committee. Justice Department prosecutors later identified another $200,000 in contributions from eleven Lippo employees in the United States that were reimbursed by Lippo wire transfers from Asia. That would place the grand total of 1992 Lippo money at $986,000, slightly shy of the $1 million Riady promised Clinton during the August limousine ride. As a way of comparison, this was more than twice the $416,000 contributed by the Democratic Party's next largest soft money donor, the National Education Association, in 1992. It was slightly less, however, than the biggest Republican soft money donor that year, the Archer Daniels Midland Co., the Decatur, Illinois–based agribusiness conglomerate.

The principal difference, however, is that all of the Lippo-Riady money may well have been in violation of the law. During the 1997 campaign finance hearings, lawyers for Senate Democrats argued that James and Aileen Riady's direct contributions to state parties were legal because Riady maintained a house in Los Angeles. (This is to be distinguished from the Riady-reimbursed donations of Lippo employees in the United States that were deemed by the Justice Department to be clearly illegal "conduit" contributions. John Huang ultimately pled guilty to his role in facilitating them.) While foreign money to U.S. political campaigns is banned, contributions from foreigners who reside in the United States are allowed under the law. But even this claim seems dubious in the case of Riady. In an unrelated civil suit, Riady himself had testified that by the summer of 1992 he had left Los Angeles and moved back to Jakarta. Of course, none of this necessarily implicates Clinton himself in any legal wrongdoing. White House aides later argued that there is no reason to believe Clinton was informed of the precise mechanics by which Riady fulfilled his limousine ride pledge. Still, one can only wonder what exactly Clinton did say when his old friend—fresh off the plane from Indonesia—told him of his intentions to give him $1 million. Under the circumstances, it seems unlikely that it was along the lines of, "Gee, James, do you think we better run this one by the lawyers?"

ACKNOWLEDGMENTS

This book could not have been written without the assistance of many others. My debts start with *Newsweek*. Washington bureau chief Ann McDaniel oversaw and directed all my reporting for the magazine. She applied her sound news judgment to all key decisions and graciously approved my leave of absence to write this book. Assistant managing editor Evan Thomas lent his considerable writing talents to all that appeared in the magazine and gave wise counsel at every stage. The editorial disagreements outlined in Chapter 20 notwithstanding, *Newsweek* president Richard Smith, editor Mark Whitaker and the late Maynard Parker were fully supportive. My *Newsweek* colleagues Mark Hosenball and Daniel Klaidman were indispensable—as well as being two of the best reporters in the business. Howard Fineman provided historical and political perspective. Wes Kosova and Matt Cooper kept me entertained. William Rafferty and Lucy Shackelford made sure I got it right. If I didn't, it's because I forgot to check with them. Steve Tuttle helped me navigate all technological obstacles with limitless patience.

Needless to say, nobody at *Newsweek* is responsible for anything in this book. I am.

At *The Washington Post,* Marilyn Thompson, Laura Stepp, Dan Balz, Lloyd Grove and David Broder were generous in sharing their recollections. So too was my former *Post* colleague Charles Shepard—an unheralded player in the Paula Jones saga. My agent Gail Ross made this book happen and was a constant source of encouragement. At Crown, editorial director Steve Ross was enthusiastic from the start and deserves my eternal gratitude. Merrill McLoughlin edited the manuscript with remarkable dexterity and good cheer. Kristin Kiser put up with my last-minute changes.

I also want to give special thanks to my parents. My mother, Trudy Isikoff, taught me to believe in myself. My father, Morris Isikoff, gave me my interest in all things political and taught me the meaning of the word integrity. My wife, Lisa Stein—with her wit and strength of character—kept me going through sometimes difficult times. My daughter, Willa, makes it all worthwhile.

INDEX

Drudge and, 144–47; investigative stories controversy, 142; and Isikoff book, 389n.1; Isikoff's move to, 96, 102; Jones cover stories, 101, 104–7, 111, 141–43, 186; Lewinsky investigative reporting, 210–12, 215, 220–21, 231, 233–35, 285–86, 290–304, 307–10, 312, 318, 354–55, 357, 396–98n.1; Lewinsky story publication debate, 321–25, 328–30, 334–36; Lewinsky story quashing, 337–38; Steele suit against, 385–86n.1; Tripp clarification letter to, 175, 387n.3, 401n.3; Willey story, 147–49, 153–61, 172, 173–75, 190, 245, 294

New York Post, 75, 184, 193, 318

New York Times, 18, 34, 75, 89, 102, 161, 335, 357, 408n.1

Nightline (TV program), 185, 343

Nixon, Richard, 8, 137, 191–92, 205, 358

Norman, Greg, 211

Nussbaum, Bernard, 109, 110, 131, 132, 133, 136

O'Connor, Sandra Day, 85, 111

Olson, Theodore (Ted), 110, 111, 257

oral sex: Clinton distinction, 23–24, 45, 405n.6; Jones and, 9, 22, 23, 25, 42, 45, 88, 111, 185–86, 327; Lewinsky and, 135, 171, 176, 331

Orin, Deborah, 318

Oxford University, 10, 26

Packwood, Bob, 54, 61, 76, 78–79

Palladino, Jack, 31, 32–33, 79, 383n.2, 398n.5

Panetta, Leon, 121, 126–27, 136, 341

Parker, Laura, 383n.1

Parker, Maynard, 104–5, 142, 309, 310

Parks, Jerry, 113

Patterson, Larry, 23, 24, 83

Pennington, Clydine, 380n.2

Pentagon City Mall, 281–82, 311, 314, 316

Penthouse, 47

Pepperdine Law School, 274

Perdue, Sally, 32, 57, 79

Perelman, Ronald, 265, 268

Peretz, Martin, 58

perjury, xiii–xiv, 250–52, 255, 269, 288, 306–307, 310, 314, 403–404n.4; as Clinton issue, 350–51, 354, 405n.6; subor-

nation charge, 313, 329, 352; Tripp's attempt to tape Lewinsky in, 279, 284–85

Perot, Ross, 30, 117

Perry, Charlotte, 55, 225

Peyronie's disease, 184, 383n.3

phone sex, 135, 171, 199, 230, 320, 324

phone tapes. *See* taped conversations; Tripp-Lewinsky tapes

Plante, Bill, 155

Podesta, John, 85, 199, 205, 206, 212, 213, 219, 283, 325–26, 338

Pond, Betsey, 131, 132

Poole, Cheryl, 133–34

Porter, Richard, 83, 84, 109, 230–31, 235, 251, 252, 256, 266, 268, 272, 354, 402–403n.1

Poveromo, Bill, 362

Price, Phil, 37, 46, 47, 48, 96, 225

privacy rights, 58, 81, 168, 264, 351, 382n.4

private investigators, 30–33, 50, 79, 255, 268, 383n.2

Prochnau, William, 383–84n.1

Provyn, Frank, 140

Purdum, Todd, 167

Purposes of the Heart (Browning), 240, 241, 395n.1

Pyke, David, 187, 235–36, 237–38, 248, 249, 267, 268, 337, 383n.3, 398n.4

Quality Management Conference, 37, 39, 46, 48

Quayle, Dan, 83, 230

Radek, Lee, 312, 313

Rader, Campbell, Fisher & Pyke, 187, 354

Rafferty, William, 114

Ray, Elizabeth, 58

Reagan, Nancy, 211

Reddy, Lynn, 127

Regnery, Al, 230, 235

Regnery Books, 138, 230

Rempel, Bill, 4, 46, 52

Reno, Janet, 36, 125, 277, 314, 334

Republican Party, 353, 354

Revlon, 246, 265, 275, 276, 277, 283

Riady, James, 170, 275, 276, 372, 373, 411–12n.6

Rice, Donna, 59, 71, 244

ABOUT THE AUTHOR

MICHAEL ISIKOFF joined *The Washington Post* in 1981, where he covered the Justice Department, Latin American drug operations, and the 1992 presidential campaign. In 1994, he moved to *Newsweek,* where he covered the Oklahoma City bombing, the Senate hearings into campaign finance abuses, and other national issues. His exclusive reporting on the Lewinsky scandal gained him nationwide attention, including profiles in *The New York Times* and *The Washington Post.* He has been a news analyst for MSNBC and a frequent guest on numerous news programs, including NBC's *Meet the Press* and PBS's *Charlie Rose.* Isikoff lives with his wife and daughter in Chevy Chase, Maryland.